Date Due

May 12'62			
Oct 6'67			
Apr 14'69			
Nov 5 69			
Feb 26'70			
May 10 78			
Dec 15 78 B			
GB	PRINTED	IN U. S. A.	

William Butler Yeats: *The Lyric of Tragedy*

William Butler Yeats

The Lyric of Tragedy

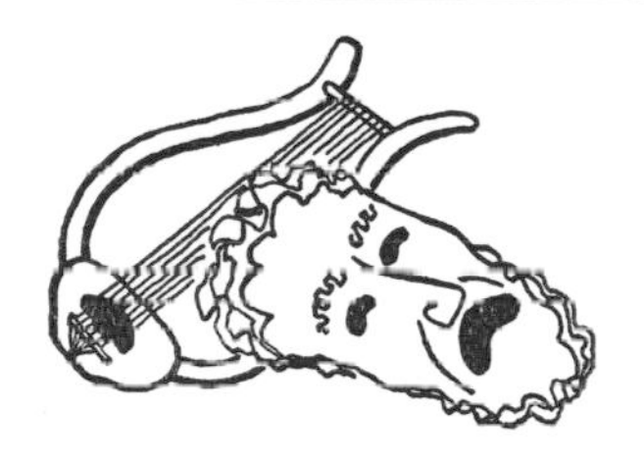

by B. L. Reid

University of Oklahoma Press

Norman

By B. L. REID

Art by Subtraction: A Dissenting Opinion of Gertrude Stein (Norman, 1958)
William Butler Yeats: The Lyric of Tragedy (Norman, 1961)

The publication of this work has been aided by a grant from The Ford Foundation

Library of Congress Catalog Card Number: 61-15147

Composed and printed at Norman, Oklahoma, U.S.A., by the University of Oklahoma Press.
First edition.

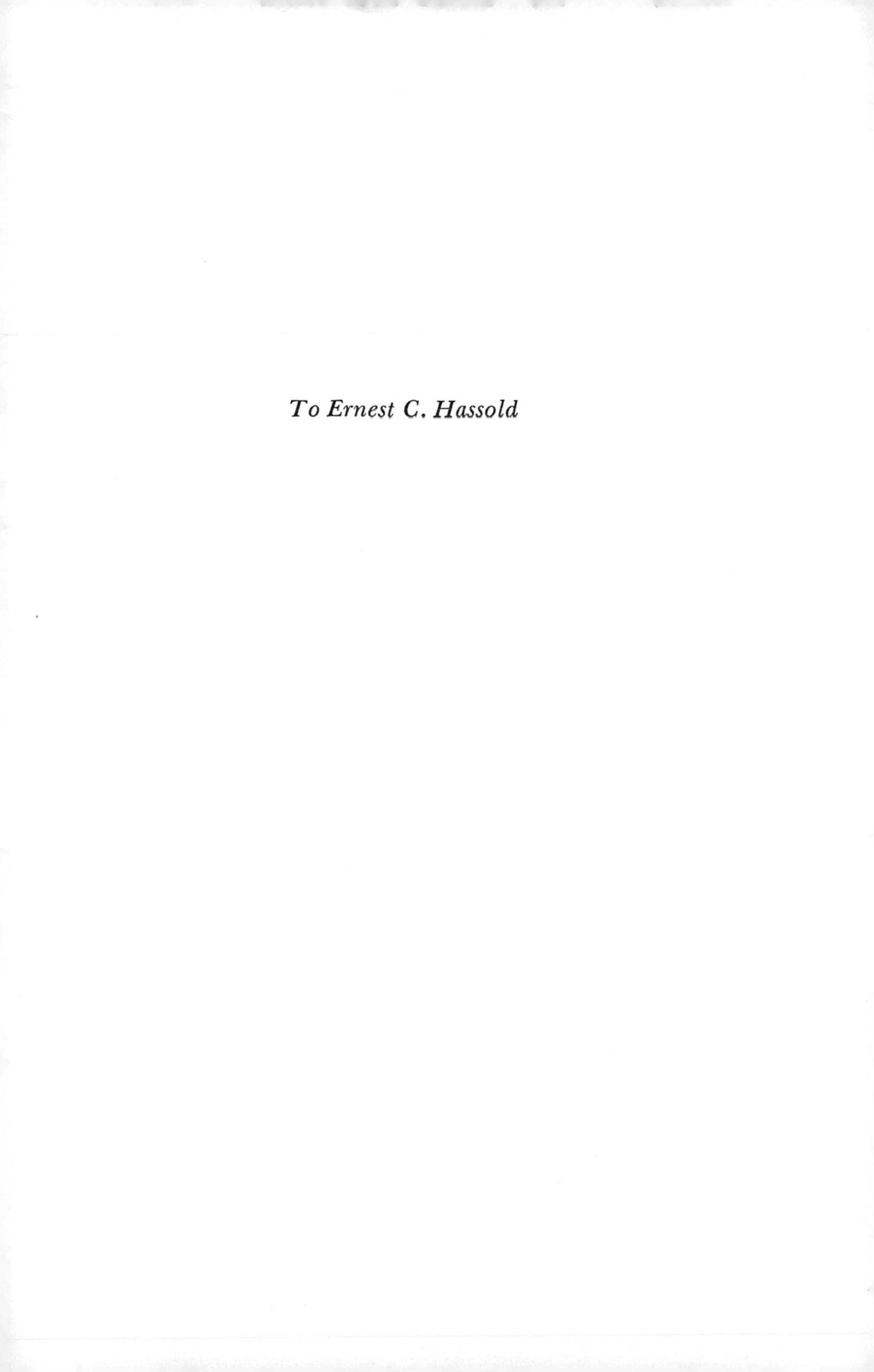

To Ernest C. Hassold

Preface

AFTER THE QUANTITY OF WORK, of excellent work, that has been done on the poems of William Butler Yeats, one needs a good justification for offering yet another public rereading. The grandest possible justification is built into the poems themselves, their unequivocal greatness as human documents and works of art; we can never learn enough about so great a poet. But I found my more particular justification in what proved for me the light-shedding experience of reading the poems within a context and a discipline which they both validate and exemplify, that of tragedy, or "the tragic," or "the tragic sense of life."

One may well wonder why, if I was interested in Yeats and in tragedy, I chose to examine the poems rather than the plays, which would appear to offer the orthodox form, the dramatic, in an appropriate critical setting. The truth is that what had come to interest me most was the frequency and power with which works pointedly not by formal definition tragedies convinced one that they yet were somehow tragedies in essence—which, abjuring the form, yet thought, spoke, and felt like tragedy.

Tragedy was born, we believe, out of primitive pagan ritual, religious in shape and function; and the ritual took its themes and structure, we believe, from men's early recognition of the physical and metaphysical rhythm in the design of their lives, the regular march of the seasons, the inevitability of suffering and death, the hope of resurrection. What happens to the original blood-knowledge that begat tragedy, in the many centuries of tragedy's codifiying and sophistication, by which the original "dung and death" becomes *"Tragedia cothurnata,* fitting Kings,/ Containing matter, and not common things"? My feeling is that the old, wonderful blood-knowledge, brute-knowledge, is still what impels true tragedy into being, still unconsciously shapes its content and its form, though we have tended to forget it as we have complicated our critical theory and accumulated our literary history. In the sufficiently difficult attempt to define and to understand formal literary tragedy, we may have codified it too stiffly, have lost touch with the reality of "informal" tragedy, the tragic sense of *life,* the ancient, vulgar knowledge of the fatal and beautiful structure of man's experience. A. C. Bradley, most classical of modern commentators on tragedy, has conceded that "the saying that every death-bed is the scene of the fifth act of a tragedy has its meaning"; but he classifies the truth as, in effect, extra-literary: "It would not be true if the word 'tragedy' bore its dramatic sense." It is the general assumption that the vulgar sense of tragedy is useless or irrelevant to literature which troubles me.

Preface

In this study I have tried to deal with the lyric poetry of Yeats as exemplifying the cross-fertilization of formal and informal tragedy, the grandeur and power that a great poet's sense of the tragic in life creates in work that is not tragedy in the specific and orthodox sense. My first chapter treats, in a necessarily general way, something of the theory and history of the criticism of tragedy. The chapters which compose the main body of the book aim to analyze Yeats's own theory and practice of tragedy in his poems and prose; biographical details have been kept to an indispensable minimum. The closing chapter seeks to formulate a critical hypothesis by reassembling the three main counters, formal and informal tragedy and the poems.

The final chapter of this book first appeared as an essay in *The Hudson Review,* Vol. XI, No. 3 (Autumn, 1958), copyright 1958 by *The Hudson Review,* Inc., and is reprinted by permission.

It is a pleasure to acknowledge the encouragement and instruction given me in early stages of this study by Professor Arthur Kyle Davis, Jr., and by Professor Frederick Gwynn. My friend and former colleague Professor Lawrence G. Nelson has tried passionately to educate me, and I thank him. My dedication testifies, inadequately, to a personal and intellectual debt that has always been deep and has now grown long.

B. L. Reid

South Hadley, Massachusetts
August 9, 1961

Contents

Illustrations

William Butler Yeats: *The Lyric of Tragedy*

CHAPTER ONE

Definitions

INTRODUCTORY

"WE BEGIN TO LIVE when we have conceived life as tragedy,"[1] William Butler Yeats wrote in 1922. In July, 1935, a brilliant and famous old man of letters, he wrote to his new friend Dorothy Wellesley of an object and its surrounding emotion which were to generate, in the course of a year, one of his capital poems, "Lapis Lazuli":

> I notice that you have much lapis lazuli; someone has sent me a present of a great piece carved by some Chinese sculptor into the semblance of a mountain with temple, trees, paths, and an ascetic and pupil about to climb the mountain. Ascetic, pupil, hard stone, eternal theme of the sensual east. The heroic cry in the midst of despair. But no, I am wrong, the

[1] *The Autobiography of William Butler Yeats* (New York, The Macmillan Company, 1938), 165.

> east has its solutions always and therefore knows nothing of tragedy. It is we, not the east, that must raise the heroic cry.[2]

Three weeks later, writing to the same correspondent, he continued the thought and cast it as credo:

> To me the supreme aim is an act of faith and reason to make one rejoice in the midst of tragedy. An impossible aim; yet I think it true that nothing can injure us.[3]

The simple size of such statements, their inclusiveness, their air of synopsis, the weight of settled philosophical conviction they seem to carry, make them imposing enough to permit us to study Yeats as a poet for whom the sense of life as tragedy was conclusive. Indeed I believe they do prepare a hypothesis which will endure testing. But has Yeats a right to set himself and his lyrical art within the frame of the tragic, and will there be any special profit in examining him within that frame?

Yeats thought about tragedy in two main ways. Occasionally and briefly, he thought about it formally, as a kind of "official" or "academic" literary and theatrical category. It is in this sense that tragedy has been discussed by many of the most brilliant critical and scholarly intelligences in the long line that begins with Aristotle. Much more often, Yeats thought about tragedy informally, in ways which might not even involve the word itself, and which certainly envisioned no dramatic vestment—our "normal," vulgar, quotidian sense of the term as describing the melancholy, mysterious, and fatal logic or illogic of existence. In such contexts, Yeats thought of tragedy as a property of art generally and of life generally: "an act of faith and reason to make one rejoice in the midst of tragedy."

Because it was the notion which chiefly occupied Yeats, we

2 *Letters on Poetry from W. B. Yeats to Dorothy Wellesley* (London, Oxford University Press, 1940), 8–9.
3 *Ibid.*, 13.

will concern ourselves mainly in this study with this broader and looser, more personal, lyrical, or vulgar concept of tragedy, describing a "sense of life," and depending on a definition of *experience* as tragic. Perhaps we may agree to call this branch "generic" tragedy. But serious students of literature are bound to remain interested in "systematic"[4] tragedy, as Richard Sewall calls it, with its long history and its elaborate accumulated rationale, its library of famous creative and critical texts. In search of the greatest profit, we ought to set orthodox tragedy and the Yeatsian kind of tragedy side by side, to see what they have to say to each other. It may be that our notions of tragedy have grown stiff and overprotective. Is tragedy only one codified thing? Might tragedy extend its spectrum to include, with profit, such a strong shade as the superb vulgarly-tragic lyrics of Yeats? The lyrics fall into configurations which suggest analogies to recognized patterns of formal tragedy; has the correspondence meaning and value? Can we learn anything about the nature of "systematic" tragedy by analyzing the behavior of Yeats's kind of intuitive or primitive or "generic" tragedy? Such questions as these have motivated the present study.

The body of interpretative thought which has grown up about tragedy is too large and rich to review other than selectively in a chapter, and I should like here to pay the small tribute of naming the works I have found most generously instructive. The classic studies are by now fairly conclusively identified as those of Aristotle, Hegel, Schopenhauer, Nietzsche, and Bradley. Herbert Weisinger's recent *Tragedy and the Paradox of the Fortunate Fall* impresses me as a study which must become part of the basic literature of the subject. Richard Sewall's *The Vision of Tragedy,* Herbert J. Muller's *The Spirit of Tragedy,* and William G. McCollom's *Tragedy* are excellent traditional synoptic studies. Fredson Bowers' *Eliz-*

[4] Richard Sewall, "The Tragic Form," *Essays in Criticism,* Vol. IV (1954), 348.

abethan Revenge Tragedy, H. D. F. Kitto's *Greek Tragedy,* Bernard Knox's *Oedipus at Thebes,* and Willard Farnham's studies of medieval and Shakespearean tragedy[5] are indispensable treatments of special aspects. Sir James Frazer, Gilbert Murray, and Jane Harrison staked out the anthropological area of ritual origins which Weisinger has brilliantly worked again. The most intelligent as well as the most eloquent of the full-length impressionistic accounts is probably W. Macneile Dixon's *Tragedy.* F. L. Lucas' *Tragedy in Relation to Aristotle's "Poetics"* is less inclusive, more idiosyncratic, and constantly stimulating. Among the hundreds of studies of essay length, there is time to notice only such important recent papers as Joseph Wood Krutch's "The Tragic Fallacy,"[6] Richard Sewall's "The Tragic Form,"[7] and the excellent collection of seven lectures at Yale, edited by Cleanth Brooks under the title of *Tragic Themes in Western Literature.*

CONSTANTS

What one may forget, watching the intestine warfare over the aesthetics of tragedy, is the really remarkable oneness persons feel in regard to what might be called the ethics of tragedy. Most of the critical battles are fought, that is, on issues of how tragedy is to be written, performed, and responded to; not what it is to say, or why it feels moved to say it. This unanimity of view is perhaps the most striking single fact about tragedy

[5] Willard Farnham, *The Medieval Heritage of Elizabethan Tragedy* (Berkeley, the University of California Press, 1936); *Shakespeare's Tragic Frontier: The World of His Final Tragedies* (Berkeley, The University of California Press, 1950).

[6] *Criticism: The Foundations of Modern Literary Judgment,* ed. by Mark Schorer, Josephine Miles, and Jordan McKenzie (New York, Harcourt, Brace and Company, 1948), 76–84.

[7] *Essays in Criticism,* Vol. IV (1954), 345–58.

in the abstract. "Tragedy is common knowledge," Lawrence G. Nelson said.[8] The reality of tragedy, that is, is archetypal reality, the sad truth we know most anciently and surely. To attempt a working formula, I suggest that systematic tragedy dramatizes the generic imbalance between the ideal and the real—what we feel life ought to be and what it is; tragedy's archetypal subject is really the loss of the perfect, the Fall of Man, "with loss of Eden," as Milton puts it. Tragedy confronts, combats, accepts at last, and makes one or another kind of peace with, the loss of that perfected state in man and nature. *Each* tragedy goes through that process in some way: tragic philosophy has never really accepted the fatality of the Fall, but must fight through to resignation, and beyond, again and again. Comedy is the true pessimist, in accepting the imperfect as the "normal" condition within which compromises are to be made; and tragedy is the true optimist, because it insists that the imperfect is "abnormal" and remedial, and because it must be repeatedly instructed in the fatality of fact.

But tragedy learns the truth; and thus Nietzsche, and Dixon after him, can speak with an assumption of agreement of an "antagonism at the heart of the world,"[9] and an "affair with the gods."[10] This ethical agreement is so sweeping, and so much more fundamental to our larger understanding of tragedy than all our disagreements as to ways and means, that we would do well to collect some few of the representative statements that make it large and plain.

Man's bewilderment and outrage, his anger and pain and fear, at the disjunction between the ideal and the real in life, at his Fall and loss of Eden, takes, typically, the form of a

8 Lecture at Sweet Briar College, February, 1956.

9 W. Macneile Dixon, *Tragedy* (London, Edward Arnold and Company, 1929, 3rd ed.), 71.

10 *Ibid.*

mystery. I am thinking, as Keats did in a similar context,[11] of Wordsworth's phrase, "the burden of the mystery," the recognition cited in "Tintern Abbey" as the sign of attained maturity. "Mystery" is a word to which commentators on tragedy find themselves repeatedly driven. Thus, Bradley says that the pity and fear in Shakespearean tragedy "seem to unite with, and even to merge in, a profound sense of sadness and mystery," and again, "Tragedy is the typical form of this mystery . . . . It forces the mystery upon us."[12] Tragedy takes as its subject the religious and philosophical mystery at the heart of the cosmic design involving man, and takes as its function the ordering of that mystery into significant dramatic focus. Tragedy is the most hubristic of the arts because it presumes to try to define man, God, and the universe, and to puzzle out the lines of their mingling.

The archetypal imbalance which constitutes the tragic subject is put most compactly and familiarly in *Hamlet,* where, though Hamlet expresses it to Rosencrantz and Guildenstern as matter of mere distempered mood, it is a radical distemper, and plainly and powerfully functions as the play's coordinating metaphor of grandeur declined, virtue corrupted, and beauty rotted—Fall of man, with loss of Eden:

> . . . it goes so heavily with my disposition that this goodly frame, the earth, seems to me a sterile promontory; this most excellent canopy, the air, look you, this brave o'erhanging firmament, this majestical roof fretted with golden fire—why, it appeareth no other thing to me than a foul and pestilent congregation of vapours. What a piece of work is a man! how noble in reason! how infinite in faculties! how like an angel! in apprehension how like a god! the beauty of the world, the

[11] Letter to John Hamilton Reynolds, May 3, 1818, *The Letters of John Keats,* ed. by Maurice Buxton Forman (London, Oxford University Press, 1952), 143.

[12] A. C. Bradley, *Shakespearean Tragedy* (New York, Meridian Books, 1955), 28–29.

paragon of animals! And yet to me what is this quintessence of dust? Man delights not me—no, nor woman neither, though by your smiling you seem to say so.—Act II, scene 2.

Miss Caroline Spurgeon, commenting on that condition of inexplicable decay for which Hamlet's speech serves as metaphor, calls it "the tragedy of *Hamlet,* as it is perhaps the chief tragic mystery of life."[13] She has drawn out an extension in meaning from Hamlet to the "mystery" I have called generic tragedy. Nietzsche, similarly, accounts for Hamlet's paralysis of will on grounds of his very recognition of the size and significance of the mystery. He has "looked deeply into the true nature of things," Nietzsche writes, he has "understood" and is "now loath to act"; and what in Hamlet "overbalances any motive leading to action, is not reflection but understanding, the apprehension of truth and its terror."[14] It is that sort of "understanding" that justifies the laconicism of Dixon's, "If we are not bewildered by life we should be,"[15] and lets F. L. Lucas call Pope's wry lines on the mystery a "transcendent commonplace":[16]

Placed on this Isthmus of a middle state,
A being darkly wise and rudely great;
With too much knowledge for the Sceptic side,
With too much weakness for a Stoic's pride,
He hangs between; in doubt, to act or rest,
In doubt to deem himself a God, or Beast,
Born but to die, and reas'ning but to err . . .
Created half to rise, and half to fall:

13 Maynard Mack, "The World of *Hamlet,*" in Cleanth Brooks, ed., *Tragic Themes in Western Literature,* 48.

14 Friedrich Nietzsche, *The Birth of Tragedy and the Genealogy of Morals,* trans. by Francis Golffing (New York, Doubleday and Company, 1956), 51.

15 *Op. cit.,* 137.

16 F. L. Lucas, *Tragedy in Relation to Aristotle's "Poetics"* (New York, Harcourt, Brace and Company, 1928), 57.

Great Lord of all things, yet a Prey to all;
Sole Judge of Truth, in endless error hurl'd;
The Glory, Jest, and Riddle of the world!

Hamlet's exclamation, "What a piece of work is a man!" and Pope's response, "The Glory, Jest, and Riddle of the world!" are echoed repeatedly by all those involved in generic tragedy —playwrights, critics, readers, who are all tragic men themselves, and know it.

Richard Sewall quotes the cry of Dostoevski's character Kalganov at the spectacle of the Karamazovs, "What are these people? What can men be after this?" and concludes: ". . . echoed in his words is the question, always implicit and often explicit, at the heart of every tragic treatment from the Book of Job down: 'What is man?' "[17] In his brilliant critique of *Oedipus,* Bernard Knox follows the savage ironic turning which Sophocles administers to Protagoras' dictum, "Man is the measure of all things," according to which "man is the center of the universe, his intelligence can overcome all obstacles, he is master of his own destiny, tyrannos, self-made ruler who has the capacity to attain complete prosperity and happiness."[18] Mr. Knox adduces the earlier chorus from the *Antigone,* with its paean to man's immense accumulation of knowledge and power: "Full of resources, he faces the future." Equipped as hero, tyrannos, "Oedipus' problem is apparently simple: 'Who is the murderer of Laius?' but as he pursues the answer the question changes shape. It becomes a different problem: 'Who am I?' " And the answer to this problem, as Mr. Knox remarks, "involves the gods as well as man."[19] Defining himself, man must also define God. He goes on to cata-

[17] "The Tragic World of the Karamazovs," in Cleanth Brooks, ed., *Tragic Themes in Western Literature,* 122–23.

[18] "Sophocles' Oedipus," in Cleanth Brooks, ed., *Tragic Themes in Western Literature,* 9.

[19] *Ibid.,* 8–10.

log the elaborate and horrible pattern of ironic reversals which composes the "action" of *Oedipus Tyrannos:*

> As the images unfold, the enquirer turns into the object of enquiry, the hunter into the prey, the doctor into the patient, the investigator into the criminal, the revealer into the thing revealed, the finder into the thing found, the savior into the thing saved . . . the liberator into the thing released . . . , the accuser becomes the defendant, the ruler the subject, the teacher not only the pupil but also the object lesson, the example.[20]

Peripeteia indeed! Sophocles' dramatic structure tells us a great deal more about tragic fact than all of Aristotle's dry analytical prescriptions. Lucas rightly draws out the bare Aristotelian formula to that extension which gives it full philosophical weight:

> In the *peripeteia,* rightly understood, is implied a whole tragic philosophy of life; and in the practice of tragedy, once we see the right meaning of the term, we shall discover with what amazing regularity the thing itself recurs. For the deepest tragedy is not when men are struck down by the blow of chance or fate like Job or Maurya in *Riders to the Sea;* nor yet when they are destroyed by their enemies like Polyxena or Henry VI; but when their destruction is the work of those that wish them well or of their own unwitting hands. For it is the perpetual tragic irony of the Tragedy of Life that again and again men do thus laboriously contrive their own annihilation, or kill the thing they love.[21]

Bradley, too, speaks again and again of this "perpetual tragic irony," which ordains the condition that "everywhere, in this tragic world, man's thought, translated into act, is transformed

20 *Ibid.,* 10–11.
21 *Op. cit.,* 94–95.

into the opposite of itself."[22] Butcher restates the proposition and cites the two most pressing of many possible instances:

> So too in tragedy those are doomed who innocently err no less than those who sin consciously. Nay, the tragic irony sometimes lies precisely herein, that . . . the very virtues of a man hurry him forward to his ruin. Othello in the modern drama, Oedipus in the ancient–widely as they differ in moral guilt–are the two most conspicuous examples of ruin wrought by characters, noble indeed, but not without defects, acting in the dark, and, as it seemed, for the best.[23]

This irony is a part of generic tragedy, the facts of life according to the tragic view, the ineluctable presence of "*evil* in the universe, whatever it is in the stars that compels, harasses, and bears man down," as Richard Sewall writes. "Tragedy wrestles with the evil of the mystery—and the mystery of the evil. And the contest never ends."[24]

"I see in him outrageous strength, with an inscrutable malice sinewing it. That inscrutable thing is chiefly what I hate; and be the white whale agent, or be the white whale principal, I will wreak that hate upon him." So rages Ahab in the most tragic of novels. The true source of Ahab's vast unease, the most ultimate of all his fears and doubts, is the question of Design. He can accept the thought of a universe subject to an Order, even an Order that countenances or perhaps encourages evil: "That intangible malignity which has been from the beginning." The thought that really maddens Ahab, and Melville, we discover in the great chapter on "The Whiteness of the Whale," is the thought that there is *no* Design. What if, when we finally "strike through the mask" of that colossal enigma, Moby Dick,

[22] Bradley, *Shakespearean Tragedy,* 32–33.

[23] S. H. Butcher, *Aristotle's Theory of Poetry and Fine Art* (London, Macmillan and Company, 1907, 4th ed.), 321–22.

[24] "The Tragic Form," *Essays in Criticism,* Vol. IV (1954), 350.

we find *nothing* behind it: "the colorless, all-color of atheism from which we shrink"? Better a malign God than no God at all; better to live in a universe of ordained torture, "the invisible spheres formed in fright," than in a universe of anarchic godlessness. "Zeus is dead but his son, Whirligig, rules in his place," muses Strepsiades in *The Clouds* of Aristophanes, after instruction by Socrates—Nietzsche's hated rationalist.

The need to find order, logic, morality in the shape of man's disaster, has been one of the greatest problems faced by tragedy and its commentators. F. L. Lucas, for example, believed that "this yearning of the human mind to believe the Universe not utterly amoral has moulded the whole history of tragedy."[25] In his own search for moral cause, Louis L. Martz makes use, as somebody should have done earlier, of the stiff little formula drawn up by precocious Stephen Dedalus in *A Portrait of the Artist as a Young Man:*

> "Aristotle has not defined pity and terror; I have. Pity is the feeling which arrests the mind in the presence of whatsoever is grave and constant in human sufferings and unites it with the human sufferer. Terror is the feeling which arrests the mind in the presence of whatsoever is grave and constant in human sufferings and unites it with the secret cause."[26]

Mr. Martz summarizes:

> Tragedy, then, seems to demand both the human sufferer and the secret cause: that is to say, the doubt, the pain, the pity of the human sufferer; and the affirmation, the awe, the terror of the secret cause. It is an affirmation even though the cause seems to affirm the existence of some universal order of things.[27]

25 *Op. cit.*, 102.

26 Quoted in Louis L. Martz, "The Saint as Tragic Hero: *St. Joan* and *Murder in the Cathedral*," in Cleanth Brooks, ed., *Tragic Themes in Western Literature*, 153.

27 *Ibid.*

I. A. Richards, rationalistically, anatomizes the cathartic effect which presumably follows from this "union" of sufferer and secret cause as a condition of no more than psychic euphoria resting on a mere moral illusion:

> Pity, the impulse to approach, and Terror, the impulse to retreat, are brought in Tragedy to a reconciliation which they find nowhere else, and with them who knows what other allied groups of equally discordant impulses. Their union in an ordered single response is the *catharsis* by which Tragedy is recognized, whether Aristotle meant anything of this kind or not. This is the explanation of that sense of release, or repose in the midst of stress, of balance and composure, given by Tragedy, for there is no other way in which such impulses, once awakened, can be set at rest without suppression . . . . Suppressions and sublimations alike are devices by which we endeavour to avoid issues which might bewilder us. The essence of Tragedy is that it forces us to live for a moment without them. When we succeed we find, as usual, that there is no difficulty; the difficulty came from the suppressions and sublimations. The joy which is so strangely the heart of the experience is not an indication that "all's right with the world" or that "somewhere, somehow, there is Justice"; it is an indication that all is right here and now in the nervous system.[28]

In his important article on "Catharsis," F. A. Pottle amends the Aristotelian doctrine as follows:

> . . . in my view the relief that comes from tragedy is really not due to an elimination of mental factors that cause uneasiness because they are present in excessive amounts, but rather to a process through which they are rendered acceptable by being given an altered significance.[29]

28 *Principles of Literary Criticism* (New York, Harcourt, Brace and Company, 1926), 245–56.

29 "Catharsis," *Yale Review*, Vol. XL (1950–51), 631.

He seconds Lucas' notion in regard to the importance of the issue of moral design, and draws an equation between the fear of amorality and the basic Aristotelian emotions:

> The greatest evil of man is . . . the haunting fear that he will be forced to admit that the universe is meaningless. The pity and terror with which tragedy deals are both reflections of this fear.[30]

Then he goes on to make his central point, the function of tragic art as the homeopathic ordering of disorder:

> Tragedy must use the material of pity and terror unsparingly, for only so can it embody our central problem; but by imposing form on pity and terror, by giving them direction, it makes us feel, at least temporarily, that there is purpose in our own afflictions and distractions. By regarding patterned pity and terror we are purged for the time being of our everyday or random pity and terror.[31]

Finally, in two later passages, Mr. Pottle traces the cathartic satisfaction to a sense, not clear or positive or logical, but one which "must be" that of union with a secret cause which *is* somehow godly and moral and salvatory. Since "proof" of such hypotheses of a supernatural "cause" is not to be had, Mr. Pottle's proposition begs the question, as all such arguments must; but his statement is admirably clear and as persuasive as it can be made. And it carries the psychological analysis of Richards a necessary further step:

> The beauty of the patterns of poetry lies within poetry and is self-justifying. The truth of the patterns of poetry lies outside poetry and is ultimately theological. The "calm of mind, all passion spent" of the nobler literary catharsis is not the

30 *Ibid.*
31 *Ibid.*

peace that passes understanding, but it may not be unrelated to it.[32]

According to these views of the matter, tragic man in flight from meaninglessness seeks wholeness and order, psychologically or religiously in the state of his nerves or the state of his soul. Mr. Pottle's analysis, especially, is interestingly Nietzschean; his emphasis on "patterned pity and terror" as one of the great poetic patterns whose truth is "ultimately theological" reminds one of Nietzsche's analysis of tragic pleasure, which he finely calls "metaphysical solace," as partly the consequence of Apollonian formalizing imposed upon the cry of the heart, partly the consequence of its ability to fabricate "those harmonious sounds of reconciliation from another world."[33] But it is chiefly generic tragedy which we are trying to understand, and in that effort the special function of tragic emotion is explained best of all by a single rich sentence of Nietzsche's:

> No matter how deeply pity moves us, that pity saves us from the radical "pity of things," even as the parable of myth saves us from the direct intuition of the cosmic idea, as idea and word save us from the undammed pouring forth of the unconscious will.[34]

Systematic tragedy dramatizes generic tragedy; by reducing chaos to ordered art, it presents a shield against an almost unbearable reality; the pity of systematic tragedy "saves us from the radical pity" of generic tragedy.

The great question raised by all these discussions is that of logic and justice. A great many sentimental attempts have been made, notoriously by certain critics of the eighteenth cen-

[32] *Ibid.*, 641.

[33] *Op. cit.*, 50, 107.

[34] *Ibid.*, 128.

tury, to reduce the logic of tragedy to the simple-minded rationale of poetic justice. Jeremy Collier made the attempt in *A Short View of the English Stage;* but John Dennis presents the true short view of tragedy:

> I conceive, that every Tragedy, ought to be a very Solemn Lecture, inculcating a particular Providence, and shewing it plainly protecting the Good, and chastizing the Bad, or at least the Violent; and that, if it is otherwise, it is either an empty Amusement, or a scandalous and pernicious Libel upon the Government of the World.[35]

But Joseph Addison soon dealt very peremptorily with this "ridiculous Doctrine in Modern Criticism" that writers of tragedy are obliged "to an equal Distribution of Rewards and Punishments, and an impartial Execution of Poetical Justice . . . . I am sure it has no Foundation in Nature, in Reason, or in the Practice of the Ancients."[36] We are pretty well driven at last to admit that injustice and illogic are fundamental properties of generic tragedy, functions of its basic "mystery."

On this central issue W. M. Dixon writes very well, and we cannot do better than to quote from several portions of his argument.

> Yet of all truths this is the most tragical . . . . In this incalculable world to act and to blunder are not two but one. The wisest and the best are but as children, and there is no truth in the doctrine either in life or tragedy, the mirror of its grievous mischances, that the afflictions of the good are necessarily the fruits of their own acts, of imperfect character or faulty judgment, that errors never creep into the reckonings of Fate or that her awards are impeccable . . . . The door to tragedy turns very easily upon its hinges. Clear as the Aris-

35 *The Advancement and Reformation of Poetry.*
36 *The Spectator,* April 16, 1711.

> totelian exposition may seem, and however it may be interpreted, the true problem is there veiled, as it is veiled for example in *Oedipus* or *Lear,* to mitigate out of consideration for our human weakness, the terror and the truth. But no more than veiled, for only in some outlandish legal or official sense does Oedipus, unconscious of guilt, deserve his fate, nor does Sophocles desire us to believe it, any more than Shakespeare desires us to believe that Lear's headstrong folly was appropriately punished. Lessing, and not for that tenderness to be blamed, finds the thought intolerable that good men may incur undeserved misery. "Religion and common sense should have convinced us . . . that to think so is as erroneous as it is blasphemous." But it is not erroneous, and the moral offensiveness we meet with in the world is, in fact, the tragic problem.[37]

It is a mark of the greatness of Aeschylus, Mr. Dixon finely says, that he accepts as a "point of departure"[38] the existence of this "moral offensiveness" at the heart of the design of things.

The effort made by "modern" tragedy to evade these facts of life, and to root the logic of tragedy in the rationale of "character" and its cause-effect behavior, Dixon says, is an emasculation of tragic truth and a retreat from the center of its strength:

> Thus modern tragedy insulates and makes more of character; with this implication, that helpless we are not altogether helpless, that another, wiser or better or stronger than the defected hero, might have met and sustained the hour and the shock—a more sustained Brutus, a wiser Othello, a saner Lear . . . . Yet we must resist those who would take advantage of our natural dullness. Faith at the best implies lack of knowledge, and the most exalted hope an uncertain issue.

[37] Dixon, *op. cit.,* 136–40.

[38] *Ibid.,* 72–73.

> Tragedy of whatever type, to remain tragedy, must refuse to make all things plain, must prostrate itself before the unknown, nor presume with the sentimentalists lightly to interpret the hieroglyphics of destiny.[39]

Dixon returns again and again to attack almost obsessively "tragedy thus ameliorated and made easy for us," by the logic of "character," or by any logic at all which would rob tragedy of its basis in mystery, that center "which seems to display the workings of a great, incalculable, natural force; that great Necessity, whatever it be, which brought us into being, governs us and removes us from the scene; before which, as before the earthquake, the flood or the thunderbolt, the heart stands still."[40]

No, he concludes at last, "There is no balsam for the world's incurable Philoctetian wound."[41] "Though in many of its aspects this visible world seems formed in love," Melville writes, "the invisible spheres were formed in fright." We are back in the presence of the "immedicable woe" of Hamlet's broken-hearted dualism: "What a piece of work is a man! . . . And yet to me what is this quintessence of dust?"

We have fallen, then, and lost Eden, yet it is our absurd grandeur that we struggle to the death to deny the fact, reach hopelessly toward the perfect. Keats, feeling that he had reached a tragic maturity by passing through the "vale of Soul-Making," spoke pityingly of his friend Dilke as a "Godwin perfectibility man."[42] Yet that desperate urge for the perfect is a part of generic tragedy—the impossibility that tragic man dies in denying. Dixon puts the case this way: "Though all desire good and only good, yet from the struggle for its various

39 *Ibid.*, 37–38.
40 *Ibid.*, 66–67.
41 *Ibid.*, 79.
42 Letter to George and Georgiana Keats, October 14–31, 1818, *op. cit.* 234.

forms or appearances arise evils and tragedies."[43] Bradley's most comprehensive summation rests on the same emphasis:

> Thus we are left at last with an idea showing two sides or aspects which we can neither separate nor reconcile. The whole or order against which the individual part shows itself powerless seems to be animated by a passion for perfection: we cannot otherwise explain its behaviour towards evil. Yet it appears to engender this evil within itself, and in its effort to overcome and expel it it is agonised with pain, and driven to mutilate its own substance and to lose not only evil but priceless good.[44]

Bradley, amazingly, locates the urge to perfection not within man but within the universal fabric itself; it seems to be his personal concept of the "secret cause":

> The ultimate power which shows itself disturbed by . . . evil and reacts against it, must have a nature alien to it. Indeed its reaction is so vehement and "relentless" that it would seem to be bent on nothing short of good in perfection, and to be ruthless in its demand for it.[45]

That would seem to return us to the Old Testament fable of the Fall. Is it *God* who desires perfection and punishes our failure? I do not know what else to call Bradley's "ultimate power" or "whole or order." "A god, a god their severance ruled!" Matthew Arnold cried, "And bade betwixt their shores to be/ The unplumbed, salt, estranging sea." We are back with Ahab's anguished doubt, too; and back with Zeus and Whirligig. Must there be a secret cause, after all? If so, is it God or Chaos? If it is God, is He a God of "love," or of "fright," or simply of "justice"? If He is a Christian God, how does His promised life-eternal affect earthly tragedy? What do we say

[43] *Op. cit.,* 108.
[44] *Shakespearean Tragedy,* 39–40.
[45] *Ibid.,* 37.

to I. A. Richards, who believed that "Tragedy is only possible to a mind which is for the moment agnostic or Manichean"?[46] But those are the unanswerable questions.

THE LINE OF GENERIC TRAGEDY

In trying to understand generic tragedy, we ought to get more help than we do from Unamuno's *The Tragic Sense of Life;* but that book dissolves into incoherent polemical philosophy and theology, and ends by supplying us with little more than the indispensable phrase of its title. Still, Unamuno offers premises which are useful, even though his development of them is disappointing. Sewall calls Unamuno's formulation that of a "sub-philosophy," "reaching deep down into temperament." "It is the sense of ancient evil, of the mystery of human suffering, of the gulf between aspiration and achievement."[47] Essentially, it is a description of what we have called generic tragedy. "Such a recognition should precede any attempt to talk 'systematically' about tragedy," Mr. Sewall agrees, "while not denying the value of the attempt itself."[48] Thus he assumes the existence of a "sub-philosophy" of generic tragedy, an operating "tragic sense of life"; but in his own essay he takes that sense for granted, and devotes himself entirely to "systematic" tragedy, analytical discussion of themes and forms of agreed monuments of tragic drama. The present study tries to reverse that emphasis—to accept "systematic" tragedy as the given, and to discuss the subphilosophical soul-environment of generic tragedy, the data of the tragic sense of life.

It is what I wish Unamuno had done. He begins promisingly, with his citation of a dialogue between "a pedant" and Solon,

[46] *Op. cit.*, 246.
[47] "The Tragic Form," *Essays in Criticism,* Vol. IV (1954), 348.
[48] *Ibid.*

who is mourning the death of his son: " 'Why do you weep thus, if weeping avails nothing?' 'Precisely for that reason—because it does not avail.' "[49] Solon's grieving, for the fact of failure—death or whatever—and for the inutility of grief, is a vivid trope for our concept of generic tragedy. But what Unamuno does is to seize upon the fact of death alone, and make it virtually the whole of tragedy. Thus his "tragic sense of life" is reduced to candid facing of the fact of the body's mortality, and the violent counter-assertion of a candidly anti-rational faith in the soul's immortality.

It is really Unamuno's solution that disturbs one, his retreat wholly into theology. With sufficient soul-searching, one comes to feel the force of his fixation on death. As he puts it, "The man who exists is infinitely interested in existing."[50] It is one of the many unprovable assumptions we are driven to make about a concept as inclusive and mysterious as generic tragedy, but I suspect that for each of us the deepest hopeless truth, the root tragic datum, is the buried knowledge of his own mortality. But whether we "think" of death or not, always somewhere alive within us is that *Pricke of Conscience,* "Ded is the most dred thing that is in all this world."[51]

That special knowledge of the immanence of death is a part of the subphilosophy of systematic tragedy, as it is of generic tragedy. But we find it, on the whole, less often in tragic writings than we would expect. We feel all that is implied of our frantic hold on life when Hardy's Jude is presented to us as the embodiment of "the coming universal wish not to be"; a resignation and decay of the will such as that signals the collapse of the race itself, a reversal of our basic

[49] Miguel de Unamuno, *The Tragic Sense of Life,* trans. by J. E. Crawford Flitch (New York, Dover Publications, 1954), 17.

[50] *Ibid.,* 108.

[51] William Van O'Connor, *Climates of Tragedy* (Baton Rouge, Louisiana State University Press, 1943), 23.

definitions of ourselves as human. Without doubt, the idea of death is central to the sense of tragedy; but what is most interesting is our subordination of it. "All consciousness," Unamuno says, "is consciousness of death and suffering."[52] "Call no man lucky until he is dead," sings the chorus at the end of *Oedipus Rex.* Systematic tragedy and generic tragedy both function through the raw materials of death and suffering, but emphasis is nearly always upon the suffering which is the standard pattern of life; death itself is only a part of that suffering, merely the last of the tragic evidences. Tragedy treats of endemic failure, and death is the last and most vivid failure of all; of the consequences of the Fall, death is the grandest, but still only one.

We are left, really, where we were, holding a multiple mystery: a mysteriously malign universe, "utterly indifferent to the will and desires of men,"[53] which we order dramatically in a mysterious art, in a sad spectacle to which we respond with emotions not only of peace but of triumph. Let us accept Gilbert Murray's description of what he calls the "tragic pattern" or the "essential tragic idea"—our generic tragedy:

> . . . in the main popular conception . . . life is seen in the tragic pattern. As the Sun every year and every morning begins weak and lovely, then grows strong and fierce, then excessive and intolerable, and then, by reason of that excess, is doomed to die, so runs the story with trees, beasts, and men, with kings and heroes and cities. Herodotus sees the history of the Persian War in the same tragic pattern: Xerxes, tall, strong, beautiful, lord of a vast empire, became proud and desired too much, was led into Ate and stricken down. Thucydides sees the history of Athens in the same pattern: incredible achievements, beauty, splendour; then pride, bat-

[52] *Op. cit.*, 112.

[53] Herbert Weisinger, *Tragedy and the Paradox of the Fortunate Fall* (London, Routledge and Kegan Paul, 1953), 194.

> tle, determination to win at all costs; crime, brutality, dishonour, and defeat after all. That is the essential tragic idea, however we translate it into modern language, climax followed by decline, or pride by judgement.[54]

He restates our old question, "Why is it that people should find not merely enjoyment, but a very high kind of enjoyment, in scenes of death and anguish, the disappointment of human hopes, the terrific punishment of slight errors, and generally the overthrow of the great?"[55]

When Aristotle speaks, "in his abrupt style, like a telegram," of the central tragic emotion as one of purgation of pity and fear and "affections of that sort," he does not carry us all the way. The "homeopathic metaphor" of catharsis, implying a cleansed emptiness, rest and peace and reconstruction, does not extend to cover our further, equally important emotions, implied perhaps in Murray's "very high enjoyment," but more nearly described by Bradley's word "exultation."[56] There is more at the end of tragedy than Milton's "calm of mind" or "new acquist," though those are well. Do we not feel, in the presence of tragic art, something beyond emptiness and peace and instruction: an excitement, an actual vicarious triumph, a sense of liberation and power, a heightening and lightening of the body and the spirit, a feeling that we transcend, even while we unite with, the tragic experience? One seems to feel a violent rising assertion of the powers of the self, as if one were nominated and qualified as racial representative, "culture hero." Why this strange exhilaration? Why does one feel, at the *end* of the tragic process, after the brutal disciplinary

54 *The Classical Tradition in Poetry* (Cambridge, Harvard University Press, 1927), 60.

55 *Ibid.*, 59.

56 "Hegel's Theory of Tragedy," in Schorer, Miles, and McKenzie's *Criticism: The Foundations of Modern Literary Judgment*, 61.

experience, an even larger confidence than the hero's at the beginning, when "full of resources, he faced the future"?

In that emotion, that increment of excitement added to catharsis, is a deeper mystery than we have yet explored. The roots of the emotion lie as deep as possible, perhaps deeper than we can dig with any tools except those of intuition. The sensation, as I say, is one of *racial* fusion and transcendence, of merging with the long past and long future, of sharing the oldest emotions of mankind. The history of tragedy has been very thoroughly canvassed by scholars, and we have their findings. But there are still things we feel we do not understand about tragedy. In searching into those we must depend upon the findings of anthropologists and their interpreters, and upon the brilliant guesswork of such psychologists as Jung. We will learn more from them, but perhaps be finally left with the heart's intuitions, with convictions as much "proved upon our pulses" as upon our reason.

But if it is generic tragedy we seek to understand, these boggy acres are where we shall have to work. It is a considerable comfort, in any case, to reflect that the solid anthropological researches into the origins of dramatic tragedy, made by Sir James Frazer, Gilbert Murray, Jane Harrison, and recently by Herbert Weisinger, rest upon the relatively spongy foundation of an indispensable intuition of Nietzsche's: the origin of Greek tragedy in Dionysiac ritual, and the general interdependence of myth and ritual in primitive cultures.[57] We need not follow Nietzsche all the way, but we may borrow certain of his premises to lead us into the anthropological areas more "scientifically" developed by the later writers. We have already seen passing references to these notions of tragic archetypes deeply buried in culture, in Murray's "main popular concep-

[57] Francis Golffing, Introduction to *The Birth of Tragedy and the Genealogy of Morals, op. cit.*, ix.

tion" of life "seen in the tragic pattern,"[58] and in Dixon's "unresolved dissonance within the universe, which popular imagination has always pictured as a conflict."[59]

What we may call the anthropological hypothesis of tragedy needs to be presented in four main stages. First, a clear statement of the hypothesis itself, which we can set down in the compact formula of Maud Bodkin, who leans in her turn upon the social psychology of Jung and the historical criticism of Gilbert Murray:

> The hypothesis to be examined is that in Poetry—and here we are to consider in particular tragic poetry—we may identify themes having a particular form or pattern which persists amid variation from age to age, and which corresponds to a pattern or configuration of emotional tendencies in the minds of those who are stirred by the theme.[60]

Miss Bodkin further names, very generally and tentatively, the particular kind of ritual which lies behind the "emotional continuity" of the history of tragedy:

> Moreover, for the knowledge of the recurrences, the rhythms and seasons of life—a knowledge almost essential to the attitudes of courage and patience in misfortune and of temperance in prosperity—we depend upon participation in a moral and psychological tradition conveyed through the great images of tragic poetry and of myth. The rising and the setting of the sun, the exultant rush of growth in early summer and then the fall of the year, are through cumulative poetic tradition so fused with human emotion as to have become for us half-mythical symbols that mirror in little span experiences brought only in the slow course of years . . . . Within the meaning communicated today to a sensitive reader or spectator of

58 See above, pp. 6, 23–24.
59 See above, pp. 6 f., 18 ff.
60 *Archetypal Patterns in Poetry* (London, Oxford University Press, 1934), 4.

> *Hamlet* or *King Lear* . . . something is present corresponding to the emotional meaning that belonged to ancient rituals undertaken for the renewal of the life of the tribe.[61]

Secondly, we ought to examine as briefly as possible the poeticized intuitions of Nietzsche. Then we must follow at greater length Murray's analysis, in virtual collaboration with Jane Harrison, of the genetic patterns of Greek tragedy; and add to that the inductions rising out of his comparative study of the "Hamlet-Saga" and the "Orestes-Saga." Finally, we need to look carefully at the conclusions of Herbert Weisinger, who traces the special significance of the archetype of the "Fortunate Fall" within the pattern of myth and ritual.

The most concise of Nietzsche's definitions runs as follows: Greek tragedy is "a Dionysiac chorus which again and again discharges itself in Apollonian images";[62] or, in reverse order: "Tragedy is an Apollonian embodiment of Dionysiac insights and powers . . . ."[63] Nietzsche's famous categories of "Apollonian" and "Dionysiac"—which he uses, on the whole, with remarkable precision—connote opposed groups of urges and manners, which commingle, as he says, to create tragic drama. The Dionysiac complex, in which rests the basic religious impulse to tragic utterance, is made of impulses which are of "music," "intoxication,"[64] "enchantment," "transformation";[65] it is full of wisdom and knowledge, but its knowledge is passionate, intuitive, poetic—folk-knowledge or blood-knowledge, rising out of a deep union with earth and time. Its habits in the transported state are wild and free and orgiastic. The Apollonian urges, by contrast, are much more cerebral, much less gaudy and interesting. They are those of "dream" rather

61 *Ibid.*, 85.
62 Nietzsche, *op. cit.*, 56.
63 *Ibid.*, 56–57.
64 *Ibid.*, 19.
65 *Ibid.*, 56.

than "intoxication," and of "plastic art" rather than "music."[66] The Apollonian urges limit and order and codify and dignify; their role is that of modest meliorism, and their slogans are *"sophrosyne,"* and "know thyself," and "nothing too much."[67] They want to give form and decorum to intuition and impulse, to "compose" rather than to "express." "Attic tragedy," Nietzsche concluded, was "the common goal of both urges; whose mysterious marriage, after long discord, ennobled itself with such a child, at once Antigone and Cassandra."[68]

It is a bit startling to see, at last, that Nietzsche's categories of "Dionysiac" and "Apollonian" correspond at least crudely to the distinction I have been trying to draw between "generic" and "systematic" tragedy. For generic tragedy is an intuitive, blood-rooted folk tragedy, however it may be sophisticated in practice; only the excesses of the Dionysiac chorus are foreign to it—and those perhaps not altogether foreign, as we shall see when we come to the last poems of Yeats. And systematic tragedy is the "Apollonian" imposition of the order, limitation, and logic of dramatic form upon generic experience and emotion.

Though Nietzsche's thought grows more and more lyrical and difficult, we must follow it somewhat further if we are to understand his poeticized contribution to the theory of the archetypes of tragedy. The Apollonian spirit, he argues, being the ordering "plastic" spirit, acts upon the tragic evidences, "the terrors and horrors of existence,"[69] and makes them bearable by reducing their immensity, and, for the moment, their significance, to the shape and compass of formal dramatic art: ". . . the Apollonian spirit rescues us from the Dionysiac

66 *Ibid.*, 19.

67 *Ibid.*, 34.

68 *Ibid.*, 36.

69 *Ibid.*, 29.

universality and makes us attend, delightedly, to individual forms."[70] And again,

> Apollo embodies the transcendent genius of the *principium individuationis;* through him alone is it possible to achieve redemption in illusion. The mystical jubilation of Dionysos, on the other hand, breaks the spell of individuation and opens a path to the maternal womb of being.[71]

Further, the fable of the drama, "tragic myth," focusing in the figure of the hero, offers the means by which generic tragic experience may be transported and sublimated; thus:

> Like a mighty titan, the tragic hero shoulders the whole Dionysiac world and removes the burden from us. At the same time, tragic myth, through the figure of the hero, delivers us from our avid thirst for earthly satisfaction and reminds us of another satisfaction and a higher delight . . . . Tragedy interposes a noble parable, *myth,* between the universality of its music and the Dionysiac disposition of the spectator and in so doing creates the illusion that music is but a supreme instrument for bringing to life the plastic world of myth.[72]

But at the same time the Dionysiac primitivism drags back against the Apollonian idealizing, and strives to return to lyricism, blood-knowledge, and union with the racial memory:

> In exchange, music endows the tragic myth with a convincing metaphysical significance, which the unsupported word and image could never achieve, and, moreover, assures the spectator of a supreme delight—though the way passes through annihilation and negation, so that he is made to feel that the very womb of things speaks audibly to him.[73]

70 *Ibid.,* 128.

71 *Ibid.,* 97.

72 *Ibid.,* 126.

In the richest of his summations, Nietzsche makes clear his belief that in tragedy the last voice is that of Dionysus:

> In the final effect of tragedy the Dionysiac element triumphs once again: its closing sounds are such as were never heard in the Apollonian realm. The Apollonian illusion reveals its identity as the veil thrown over the Dionysiac meanings for the duration of the play, and yet the illusion is so potent that at its close the Apollonian drama is projected into a sphere where it begins to speak with Dionysiac wisdom, thereby denying itself and its Apollonian concreteness.[74]

What he is dealing with is the great problem of the residual emotion of tragedy, which Aristotle accounted for on the basis of catharsis—the word we have called too small to include our emotions of excited joy and transcendence: in Nietzsche's own phrase, "raised to a kind of omniscience."[75] He accounts for these emotions in terms of metaphor which is intensely persuasive. In a series of eloquent phrases, he traces the highest tragic emotion to the most ancient blood-kinship among the tragic spectator, the dramatized tragic fable, and the tragic materials of racial memory in which both are rooted. "In that myth," he writes, "the world of appearance is pushed to its limits, where it denies itself and seeks to escape back into the world of primordial reality."[76] Our union, he says, is with "the very womb of things,"[77] the "Original Mother,"[78] the "maternal womb of being,"[79] with the "mothers of being, whose names are Wish, Will, Woe."[80] In the Dionysiac rite, Nietzsche

73 *Ibid.*
74 *Ibid.*, 131.
75 *Ibid.*
76 *Ibid.*, 132.
77 *Ibid.*, 126.
78 *Ibid.*, 102.
79 *Ibid.*, 97.
80 *Ibid.*, 124.

says, "nature herself . . . rises again to celebrate the reconciliation with her prodigal son, man."[81]

In the midst of that deep mingling, tragedy "sits in noble ecstasy,"[82] the crown of which is a self-forgetful joy: "The metaphysical solace . . . that, despite every phenomenal change life is at bottom indestructibly joyful and powerful."[83] The same idea amplified:

> Music alone allows us to understand the delight felt at the annihilation of the individual. Each single instance of such annihilation will clarify for us the abiding phenomenon of Dionysiac art, which expresses the omnipotent will behind individuation, eternal life continuing beyond all appearance and in spite of destruction. The metaphysical delight in tragedy is a translation of instinctive Dionysiac wisdom into images. The hero, the highest manifestation of the will, is destroyed, and we assent, since he too is merely a phenomenon, and the eternal life of the will remains unaffected. Tragedy cries, "We believe that life is eternal!" and music is the direct expression of that life. The aims of plastic arts are very different: here Apollo overcomes individual suffering by the glorious apotheosis of what is eternal in appearance: here beauty vanquishes the suffering that inheres in all existence, and pain is, in a certain sense, glossed away from nature's countenance. That same nature addresses us through Dionysiac art and its tragic symbolism, in a voice that rings authentic: "Be like me, the Original Mother, who, constantly creating, finds satisfaction in the turbulent flux of appearances."[84]

To intuitions of such passion and brilliance, one can respond only intuitively: "this is lyrical nonsense"; or "it must be so." I am deeply impressed; and convinced, in any case, that we

81 *Ibid.,* 23.
82 *Ibid.,* 124.
83 *Ibid.,* 50.
84 *Ibid.,* 101–102.

can approach understanding of an emotion so complex as the full tragic emotion only by some such "inspirational" process as that of Nietzsche.

His intuitions are given a considerable thickening and sobering by more scholarly and scientific critics, of whom Gilbert Murray is the most serviceable. We may follow out Nietzsche's line in two of Murray's essays, his "Excursus on the Ritual Forms Preserved in Greek Tragedy," published as part of Jane Harrison's *Themis* in 1912, and his Charles Eliot Norton lecture, "Hamlet and Orestes," published in 1927.

Murray's thesis takes as a point of departure Miss Harrison's isolation and elevation of the all-important archetypal Spirit of primitive ritual, the "Eniautos- or Year-Daimon, who lies behind each and every primitive god."[85] In his "Excursus," Murray speaks only of Greek tragedy. His basic assumption is that tragedy rose out of vegetation or fertility ceremony, "a Ritual Dance, a *Sacer Ludus,*" which conceived Dionysus as an " 'Eniautos-Daimon,' or vegetation god, like Adonis, Osiris, etc., who represent the cyclic death and rebirth of the Earth and the World, i.e., for practical purposes, of the tribe's own lands and the tribe itself."[86] He argues that, whereas the content of Greek tragedy wandered far from the content of the Dionysiac ritual-drama, the actual forms of the ritual structure showed a remarkably stubborn constancy: " . . . the forms of tragedy retain clear traces of the original drama of the Death and Rebirth of the Year Spirit."[87] He then catalogs the elements which occur, in a "normal sequence" of startling regularity, in characteristic Eniautos celebrations; we find that most of the terms are familiar to us from Aristotle:

85 *Themis: A Study of the Social Origins of Greek Religion* (Cambridge, Cambridge University Press, 1927, 2nd ed.), vii.

86 Gilbert Murray, "Excursus on the Ritual Forms Preserved in Greek Tragedy," in Jane Harrison's *Themis,* 341.

87 *Ibid.,* 342.

1. An *Agon* or Contest, the Year against its enemy, Light against Darkness, Summer against Winter.
2. A *Pathos* of the Year-Daimon, generally a ritual or sacrificial death, in which Adonis or Attis is slain by the tabu animal, the Pharmakos stoned, Osiris, Dionysus, Pentheus, Orpheus, Hippolytus torn to pieces....
3. A *Messenger*. For this Pathos seems seldom or never to be actually performed under the eyes of the audience .... "The news comes" that Pan the Great, Thammuz, Adonis, Osiris, is dead, and the dead body is often brought in on a bier ....
4. A *Threnos* or Lamentation ... a clash of contrary emotions, the death of the old being also the triumph of the new ....
5. and 6. An *Anagnorisis*—discovery or recognition—of the slain and mutilated Daimon, followed by his Resurrection or Apotheosis or, in some sense, his Epiphany in glory. This I shall call by the general name *Theophany*. It naturally goes with a *Peripeteia* or extreme change of feeling from grief to joy.[88]

The terms are listed in "the sequence in which these should normally occur."

Murray next deals briefly with the problem of what seems to have been "a special final Peripeteia," that from grief to joy, accompanying the Anagnorisis and Theophany of the close of the ceremony. The fact that that primitive element is missing from extant tragedy must be due, he concludes, to the disappearance of the satyr play, the fourth member of the early tragic tetralogies.[89] (Nietzsche thought the same: the chorus of satyrs expressed the conviction that "life is at bottom indestructibly joyful and powerful.")[90] This matter, on which Murray spends little space, is to me intensely interesting and im-

88 *Ibid.*, 343–44.
89 *Ibid.*, 344–45.
90 *Op. cit.*, 50.

portant, and I hope to show eventually that it has a special relevance to Yeats; further, it seems to me plainly related to the vital increment of emotion added to the Aristotelian catharsis, which I have tried, unscientifically and with the help of Nietzsche, to associate with some such mysterious phenomenon as the racial memory.

In the main body of his "Excursus," Murray analyzes, briefly but closely, the degree to which each of the extant Greek tragedies follows or fails to follow the characteristic form of the ritual of the Year-Spirit. His finding is that, whereas there is a great deal of individual variation, there occurs also a wholly remarkable tendency, and that most notably of all in the latest plays of Euripides, to reproduce "the whole sequence of Contest, Tearing-Asunder, Messenger, Lamentation, Discovery, Recognition, and Resurrection which constituted the original Dionysus-mystery."[91] And his deeply moved and moving conclusion:

> An outer shape dominated by tough and undying tradition, an inner life fiery with sincerity and spiritual freedom; the vessels of a very ancient religion overfilled and broken by the new wine of reasoning and rebellious humanity, and still, in their rejection, shedding abroad the old aroma, as of eternal and mysterious things: these are the fundamental paradoxes presented to us by Greek tragedy. The contrasts have their significance for other art also, perhaps for all great art.[92]

Murray's essay on Hamlet and Orestes, solid in its scholarship and exciting in its speculations, is a daring foray into the "unconscious tradition" in poetry. His aim is a comparative study of the two heroes, "most central and typical" representa-

[91] "Excursus on the Ritual Forms Preserved in Greek Tragedy," in Jane Harrison's *Themis*, 362.

[92] *Ibid.*, 362–63.

tives of ancient and modern tragedy, as "traditional types."[93] We cannot take the time here to follow Murray's painstaking compilation of detailed correspondences among the numerous extant forms of the sagas and dramas involving his two heroes. Suffice it to say that one is shaken and impressed, as Murray is. What must occupy us is his conclusions. He can find no historical reason for the overlapping patterns, and no chance of imitations. For a moment he considers the "terrifying hypothesis" that the basic materials of tragedy are "by nature so limited that these similarities are inevitable";[94] but he lays that speculation aside, not without suspecting some truth in it. Then he turns to his central question:

> . . . can there be some original connection between the myths, or the primitive religious rituals, on which the dramas are ultimately based? And can it be that in the last analysis the similarities between Euripides and Shakespeare are simply due to the natural working out, by playwrights of special genius, of the dramatic possibilities latent in that original seed? If this is so, it will lead us to some interesting conclusions.[95]

The conclusions are interesting indeed. What we have in the Orestes saga is "the world-wide ritual story of the Golden Bough Kings. That ritual story is . . . the fundamental conception that forms the basis of Greek tragedy . . . ."[96] And, Murray reminds us, "It is no pale myth or allegory that has so deeply dyed the first pages of human history"; these are life-and-death matters that lie at the brute sources of life: "It is man's passionate desire for the food that will save him from starvation, his passionate memory of the streams of blood,

[93] "Hamlet and Orestes," *The Classical Tradition in Poetry,* 205.
[94] *Ibid.,* 226.
[95] *Ibid.,* 226–27.
[96] *Ibid.,* 228.

willing and unwilling, that have been shed to keep him alive."[97] But can the same things be said of the Hamlet saga? Here, in an area where he is not a specialist, Murray is more diffident; but he is sure it is true, and he cites the strong confirmations of the researches of Gollancz, Zinzow, Rydberg, and Bertha V. Phillpotts. Thus " . . . we finally run the Hamlet-saga to earth in the same ground as the Orestes-saga," he concludes, "in that prehistoric and worldwide ritual battle of Summer and Winter, of Life and Death, which has played so vast a part in the mental development of the human race . . . ."[98] More lyrically and imaginatively:

> The things that thrill and amaze us in *Hamlet* or the *Agamemnon* are not any historical particulars about medieval Elsinore or prehistoric Mycenae, but things belonging to the old stories and the old magic rites, which stirred and thrilled our forefathers five and six thousand years ago; set them dancing all night on the hills, tearing beasts and men in pieces, and giving up their own bodies to a ghastly death, in hope thereby to keep the green world from dying and to be the saviours of their own people.[99]

Murray sums up the implications of his hypothesis. It envisions, he says, "a great unconscious solidarity and continuity, lasting from age to age, among all the children of the poets, both the makers and the callers-forth, both the artists and the audiences."[100] Ancient subjects show "a curious power of almost eternal durability"[101]—a conception of art which will seem less strange if we recall that the durability and the interconnectedness of primitive beliefs and rites is a commonplace

[97] *Ibid.*, 229.

[98] *Ibid.*, 234.

[99] *Ibid.*, 236.

[100] *Ibid.*, 237.

[101] *Ibid.*

of the history of religion. Tragedy began as religion, and when has it ceased to be religious? He wonders, in terms interestingly Jungian, whether the archetypal stories and situations may not be

> deeply implanted in the memory of the race, stamped, as it were, upon our physical organism. We have forgotten their faces and their voices; we say that they are strange to us. Yet there is that within us which leaps at the sight of them, a cry of the blood which tells us we have known them always.[102]

At the end of this extraordinary essay, Murray quiets our strongest objection to his argument by recognizing the function of the creative artist, who must always apply his own life-sense and his own ordering imagination to the blood myth to make new art of it. This time, his terms are unconsciously Nietzschean:

> And in the greatest ages of literature there seems to be, among other things, a power of preserving due proportion between these opposite elements—the expression of boundless primitive emotion and the subtle and delicate representation of life. In the plays like *Hamlet* or the *Agamemnon* or the *Electra* we have certainly fine and flexible character-study, a varied and well-wrought story, a full command of the technical instruments of the poet and the dramatist; but we have also, I suspect, a strange, unanalyzed vibration below the surface, an undercurrent of desires and fears and passions, long slumbering yet eternally familiar, which have for thousands of years lain near the root of our most intimate emotions and been wrought into the fabric of our most magical dreams. How far into past ages this stream may reach back, I dare not even surmise; but it seems as if the power of stirring it or moving with it were one of the last secrets of genius.[103]

102 *Ibid.,* 238–39.

103 *Ibid.,* 239–40.

A bit Dionysiac, perhaps; but intensely exciting and containing, one feels, a luminous insight.

We have followed out what I take to be the basic line of the anthropological hypothesis of tragedy. In *Tragedy and the Paradox of the Fortunate Fall* (1953), Herbert Weisinger, too, follows this hypothesis, and takes account of the vast scholarship which has grown up about it since Frazer. He takes as his special task the historical and analytical survey of a single important mythical and ritual configuration which he calls, following Lovejoy's famous essay on *Paradise Lost,* "the paradox of the fortunate fall."

It is as a piece of "the ultimate stuff out of which meaning is derived," "so old and so basic,"[104] that Mr. Weisinger approaches the history of the archetype of the fortunate fall. The familiar Miltonic expression occurs in lines 473–78 of Book XII of *Paradise Lost*: "Full of doubt I stand," says Adam,

> *Whether I should repent me now of sin*
> *By me done or occasioned, or rejoice*
> *Much more that much more good thereof shall spring–*
> *To God more glory, more good will to men*
> *From God–and over wrath grace shall abound.*

The element of paradox is plain: on the one hand, "loss of Eden," and all therein implied; on the other hand, Incarnation and Redemption.

Mr. Weisinger postulates a genetic process in the coming-to-be of art which runs from "experience," to "myth," to "literature." The paradox of the Fortunate Fall, he believes, is an indispensable medial step between myth and tragedy, a step "which translates the emotional overtones of myth into the conscious creation of tragedy."[105] We should set down his more

104 Weisinger, *op. cit.,* 10.

105 *Ibid.,* 29.

detailed postulate of a standard "chain of response to tragedy,"[106] a chain of four links, as it stands in this telescoped statement:

> First, experience, the repeated primeval traumatic shocks ultimately crystallizing themselves into the archetype of rebirth; then, the myth and ritual mould of the ancient Near East, concretizing the archetype of rebirth into a pattern of behaviour and belief infused with conviction and faith; then, the paradox of the fortunate fall, summing up in brief the essence of the myth and ritual of the ancient Near East, sharper in its formulation, more ideological, yet, at the same time, carrying with it the emotional aura of the myth and ritual pattern, and finally, tragedy, the deliberate work of art, using the paradox of the fortunate fall as its ideological backbone, so to speak, but divergent in kind from the archetype of rebirth, from the myth and ritual of the ancient Near East, and from the paradox of the fortunate fall, yet partaking of the force of each, and adding to them the conscious choice of materials and meaning which distinguishes art from the stuff out of which it is made.[107]

Regretfully but understandably, Mr. Weisinger confines himself to the second and third of these huge "links." His conviction in regard to "the secret of the hold which tragedy has on us" is precisely the conviction we have been developing for a good many pages:

> . . . our reaction to tragedy goes far deeper than at first we might have suspected . . . in fact, because it is made up of links in so long a chain, it binds us to a pattern of belief so strong in its grip on the mind of man that in whatever form we encounter it we cannot but respond, and respond deeply, to it.[108]

106 *Ibid.*, 10.
107 *Ibid.*, 29.
108 *Ibid.*, 10.

In the body of his book, trying to assemble the "ideological backbone" of tragedy, Mr. Weisinger traces out the scores of linked variants of the myth and ritual of the Fortunate Fall, showing their intricately overlapping patterns and interlocking symbolisms, through the many centuries of their progress, from their rise in the ancient Near East, their development in Mediterranean, Aegean, and Hebrew thought, their transformation into Christian practice and into medieval theology, and into such codifications as that of the Easter Even Hymn which gives us the actual phrase with which both he and Lovejoy work: *"O certe necessarium Adae peccatum, quod Christi morte deletum est! O felix culpa, quae talem ac tantum meruit habere redemptorem!"* Such an elaborate progress we can hope to review only in the sketchiest fashion. In any case, T. S. Eliot, if not Frazer and Murray, has made the broad outlines familiar to students of poetry.

In its primitive form, "at least six thousand years old," the ritual centers upon a king, conceived as divine, who was killed every year and reborn in the figure of his successor. As the ritual slowly developed, the killing was made symbolic, rather than literal, in an annual rite which terminated, of course, in an equally symbolic resurrection.[109] Thus it is perfectly clear that this figure of focus, the king-god, is simply another of what Murray, following Frazer, calls the Golden-Bough Kings; and his ritual is that most ancient and fundamental ceremony of sympathetic magic, the figurative death and rebirth of the Scapegoat. The king was killed and resurrected because in him centered the whole well-being of the people, dependent upon his supposed control of the processes of nature, the sustainers of life itself.[110] Mr. Weisinger draws up a table of the steps in the standard ritual:

[109] *Ibid.*, 31.
[110] *Ibid.*, 37–38.

(1) the indispensable role of the divine king;
(2) the combat between the God and an opposing power;
(3) the suffering of the God;
(4) the death of the God;
(5) the resurrection of the God;
(6) the symbolic reaction of the myth of creation;
(7) the sacred marriage;
(8) the triumphal procession; and
(9) the settling of destinies.[111]

The parallel to the life, death, and resurrection of Christ will have almost certainly sprung to the reader's mind at once. The detailed likeness of Mr. Weisinger's sequence to the Eniautos-ritual recorded by Murray is also unmistakable: "Agon, Pathos, Messenger, Threnos, Anagnorisis, Theophany."[112] And Nietzsche, as usual, had anticipated the whole pattern of these conclusions:

> The legend of Prometheus is indigenous to the entire community of Aryan races and attests to their prevailing talent for profound and tragic vision. In fact, it is not improbable that this myth has the same characteristic importance for the Aryan mind that the myth of the Fall has for the Semitic, and that the two myths are related as brother and sister.[113]

Pursuing his gradual focus upon Christian thought through the practices of the ancient Mediterranean cultures, Mr. Weisinger concludes:

> By the time of the rise of Christianity, the Mediterranean world was pulsating with beliefs, which, however they might differ in details, tended towards one general form, that of salvation through rebirth.[114]

111 *Ibid.*, 39.

112 Murray, "Excursus on the Ritual Forms Preserved in Greek Tragedy," in Jane Harrison's *Themis,* 344.

113 *Op. cit.*, 63.

114 Weisinger, *op. cit.,* 114.

To that he joins the pressure of Aegean thought, so that "two great streams of similar ideas, one rising in the Near East, and the other in the Aegean area, slowly converged on Palestine to form one single sea out of which Christianity emerged."[115] Thus far, such mutations as he has found in the archetype of the Fortunate Fall have been orderly and unspectacular. But the Hebrews made a radical addition; through their "unique and tenacious insistence on the mercy of their transcendent God," they introduced a vital new metaphysical extension, making possible "the dialectical leap from out of the endless circle on to a different and higher stage of understanding."[116] Placing his faith in a God such as that of the Hebrews, man enters into an "eternal" relation with that God, and escapes his helpless entrapment in the temporal cycle; he enters a kind of divine time-scheme which surrounds, encloses, and makes little of, human time. This is a personal relationship with a personal God, into which man enters by his own will. The Hebrews "showed that man can, by himself, transcend" an "indifferent universe."[117]

For his recapitulation of the long evolutionary process which prepared the way for Christ, the greatest of the Scapegoats, Mr. Weisinger depends upon the five-stage formula of Professor Theodore H. Gaster, which I will paraphrase. The first stage is that in which men, recognizing the basic presence of cyclical regularity in nature, concludes that " 'Life is a series of leases,' " over which he may be able to gain magical control by regular communal practice of mimetic ceremony. In the second stage, these motives are brought to focus in the figure of the king, who "represents" the whole life-and-death struggle. The third stage carried ritual into theology, with the recognition that "the

115 *Ibid.*, 131.
116 *Ibid.*, 189.
117 *Ibid.*

series of leases is in fact a continuum" presided over by a single eternal God-personality: this, I take it, is the stage achieved by Hebrew thought. In the fourth stage, the mythic fable is "moralized," and the figure of focus grows into a "Divine King," who has the actual power of transforming life into a scene of bliss, and who does not merely renew energy but can secure actual forgiveness of sin. This is clearly the pattern which includes Christ, and it prepares the fifth and last stage, which sees life as everlasting, breaks down the separation between life and death, and sees death as a mere point of transition in an eternal continuum:[118] "One short sleep past, we wake eternally," says Donne in classic Christian terms; "Death, thou shalt die."

The chain comes to rest, then, at least for the moment of the last two thousand years, in Christian theology. And Mr. Weisinger makes clear the immense concentration of emotion and meaning which fills the figure of Christ, after the long accumulation of man's suffering, rationalising, and dramatizing of generic tragedy. Of generic tragedy, the tragic hero is the race, man at large, the creature who "asserts in the face of all the evidence to the contrary the reality of his hopes and ideals."[119] Our tragic line, then, is very clearly drawn from the Golden-Bough King to the modern tragic hero; they are one flesh. "Christ, Adam, Everyman—each suffers, yet each is triumphant; and in the wings stands Hamlet."[120]

Though this introductory survey of theories of tragedy has been long, my real temptation was to make it longer, for much is left unsaid. I hope mainly to have shown that the case of tragedy remains "open," that we are still trying to understand

118 *Ibid.*, 191–92.
119 *Ibid.*, 194.
120 *Ibid.*, 218.

it; that tragedy may be talked about in at least two basic senses: in the usual sense of "systematic" tragedy, a formal art, generally dramatic, and in the less common sense of "generic" tragedy, an ancient and universal "sub-philosophical" "sense of life," which may be dumb, or may express itself in art in almost any form. To illustrate the practice of tragedy in this latter sense, and to show the cross-fertilization between the two senses, we have the grand example of the tragic lyricism of Yeats.

CHAPTER TWO

Yeatsian Definitions

TURNING AT LAST to the poetry of Yeats, we need to recall the cardinal texts with which we began. First, the resonant statement from that portion of his *Autobiography* first published in 1922: "We begin to live when we have conceived life as tragedy";[1] then the rumination on the carved Chinese stone which led to the great poem "Lapis Lazuli":

> Ascetic, pupil, hard stone, eternal theme of the sensual east. The heroic cry in the midst of despair. But no, I am wrong, the east has its solutions always and therefore knows nothing of tragedy. It is we, not the east, that must raise the heroic cry;[2]

then the same thought elevated into credo:

1 Page 165.

2 *Letters to Dorothy Wellesley*, 8–9.

> To me the supreme aim is an act of faith and reason to make one rejoice in the midst of tragedy. An impossible aim; yet I think it true that nothing can injure us.[3]

It was the philosophical gravity of such statements which declared the legitimacy of reading the lyrics of Yeats in a tragic frame of reference.

This is not to claim that it is safe to trust as solid doctrine every pronouncement of his which carries an air of synopsis. Yeats loved to speak ex cathedra, and whereas he was an able pontificator, he was a far from consistent one. Yet the inconsistencies, on the other hand, are often only seeming, and result from Yeats's fiery transcendentalism and pronounced Heraclitean sympathies. He was a dynamist, a "perner" in "gyres" between antinomies, a devotee of process—of flux and change and cycle. The seeming whimsicality of thought which follows from philosophical dynamism of this sort sets hard problems for the reader who tries to search out dominant lines. But Yeats's prose and verse do draw dominant lines, and I believe that his definition of life as tragedy, if we can read it with enough patience and variety, will prove to be one great determining constant in the purposefully shifting ground of his speculation.

From the texts above we may mine a half-dozen interrelated premises: (1) life is "tragedy"; (2) maturity depends upon one's recognition of the fact that life is "tragic"; (3) the tragic sense is available only to those who lack "solutions"; (4) art itself is one response to the fact of tragedy; (5) the specific function of art is transmutation of tragedy into joy: it is "an act of faith and reason to make one rejoice in the midst of tragedy"; (6) the individual is ultimately impervious: "nothing can injure us." Works of art are fragments to be shored against ruins.

[3] *Ibid.*, 13.

What we need to know is whether these are Yeats's settled views of life and art; how consistently he adhered to his sense of life as tragedy; how he fleshed out and how he varied the ideas formulated here; whether any other side of his thought seriously undercuts these views; what kind of art results from this response to life as tragedy—what is the nature and what the stature of his personal "acts of faith and reason"; finally, what value may we place, critically, upon an art which calls itself "tragic" yet differs so widely from the accepted forms of "systematic" tragedy?

We must begin by noticing firmly that Yeats uses the word tragedy in the passages above, and in fact uses it characteristically, not in any formal academic or literary-historical sense, Aristotelian or otherwise, but in the broadly useful vulgar conception of the term. He is talking about what W. M. Dixon called the "moral offensiveness" of the organization of things, *lacrimae rerum* and *vanitas vanitatum*, about the vale of tears, mutability and mortality, decay and death, congenital defeat, endemic sadness—the gulf between our dream of life and life itself, what we want and what we get. Perhaps it is best to call this, for the moment, a romantic concept of tragedy, because of its roots in subjective emotion and its dependence upon the experiences of the self for evidence. It is best to confess, too, that academic stringency might with propriety insist that this Romantic tragedy is really only pathos. But perhaps we may lay down the condition that this pathos approaches the size and seriousness of tragedy only insofar as it succeeds in objectifying and universalizing the data of the suffering self in the work of art. Yeats was not a university man, and never a systematic scholar. Yet I should say he made himself the most interestingly learned poet of his time. He read hugely and passionately and at the same time prejudicially and idiosyncratically; he read, that is, the literature and history and philosophy that would buttress with illustration and sympathy his special crotchets of Celticism, Transcendentalism, and Gnosticism. This is to say again that we will not get far if we pursue Yeats with strict academic terminology; that vocabulary will jibe only coincidentally with his, and we will work more profitably if we can accommodate ourselves to his conventions of thought and speech—a task difficult enough in all conscience.

Let us begin by making a tentative collection of some of the texts which will suggest Yeats's personal definitions of tragedy. For the time being we want only enough members to piece together the general skeleton of his belief. Giving life and body to that will involve us with most of Yeats's poetry and will need all our remaining time and space.

It is odd, considering the clearly central position of an idea of tragedy in Yeats's matter and his manner, that almost nothing has been written of him from the point of view of tragedy. Is the case too obvious, or too difficult? Neither, I should say. It is some comfort to see John Crowe Ransom remark in passing, "The body of his poetry breathes a tragic sense. His gods are true gods rather than easy ones."[4] Louis MacNeice gives Yeats's idea of tragedy a few interesting, arguable paragraphs. The title of Vivienne Koch's study, *W. B. Yeats: The Tragic Phase,* promises an investigation, but the text scarcely delivers it: she has little specifically to say of tragedy, Yeatsian or otherwise. Probably the best extant treatment of the subject is Walter E. Houghton's analysis, keen but small in scope, of a late sequence of poems, in his essay "Yeats and Crazy Jane: The Hero in Old Age."[5] This essay, too, we may consult in context. My point now is that Yeats's orientation to tragedy was sufficiently obvious to himself that he spoke of it in the most

[4] "Yeats and His Symbols," in James Hall's and Martin Steinmann's *The Permanence of Yeats* (hereinafter referred to as *PY*), 107.
[5] *PY,* 365–88.

laconic terms, as when he described his plays in a letter to his father in 1912 as "tragic work of my sort,"[6] or when he wrote to Lady Gregory a year later of "The Three Hermits" as "my first poem which is comedy or tragi-comedy,"[7] or when he likened Liam O'Flaherty's novels to the dramatic "line" of the Abbey Theatre which he had been so instrumental in establishing: "I think they are great novels and too full of abounding natural life to be terrible despite their subjects. They are full of that tragic farce we have invented."[8]

Already in these fragmentary statements we find undertones that make us feel, perhaps uneasily, that Yeats's definition of tragedy will be an eccentric one. The phrase "of my sort," the easy coupling of tragedy and comedy, and tragedy and farce, sound like better Yeats than Aristotle. And so they are. That Yeats was ready with cant Aristotelianism by 1889 is clear by the advice he gave to an unnamed "writer of poetical plays":

> I suggested that he should begin with a pastoral play, because nobody would expect from a pastoral play the succession of nervous tremours which the plays of commerce, like the novels of commerce, have substituted for the purification that comes with pity and terror to the imagination and intellect.[9]

At this early date, Yeats was apparently willing to accept Aristotle's purgative ideal as his ideal, and to borrow the standard phrasing. But this is the only bit of pure Aristotelianism I have been able to find in Yeats; and this bit takes on a lip-service air as he goes on in the maturing of his theory and of his vocabulary.

In point of fact Yeats's formal discussions of tragedy are

[6] *The Letters of W. B. Yeats* (hereinafter referred to as *Letters*), ed. by Allan Wade (New York, The Macmillan Company, 1955), 567.

[7] *Ibid.*, 577.

[8] *Ibid.*, 722.

[9] "The Theatre," *Ideas of Good and Evil,* 257.

relatively few and never extended, and much of our evidence will thus have to be fragmentary and suggestive rather than positive and doctrinal; but his attitude does come slowly clear. Yeats's longest and most concentrated pronouncement on a technical conception of tragedy is to be found in an essay of 1910, "The Tragic Theatre." The essay is not easy to work with, couched as it is in that remarkable manner of his early critical prose—still Pateresque, beautifully but almost too consciously rhythmical, impressionistic and elliptical, richly emotive; but it contains important matter that must be quoted at length and examined with some care. Three interrelated concepts will interest us chiefly: tragedy's transcendence of the empirical situation and its ascent into the timeless, abstract, and transparent; the location of "character" in comedy rather than in tragedy and the corollary anonymity of the tragic personae; and the merging of tragedy and passion.

Yeats wrote this brief essay because he felt the contrast between his own views and those of other critics of the performance of the tragic play, *Deirdre of the Sorrows,* which Synge left unrevised at his death in 1909:

> I did not find a word in the printed criticism . . . about the qualities that made certain moments seem to me the noblest tragedy, and the play was judged by what seemed to me but wheels and pulleys necessary to the effect, but in themselves nothing.[10]

Most of the play, Yeats says, had affected him only drably as "a Master's unfinished work, monotonous and melancholy, ill arranged, little more than a sketch of what it would have grown to."[11] But there arrived at last the great ironic moment

[10] "The Tragic Theatre," *The Cutting of an Agate* (hereinafter referred to as *CA*), 196.

[11] *Ibid.,* 197–98.

NATIONAL PORTRAIT GALLERY, LONDON

John Butler Yeats, 1839–1922

The father of William Butler Yeats, from a self-portrait, signed and dated 1920.

NEW YORK PUBLIC LIBRARY PICTURE COLLECTION

John M. Synge, 1871–1909

From the original drawing by John B. Yeats, dated 1907.

when Deirdre and her lover quarrel beside the open grave, "losing all they had given their life to keep":

> "Is it not a hard thing that we should miss the safety of the grave and we trampling its edge?" That is Deirdre's cry at the outset of a reverie of passion that mounts and mounts till grief itself has carried her beyond grief into pure contemplation.[12]

Assembled here in a sort of shorthand notation are ideas which turn out to be major counters in Yeats's formal definition of tragedy. Notice the focus on passion, and the description of tragedy's soaring ascension toward the abstract: perfect realization of an emotion eventually destroys the emotion itself and leaves only a confrontation of absolutes; note too the suggested location of tragic emotion in "reverie" rather than in action.

Yeats goes on to elaborate lyrically his responses to the created tragic emotion:

> . . . now I listened breathless to sentences that may never pass away, and as they filled or dwindled in their civility of sorrow, the player, whose art had seemed clumsy and incomplete, like the writing itself, ascended into that tragic ecstasy which is the best that art—perhaps that life—can give. And at last when Deirdre, in the paroxysm before she took her life, touched with compassionate fingers him that had killed her lover, we knew that the player had become, if but for a moment, the creature of that noble mind which had gathered its art in waste islands, and we too were carried beyond time and persons to where passion, living through its thousand purgatorial years, as in the wink of an eye, becomes wisdom; and it was as though we too had touched and felt and seen a disembodied thing.[13]

[12] *Ibid.*, 197.
[13] *Ibid.*, 198.

The passage virtually completes this portion of Yeats's definition. He has used a new word, "ecstasy," to describe the pinnacle moment in the tragic effect; reaffirmed his conviction that that moment is the crown of art and possibly of life—comforting the thesis of this study; remarked tragedy's tendency, at least in this instance, to dissolve motives and to blend all in the paradox of pity; restated his sense of tragedy's transcending gesture, "beyond time and persons," and its transmuting function in which "passion . . . becomes wisdom"; and announced the crucial word, "disembodied."

The "disembodiment" of tragedy for Yeats is a concept of which we must have much to say. At the moment its office is to lead him to an important corollary idea. He is about to quarrel elaborately with the convention of dramatic criticism which insists upon definiteness of characterization, upon conflict between clearly demarcated persons, and upon the antipathy of clear characterization to lyrical verse. One feels grumbling under the breath of this argument Yeats's anger at insults directed at his own dramatic method, with its ardent lyricism and its vagueness of character conception. But though he is not disinterested, his rationale is impressive and interesting. His own conviction is that right reading of the great dramas of the past proves that the dogma of character as inconsistent with lyricism is faulty: " . . . character grows less and less and sometimes disappears, and there is much lyrical feeling . . . ."[14] This new conviction presents him with the thesis which occupies him in the rest of the essay: character is really the property of comedy, and character in tragedy is sublimated by intensity of feeling into anonymous archetypal postures in which personality grows irrelevant; we know now what he meant above by "a disembodied thing."

[14] *Ibid.*, 199.

> Suddenly it strikes us that character is continuously present in comedy alone, and that there is much tragedy, that of Corneille, that of Racine, that of Greece and Rome, where its place is taken by passions and motives, one person being jealous, another full of love or remorse or pride or anger. In writers of tragi-comedy (and Shakespeare is always a writer of tragi-comedy) there is indeed character, but we notice that it is in the moments of comedy that character is defined, in Hamlet's gaiety let us say; while amid the great moments, when Timon orders his tomb, when Hamlet cries to Horatio, "absent thee from felicity awhile," when Anthony [*sic*] names "Of many thousand kisses the poor last," all is lyricism, unmixed passion, "the integrity of fire." Nor does character ever attain to complete definition in these lamps ready for the taper, no matter how circumstantial and gradual the opening of events, as it does in Falstaff who has no passionate purpose to fulfill, or as it does in Henry the Fifth whose poetry, never touched by lyric heat, is oratorical . . . .[15]

Now Yeats is ready to pack his whole distinction into a neat formula: " . . . tragedy must always be a drowning and breaking of the dykes that separate man from man, and . . . it is upon those dykes comedy keeps house."[16] His emphasis, we see, is upon a quantity and quality of passion which takes on such pressing fluidity that it overpowers distinctions of character precisely because it is not personal but representative; it is "heroic" passion, but it is not the property of a given hero; "character," strictly defined, is irrelevant to tragedy: tragedy deals with man, not men.

Yeats proceeds next to refine his distinction by contrasting the manners which he calls "an art of the flood" and "an art that we call real." The terms are significant: the former, the tragic "art of the flood," recalling of course "the drowner of

[15] *Ibid.*, 199–200.
[16] *Ibid.*, 201.

dykes" and being an art of fullness and fluidity and hyperbole, larger than life and pointing toward frenzy or, we shall see, trance; tragedy being sharply separated from "the real" and its art, to which we respond adequately with our merely quotidian sensibility—"through a delicate discrimination of the senses which is but entire wakefulness, the daily mood grown cold and crystalline."[17] Now, the prose lyricism thickening as Yeats's visionary mood intensifies, he goes on to speak of the art of the flood's functional distortions of "the real" as it edits experience into abstract significance:

> We may not find either mood in its purity, but in mainly tragic art one distinguishes devices to exclude or lessen character, to diminish the power of that daily mood, to cheat or blind its too clear perception. If the real world is not altogether rejected, it is but touched here and there, and into the places we have left empty we summon rhythm, balance, pattern, images that remind us of vast passions, the vagueness of past times, all the chimeras that haunt the edge of trance; and if we are painters, we shall express personal emotion through ideal form, a symbolism handled by the generations, a mask from whose eyes the disembodied looks, a style that remembers many masters, that it may escape contemporary suggestion; or we shall leave out some element of reality as in Byzantine painting, where there is no mass, nothing in relief, and so it is that in the supreme moment of tragic art there comes upon one that strange sensation as though the hair of one's head stood up.[18]

Finally, in the ultimate lyricism of the sentences which close his essay, Yeats recapitulates all his terms, then pushes all abruptly toward that rich paradox of dynamic stasis, or

[17] *Ibid.*, 203–204.
[18] *Ibid.*, 204.

opaque transparency, or loud silence, which has been hesitating within his thought throughout:

> Tragic art, passionate art, the drowner of dykes, the confounder of understanding, moves us by setting us to reverie, by alluring us almost to the intensity of trance. The persons upon the stage, let us say, greaten till they are humanity itself. We feel our minds expand convulsively or spread out slowly like some moon-brightened image-crowded sea. That which is before our eyes perpetually vanishes and returns again in the midst of the excitement it creates, and the more enthralling it is, the more do we forget it.[19]

In sum, then, in his formal definitions Yeats has concluded that tragedy dramatizes or, more properly, mimes, that inscrutable heart of fate which Wordsworth called, and Keats after him, "the burden of the mystery." True tragedy is lyrical and rhythmical and incantatory and it lures us through intense contemplative excitement to trance. Its great moments are instances of passionate reverie ending in an ecstasy of identification, rising out of time and space to stare hypnotized at absolutes. Key words are "passion," "ecstasy," "lyrical," "reverie," "flood," and "disembodied." All these words tag concepts with which we shall have further dealings.

In his distinctions as so far formulated two tendencies seem to me most interesting and most Yeatsian. First is the informing transcendentalism of his whole argument, its drive upward toward "ecstasy" or toward "wisdom," its fascinated contemplation of absolutes, a vaulting vision aiming at ultimates: tragedy seen as an essentially metaphysical art, by a man for whom "the daily life" is a hampering and ignoble condition. Second is the emphasis on "moments," knots of

[19] *Ibid.*, 207.

passion and insight as the repositories of all that is valuable in tragedy: which moments always give rise to that "reverie" of drenched but controlled emotional excitement which becomes a kind of transfixed epiphany. The point to be insisted upon here is that in the smallness of its significant units, its absence of movement, and its worship of feeling, Yeats's concept of the tragic is essentially lyrical rather than dramatic, and we must expect it to take that form even when its vesture is nominally dramatic. By this particular aesthetic and technical emphasis, he takes a distinct step away from "systematic" tragedy. These postures, the lyrical sublimation and the effort at transcendent perfection of passion, or of insight, or of form, become constants in Yeats. Eric Bentley presents at the end of his essay "Yeats As a Playwright" a summary of Yeats's habits in his plays which reviews the whole case for us in simple and useful terms:

> . . . he starts from a dramatic situation and resolves it in a single incident; . . . he employs the non-verbal arts while subordinating them to the words; . . . he asks for absolutely un-Stanislavskyan actors who dance, and speak behind masks; . . . his situation is not used to define individual character or as the starting point of a plot but as the gateway to the "deeps" of the "soul life"; and, finally, . . . we are not left holding a mere Maeterlinckian mood, but are given a theme, namely, that, if we are to live, our wintry and saintly virginity must descend into the dung of passion.[20]

But Mr. Bentley's reference to passion here, "the dung of passion," really gives us a view of an end we shall reach long hence; there is plenty of dung in Yeats's late passion, but it is important to distinguish that tougher emotion from the "passion" of his early essay, which is the passion of stylized

[20] *PY*, 247.

reverie and an almost static lyricism. The equation of passion and tragedy is a great permanent equation in Yeats's thought, as we shall see, and perfectly central to both theme and manner in his art. He means, eventually, a number of things by "passion," and all of them important; at the moment it is necessary to confess the vague monumentality of his early uses of the term, in which it serves as an envelope to contain all those complex and half-articulate feelings and thoughts and attitudes he believed composed the true tragic emotion. Perhaps this brilliant vagueness is caught best in "The Death of Synge," where he analyzes the subtle inadequacy of a performance by the actress Maire O'Neill (Molly Allgood Synge):

> Molly had personal charm, pathos, distinction even, fancy, beauty, but never passion—never intensity; nothing out of a brooding mind. All was but observation, curiosity, desire to please. Her foot never touched the unchanging rock, the secret place beyond life; her talent showed . . . social, modern, a faculty of comedy. Pathos she has, the nearest to tragedy the comedian can come, for that is conscious of our presence and would have our pity. Passion she has not, for that looks beyond mankind and asks no pity, not even of God. It realises, substantiates, attains, scorns, governs, and is most mighty when it passes from our sight.[21]

Yeats's thought and expression at this stage, like his stated ideal of tragic style, "remembers many masters." One thinks of Keats, who believed that "the excellence of every art is its intensity";[22] of the impassioned, visionary other-worldliness of Blake; and of the loose heroic idealizing of Shelley. But there is also much that is personal and promising in a

[21] *Dramatis Personae,* 151–52.

[22] Letter to George and Thomas Keats, December 21, 1817, *The Letters of John Keats,* 70.

passage such as the foregoing: an alert, realistic, common-sense attentiveness to facts of action and personality—to temper the dreaming abstractness; and a largeness, elevation, and objectivity of aim which amounts to a kind of unconscious native classicism. Yet the whole is still distinctly twilit and subjective, and thus the most important word in the whole statement may well be "brooding."

CHAPTER THREE

Transitions

EARLY POEMS

THE GREAT DOGMAS cited at the beginning of this study are relatively late pronouncements; just when does the tragic sense actually begin in Yeats? I think it was never not there, but that it became peculiarly and focally his own tragic sense just after the turn of the century. One even wonders, finally, if it is not possible to date the definitive shift precisely, in 1903, when Maud Gonne married John MacBride: which is to suggest again the romantic center of the phenomenon. It is a critical commonplace to remark that Yeats's poetic career breaks rather sharply into two parts with his renunciation of his "Celtic Twilight" phase, and that thereafter Yeats writes a different and for most tastes a finer poetry. Commentary of the past twenty years or so has tended to dismiss the productions of the first fifteen years of Yeats's career as interesting but finally uncharacteristic apprentice work, at best fineness in an inferior genre. Delmore Schwartz, for example, says flatly, "The poems which begin with the volume called *The Green Helmet* and end with *Last Poems and Plays* are for most readers the only reason why the rest of Yeats's work has anything but incidental interest."[1] John Crowe Ransom calls Yeats's original effort "to establish his poetry within the frame of the Ossianic or Irish mythology" "a creative effort long sustained and all but wasted."[2] This is a judgment with which, on grounds of taste, I am inclined to concur. Certainly Yeats concurred, and saw himself as laboring to perfect a new idiom and a new and more adult response to life. After all, his "true Mask" was "simplification through intensity," and it was his job to seek that mask.

Yeats himself speaks of his shift in sensibility as a process already part of the past in an essay dated 1906:

> Without knowing it, I had come to care for nothing but impersonal beauty. I had set out on life with the thought of putting my very self into poetry, and had understood this as a representation of my own visions and an attempt to cut away the non-essential, but as I imagined the visions outside myself my imagination became full of decorative landscape and of still life. I thought of myself as something unmoving and silent living in the middle of my own mind and body, a grain of sand in Bloomsbury or in Connacht that Satan's watch fiends cannot find. Then one day I understood quite suddenly, as the way is, that I was seeking something unchanging and unmixed and always outside myself, a Stone or an Elixir that was always out of reach, and that I myself was the fleeting thing that held out its hand. The more I tried to make my art deliberately beautiful, the more did I follow the opposite of myself, for deliberate beauty is like a

1 "An Unwritten Book," *PY*, 320–21.
2 "Yeats and His Symbols," *PY*, 100.

> woman always desiring man's desire. Presently I found that I entered into myself and pictured myself and not some essence when I was not seeking beauty at all, but merely to lighten the mind of some burden of love or bitterness thrown upon it by the events of life. We are only permitted to desire life, and all the rest should be our complaints or our praise of that exacting mistress who can awake our lips into song with her kisses.[3]

Though the softness of his prose is full of lingering Pre-Raphaelitism, it is actually his own Pre-Raphaelite youth that Yeats is deriding. "I was in all things pre-Raphaelite," he writes in "The Trembling of the Veil."[4] Rereading his early poems, he says in "Reveries," "I find little but romantic convention, unconscious drama. It is so many years before one can believe enough in what one feels even to know what the feeling is."[5] Clearly Yeats is not thinking specifically of tragedy in all this; he speaks of a newly objectified exploration of the self, of a new normalcy and passion and discipline, of "simplification through intensity." But the point is that these are counters in the system he came at last to name tragedy and which we need to name so from start to finish. These passages mark Yeats's crucial recognition that his early art was little more than pathos.

The special qualities of the early Yeats, of *Crossways, The Rose*, *The Wind Among the Reeds,* and *The Wanderings of Oisin,* are well enough known—the subject matter drawn from Irish myth or prehistory or from the melting stylized psyche of the poet, the stock sadness and the stock adorations, the lush mood and languid tempo, the derivative "poetic" diction. That Yeats was writing here probably the best Eng-

3 "Discoveries," *CA,* 68–70.

4 *Autobiography,* 100.

5 *Ibid.,* 91.

lish poetry of these years—Hopkins being silent, and Hardy yet to renounce the novel—is less a credit to him than a deserved insult to his contemporaries. Saturated with Shelley, Blake not yet digested, Yeats was writing a throw-back poetry of almost purer romanticism than that of the formal Romantics of the early century. "We were the last romantics,"[6] he confessed in a famous line. The tragic sense waits in foetal form in these early poems, as I have suggested; but it seems to me stock and standard, academic and softly theatrical, and it moves with that distance and formality which expresses an impure emotion, half-felt and half-understood. This stylized romantic pathos, though it is only pathos, is still the dominant note in these early volumes. It rests with time to mature Yeats's simple, undissolved, adolescent *Weltschmerz* into an adult tragic sense. But its direction is the necessary one.

For example, the tears in all things, the indifference of the cosmos to man, are the burden of the second poem of the first volume, "The Sad Shepherd," with its dim personified abstractions and its cloying feminine shyness. And the literally escapist side of Yeats's early pathetic manner is best revealed in the exquisitely romantic refrain of one of the best known of the poems of these years, "The Stolen Child":

> *Come away, O human child!*
> *To the waters and the wild*
> *With a faery, hand in hand,*
> *For the world's more full of weeping*
> *than you can understand.*

There is a far more promising stringency in the refrain of "The Meditation of the Old Fisherman": *"When I was a boy with never a crack in my heart."* And "Who Goes With Fergus?", probably the finest of all these earliest poems, in-

[6] "Coole Park and Ballylee, 1931," *Collected Poems,* 239.

corporates a true foretaste both of that aristocratic strictness of discipline and that element of irrational mystery which become parts of the adult vision—though still spongy and crepuscular in image and mood:

> *Who will go drive with Fergus now,*
> *And pierce the deep wood's woven shade,*
> *And dance upon the level shore?*
> *Young man, lift up your russet brow,*
> *And lift your tender eyelids, maid,*
> *And brood on hopes and fear no more.*
>
> *And no more turn aside and brood*
> *Upon love's bitter mystery;*
> *For Fergus rules the brazen cars,*
> *And rules the shadows of the wood,*
> *And the white breast of the dim sea*
> *And all dishevelled wandering stars.*

We may take brief notice of prose equivalents of these signs of Yeats's primitive but developing tragic sense—still for the most part confined to that negative conviction of *lacrimae rerum* which is unoriginal but from which all springs. One should recall from this same period his famous advice to Synge in his Paris attic to decamp to the Aran Islands; because, Yeats says, "I had just come from Aran, and my imagination was full of those grey islands where men must reap with knives because of the stones."[7] In one of the earliest of his essays, his beautiful appreciation of "Lady Gregory's Translations," we find him admiring the mythical Irish hero Cuchulain as one "whose life is vehement and full of pleasure, as though he always remembered that it was to be soon over."[8] And we feel Yeats's lingering perfectionism already mortally wounded in a more synoptic passage from the same essay:

7 "Preface to the First Edition of *The Well of the Saints,*" *CA,* 37–38.
8 *CA,* 9.

> Children play at being great and wonderful people, at the ambitions they will put away for one reason or another before they grow into ordinary men and women. Mankind as a whole had a like dream once; everybody and nobody built up the dream bit by bit, and the ancient story-tellers are there to make us remember what mankind would have been like, had not fear and the failing will and the laws of nature tripped up its heels.[9]

These are elementary prose responses to the harsh face of life, but confessing, notably, that it was life and that it was harsh; this is denser than academic sadness. In the poetry of the first years of the new century these responses begin to get dramatized in a new stripped, acidulous lyricism which begins to be capable of saying tragic truths. One feels the new tension and the maturing conviction in scattered lines and in a few whole poems of the volume of 1904, *In the Seven Woods.* The quality of brutal passion and the genuinely personal irony in these lines from the first poem of that volume, for example, are unmistakably something new; he is saluting the passing of Victoria and the ascension of Edward:

I have forgot awhile
Tara uprooted, and new commonness
Upon the throne and crying about the streets
And hanging its paper flowers from post to post,
Because it is alone of all things happy.

In the same way, the pressure of a real love and a real deprivation underlies the harsh immediacy of the opening lines of the poem that follows: "I thought of your beauty, and this arrow,/ Made out of a wild thought, is in my marrow." And a more than subjective pity heats this fulmination in "Adam's Curse" upon the fate of his class:

[9] *Ibid.,* 20–21.

Better go down upon your marrow-bones
And scrub a kitchen pavement, or break stones
Like an old pauper, in all kinds of weather;
For to articulate sweet sounds together
Is to work harder than all these, and yet
Be thought an idler by the noisy set
Of bankers, schoolmasters, and clergymen
The martyrs call a world.

But the first full flowering of the new Yeats takes place in the volume of 1910, *The Green Helmet.* The vital precipitating motive, it seems clear, was the disaster in his affair with Maud Gonne. What Yeats felt for Maud was the Grand Passion itself; there is no greater factor in the career of Yeats than that passion. His affair with that "Woman Homer Sung" offers surely the greatest public passional spectacle in modern English letters, at least since that of the run-away Brownings; and Yeats's spectacle, though scattered and a failure, is gaudier than theirs. The relationship had its endearing comic side, with the needy Yeats borrowing pence to provide galas for Maud, piling her into railway carriages with her caged singing birds and Donegal hawks, proposing to her daughter after Maud had refused him for the last of many times in almost thirty years. Undoubtedly, too, his love for her had a strong bookish cast: he worshipped in Maud his heroic idea of woman as much as the woman herself. For a man of Yeats's feverish and literary idealism this was inevitable, given such a superb personification as Maud Gonne, and it makes no real difference; his idealism does not weakly qualify his adoration, makes it if anything all the richer. A significant passage in *A Vision,* though it names no names, seems to me almost certainly a rationalization in "systematic" terms of his loss of Maud. He is speaking of the difficult search for "unity of being" of a man of his own Phase 17:

> The *Body of Fate* . . . is "loss", and works to make impossible "simplification by intensity". The being, through the intellect, selects some object of desire for a representation of the *Mask* as Image, some woman perhaps, and the *Body of Fate* snatches away the object. Then the intellect . . . which . . . were better described as imagination, must substitute some new image of desire; and in the degree of its power and of its attainment of unity, relate that which is lost, that which has snatched it away, to the new image of desire, that which threatens the new image to the being's unity.[10]

Maud was in his mind until he died. "My poetry all comes from rage or lust,"[11] he wrote to Dorothy Wellesley in 1936; much of the rage and ultimately all the lust rose out of Maud and returned to her in his poetic speech. Poems he wrote virtually on his deathbed summon up her undecayed image.

But now the point to be established is that a fatal crisis in his relationship with Maud set under way a permanent motive in Yeats's tragic vision. When Maud made the Great Refusal by marrying John MacBride in 1903, Yeats's disappointment was not ordinary but heroic. The quality of his passion, his subjectivity, and his need for self-dramatization were such that his grief inevitably seemed to him to reach tragic stature and sought to express itself in tragic form. The bitter news reached him in a telegram from Maud Gonne as he stood on a lecture platform; Yeats said later that he was reduced to such a state of shock that though he went through with the lecture, apparently in perfect form, afterward he could never remember a word of what he had said.[12] The whole experience and some of its consequences are compressed into the taut lyric "Reconciliation," which recreates the physical im-

10 (New York, The Macmillan Company, 1956), 142.

11 *Letters to Dorothy Wellesley,* 120.

12 A. Norman Jeffares, *W. B. Yeats: Man and Poet* (New Haven, Yale University Press, 1949), 315, n. 34.

agery of his stunned dismay, describes the compensatory shift (in the plays) to a detached heroic subject matter to which his deprivation has driven him, professes a defiant "laughing-weeping" oxymoron; then closes with the simple heartbroken confession: nothing will do, he is helpless and broken without her:

> *Some may have blamed you that you took away*
> *The verses that could move them on the day*
> *When, the ears being deafened, the sight of the eyes blind*
> *With lightning, you went from me, and I could find*
> *Nothing to make a song about but kings,*
> *Helmets, and swords, and half-forgotten things*
> *That were like memories of you—but now*
> *We'll out, for the world lives as long ago;*
> *And while we're in our laughing, weeping fit,*
> *Hurl helmets, crowns, and swords into the pit.*
> *But, dear, cling close to me; since you were gone,*
> *My barren thoughts have chilled me to the bone.*

About half the short poems of this short volume testify in one way or another to the height of his adoration, the depth of his heartbreak, or the stubbornness of his infatuation for Maud Gonne and her image. He refers constantly with grief and awe to her heroic beauty ("outrageously beautiful,"[13] Shaw called her) and her violent innocence, "Half lion, half child," and broods bitterly over the pallor of his life of letters as contrasted to her life of political passion. The last stanza of "A Woman Homer Sung" puts it this way:

> *For she had fiery blood*
> *When I was young,*
> *And trod so sweetly proud*
> *As 'twere upon a cloud,*

[13] Quoted in Joseph Hone, *W. B. Yeats* (New York, The Macmillan Company, 1943), 163 n.

A woman Homer sung,
That life and letters seem
But an heroic dream.

And the closing stanza of "Words" develops the same theme:

. . . every year I have cried, "At length
My darling understands it all,
Because I have come into my strength,
And words obey my call";
That had she done so who can say
What would have shaken from the sieve?
I might have thrown poor words away
And been content to live.

In "No Second Troy," perhaps the tensest and harshest as well as the most forgiving of these lyrics, Yeats confesses the sad fatality of Maud's nature and dismisses himself as an incidental casualty:

Why should I blame her that she filled my days
With misery, or that she would of late
Have taught to ignorant men most violent ways,
Or hurled the little streets upon the great,
Had they but courage equal to desire?
What could have made her peaceful with a mind
That nobleness made simple as a fire,
With beauty like a tightened bow, a kind
That is not natural in an age like this,
Being high and solitary and most stern?
Why, what could she have done, being what she is?
Was there another Troy for her to burn?

What must have hurt most bitterly was Yeats's helpless feeling that he had presumed fatuously to title to a being different and larger than himself; Maud's rejection, it must have seemed, defined him as a type while it despised him as an individual. For in capitulating to the military roisterer MacBride, she rejected with painful pointedness Yeats's kind of dreamy, ascetic sensitivity: Yeats now knew he was not the hero to deserve that "form/ That could show what Homer's age/ Bred to be a hero's wage."

Yeats responded to all that deep invidiousness, it seems to me, in exactly the most fruitful way. He left off his rather stagey posturing at political hustings and began to practice his heroics in his verse: in a new warmth and immediacy of subject matter, in an impressive adamancy of attitude, and in the discipline of the shape, the speech, the movement and muscle tone of his poems. These forces are at work already in the poems quoted above; and they are more compactly obvious in the new toughness of form and content of one of the first of those many little poems of four to twelve lines in which Yeats dramatized an astringent epigrammatism, full of knowledge and self-knowledge. In "The Coming of Wisdom With Time" he at once takes formal leave of youth and Twilight and demonstrates, in texture and diction, how the new resolution is to be implemented poetically.

> *Though leaves are many, the root is one;*
> *Through all the lying days of my youth*
> *I swayed my leaves and flowers in the sun;*
> *Now I may wither into the truth.*

The candor of "lying," the self-scorn of "swayed my leaves and flowers in the sun," and the sudden charge of energized bitterness that enters the verse with "wither into the truth," all recall vividly the same sharp shift that occurs in Keats in the middle of the "Ode on Melancholy" with the procession of harsh verbs inaugurated by "glut" and continuing through "emprison," "rave," and "feed."

In the important short poem that stands next to last in

The Green Helmet, "All Things Can Tempt Me," Yeats depreciates his passion for Maud, cries curse upon Irish public life, lumps the two among the unworthy preoccupations which choke his art, and closes with praise of silence:

> *All things can tempt me from this craft of verse:*
> *One time it was a woman's face, or worse—*
> *The seeming needs of my fool-driven land;*
> *Now nothing but comes readier to the hand*
> *Than this accustomed toil. When I was young,*
> *I had not given a penny for a song*
> *Did not the poet sing it with such airs*
> *That one believed he had a sword upstairs;*
> *Yet would be now, could I but have my wish,*
> *Colder and dumber and deafer than a fish.*

Here is the definite farewell to the Twilight in poetic form, taking leave of "youth," of Pre-Raphaelitism, of romantic excess and wishfulness generally. And again both the diction and the theme have to be called classical. Is it the *sprezzatura* of Landor—a permanent idol—that is now guiding his hand and thought?

But Yeats is not vowing silence, though he is praising it, nor is he announcing a merely stoical renunciation; what we really have here is a vow not to abjure art but to deserve his gift: and to prove his desert by maturing the art into tragic strictness and restraint. He will "wither into the truth," or, in the idiom of the great short poem which closes his next volume, he will "walk naked":

A COAT

> *I made my song a coat*
> *Covered with embroideries*
> *Out of old mythologies*
> *From heel to throat;*
> *But the fools caught it,*

Wore it in the world's eyes
As though they'd wrought it.
Song, let them take it,
For there's more enterprise
In walking naked.

But this is to look ahead, and neither of these poems sounds the right note for closing a discussion of *The Green Helmet.* Yeats himself felt this and chose to end his volume with a softer lyric which looks back at "All Things Can Tempt Me," admits that it was unjust to his true feeling for Maud and to his own sense of her loss, and gently and sadly redresses that balance: "Ah, penny, brown penny, brown penny,/ I am looped in the loops of her hair." Yeats was that not common thing, a completely honest poet.

EARLY PROSE

Our overview of the early poems has carried us forward almost too hurriedly, and it is time to go back a bit and fill out the theoretic side of Yeats's tragic sense by a further look at his prose. Especially we need to return admonitorily to that mystical, perfectionist transcendentalism of his that loomed so large in the formulas of "The Tragic Theatre." For this side of Yeats did not pass with the passing of the Twilight. We have emphasized the new dogmas announcing renunciation of the vague luxuriance and the dim escapism of the earliest poems; and have commented on new qualities which promise to last—the tautness, the passion, the bitterness, the close pragmatic subjectivity of many poems in the volumes of 1904 and 1910. But these qualities may lead us to expect and to find too easily in the later Yeats a "realistic" art, one tied quite literally and exclusively to "life." In fact, Yeats does not practice this literalism henceforth. What he seeks and what he seems to me brilliantly to achieve is a rich dualistic art which will counterpoint the real and the ideal, the literal and the symbolic, which will rise out of the actual and labor or soar, as the case may be, toward that sense of revelation which he was to call, at the end, "the madness of vision": "You must feel plunged as I do into the madness of vision, into a sense of the relation between separated things that you cannot explain, and that deeply disturbs emotion."[14] The transcendental drive of Yeats's spirit survived every change of style, every shift of philosophical masters, all vicissitudes of experience.

We can demonstrate the dualism in Yeats's thinking here at the point of egress from the Twilight by juxtaposing a few texts from the early essays. Prose support for the new empiricism, on the one hand, is not hard to find. In "Discoveries," for example, Yeats makes use of Matthew Arnold's famous trope to show that by 1906 he had come to find "Shelley plain" too thin for his blood:

> Shelley seemed to Matthew Arnold to beat his ineffectual wings in the void, and I only made my pleasure in him contented pleasure by massing in my imagination his recurring images of towers and rivers, and caves with fountains in them, and that one star of his, till his world had grown solid underfoot and consistent enough for the soul's habitation.[15]

Describing his reaction to two paintings, by Canaletto and Franz Francken, which he saw together, probably at Lady Gregory's "great house," Coole Park, he rejects the abstract and comes out strongly, in vividly sensuous images, for the quality of physical identification:

> Neither painting could move us at all, if our thought did not

[14] *Letters to Dorothy Wellesley*, 149–50.
[15] *CA*, 110.

> rush out to the edges of our flesh, and it is so with all good art, whether the Victory of Samothrace which reminds the soles of our feet of swiftness, or the Odyssey that would send us out under the salt wind, or the young horsemen on the Parthenon, that seem happier than our boyhood ever was, and in our boyhood's way. Art bids us touch and taste and hear and see the world, and shrinks from what Blake calls mathematic form, from every abstract thing, from all that is of the brain only, from all that is not a fountain jetting from the entire hopes, memories, and sensations of the body.[16]

And in a text that is permanently important, however qualified eventually by his dualism, Yeats canonizes passionate normality and locates it in both artist and artifact:

> I have always come to this certainty: what moves natural men in the arts is what moves them in life, and that is, intensity of personal life, intonations that show them in a book or a play, the strength, the essential moment of a man who would be exciting in the market or at the dispensary door. They must go out of the theatre with the strength they live by strengthened with looking upon some passion that could, whatever its chosen way of life, strike down an enemy, fill a long stocking with money or move a girl's heart . . . . An exciting person, whether the hero of a play or the maker of poems, will display the greatest volume of personal energy, and this energy must seem to come out of the body as out of the mind.[17]

But the other face of the coin, the metaphysical as opposed to the physical passion, is importantly present in the same group of little essays dated 1906. We may satisfy the case with a couple of bits of that prose gorgeousness which reflects subject matter and which sometimes seems to approach nonsense because it tries to say almost unsayable things, and in which

[16] *Ibid.*, 107.
[17] *Ibid.*, 56–57.

meaning moves as much in the exaltation of the tone and rhythm as in the basic denotation of the language. Thus as the end of "The Holy Places" Yeats writes:

> I am orthodox and pray for a resurrection of the body, and am certain that a man should find his Holy Land where he first crept upon the floor, and that familiar woods and rivers should fade into symbol with so gradual a change that he never discover, no, not even in ecstasy itself, that he is beyond space, and that time alone keeps him from Primum Mobile, the Supernal Eden, and the White Rose over all.[18]

And he closes "The Subject Matter of Drama" with one of the most beautiful and richly fantastic of all his sentences:

> All art is dream, and what the day is done with is dreaming ripe, and what art has moulded religion accepts, and in the end all is in the wine cup, all is in the drunken fantasy, and the grapes begin to stammer.[19]

The passage, again, "remembers many masters." The thought comes from Blake, from the long Hermetic tradition, and from Celtic mysticism; the rhythm and the soft texture of the prose are Pater's. The ideal is that of Nietzsche's Dionysiac wisdom; and Neitzsche may well be the most immediate of Yeats's sources here. Yeats read that "strong enchanter," as he calls him,[20] with excitement after the turn of the century, and placed him in the line growing out of his Blake studies: "Nietsche completes Blake and has the same roots."[21] He felt, too, that Nietsche possessed the same "curious astringent joy" as Synge.[22] The German's Apollonian-Dionysiac distinction, Yeats wrote to John Quinn, expressed a convic-

18 "Discoveries," *CA,* 115.
19 *Ibid.,* 92–93.
20 *Letters,* 379.
21 *Ibid.*
22 *Ibid.*

tion that he himself had "always felt": " . . . the soul has two movements primarily: one to transcend forms, and the other to create forms."[23] But the personal note is unmistakable, in any case, and both style and conviction, whatever their first sources, have become genuinely personal property.

To put his case more simply and in more conventional but still Yeatsian metaphor, we may recall this passage from three years earlier:

> Poets have chosen their themes more often from stories that are all, or half, mythological, than from history or stories that give one the sensation of history, understanding, as I think, that the imagination which remembers the proportions of life is but a long wooing, and that it has to forget them before it becomes the torch and the marriage-bed.[24]

The physical and the metaphysical begin to coalesce in a passage from 1903 which is still within the Twilight in its emphasis upon the intuitive knowledge of the folk; we may note in passing how Yeats's head is stuffed already with the astrological symbolism which, in about fifteen years, his mysterious "instructors" would play upon, shift and change, to put together the mystical "system" of *A Vision.*

> Old writers had an admirable symbolism that attributed certain energies to the influence of the sun, and certain others to the lunar influence. To lunar influence belong all thoughts and emotions that were created by the community, by the common people, by nobody knows who, and to the sun all that came from the high disciplined or individual kingly mind. I myself imagine a marriage of the sun and moon in the arts I take most pleasure in; and now bride and bridegroom but exchange, as it were, full cups of gold and silver, and now they are one in a mystical embrace.[25]

23 *Ibid.,* 403.
24 "Lady Gregory's Translations," *CA,* 8.
25 *Ibid.,* 27–28.

But the true fusion occurs in a rather long and densely lyrical passage in "The Tree of Life," also of 1906; and develops as a union of several important motives, among them an epicene Pateresque subjectivity, the new pragmatic and passional subjectivity, and that constant mystical idealism I have been calling transcendental. A portion of this passage we have seen before; now we may set it more firmly in context:

> The more I tried to make my art deliberately beautiful, the more did I follow the opposite of myself, for deliberate beauty is like a woman always desiring man's desire. Presently I found that I entered into myself and pictured myself and not some essence when I was not seeking beauty at all, but merely to lighten the mind of some burden of love or bitterness thrown upon it by the events of life. We are only permitted to desire life, and all the rest should be our complaints or our praise of that exacting mistress who can awake our lips into song with her kisses. But we must not give her all, we must deceive her a little at times, for, as Le Sage says in *Diable Boiteux* the false lovers who do not become melancholy or jealous with honest passion have the happiest mistresses and are rewarded the soonest and by the most beautiful. Our deceit will give us style, mastery, that dignity, that lofty and severe quality Verlaine spoke of. To put it otherwise, we should ascend out of common interests, the thoughts of the newspapers, of the market-place, of men of science, but only so far as we can carry the normal, passionate, reasoning self, the personality as a whole. We must find some place upon the Tree of Life for the Phoenix nest, for the passion that is exaltation and the negation of the will, for the wings that are always upon fire, set high that the forked branches may keep it safe, yet low enough to be out of the little wind-tossed boughs, the quivering of the twigs.[26]

It is a difficult passage, because of its multiple motives;

[26] "Discoveries," *CA*, 69–70.

but it does come clear, and it promises a healthy, interesting, and lofty art. Yeats abjures the conscious search for beauty; beauty will be the earned increment of honest expression of true emotion. But not quite "honest," either: emotion is not to be simply "expressed," in all its fulsome native heat; instead it is to be "deceitfully" edited—cooled and dried. Yet, on the other hand, it must not be utterly limited and rationalized, not stripped of mystery; room must be left for the Phoenix nest and the fiery wings. Basically, then, the motives are three, which we may call realistic in emotional impulse, classic in form and expression, and romantic in theme. The theory describes an art which is at least potentially tragic, and richly so: Apollonian and Dionysiac, Greek and Shakespearean—if the genius can be brought to match the vision.

CHAPTER FOUR

Maturity

THE BASIC LINE OF TRAGEDY

In remaining essays of *The Cutting of an Agate* and in the *Per Amica Silentia Lunae* of 1918, which might be called the first of his Prophetic Books, Yeats continues to shade in the tentative sketch of his tragic vision drawn thus far, and to add and shift perspectives. He supports anew his basic negative conviction, the radical definition of life itself as tragic phenomenon; repeatedly he makes it clear that this recognition is his touchstone for full seriousness in artist and art. Thus in the long essay of 1910, "Synge and the Ireland of His Time," which is the most formal of Yeats's variously heart-broken responses to the recent death of his friend, he does not hesitate to make a full equation of the tragic and the real; the real is the tragic, and the truly "happy" is a state achieved only through the tragic initiation:

> All minds that have a wisdom come of tragic reality seem morbid to those that are accustomed to writers who have not faced reality at all; just as the saints, with that Obscure Night of the Soul, which fell so certainly that they numbered it among spiritual states, one among other ascending steps, seem morbid to the rationalist and the old-fashioned Protestant controversialist. The thought of journalists, like that of the Irish novelists, is neither healthy nor unhealthy, for it has not risen to that state where either is possible, nor should we call it happy; for who would have sought happiness, if happiness were not the supreme attainment of man, in heroic toils, in the cell of the ascetic, or imagined it above the cheerful newspapers, above the clouds?[1]

About seven years later, in "Anima Hominis," there appear a couple of sentences which compress this distinction:

> Some thirty years ago I read a prose allegory by Simeon Solomon, long out of print and unprocurable, and remember or seem to remember a sentence, "a hollow image of fulfilled desire." All happy art seems to me that hollow image, but when its lineaments express also the poverty or the exasperation that set its maker to work, we call it tragic art.[2]

At the moment the point to be made is that, for Yeats, literary seriousness must begin in personal need and deprivation and difficulty and raise itself from those negatives to the positive of tragedy. Later in "Anima Hominis" he phrases this conviction more imposingly:

> It is not permitted to a man, who takes up pen or chisel, to seek originality, for passion is his only business, and he cannot but mould or sing after a new fashion because no disaster is like another. He is like those phantom lovers in the Japanese

1 "Synge and the Ireland of His Time," *CA*, 165.

2 "Anima Hominis," *Per Amica Silentia Lunae* (hereinafter referred to as *PASL*), 25–26.

> play who, compelled to wander side by side and never mingle, cry: "We neither wake nor sleep and passing our nights in a sorrow which is in the end a vision, what are these scenes of spring to us?"[3]

The note of laconic certainty, once more, shows Yeats's settled conviction; there is no question in his mind of the rightness of his view: disaster is the defining condition of life and of art. We should underscore, too, the reassertion of "passion" as art's center; and take considerable comfort from the size that personal passion is taking on in Yeats's system of thought about tragedy: this "sorrow which is in the end a vision." Yeats's fundamental tragic line is now drawn: from disaster, to passion, to vision, to tragedy.

THE CREATIVE OPPOSITION

We ought to look now with some patience at what remains of "Anima Hominis," for Yeats adumbrates there concepts which grow to be central in his total philosophical system, as well as in that important branch of the system which composes his thought about tragedy. His concepts of "Mask" and "Daemon" and "the path of the Serpent," which he touches upon in "Anima Hominis," are ultimately to be developed in *A Vision* to an extreme complexity which is happily outside our province. Here what we want to see is that Yeats is beginning to formulate an ethic and an aesthetic of tragedy which posits a creative dynamism of opposed states, vacillating productively in a pattern of alternating rhythm which is quasi-deterministic. In a superb long paragraph beginning with a famous sentence, he lays down a typically vague-vivid image of that demanding passionate "reality," the certainty of man's "uncertainty," his "solitude" and his "difficulty," which he

[3] *Ibid.*, 44–45.

saw as the qualifying condition of tragic discipline, the seed-bed of the only valuable art. At the center of the thought is an image he recalls from a beautiful and moving letter written him by his father, then a voluntary exile in New York, and identified anonymously here as "an old artist."[4]

> We make out of the quarrel with others, rhetoric, but of the quarrel with ourselves, poetry. Unlike the rhetoricians, who get a confident voice from remembering the crowd they have won or may win, we sing amid our uncertainty; and smitten even in the presence of the most high beauty by the knowledge of our solitude, our rhythm shudders. I think, too, that no fine poet, no matter how disordered his life, has ever, even in his mere life, had pleasure for his end. Johnson and Dowson, friends of my youth, were dissipated men, the one a drunkard, the other a drunkard and mad about women, and yet they had the gravity of men who had found life out and were awakening from the dream; and both, one in life and art and one in art and less in life, had a continual preoccupation with religion. Nor has any poet I have read of or heard of or met with been a sentimentalist. The other self, the anti-self or the antithetical self, as one may choose to name it, comes but to those who are no longer deceived, whose passion is reality. The sentimentalists are practical men who believe in money, in position, in a marriage bell, and whose understanding of happiness is to be so busy whether at work or at play, that all is forgotten but the momentary aim. They find their pleasure in a cup that is filled from Lethe's wharf, and for the awakening, for the vision, for the revelation of reality, tradition offers us a different word—ecstasy. An old artist wrote to me of his wanderings by the quays of New York, and how he found there a woman nursing a sick child, and drew her story from her. She spoke, too, of other children who had died: a long tragic story. "I wanted to paint her," he wrote, "if I

[4] J. B. Yeats, *J. B. Yeats: Letters to His Son W. B. Yeats and Others*, ed. by Joseph Hone (New York, E. P. Dutton and Company, 1946), 163.

> denied myself any of the pain I could not believe in my own ecstasy." We must not make a false faith by hiding from our thoughts the causes of doubt, for faith is the highest achievement of the human intellect, the only gift man can make to God, and therefore it must be offered in sincerity. Neither must we create, by hiding ugliness, a false beauty as our offering to the world. He only can create the greatest imaginable beauty who has endured all imaginable pangs, for only when we have seen and foreseen what we dread shall we be rewarded by that dazzling unforeseen wing-footed wanderer. We could not find him if he were not in some sense of our being and yet of our being but as water with fire, a noise with silence. He is of all things not impossible the most difficult, for that only which comes easily can never be a portion of our being, "Soon got, soon gone," as the proverb says. I shall find the dark grow luminous, the void fruitful when I understand I have nothing, that the ringers in the tower have appointed for the hymen of the soul a passing bell.[5]

Yeats's counters here, obviously, are those we have seen him associating with tragedy: "passion," "reality," "ecstasy." But what is especially interesting—aside from his equation of the tragic view and full seriousness, and his dismissal of any shorter vision as "rhetoric" and "sentiment," attitudes which by now are expected—is Yeats's conception of the creative state as an achieved antithesis, a state of rhythmical recurrence, of paradoxical union with the artist's opposite, his "mask," or "anti-self." He posits here and frequently elsewhere a "Daemon," or "Gate-Keeper," who is the essential midwife for the artist seeking to fructify, whose office is specifically to bring the seeker face to face with the most exacting of all images and all efforts—confronting the "mask": which confrontation Yeats believed was the only true fertile condition. The artist earns the right to the great challenge of his "Daemon" by sufficiency of "pas-

[5] "Anima Hominis," *PASL*, 29–32.

NATIONAL PORTRAIT GALLERY, LONDON

William Butler Yeats about 1907

From the original drawing by Augustus Edwin John

NATIONAL PORTRAIT GALLERY, LONDON

Another drawing of W. B. Yeats by Augustus Edwin John, dated 1907.

sion" and by insight into the tragic nature of "reality." This idea of the dynamism which follows from a creative vacillation between antithetical states or tendencies is probably the most important single idea in Yeats. We find in *A Vision* that it is for him the true life-principle. Without this rhythmical tension, figured in his capital symbol of the interlocking gyres, life ceases; and by its operation is determined not only the bias of individual personality but the character of eras, of civilizations—ultimately the whole pattern of human history.

But we need only to understand a smaller thing, his definition of individual artistic creativity in terms of fertile tension. I am most interested at the moment in the pointedly paradoxical nature of Yeats's image, its union of pain and pleasure, of attraction and repulsion, of rocky obduracy and soft capitulation, for all of these seem to me components that are beginning to fuse in the tragic definition he is still in process of developing. He rephrases the paradox in a couple of sentences:

> . . . I think it was Heraclitus who said: the Daemon is our destiny. When I think of life as a struggle with the Daemon who would ever set us to the hardest work among those not impossible, I understand why there is a deep enmity between a man and his destiny, and why a man loves nothing but his destiny.[6]

Now he clarifies the way of the poet by contrast to that of the "saint." The basic distinction, we find, is that the poet remains *in* the world, which is to say in the condition of the tragic, whereas the saint, by abnegation of will, becomes essentially nonhuman in abjuring the creative struggle:

> The poet finds his mask in disappointment, the hero in defeat. The desire that is satisfied is not a great desire, nor has

6 *Ibid.*, 38.

> the shoulder used all its might that an unbreakable gate has never strained. The saint alone is not deceived, neither thrusting with his shoulder nor holding out unsatisfied hands. He would climb without wandering to the antithetical self of the world, the Indian narrowing his thought in meditation or driving it away in contemplation, the Christian copying Christ, the antithetical self of the classic world.[7]

Now, in a concentrated, poetical passage, Yeats mingles his several current concerns, the way of the artist on *Hodos Chameliontos,* "the path of the serpent," the contrasting way of "saint or sage," his deterministic notion of human processes, and expresses these ideas in images that are to become permanent figures in his symbolism:

> Many years ago I saw, between sleeping and waking, a woman of incredible beauty shooting an arrow into the sky, and from the moment when I made my first guess at her meaning I have thought much of the difference between the winding movement of nature and the straight line, which is called in Balzac's *Seraphita* the "Mark of Man," but comes closer to my meaning as the mark of saint or sage. I think that we who are poets and artists, not being permitted to shoot beyond the tangible, must go from desire to weariness and so to desire again, and live but for the moment when vision comes to our weariness like terrible lightning, in the humility of the brutes. I do not doubt those heaving circles, those winding arcs, whether in one man's life or in that of an age, are mathematical, and that some in the world, or beyond the world, have foreknown the event and pricked upon the calendar the life-span of a Christ, a Buddha, a Napoleon: that every movement, in feeling or in thought, prepares in the dark by its own increasing clarity and confidence its own executioner. We seek reality with the slow toil of our weakness and are smitten from the boundless and the unforeseen. Only when we are saint or sage,

[7] *Ibid.,* 40–41.

> and renounce Experience itself, can we, in the language of the Christian Caballa, leave the sudden lightning and the path of the serpent and become the bowman who aims his arrow at the center of the sun.[8]

For us the important thing is not the symbolism but the content of Yeats's argument, and what seems to me most striking and conclusive in the passage above is the fact that Yeats's determinism does not, for him at least, rule out tragedy or seriously qualify its validity. One of the major questions to be asked of Yeats's formula of tragedy is whether it wholly survives his "systematic" definition of experience as an alternating or cyclical pattern to greater or lesser extent *imposed* upon the individual will by cosmic law. How automatic and complete is this process? Does man merely accept it helplessly and passively? Has he significant remnants of self-determination? Or is the process so obscured to his view, perhaps, that he has the illusion of more or less complete autonomy? These are questions to which it is difficult to find clear answers in Yeats's later thought; the argument of *A Vision* is exasperatingly blurred on these subjects. Yet any mature theory of tragedy, one feels, must envision the tragic personae as involved in a struggle and conflict which, however ultimately hopeless, is mediately logical and always dignified; that logic and that dignity must come from the sense of free will in the personae, even if only as a convinced illusion. If the logic is missing we get farce; if the dignity is missing we get pathos. Thus the argument of "Anima Hominis" on this head becomes peculiarly significant.

The passage above and later paragraphs give compact and positive answers to our questions, and they preserve, at least wishfully, Yeats's established ideas of tragedy. Here it seems clear that Yeats's determinism is not really denying free will

[8] *Ibid.*, 45–47.

and certain that he is not jettisoning his idea of tragedy. His "sentimentalists," apparently, are men who have played deaf to their Daemon: they have rested content with less than the ultimate challenge—by, it must be, an act of will. Similarly, saint and sage must will their supervention of cycle and hence of total reality. And clearly the fully sentient man, avid for his Daemon, is involved in a process notably willed and dynamic: "We seek reality with the slow toil of our weakness." The fact that "every movement . . . prepares its own executioner," and that the seeker is infallibly "smitten from the boundless and the unforeseen" declares tragedy deterministic while retaining dynamism and hence dignity in the personae. "Experience itself" is tragic reality, and the artist will not leave off involvement in that.

That Yeats pictures man's life as something very different from passive waiting upon an imposed fate, is clear in his own elaborate summary metaphor in *A Vision;* he is speaking only of his own kind of man, "antithetical" man, but that will serve our purpose:

> When I wish for some general idea which will describe the Great Wheel as an individual life I go to the *Commedia dell' Arte* or improvised drama of Italy. The stage-manager, or *Daimon,* offers his actor an inherited scenario, the *Body of Fate,* and a *Mask* or role as unlike as possible to his natural ego or *Will,* and leaves him to improvise through his *Creative Mind* the dialogue and details of the plot. He must discover or reveal a being which only exists with extreme effort, when his muscles are as it were all taut and all his energies active.[9]

And the basic definition of personality itself shows that even that is a hard-won thing: "Personality, no matter how habitual, is a constantly renewed choice."[10] *Sturm und Drang* are the

[9] *A Vision* (New York, The Macmillan Company, 1956), 83–84.
[10] *Ibid.,* 84.

very qualifying conditions of existence: "Without this continual Discord . . . there would be no conscience [i.e., consciousness], no activity."[11] So terribly exacting is this vital process that Yeats invents a condition of palliative "Automatism," to be resorted to, legitimately, only in moments of exhaustion.[12] "Life," he says in synopsis, "is an endeavor, made vain by the four sails of its mill, to come to a double contemplation, that of the chosen Image, that of the fated Image."[13]

He means that we constantly seek, and constantly fail, to bring into "register," a single focus, "chance being one with choice at last" (as he will put it in "Solomon and the Witch"), our ideal of life and the reality of life. That search and failure are what it means to be human. And this dynamic incongruity, we now remember, is that of one of our proffered definitions of tragedy: "Tragedy dramatizes the imbalance between the ideal and the real." *"The Body of Fate,"* Yeats says with a note of laconic acceptance, "is inimical to *antithetical* natures."[14] Still, they set about the hopeless task of its reformation, and continue that struggle to the end.

Whether man will ever leave off that involvement is in fact the last question which occupies Yeats in "Anima Hominis." His answer is no. Here his persona is Landor—always, like Blake and Swift, a hero to Yeats—and functioning like them as an image of splendid old age, bloody-unbowed, "ridiculous and unconquered"; and accompanying Yeats into his own old age, where he wrote what must surely be the greatest old man's poetry in the language.

> A poet, when he is growing old, will ask himself if he cannot keep his mask and his wisdom without new bitterness, new

11 *Ibid.*, 94.
12 *Ibid.*, 95.
13 *Ibid.*, 94.
14 *Ibid.*, 91.

> disappointment. Could he if he would, knowing how frail his vigour from youth up, copy Landor who lived loving and hating, ridiculous and unconquered, into extreme old age, all lost but the favour of his muses.
>
> . . . .
>
> Surely, he may think, now that I have found vision and mask I need not suffer any longer. He will buy perhaps some small old house where like Ariosto he can dig his garden, and think that in the return of birds and leaves, or noon and sun, and in the evening flight of the rooks he may discover rhythm and pattern like those in sleep and so never awake out of vision. Then he will remember Wordsworth withering into eighty years, honoured and empty-witted, and climb to some waste room and find, forgotten there by youth, some bitter crust.[15]

Yeats wanted to wither, we remember, not into honor but into truth; to do so he will sustain himself upon that essential food of any age, the bitter crust, the tragic.

TRAGIC JOY

We need now to look a little longer at that side of Yeats's tragic theory which emphasizes the quality of paradox, especially at that pole of the paradox which he denominates as "joy." It happens that he provides us an entry into this side of his thought through some further remarks upon Synge. Though it seems, from what we can partly know and partly guess about Synge, that Yeats estimated him justly as well as fondly as a man, he no doubt overvalued him somewhat as an artist. His motives in doing so—involvement with him in the difficult idealistic business of the Abbey Theatre, his sense of a deep artistic kinship, his notion of himself as Synge's savior and "maker"—are themselves creditable and interesting. But if Synge was not quite the giant of drama that Yeats wanted

[15] "Anima Hominis," *PASL*, 49–50.

to believe him, there can be no doubt of his importance to Yeats as a theorist of tragedy and, sadly, as a walking embodiment of the tragic condition of man. Synge as a tragic model we find in this grieved and moving tribute phrased shortly after his death:

> The misfortune was for the living certainly, that must work on, perhaps in vain, to magnify the minds and hearts of our young men, and not for the dead that, having cast off the ailing body, is now, as I believe, all passionate and fiery, an heroical thing. Our Daimon is as dumb as was that of Socrates, when they brought in the hemlock; and if we speak among ourselves, it is of the thoughts that have no savour because we cannot hear his laughter, of the work more difficult because of the strength he has taken with him, of the astringent joy and hardness that was in all he did, and of his fame in the world.[16]

Synge's offices of model and preceptor are joined in this statement Yeats quotes from him and in Yeats's analysis of the personality of the speaker as embodying the central paradox:

> He once said to me, "We must unite asceticism, stoicism, ecstasy; two of these have often come together, but not all three": and the strength that made him delight in setting the hard virtues by the soft, the bitter by the sweet, salt by mercury, the stone by the elixir, gave him a hunger for harsh facts, for ugly surprising things, for all that defies our hope.[17]

What is missing in that catalog, we see, is the quality of "astringent joy" from the passage above. In a slightly later passage Yeats puts together a composite judgment which joins most of the significant elements—the discipline of conflict, the condition of art addressed to suffering, the quality of passion—and adds the new element, joy. It is this joy, we see, which purifies the *merely* sad and conducts its transcendence:

[16] "Preface to the First Edition of *The Well of the Saints*," *CA*, 139–40.
[17] *Ibid.*, 143.

> I think that all noble things are the result of warfare; great nations and classes, of warfare in the visible world, great poetry and philosophy, of invisible warfare, the division of a mind within itself, a victory, the sacrifice of a man to himself. I am certain that my friend's noble art, so full of passion and heroic beauty, is the victory of a man who in poverty and sickness created from the delight of expression, and in the contemplation that is born of the minute and delicate arrangement of images, happiness, and health of mind. Some early poems have a morbid melancholy, and he himself spoke of early work he had destroyed as morbid, for as yet the craftsmanship was not fine enough to bring the artist's joy which is of one substance with that of sanctity . . . . Later on, he can see himself as but a part of the spectacle of the world and mix into all he sees that flavour of extravagance, or of humour, or of philosophy, that makes one understand that he contemplates even his own death as if it were another's and finds in his own destiny but as it were a projection through a burning glass of that general to men. There is in the creative joy an acceptance of what life brings, because we have understood the beauty of what it brings, or a hatred of death for what it takes away, which arouses within us, through some sympathy perhaps with all other men, an energy so noble, so powerful, that we laugh aloud and mock, in the terror or the sweetness of our exaltation, at death and oblivion.[18]

Note that Yeats is now introducing into the catalog of tragic properties the fundamental idea of the projection of individual fate into archetypal experience: personal, romantic tragedy firms and grows here into datum of experience "general to men." That is the elevating and liberating emotion which transcends pathos. Subsequent passages show him making the crucial fusion of strength and wisdom, laughing and mourning, and pushing all together toward that intricate para-

18 "Synge and the Ireland of His Time," *CA*, 162–64.

doxical "ecstasy" we have heard him call the crown of tragedy's emotion. "Who should be free if he were not?" he asks of the artist, and goes on, in two long, eloquent paragraphs which I must quote nearly in their entirety because they are so central and so synoptic, to reassemble virtually all the components of his early tragic vision—including, at the last, that transcendentalism we have again lost sight of for some time:

> It it the playing of strength when the day's work is done, a secret between a craftsman and his craft, and is so inseparate in his nature, that he has it most of all amid overwhelming emotion, and in the face of death. Shakespeare's persons, when the last darkness has gathered about them, speak out of an ecstasy that is one half the self-surrender of sorrow, and one half the last playing and mockery of the victorious sword, before the defeated world . . . . This joy, because it must be always making and mastering, remains in the hands and in the tongue of the artist, but with his eyes he enters upon a submissive, sorrowful contemplation of the great irremediable things, and he is known from other men by making all he handles like himself, and yet by the unlikeness to himself of all that comes before him in a pure contemplation . . . . Timon of Athens contemplates his own end, and orders his tomb by the beachy margent of the flood, and Cleopatra sets the asp to her bosom, and their words move us because their sorrow is not their own at tomb or asp, but for all men's fate. That shaping joy has kept the sorrow pure, as it had kept it were the emotion love or hate, for the nobleness of the Arts is in the mingling of contraries, the extremity of sorrow, the extremity of joy, perfection of personality, the perfection of its surrender, overflowing turbulent energy, and marmorean stillness; and its red rose opens at the meeting of the two beams of the cross, and at the trysting-place of mortal and immortal time and eternity.[19]

[19] "Poetry and Tradition," *CA,* 128–31.

CHAPTER FIVE

Middle Poems

"RESPONSIBILITIES"

WE MAY TRY NOW to fit the relevant poems of the volumes which fall roughly at the mid-point of Yeats's long career, those of 1914, 1919, and 1921, into the frame of his tragic theory as we have managed to amplify it.

John Middleton Murry felt that *The Wild Swans at Coole* of 1919 signaled a fatal falling away of Yeats's powers—that it was "indeed a swan song."[1] Ultimately Yeats proved him amusingly far wrong. My own feeling is that *The Wild Swans at Coole* is one of Yeats's greatest successes, and that such falling away as there is in Yeats in mid-career needs to be located in the preceding volume, *Responsibilities.* In fact, we might feel no declension even there if the magnificent epigraph poem, that which Eliot called "the violent and terrible epistle

[1] "Mr. Yeats's Swan Song," *PY,* 12.

dedicatory,"[2] promised less than it does. There, in terms of shamed reverence that roughens to grinding bitterness, Yeats begs pardon—"Pardon, old fathers, if you still remain/ Somewhere in earshot for the story's end"—of the ranked shades of his Yeats and Pollexfen ancestors who linger in his mind as images of nobility and learning and passion: "Merchant and scholar who have left me blood/ That has not passed through any huckster's loin." Particularly he addresses the shade of his old grandfather William Pollexfen, that "silent and fierce old man" whom Yeats, when he was a boy, had confused with God.[3] In his autobiography Yeats pays him the handsome tribute of likening him to Lear and associating him both with his lifelong devotion to that play and with his lifelong worship of passion: "Even to-day when I read *King Lear* his image is always before me and I often wonder if the delight in passionate men in my plays and in my poetry is more than his memory."[4] Here in his "Introductory Rhymes," William Pollexfen is recollected in the same terms stripped and heightened:

> *You most of all, silent and fierce old man,*
> *Because the daily spectacle that stirred*
> *My fancy, and set my boyish lips to say,*
> *"Only the wasteful virtues earn the sun."*

After so much tense elevation, Yeats's own self-contempt falls, as it is calculated to fall, with the shock of bitter anticlimax:

> *Pardon that for a barren passion's sake,*
> *Although I have come close on forty-nine,*
> *I have no child, I have nothing but a book,*
> *Nothing but that to prove your blood and mine.*

The verse is acidly alive, but the posture out of which it

[2] "The Poetry of W. B. Yeats," *PY*, 331.
[3] *Autobiography*, 9.
[4] *Ibid.*, 10.

rises is slack and dull, and some of that flaccidity attenuates and weakens the poems of the volume. Yeats is gnawed, we see, by two of his old bosom serpents, the poet's standard professional embarrassment and his feeling that Maud Gonne has fatally wounded him; and to these he adds a third, the heavy sense of entering upon what promises to be a sterile and lonely middle or old age.

He writes these poems in his middle forties, in a mood of lassitude and impotence, a kind of artificial menopause. Many things conspire to make him feel weak and peevish—his failure as a lover and political comrade of Maud Gonne, the labor and frustrations of the Abbey Theatre program, current perversions in politics and the arts of his dreams of Celtic glory as a practical national fact. He has a general sense of himself as "ineffectual angel," he feels that his life lacks purpose and concentration, feels his talents and energies scattered in that "dispersal" which was his "false mask." It is a mood which breaks up only with his marriage, the coming of the revelations of *A Vision* and the excitement of work on that, and the birth of his daughter in 1919. Pending those events, his epigraph poem shows his painful sense of his own sterility; he is a break in the virility of his ancestral line. All these, obviously, are negative emotions, and they promise a rather maundering and self-sorrowful dyspepsia. But though quality is lower here, the volume still contains a very considerable richness. Fair Yeats may be excellent poetry. Edmund Wilson, in *Axel's Castle,* points to this volume as marking Yeats's achievement of a "Dantesque mask," the power to "sustain a grand manner through sheer intensity without rhetorical heightening."[5] And *Responsibilities* contains valuable data to add to his cumulative view of tragedy.

Yeats's response to what he saw as betrayals in Dublin pub-

[5] "W. B. Yeats," *PY,* 23.

lic life of the idealism and self-sacrifice of the Irish patriots is by turn hotly or coldly furious, aloofly suffering, or elegantly scurrilous. At the center of the emotion in this book is the wound of his defeat in love, and all his sensitivity spreads out from there. Frustrations in public life join with the frustration in love, and express the bitter norm of experience. In *Responsibilities* his lines are full of insult for the Dublin crowds, for their ignoble crassness and conventionality—"Indignant at the fumbling wits, the obscure spite/ Of our old Paudeen in his shop." The most elaborate of these insults composes "September 1913," where he phrases a bitter condemnation of the Irish public; the Post Office Massacre of 1916 was shortly to drive him to the vivid overcompensatory gesture of "Easter 1916." In the former poem he counterpoises the huddling crowd, for whom he coins the motto, "Men were born to pray and save," against the noble images of the classic Irish heroes Fitzgerald, Emmet, and Tone, and turns a bitterly wistful refrain on the name of his own idol, John O'Leary: "Romantic Ireland's dead and gone,/ It's with O'Leary in the grave." These names make for him images of selfless recklessness to hang golden and homeless in the modern Dublin air: "They weighed so lightly what they gave."

To see the radical shift that has occurred in Yeats's thought about Ireland, it is enough to return to an early letter, written to George Russell (Æ) in January, 1898. He speaks in the most matter-of-fact terms of the most visionary and idealist schemes for the future:

> I am deep in "Celtic Mysticism," the whole thing is forming an elaborate vision. Maud Gonne and myself are going for a week or two perhaps to some country place in Ireland to get as you do the forms of gods and spirits and to get sacred earth for our evocation . . . Maud Gonne has seen vision of a little temple of the heroes which she proposes to build somewhere

> in Ireland when '98 is over and to make the centre of our mystical and literary movement.[6]

"Absorb Ireland and her tragedy," he advises Russell, "and you will be the poet of a people, perhaps the poet of a new insurrection."[7] By 1914, the date of *Responsibilities,* Yeats's idealism had soured and hardened, his social sympathies had turned aristocratic, his political sympathies conservative; he had lost almost all faith in the mass of the Irish people: "weasels fighting in a hole," he would call them in "Nineteen Hundred and Nineteen."

The Irish failings, he felt, were class failings, mainly those of that same lower middle class who provide Joyce with his unforgettable subjects. In his diary of 1909, Yeats denounced the class in exactly the terms of his "eunuch" image of the poem "On Those Who Hated The Playboy of the Western World":

> The root of it all is that the political class in Ireland—the lower-middle class from whom the patriotic associations have drawn their journalists and their leaders for the last ten years—have suffered through the cultivation of hatred as the one energy of their movement, a deprivation which is the intellectual equivalent to a certain surgical operation. Hence the shrillness of their voices. They contemplate all creative power as the eunuchs contemplate Don Juan as he passes through Hell on the white horse.[8]

In "To a Shade" Yeats advises the ghost of Parnell to adopt one of his own attitudes of this period, that of lofty, heartbroken withdrawal:

[6] *Letters,* 295.

[7] *Ibid.*

[8] *Dramatis Personae,* 111–12.

Go, unquiet wanderer,
And gather the Glasnevin coverlet
About your head till the dust stops your ear,
The time for you to taste of that salt breath
And listen at the corners has not come;
You had enough of sorrow before death—
Away, away! You are safer in the tomb.

Comparable, but more interesting for its extra dimensions of blood-pride and laughing defiance, a variant of his "tragic joy," is his beautiful little poem to Lady Gregory, "To a Friend Whose Work Has Come to Nothing"; here the close texture and tense restraint of movement endow a classical discipline that underscores the theme:

Now all the truth is out,
Be secret and take defeat
From any brazen throat,
For how can you compete,
Being honour bred, with one
Who, were it proved he lies,
Were neither shamed in his own
Nor in his neighbors' eyes?
Bred to a harder thing
Than Triumph, turn away
And like a laughing string
Whereon mad fingers play
Amid a place of stone,
Be secret and exult,
Because of all things known
That is most difficult.

Elsewhere he is more hotly involved. Yeats had great vituperative powers, a talent for bitterness that is sometimes only malice, sometimes an elegant scarifying scorn which rises above self to serve an ideal. Keats would have found him, with Hazlitt, a "good damner,"[9] and Pound calls him an "exultant slaughtermaster."[10] In this volume we have one of his finest insults in the little poem addressed to "Those That Hated 'The Playboy of the Western World,' 1907":

> *Once, when midnight smote the air,*
> *Eunuchs ran through Hell and met*
> *On every crowded street to stare*
> *Upon great Juan riding by:*
> *Even like these to rail and sweat*
> *Staring upon his sinewy thigh.*

Yet now, oddly and touchingly, after all this concentrated bitterness and disillusion, Yeats looks into his own heart and concludes that he too shares in the failures of the Irish public; in this mood ignobility seems to him sadly a part of the racial composition. So he argues in "When Helen Lived":

> *We have cried in our despair*
> *That men desert,*
> *For some trivial affair*
> *Or noisy, insolent sport,*
> *Beauty that we have won*
> *From bitterest hours;*
> *Yet we, had we walked within*
> *Those topless towers*
> *Where Helen walked with her boy,*
> *Had given but as the rest*
> *Of the men and women of Troy,*
> *A word and a jest.*

That image, too, comes out of the 1909 diary: "I dreamed this

[9] Letter to Benjamin Robert Haydon, March 14, 1818, *The Letters of John Keats,* 118.

[10] Quoted in T. R. Henn, *The Lonely Tower: Studies in the Poetry of W. B. Yeats* (Pellegrini and Cudahy, 1952), 96.

thought two nights ago: 'Why should we complain if men ill-treat our Muses, when all that they gave to Helen while she still lived was a song and a jest?' " "They" there becomes "we" in the poem, and Yeats shares the guilt.

Four poems especially in this volume of 1914 continue to exploit Yeats's fanatical love for Maud Gonne. They are interestingly different, but all show him trying to come to terms with that passion which is hopeless but still far from spent, and which, if it cannot be resolved in the flesh, still must explain itself humbly or "savagely" in speech. One of these love poems is another of those extraordinary condensations of his, in which a violent image and a violent response are pressed into a tense ordered structure, the discipline of which seems to contain, barely, the emotion and so make it supportable. In this case the rhetorical structure is a single modulated sentence in which, in the second half, a striking syncopated falling rhythm seems to understand and to forgive all.

THAT THE NIGHT COME

She lived in storm and strife,
Her soul had such desire
For what proud death may bring
That it could not endure
The common good of life,
But lived as 'twere a king
That packed his marriage day
With banneret and pennon,
Trumpet and kettledrum,
And the outrageous cannon,
To bundle time away
That the night come.

In "A Memory of Youth" Yeats reawakens a scene that is palpably real, a recollected moment in which the lovers are saved in the midst of the revelation of the tragic mutability of all relationships by a kind of cosmic demonstration of the power of intense emotion, here embodied in the personified "Love," to transcend for a time that tragic awareness. I quote the last lines of the poem:

> *We sat as silent as a stone,*
> *We knew, though she'd not said a word,*
> *That even the best of love must die,*
> *And had been savagely undone*
> *Were it not that Love upon the cry*
> *Of a most ridiculous little bird*
> *Tore from the clouds his marvellous moon.*

But there is little enough of this kind of romantic satisfaction in the volume. The reality for Yeats is an enveloping passion that is still for him the whole of life, and whose bitterness can never make him forget that lost "sweetness" which still shakes and fills him. In "Friends," he sets out to praise "Three women that have wrought/ What joy is in my days," and after a dozen lines of intimate but formal tribute directed, as I guess, to Olivia Shakespear, his long-time friend and mother of the wife of Ezra Pound, and Lady Gregory, his dear friend, patron, and fellow artist, the poem, as it approaches Maud, slips its bond and becomes a hot cry from the heart in which once more only the discipline of verse contains an emotion otherwise uncontrollable, and the vibrancy of which makes the opening lines seem bookish and remote:

> *And what of her that took*
> *All till my youth was gone*
> *With scarce a pitying look?*
> *How could I praise that one?*
> *When day begins to break*
> *I count my good and bad,*
> *Being wakeful for her sake,*
> *Remembering what she had,*

What eagle look still shows,
While up from my heart's root
So great a sweetness flows
I shake from head to foot.

Still, the most extraordinary and interesting of these bittersweet love poems is the visionary lines "The Cold Heaven." T. R. Henn calls it "the most impressive poem in the volume,"[11] and I agree. Here the emotion seems to break almost entirely from restraint, the rhythm is harsh and prosaic, impatient of form, the images soar to fantasy and descend again to outright torture of the physical body: "I cried and trembled and rocked to and fro,/ Riddled with light." And in the closing lines Yeats draws a shocking equation between his own heart, an agonized ghost after its defeat, and the ultimate ghost of the whole self, subjected to the malevolence of the cosmos. We must keep insisting that his love for Maud was no ordinary passion; it was immense and significant, for many years the most intimate presence for him of cosmic tragedy: further romanticism, I suppose, but larger than pathos, and most moving. Here is the complete poem:

Suddenly I saw the cold and rook-delighting heaven
That seemed as though ice burned and was but the more ice,
And thereupon imagination and heart were driven
So wild that every casual thought of that and this
Vanished, and left but memories, that should be out of season
With the hot blood of youth, of love crossed long ago;
And I took all the blame out of all sense and reason,
Until I cried and trembled and rocked to and fro,
Riddled with light. Ah! when the ghost begins to quicken,
Confusion of the death-bed over, is it sent
Out naked on the roads, as the books say, and stricken
By the injustice of the skies for punishment?

11 *The Lonely Tower*, 92.

Responsibilities contains three other short poems which stand apart, thematically, from those we have been examining and from each other, but which still need to be fitted into Yeats's tragic system at this middle stage. "The Magi" is a first preliminary essay in the matter which later occupied him so often, his conception of history as cyclical sequence or alternation of antinomies. His view was later to grow both softer and more complex. In "The Magi," it seems, he is occupied with a single, simple, and shocking irony (recalling Eliot's gentler version in "The Journey of the Magi"): his conviction that the Christian epiphany was not single and sufficient, but only one passing revelation in a fixed and insatiable historical rhythm:

Now as at all times I can see in the mind's eye,
In their stiff, painted clothes, the pale unsatisfied ones
Appear and disappear in the blue depth of the sky
With all their ancient faces like rain-beaten stones,
And all their helms of silver hovering side by side,
And all their eyes still fixed, hoping to find once more,
Being by Calvary's turbulence unsatisfed,
The uncontrollable mystery on the bestial floor.

The brief verses paired as "The Witch" and "The Peacock" dramatize, in the former, Yeats's bitting contempt for the merely acquisitive life:

Toil and grow rich,
What's that but to lie
With a foul witch
And after, drained dry,
To be brought
To the chamber where
Lies one long sought
With despair?

and, in the latter, his artist's compensation in the superiority of the creative spirit to "things" and to despair; the artist in the tragic vision feeds boldly on despair and—as in Yeats's prose datum of the life of Synge—transmutes it into joy. "The Peacock" impresses me as, technically, one of the greatest short poems of Yeats—in its close economic fusion of rhetoric, speech, and rhythm. Thematically it is still just a bit depressingly art-for-art:

> *What's riches to him*
> *That has made a great peacock*
> *With the pride of his eye?*
> *The wind-beaten, stone-grey,*
> *And desolate Three Rock*
> *Would nourish his whim.*
> *Live he or die*
> *Amid wet rocks and heather,*
> *His ghost will be gay*
> *Adding feather to feather*
> *For the pride of his eye.*

I have already quoted entire the little poem "A Coat,"[12] which stands last in the volume, stands there revealingly as curse and credo. "A Coat" makes perfectly, in theme and in poetic embodiment of theme, the point I have been trying to make about Yeats's maturing poetic manner: its toughening and simplifying—"walking naked," "simplification through intensity"—in harmony with his accumulating bitterness in his sense of life, and his accumulating resolve and consonant capacity to face the facts of life erect, wide-eyed, and tearless. But the last poem one should read in *Responsibilities* is "The Three Hermits," the poem which Yeats described in his letter to Lady Gregory as "my first poem which is comedy or tragi-comedy."[13] The latter term is the more accurate and of course

[12] See above, p. 70.
[13] *Letters,* 577.

to me the more significant, approaching as it does Yeats's concept of tragic joy; and what delights me most in this vivid farcical poem is its rich union of passion, humor, and depth. The refrain lines devoted to the third hermit, the one who is given to "falling asleep when he should pray," will suggest its flavor:

> *While he'd rummaged rags and hair,*
> *Caught and cracked his flea, the third,*
> *Giddy with his hundredth year,*
> *Sang unnoticed like a bird.*

"THE WILD SWANS AT COOLE"

In *The Wild Swans at Coole* of 1919, Yeats explores most of the old passions and some new ones, but with a different tonality and tempo. These poems are lower in key, calmer and more solemn in tone, slower and more stately in movement; many lines are markedly more open in texture. The poems fall naturally into a half-dozen loose thematic clusters which can help us in a necessarily summary analysis. The largest number, at least a dozen, are again as usual love poems, and almost all of those are again responses to Maud Gonne; a small but important group might be called anti-intellectual, or poems of "ignorance," celebrating Yeats's favorite new persona "the normal passionate man"; a half-dozen poems deal specifically, and numerous others deal incidentally, with the pressing sense of oncoming age which we saw begin in *Responsibilities;* another half-dozen may be seen as united by a special ironic mood directed in varying tones at self or world; perhaps the volume's most imposing nexus is that intimate yet stately occasional mode which henceforth remains so important in Yeats, here centering on the death of valued friends, Robert Gregory, Alfred Pollexfen, Mabel Beardsley; and finally, a half-dozen enigmatic and important poems which close the volume explore Yeats's great continuing mystical dialectic and take on a special hermetic unity from their use of the idiom and the imagery which, in the background of the poems, are being woven into *A Vision*. We cannot hope to examine all these poems and we need not even sample all these categories, since not all are strictly relevant to our context of tragedy. The group of mystical poems, for example, have relatively little to say to us. As it happens, the poems of this sort, as being especially difficult and strange, yet especially characteristic of one side of Yeats, have been almost overanalyzed by his commentators (without by any means giving up all their mysteries), and our time on them had better be limited to strictly relevant aspects. But it is important to assert that none of these classes of poems is actively hostile to our context.

Although he is only just past fifty as he composes this volume—"now that I have come to fifty years/ I must endure the timid sun"—Yeats is feeling keenly and variously a premature old age. What mainly disturbs him is a sense of altered and lowered passions: folding horizons, colder flames, duller dreams. In "Lines Written in Dejection" he puts the case this way:

> *When have I last looked on*
> *The round green eyes and the long wavering bodies*
> *Of the dark leopards of the moon?*
> *All the wild witches, those most noble ladies,*
> *For all their broom-sticks and their tears,*
> *Their angry tears, are gone.*
> *The holy centaurs of the hills are vanished;*
> *I have nothing but the embittered sun;*
> *Banished heroic mother moon and vanished,*
> *And now that I have come to fifty years*
> *I must endure the timid sun.*

In "A Song" the italicized refrain runs, "O who could have foretold/ That the heart grows old?" And in "Men Improve With the Years" he paints himself "worn out with dreams;/ A weather-worn, marble triton/ Among the streams." In "On Being Asked for a War Poem" he justifies his refusal to write the poem on grounds of his own slack inadequacy to the heroic context; he is, he says, merely one "who can please/ A young girl in the indolence of her youth,/ Or old men upon a winter's night."

Actually, in view of the quantity of passion we will find elsewhere in *The Wild Swans at Coole,* Yeats's emotional menopause seems stagey and unreal. No doubt he had reached something of an emotional plateau midway between the exacting peaks of his youth and the more terrible mountains still to develop in the richer philosophical excitements of his coming years. But Yeats is self-indulgent in his sadness here, and the fact makes a small but disturbing eddy in the stream of tragedy; the point is the untrustworthy subjectivity of the mood: he has lost perspective, momentarily, and confuses order with absence. The new quality of control in his passion, which is the truer pitch of this volume, is caught much more accurately by a stanza such as the following from "To a Young Beauty," where he accepts with calm confidence the storms of the past, asserts a tough integrity, and salutes his passional masters, all in verse which in speech and pace demonstrates an achieved maturity—not flaccid defeatism:

I know what wages beauty gives,
How hard a life her servant lives,
Yet praise the winters gone:
There is not a fool can call me friend,
And I may dine at journey's end
With Landor and with Donne.

Some of the most important and symptomatic of all Yeats's scores of love poems are those in *The Wild Swans at Coole.* Much of their interest and special poignancy must be admitted to come from the fact that though Yeats is now a solidly married man, almost all these love poems center squarely on Maud Gonne and testify helplessly to the insistence of that old chronic passion. It is true there are moments of detachment from Maud among these poems: "Solomon to Sheba" celebrates merely the genus passion with its perfectly Yeatsian conclusion, "There's not a thing but love can make/ The world a narrow pound"; but the true burden is still Maud and new, a trifle calmer, efforts to make peace with "that monstrous thing/ Returned and yet unrequited love." A group of seven of these poems, framed by two brief stanzas of terse understatement, "Memory" and "A Deep-Sworn Vow," stands bluntly in the middle of the volume.

But the function of all this in Yeats's notions of tragedy needs to be established. My feeling is that Yeats's emotions as a lover, especially as the rejected lover of the heroic woman Maud Gonne, his failure as a persona in the drama of the grand passion, have a significant relevance to his tragic sense of life. It is of course the intimacy of the matter which may trouble us, if we are seeking to set "tragedy" in a conceptual and abstract frame beyond the self—its "merely" personal significance, "mere" subjectivity. Actually it is just this which seems to me so interesting and important about this aspect of Yeats's thought and feeling: that it begins as intimate emotion and develops into evidence of a generic truth, then becomes the material of the figurative pattern in the art object, the poem. Yeats's failure with Maud was for him a prime piece of evidence supporting his cumulative conviction that life is tragic—a factor in his definition. Our major texts need to be recalled to service here. "To me the supreme aim is an act of faith and reason to make one rejoice in the midst of tragedy." Yeats's conviction that life is an affair of tragedy works in two directions in his love poems; the love experience serves its documentary purpose among the data defining life as tragic, then that conviction turns back to dictate the *manner* in which the emotion is to be treated: the artifact must honor its significance, it must have the size and the gravity of "an act of faith and reason." Yeats seeks to give his love poems a coloring and a tone and a pace appropriate to tragedy: hence the dignity, the order, the heroic imagery, the constant classical analogy, the quantity of what Henry James called "solidity of specification," or fullness of concrete reference; above all, the insistence on, and the verbal proof of, the heroic stature of the affair—the ardor and size of the affection and the deprivation. The passion is Yeats's passion but it is a great passion, thus heroic and generic, man's passion, "general to men," as he said in reference to Synge. Defeats of man's passion are tragic evidences.

Finally, the *quality* of the passion, though set in an unbreakable discipline of negativism and emotional disaster, provides the missing tragic element of reconciliation and reconstitution: great passion, nobly acted, makes it possible to "rejoice in the midst of tragedy"—it aims to cancel, by an assertion of spirit, the fact of defeat. Remember that Yeats equated recognition of tragedy with full consciousness: "We begin to live when we have conceived life as tragedy"; and that he equated tragedy with great passion. Thus to be passionately committed is to be fully conscious, and to be fully conscious is to face and welcome the fact of tragedy. It is this kind of bitter-joyous commitment to a brilliantly hopeless passion that Yeats salutes in this volume in "On Woman," where he places himself and Maud in the company of ancient heroes of love, anatomizes his torture in defeat, yet prays that reincarnation will but return him to the same anguished drama:

What else He give or keep
God grant me—no, not here,
For I am not so bold
To hope a thing so dear
Now I am growing old,
But when, if the tale's true,
The Pestle of the moon
That pounds up all anew
Brings me to birth again—
To find what once I had
And know what once I have known,
Until I am driven mad,
Sleep driven from my bed,
By tenderness and care,
Pity, an aching head,
Gnashing of teeth, despair;
And all because of some one
Perverse creature of chance,
And live like Solomon
That Sheba led a dance.

Tragedy treats of failure, and failures in love may be tragic failures. They may be central to the tragic action, as with Romeo and Juliet or Antony and Cleopatra, or marginal to it, as with Hamlet and Ophelia. *Hamlet* makes the closest analogy to Yeats; in both cases the failure of love is evidential, "documentary," an instance of imperfection and disaster which is taken to stand for an endemic imperfection at the center of things—"the antagonism at the heart of the world," in Nietzsche's phrase. The basic distinction between the love affair in *Hamlet* and such a love affair as that of Yeats remains the distinction between the objectivity of the dramatic poet and the subjectivity of the lyric poet; that is, it is a distinction of chosen vestment, of form. And that distinction seems to me to grow less and less fundamental, more and more merely technical, as one thinks about the case. How important is the fact that the tragic evidence arises from the experience of the poet, or even that, in effect, it remains in the poet's experience in its lyrical form of utterance? Tragic sources, I should argue, are ultimately all one, and all personal—the experience, and the emotional response to experience, of the poet. Those are the ground of tragedy; and "systematic," "dramatic," "objective," "non-lyrical" tragedy is a chosen, but not a necessary, way of uttering *generic* tragedy. The essence of tragedy is not alone the form but the experience and the emotion, and the philosophical structure erected on the base of experience and emotion.

The "occasional" poems of *The Wild Swans at Coole,* three of which seem to me to rank among Yeats's capital poems, fit with a simpler and more obvious appropriateness into the frame of the tragic. Their more obvious relevance is due to the fact that five of the six poems we may call occasional are ruminations on death and four of them are specific efforts to make peace with the tragic fact of early death blotting out vivid and beloved lives—those of Robert Gregory and Mabel Beardsley. Yeats's habit of projecting and elevating himself and his friends into dramatis personae, creatures of representative fable or myth, which I have noted in speaking of his poems on Maud Gonne, is active and important in the occasional poems. I shall discuss briefly the three poems I have called capital—"In Memory of Major Robert Gregory," "Shepherd and Goatherd," and "Upon a Dying Lady"—and virtually ignore the other occasional poems, which seem to me inferior Yeats. The vicarious emotion of "An Irish Airman Foresees His

Death" seems formalized and unreal. "In Memory of Alfred Pollexfen" is a perfunctory duty-piece, touched with Yeats's distinction of phrase and rhythm, but ruminating shallowly an emotion not deeply felt. The volume's title poem, while it rises out of a deeper level of feeling and shows the true technical magic, seems now rather to court a mood of quietism and senescence which is subordinate in the volume and which our discussion has passed beyond: "Their hearts have not grown old," Yeats says of the "nine-and-fifty swans," "Passion or conquest, wander where they will,/ Attend upon them still."

"In Memory of Major Robert Gregory" is, quite simply, a great elegiac poem in twelve eight-line stanzas—Yeats's most impressive poem to date, and the ensign of his arrival at an unshakable poetic maturity. It is the first of his many roll-calling poems, in which he assembles the cast of his archetypes, living and dead, the personae of his tragic fable. The poem's most striking achievement is the creation of an almost shocking illusion of intimacy and dynamism; one feels the vivid *presence* of the emotion and the persons, and feels present, too, not so much at the performance of a completed poem as at its composition: an ongoing process in which the reader is commanded to take a personal part in the thought, the feeling, and the consequent artifact. The poem's speech is elegantly simple, its movement fluent and graceful yet inconspicuously and forcefully ordered, the mood that of an achieved composure enclosing heartbreak, the tone gravely conversational—all enlisting the reader, as I say, in the dynamics of an emotion *in act* of formulating a poem. Allen Tate has spoken very handsomely of "In Memory of Major Robert Gregory"; "I would select this poem out of all others of our time as the most completely expressed: it has a perfect articulation and lucidity which cannot be found in any other modern poem in English."[14]

14 "Yeats's Romanticism: Notes and Suggestions," *PY*, 115.

The scene is set in Yeats's new sanctuary, the famous tower, Thoor Ballylee. Having come to this interval with its air, for him, of a coming psychic wholeness never before in his reach, and this place, with its beauty, its wildness, its rough ancientness, Yeats sets out to summon to mind all those great old friends whom he cannot summon in the flesh: "I'll name the friends that cannot sup with us/ Beside a fire of turf in th' ancient tower." Having reached at last the time and the place, he would assemble all those he values and bring them face to face "In the affections of our heart." But "all that come into my mind are dead." An easy, compact stanza to each, Yeats addresses those whom he has loved and honored. Of Lionel Johnson he recalls how "much falling he/ Brooded upon sanctity." Then he calls up the shade of "that enquiring man John Synge . . ./ That dying chose the living world for text," and in the remaining lines he accords him, reviews that important side of his tragic ideal for which Synge always stood to him:

> *long travelling, he had come*
> *Towards nightfall upon certain set apart*
> *In a most desolate stony place,*
> *Towards nightfall upon a race*
> *Passionate and simple like his heart.*

We shall look soon at other instances of this passionate-simple archetype in other poems of the volume.

George Pollexfen next receives the poem's most neutral stanza. But now, in the beautifully understated stanza that closes the first half of the poem, Yeats takes leave of these beloved but veteran dead and turns midway, as with a clutch of the heart, to whisper of the novice dead, the brilliant young man the thought of whose taking now seizes the poem and the poet and converts time and place and persons into tragic fable:

They were my close companions many a year,
A portion of my mind and life, as it were,
And now their breathless faces seem to look
Out of some old picture-book;
I am accustomed to their lack of breath,
But not that my dear friend's dear son,
Our Sidney and our perfect man,
Could share in that discourtesy of death.

What takes hold of one there is the bold understatement of tragic fact in the last phrase, "that discourtesy of death," in which Yeats catches our primitive astonishment and outrage at the workings of a power which reduces, gratuitously and shockingly, our animation to stiffness and our speech to silence.

In stanza 7, Yeats points about him to describe the tower's wild and lonely setting whose beauty is newly poignant because now it is lost to Robert Gregory. Stanza 8 recalls the young man's feats of bold horsemanship. Stanza 9 describes Robert Gregory's nature as an artist—he was a painter and stage designer, among other things—in significant terms of Yeats's own reading of ideal Irish art:

We dreamed that a great painter had been born
To cold Clare rock and Galway rock and thorn,
To that stern colour and that delicate line
That are our secret discipline
Wherein the gazing heart doubles her might.

(Has Yeats unconsciously recalled John Butler Yeats's boast of himself and his son, "By marriage with the Pollexfens I have given a tongue to the sea cliffs"?)[15] In stanza 10 the poet mourns the loss to the tower of Robert Gregory's taste, knowledge, and skill "In all lovely intricacies of a house," and presents the

15 *Autobiography*, 22.

dead young man as a sort of Renaissance embodiment expressing another of his own great ideals, a branch of that which he comes to call in *A Vision* and elsewhere "unity of being": "Soldier, scholar, horseman, he,/ And all he did done perfectly/ As though he had but that one trade alone." (The first of these lines falls as a sixth-line refrain in stanzas 9, 10, and 11.) Stanza 11 is one of Yeats's great stanzas, and one of his most significantly thematic. For Robert Gregory represents for him his ideal image of life lived hotly at the pitch of passion, opposed to an ignoble defensiveness, the life of the high key scornfully contrasted to the life of the low, and the whole set simply, candidly, and bitterly, in the last line's folk phrase, in the tragic context of evanescence:

> *Some burn damp faggots, others may consume*
> *The entire combustible world in one small room*
> *As though dried straw, and if we turn about*
> *The bare chimney is gone black out*
> *Because the work had finished in that flare.*
> *Soldier, scholar, horseman, he,*
> *As 'twere all life's epitome.*
> *What made us dream that he could comb grey hair?*

The poem's amazing last stanza, dumbly moved and deeply moving, reverts to the opening situation of the poet in his tower, involved in the ceremonial urge to summon the dead, yet stricken mute, he says in a daring paradoxical sleight, by the intimate reality of death. Tragic reality is caught here in the saturated understatement of a single metaphor, the ambiguous descriptive parenthesis of "seeing how bitter is that wind/ That shakes the shutter." The poem's grieving conversational immediacy is at its closest and most touching here, and it is managed by the brilliantly artificial yet philosophically honest assertion, in the midst of all the poem's rich elegiac eloquence, of the poet's broken-hearted muteness:

I had thought, seeing how bitter is that wind
That shakes the shutter, to have brought to mind
All those that manhood tried, or childhood loved
Or boyish intellect approved,
With some appropriate commentary on each;
Until imagination brought
A fitter welcome; but a thought
Of that late death took all my heart for speech.

W. H. Auden has written that one of the two "main legacies" of Yeats to modern poetry was his transformation of "a certain kind of poem, the occasional poem, from being either an official performance of impersonal virtuosity or a trivial *vers de société* into a serious reflective poem of at once personal and public interest." "A poem such as *In Memory of Major Robert Gregory,*" he goes on to say, "is something new and important in the history of English poetry."[16] The whole poem strikes me, as I say, as at once a brilliant exercise in tactics and a deeply moving human document. The poem's bare bones of structure and the poet's naked emotion are first made openly articulate, then disclaimed as impossible, then placed in perfect activation. The poem is a definition, a denial, and a demonstration of the ways of poetry and the ways of feeling.

"Shepherd and Goatherd" affects me as another of Yeats's greatest poems. It is another effort at psychic adjustment, a second attempt to reconcile the emotion of himself and Lady Gregory's circle to the fact of the death of their brilliant young man. Yeats functions here as court poet, making an offering, both contrite and proud, of an artifact, "rhymes on strips of new-torn bark," to the grieving family of the prince, an offering which "May be a quiet thought to wife and mother,/ And children when they spring up shoulder-high." The poem is

16 "Yeats as an Example," *PY,* 350.

a "version of pastoral"[17] in which two rustic poets, a shepherd and a goatherd (Yeats), meet on a rocky hillside to ruminate the news of the death of a young piper who has "thrown the crook away/ And died in the great war beyond the sea." Their dialogue makes explicit the implied conversational mode of "In Memory of Major Robert Gregory." As in that poem the tone is solemn and sad, but the mood is less understated, makes a more objective equivalent to the impelling emotion; the texture of the lines is looser here, a fabric consciously and beautifully homespun; diction is both more "poetic" and, logically, more primitive, and full of words which economically evoke the setting and the speakers; movement is swaying and ambulatory, giving a sense of physical activity to contrast to the intellectual and rhetorical animation of "In Memory of Major Robert Gregory." Tone, diction, and pace all suggest mastered lessons of Synge lingering in Yeats's mind and called up now by the need to confront in art an elemental tragic event. In the presence of tragedy, as always, the poet turns to art to make life bearable again: "I thought of rhyme alone,/ For rhyme can beat a measure out of trouble/ And make the daylight sweet once more."

Shepherd and goatherd speak antiphonally in formally cadenced mourning; the shepherd sets the theme with his first description of the vanished Corydon:

> *He that was best in every country sport*
> *And every country craft, and of us all*
> *Most courteous to slow age and hasty youth,*
> *Is dead.*

The goatherd's response pictures Robert Gregory in terms that directly recall the ninth stanza of the other poem, as a young artist with a right insight into the rough obduracy of nature

[17] Tate, "Yeats's Romanticism: Notes and Suggestions," *PY,* 116.

as well as its difficult joys—the negative and positive poles of the tragic definition:

> *He had often played his pipes among my hills,*
> *And when he played it was their loneliness,*
> *The exultation of their stone, that cried*
> *Under his fingers.*

The next interchange plays sadly upon country tropes to turn attention to the bereft family, the children and especially the mother; in the lofty simplicity with which the goatherd expresses his own gratitude Yeats pays the most handsome and affecting of all his tributes to Lady Gregory and to her complex generosity to him:

> SHEPHERD. *I had it from his mother,*
> *and his own flock was browsing at the door.*
>
> GOATHERD. *How does she bear her grief?*
> *There is not a shepherd*
> *But grows more gentle when he speaks her name,*
> *Remembering kindness done, and how can I,*
> *That found when I had neither goat nor grazing*
> *New welcome and old wisdom at her fire*
> *Till winter blasts were gone, but speak of her*
> *Even before his children and his wife?*

The shepherd describes the mother's courage, "erect and calm," then goes on to speak of what had seemed the dead man's intuition that he was "a cuckoo,/ No settled man," and his consequent failure to amass possessions; thus there remains of him only the touching relics of his spirit: "now that he is gone/ There's nothing of him left but half a score/ Of sorrowful, austere, sweet, lofty pipe tunes."

Shepherd and goatherd now set themselves to speak alternatively their formal lines of tribute to the dead. The shepherd's rhyme strikes one as soft and sad, a subtle throwback to pure early Yeats. The goatherd, amusingly, confirms that impression when he says that his companion's lines have roused his own nostalgia:

> *You sing as always of the natural life,*
> *And I that made like music in my youth*
> *Hearing it now have sighed for that young man*
> *And certain lost companions of my own.*

In inviting the goatherd's rhymes, the shepherd points suggestively to Yeats's mystical speculations:

> *They say that on your barren mountain ridge*
> *You have measured out the road that the soul treads*
> *When it has vanished from our natural eyes;*
> *That you have talked with apparitions.*

The goatherd confirms the case:

> *Indeed*
> *My daily thoughts since the first stupor of youth*
> *Have found the path my goats' feet cannot find.*

And before he begins his song, he asserts a bluff confidence in the powers of his magic: "They have brought me from that ridge/ Seed-pods and flowers that are not all wild poppy." The song itself is a lyricising of Yeats's convictions about the soul's immortality, one of the earliest and clearest of all his exegeses of that posthumous process of "dreaming back" to new infancy and reincarnation which he believed was "the road the soul treads/ When it has vanished from our natural eyes." I find these lines among the most persuasive and affecting of all Yeats's embodiments of his arcane symbolism; here the affair makes perfect sense, with no prescriptive reality claimed for it, and set with perfect appropriateness between grief and salvatory aspiration:

"Jaunting, journeying
To his own dayspring,
He unpacks the loaded pern
Of all 'twas pain or joy to learn,
Of all that he had made.
The outrageous war shall fade;
At some old winding whitethorn root
He'll practice on the shepherd's flute,
Or on the close-cropped grass
Court his shepherd lass,
Or put his heart into some game
Till daytime, playtime seem the same;
Knowledge he shall unwind
Through victories of the mind,
Till, clambering at the cradle-side,
He dreams himself his mother's pride,
All knowledge lost in trance
Of sweeter ignorance."

The closing speech of the shepherd, like the final stanza of the other elegy, shifts back to the dramatic context, humbly understates the poem's accomplishment, and controls emotion by compressing it in perfectly balanced speech, image, and cadence—again a brilliant equation between emotion and form:

When I have shut these ewes and this old ram
Into the fold, we'll to the woods and there
Cut out our rhymes on strips of new-torn bark
But put no name and leave them at her door.
To know the mountain and the valley have grieved
May be a quiet thought to wife and mother,
And children when they spring up shoulder-high.

We should next examine, briefly because they are less complex, though almost as significant in theme, a few poems in *The Wild Swans at Coole* which group themselves loosely around a kind of ironic primitivism of attitude. The shortest of them may serve handily as a text for the group:

> *Hands, do what you're bid:*
> *Bring the balloon of the mind*
> *That bellies and drags in the wind*
> *Into its narrow shed.*

"The Collar-Bone of a Hare" is a skilled bit of proto-tragic irony, brilliantly done but facile and a bit disappointing in its end-stopped negativism. The first stanza sketches, like a scene from Watteau—"the comely trees and the lawn,/ The playing upon pipes and the dancing"—a place of easy and sardonic love which is to serve the second stanza as a locus for haughty and oblique scrutiny of the world of normal illusions:

> *I would find by the edge of that water*
> *The collar-bone of a hare*
> *Worn thin by the lapping of water,*
> *And pierce it through with a gimlet, and stare*
> *At the old bitter world where they marry in churches,*
> *And laugh over the untroubled water*
> *At all who marry in churches,*
> *Through the white thin bone of a hare.*

Technically, with its precision of speech, its restrained tone and movement, its functional colorlessness of sound, and its quick surrealism of image, it is a dazzling stanza. But it fails to convince; one concludes at last that this studied nihilism is really only a covert and stylized response, once more, to Maud's jilting. As far as the tragic sense is concerned, this is not quite the thing itself.

"Tom O'Roughley," by contrast, presents one of the most honestly engaging of Yeats's raffish folk heroes. Here the revolt is from the "logic-choppers" and the fascinated-purposeful who have "marked a distant object down"; the affirmation is of the spontaneous, the intuitive, the toughly gay: "An aimless joy is a pure joy," says Tom; "And wisdom is a butterfly/ And not a gloomy bird of prey." In the second stanza, though the tone does not shift, the context deepens and with it the poem's achievement—to make this little unpretentious poem one of the solid accomplishments of Yeats's laconic mode:

> *"If little planned is little sinned*
> *But little need the grave distress.*
> *What's dying but a second wind?*
> *How but in zig-zag wantonness*
> *Could trumpeter Michael be so brave?"*
> *Or something of the sort he said,*
> *"And if my dearest friend were dead*
> *I'd dance a measure on his grave."*

Perhaps the most specific and important of those ironical-primitive poems are the two, "The Dawn" and "The Fisherman," which phrase most candidly Yeats's revolt against intellect and against vulgarity and his positive alternatives of passion and instinct. The negative impulse and the response of loftily embittered withdrawal are attitudes mainly peculiar to this interval in Yeats's career; but his positive answering stance —that oblique and elevated objectivity which he denominates "ignorance," the ideal of cold and muscular cerebration, of austere but fully committed passion—becomes a standard "mask," part of his configuration of true values. And the fisherman himself, though he seems to Yeats in his bitter mood of the time "A man who does not exist,/ A man who is but a dream," sticks in his mind with the stature and the seductiveness of archetype and myth; one side of him yearned from now on till the end to speak to that folk-heroic and perfect hearer. This personage materializes in a very interesting passage in *A Vision,* where Yeats is discussing again the habits of the man of Phase 17. It is a passage very close to his current mood of conflict between urges to plunge into public life and to withdraw from it, his "false mask" of "dispersal" and his "true mask" of "simplification":

> Because of the habit of synthesis, and of the growing complexity of the energy, which gives many interests, and the still faint perception of things in their weight and mass, men of this phase are almost always partisans, propagandists and gregarious; yet because of the *Mask* of simplification, which holds up before them the solitary life of hunters and of fishers and the "groves pale passion loves," they hate parties, crowds, propaganda.[18]

Aside from its thematic text—"I would be—for no knowledge is worth a straw—/ Ignorant and wanton as the dawn"—"The Dawn" is chiefly impressive for its concentrated epithetical brilliance, that inspired power of vision packed and crowded into compressed speech which may be Yeats's greatest legacy to modern poetry. Here I should single out "pedantic Babylon," "careless planets," "glittering coach," "cloudy shoulders" as instances of that rich economy. "The Fisherman" is impressive in every poetical way, and deserves extensive quotation. Yeats summons here, anatomizes, and sets in physical and philosophical motion his "wise and simple man," "The freckled man who goes/ To a grey place on a hill/ In grey Connemara clothes." The verse clumps harshly ahead with the rude muscularity, the preoccupied and functional gracelessness, and the intractable integrity that Yeats imagines as defining his tough country persona. After the introductory lines, the first stanza cries vivid anathema upon the contrast between the ideal and the real in his poet's experience. His bitter denunciation of the vulgarization in Irish public life hardens into

18 Page 143.

an almost incantatory curse—incantatory in effect because of the largely end-stopped lines, wholly without internal pause, with the staccato counterpoint of ritualistic responses:

All day I'd looked in the face
What I had hoped 'twould be
To write for my own race
And the reality;
The living men that I hate,
The dead man that I loved,
The craven man in his seat,
The insolent unreproved,
And no knave brought to book
Who has won a drunken cheer,
The witty man and his joke
Aimed at the commonest ear,
The clever man who cries
The catch-cries of the clown,
The beating down of the wise
And great Art beaten down.

After this complex negative, the equally harsh affirmation of the second stanza does not disappoint. The man himself is vigorously evoked in a taut union of speech, image, and tone, and Yeats's passionate-dispassionate resolve falls perfectly into the prepared context and completes a grandly simple exercise of rhetoric and the spirit:

Maybe a twelvemonth since
Suddenly I began,
In scorn of this audience,
Imagining a man,
And his sun-freckled face,
And grey Connemara cloth,
Climbing up to a place
Where stone is dark under froth,

And the down-turn of his wrist
When the flies drop in the stream;
A man who does not exist,
A man who is but a dream;
And cried, "Before I am old
I shall have written him one
Poem maybe as cold
And passionate as the dawn."

This "cold" passion is only one of Yeats's passions, but it is an important one, and its place in the tragic scheme needs to be carefully noted. It seems to me it is a specifically tragic essence, and its function is chiefly disciplinary. It is adopted, in the first place, as an affirmative and defiant attitude made necessary by the brute fact of tragic limitation in intimate human experience; it is a spiritual regrouping after tactical defeats of the psyche and the flesh. It asserts that, essentially, "nothing can injure us." As a spiritual and intellectual gesture it is ordering and reconstitutive and therapeutic; it practices tragedy's function of reconcilement by objectifying and universalizing the private catastrophe.

A final group of poems in *The Wild Swans of Coole* need not occupy us long; these are the specifically mystical or "systematic" poems—"Ego Dominus Tuus," "The Phases of the Moon," "The Cat and the Moon," "The Saint and the Hunchback," and "The Double Vision of Michael Robartes"—in which Yeats is versifying brilliantly and enigmatically the concepts of psyche and cycle which are forming *A Vision,* and which consume one-half his intellectual and emotional being now and henceforth. Yeats appears, personally, very engagingly in this group of poems. He understands his ridiculousness to the practical public eye and projects that public image of himself with ironic wit and dry self-knowledge; but at the same time he is profoundly stirred and convinced by his new vision, and returns equally quiet and equally public thanks to the bringers of illumination, the "unknown instructors":

> *And after that arranged it in a song*
> *Seeing that I, ignorant for so long,*
> *Had been rewarded thus*
> *In Cormac's ruined house.*

These poems are, of course, anything but trivial in content, and technically they are of first excellence, but their themes have, in general, only marginal relevance to our frame of tragedy; I will examine them only briefly, to try to clinch, in poetry, the argument I have already conducted with the prose: that the determinism of Yeats's system is still hospitable to his idea of tragedy.

The problem centers for us in the concept of the mask, which we have seen Yeats beginning to develop in *Per Amica Silentia Lunae* and expanding in *A Vision*. In "The Phases of the Moon," for example, the important thing to see is the terrific struggle and obduracy which lingers within and qualifies with its passion the deterministic quality of the cycle of the "phases." In the phases from 8 to 22 (exclusive of the desert fifteenth phase of the "full"), which are the creative phases, the productive struggle toward the mask or opposite is described, we see, in terms which make perfectly clear the "scarifying" and "drudging" nature of this dynamism; there is a a difference between helplessness and passivity:

> *From the first crescent to the half, the dream*
> *But summons to adventure and the man*
> *Is always happy like a bird or a beast;*
> *But while the moon is rounding towards the full*
> *He follows whatever whim's most difficult*
> *Among whims not impossible, and though scarred*
> *As with the cat-o'-nine-tails of the mind,*

His body molded from within his body
Grows comelier.

. . . .

And after that the crumbling of the moon.
The soul remembering its loneliness
Shudders in many cradles; all is changed,
It would be the world's servant, and as it serves,
Choosing whatever task's most difficult
Among tasks not impossible, it takes
Upon the body and upon the soul
The coarseness of the drudge.

And in the haunting poem "Ego Dominus Tuus," where the "objective," "primary" *Hic* and the "subjective," "antithetical" *Ille* discourse in stately counterpoint of the life of art, *Ille,* who is Yeats, makes movingly concrete his sense of the creative process as harrowing dialectic, "tragic war." In the dialogue *Ille* begins by announcing the doctrine of the mask: "By the help of an image/ I call to my own opposite, summon all/ That I have handled least, least looked upon"; and *Hic* expresses his contrary urge: "I would find myself and not an image." "That is our modern hope," *Ille* laments,

and by its light
We have lit upon the gentle, sensitive mind
And lost the old nonchalance of the hand;
Whether we have chosen chisel, pen or brush,
We are but critics, or but half create . . .

Hic counters with the example of "The chief imagination of Christendom/ Dante Alighieri," as one who

so utterly found himself
That he has made that hollow face of his
More plain to the mind's eye than any face
But that of Christ.

But immediately *Ille* pre-empts the figure to prove his own case, and in lines of exalted conviction harshly and vividly evokes the image of Dante as a supreme example of "antithetical" achievement:

> *is that spectral image*
> *The man that Lapo and that Guido knew?*
> *I think he fashioned from his opposite*
> *An image that might have been a stony face*
> *Staring upon a Bedouin's horse-hair roof*
> *From doored and windowed cliff, or half upturned*
> *Among the coarse grass and the camel-dung.*
> *He set his chisel to the hardest stone.*
> *Being mocked by Guido for his lecherous life,*
> *Derided and deriding, driven out*
> *To climb that stair and eat that bitter bread,*
> *He found the unpersuadable justice, he found*
> *The most exalted lady loved by a man.*

Hic would still like to reduce and simplify and familiarize the way of art:

> *Yet surely there are men who have made their art*
> *Out of no tragic war, lovers of life,*
> *Impulsive men that look for happiness*
> *And sing when they have found it.*

Now Keats is his example: "No one denies to Keats love of the world;/ Remember his deliberate happiness." But again *Ille* pre-empts the figure and defines Keats's "happiness" as merely deliberate compensatory behavior, a mask assumed to make art possible in the climate of deprivation:

> *His art is happy, but who knows his mind?*
> *I see a schoolboy when I think of him,*
> *With face and nose pressed to a sweet-shop window,*
> *For certainly he sank into his grave*

His senses and his heart unsatisfied,
And made—being poor, ailing and ignorant,
Shut out from all the luxury of the world,
The coarse-bred son of a livery-stable keeper—
Luxuriant song.

To read Keats's art as merely "happy" is almost absurdly oversimple. But as a reading of personality and motivation, Yeats's view strikes one as unoriginal but essentially accurate, even though it underestimates Keats's manliness and phrases his personal tragedy in terms far too softly and lushly pathetic. Dramatically, however, Yeats's tone is right, as it is contrastingly right in his handling of Dante. In any case, for our context of tragedy, Yeats's position in these poems is both important and clear. The artist, like all men, is fixed in a deterministic process which spins him more or less helplessly along a fixed orbit. But helplessness, as I have said, is not necessarily passivity; and Yeats himself supports my analysis of this process with a crucial phrase: "tragic war." The artist's special nature makes that process for him tragically harsh and exacting: his antithetical nature drives him brutally toward the mask, that opposite of himself which exists in a locus neighbor to the hopelessly unattainable. Thus his dynamism is literally the most difficult possible: "Choosing whatever task's most difficult/ Among tasks not impossible." Further, the artist is driven in a special homeless sense "out of" life. For his destiny enjoins him to order life by assuming a vantage point obliquely detached from it—not as a hater of life but as a lover for whom consummation, by bringing false stasis, would destroy vitality and right relation; like Frost, Yeats had "a lover's quarrel with the world." In this latter ideal of withdrawal—which Yeats frequently forgot in that hot involvement in life which renders the abstract conviction to some extent ridiculous—he really has in mind, I think, his reading of the attitude of powerful objectivity of classical masters of epic and tragedy: "We have lit upon the gentle, sensitive mind/ And lost the old nonchalance of the hand."

"MICHAEL ROBARTES AND THE DANCER"

The thin volume of 1921—thin qualitatively as well as quantitatively—*Michael Robartes and the Dancer,* offers only a few poems that need careful analysis. Yeats seems to be drawing breath in preparation for the concentrated richness of *The Tower* of 1928 and the complex poetry of his astonishing old age which begins there. *Michael Robartes and the Dancer* contains one of the greatest of all Yeats's lyrics, "The Second Coming," and the well-known "A Prayer for My Daughter" which, while not a capital poem, is technically and psychologically interesting; but elsewhere the wick of inspiration seems to be turned rather low in the volume. It seems logical to assume that this comparative lyrical thinness and scarcity results from the hard writing and thinking Yeats was concurrently giving to the prose system of *A Vision.*

Thematically, on the other hand, the volume presents a fairly typical Yeatsian assortment. Stirred and shaken by the Easter Rebellion, he returns in half a dozen poems to the theme of Irish partisan politics largely suspended in *The Wild Swans at Coole.* The best and most famous of this group is "Easter 1916," with its vivid catalogue of improbable heroes incarnated in the refrain of transformation, "All changed, changed utterly:/ A terrible beauty is born." Several poems explore, rather tentatively and in assorted tones, the idea of "unity of being," an important new theme shaping itself out of the reflections of *A Vision.* Several others return, with slackened emotion and a pathetic feeling of distance and unreality, to images recalled from the beloved Sligo of his boyhood. Two poems from the volume, "Solomon and the Witch" and "The Second Coming," have the closest relevance to our question, and we may confine our discussion to those.

In "Solomon and the Witch" Yeats brings on again two of his favorite personae, the great lovers Solomon and Sheba, and sets them to love and speculation in a visionary landscape. The poem's special importance lies in its fusion of Yeats's constant ideal of splendid human passion with his new esoteric notions of history and psychology. In lines of tense dialectic, in speech that half controls and half liberates strong emotion, Yeats dramatizes his speculation that the marriage-bed may offer the closest human equivalent, this side the grave, of "unity of being," and that perfect attainment of that perfect mingling may in fact be taken to signalize the Apocalypse. As *A Vision* presents the figure, "The marriage bed is the symbol of the solved antinomy, and were more than symbol could a man there lose and keep his identity, but he falls asleep. That sleep is the same as the sleep of death."[19] Sheba reports to the witch that in Solomon's embrace the previous night she had found herself inexplicably crying out in a strange tongue neither hers nor Solomon's. The witch, who is described in some of Yeats's most fantastic lines as one who fathomed "Whatever has been said, sighed, sung,/ Howled, miau-d barked, brayed, belled, yelled, cried, crowed," replies to the effect that the strange voice had been that of the eschatological cock who had been lured by the splendor of their passion to believe the hour had come for his apocalyptic signal:

> *"A cockerel*
> *Crew from a blossoming apple bough*
> *Three hundred years before the Fall,*
> *And never crew again till now,*

[19] Page 52.

And would not now but that he thought,
Chance being at one with Choice at last,
All that the brigand apple brought
And this foul world were dead at last."

The witch goes on to explain the generic psychology of the case. Love, she says, "has a spider's eye/To find out some appropriate pain"; love, like creativity, is a bitterly difficult "cruelty" of "Choice and Chance." The perfect bride-bed will merge Choice and Chance; yet "normal" love falls disappointingly short of the ideal fusion: "Maybe the bride-bed brings despair./ For each an imagined image brings/ And finds a real image there." But Solomon and Sheba, the witch concludes, had counterfeited the ideal oneness convincingly enough to fool the cock: "Therefore a blessed moon last night/ Gave Sheba to her Solomon." Yet the world remains, "stays," as sign that they have failed, though so gloriously that the cock "thought it worth a crow." The poem ends with Sheba reinvoking the mystical setting, its furnishings of passion and disaster, and yearning wildly at the last to make a grand assault upon the perfected passion:

"The night has fallen; not a sound
In the forbidden sacred grove
Unless a petal hit the ground,
Nor any human sight within it
But the crushed grass where we have lain;
And the moon is wilder every minute.
O! Solomon! let us try again."

The poem complicates and extends Yeats's tragic framework. Once again he has set all human experience, even the richest, in the discipline of despair, assumed as the ineluctable environment of experience. He defines love as sharing in the exacting dynamism of all creative endeavor: it is "cruel," "murderous." The perfect he has bluntly equated with the millennial; it is not a property of this life. The dignity and the pathos of human love lie in the fact that it creates a state which is the closest possible human earthly approximation to a state transcending the tragic discipline. But true unity of being is a perfected state that is beyond life, superhuman. In the terms of *A Vision,* we remember, "all unity is from the *Mask,*" and the "antithetical mask" is a "form created by passion to unite us to ourselves";[20] the "form" takes the shape of one's "direct opposite, that object of desire or moral ideal which is of all possible things the most difficult."[21] Man drives and is driven toward that condition by rhythmically counterpointed pressures—spins in his fated orbit, or "perns" in his "gyres"—which are largely controlled by the mystic will outside himself which orders all things. That force pushes him where he must go and draws the line of failure, of tragic incompleteness short of unity of being, beyond which he may not pass.

Unity of being "occurs," in the ineffectual sense in which it may be said to occur, at Phase 15. Yeats describes this phase as one of "complete beauty,"[22] and goes on to set down its characteristics:

> Thought and will are indistinguishable, effort and attainment are indistinguishable . . . nothing is apparent but dreaming *Will* and the Image that it dreams . . . . The being has selected, molded and remolded, narrowed its circle of living, been more and more the artist, grown more and more "distinguished" in all preference. Now contemplation and desire, united into one, inhabit a world where every beloved image has bodily form, and every bodily form is loved. This

20 Page 82.

21 Page 83.

22 *A Vision,* 135.

> love knows nothing of desire, for desire implies effort, and though there is still separation from the loved object, love accepts the separation as necessary to its own existence . . . . Chance and Choice have become interchangeable without losing their identity. As all effort has ceased, all thought has become image, because no thought could exist if it were not carried towards its own extinction, amid fear or in contemplation; and every image is separate from every other, for if image were linked to image, the soul would awake from its immovable trance.[23]

But space is left for human will inside the fatal dialectic; man both drives and is driven, as I have said, and the fact that his sense of free-agency is largely illusion is finally beside the point. The workings of this deluded will give the order of life such dynamism as it has, and its workings alone make creativity possible. The creative spirit both *seeks* its opposite and *accepts* its Daemon as conductor toward those tasks "most difficult among tasks not impossible"; performing those tasks is the spirit's creative act. The infallibility of man's failure is the defining condition of his tragedy. His refusal to admit this infallibility and his willed commitment to the passionate and hopeless struggle—his vital absurdity—are his qualifying conditions for tragic dignity. His participation is full only when his commitment is total, and his commitment is total in acts of supreme passion. Thus in "Solomon and the Witch" and in many later poems, the embrace of love, performed with full passion by heroic persons, becomes the dramatized symbol (both really and ideally true) of man's noblest approximation to unity of being; the act will fail, but it is incandescent and beautiful because it embodies aspiration and will at the peak of passion.

In sum, this seems to leave us three Yeatsian propositions:

[23] *Ibid.*, 135–36.

(1) man's life is a discipline of contrapuntal Chance and Choice; (2) Chance and Choice coincide and make unity of being, historically, only at millennial epochs, and, individually, only beyond life; (3) man approaches the fated limits of his achievement only in the fullness of passion. All this elaborate and certainly overstrained rationale of the doctrinal and representative function of great love and great lovers helps us to understand—almost—Yeats's sense of the grandeur of his love for Maud Gonne and the immense and special poignancy of his failure there. He and Maud had really failed at a priestly and sacramental office.

Although it is philosophically simpler, "The Second Coming" is aesthetically a far finer poem; it is surely one of the great lyrics of the century. Thematically the poem needs no elaborate gloss; it rises out of difficulty and above it, and reduces the complex to a blinding simplicity. The figure the poem makes, to adapt Frost's phrase, is possibly the most pressingly memorable figure achieved by any English poet since Blake. Yeats makes that figure by cutting into our psychic sense of our time and inserting into that open memory an embodied colossal malignity. The poem constructs an ironic apocalypse, of a terrible near-vagueness, and embodies that apocalypse in a single huge symbol, that "shape," that "rough beast" who reactivates Chaos and whose function is to harrow out the age of Christ and install his own anarchic millennium. R. P. Blackmur has called attention to Yeats's description of the monstrous beast of the poem as an image he had personally seen many times, "always at my left side just out of the range of sight, a brazen winged beast that I associated with laughing, ecstatic destruction."[24] "The Second Coming" is at once a representation of Yeatsian dialectic, his cyclical theory of history, the "primary-antithetical" oscillation, and of his heartbroken

[24] "The Later Poetry of W. B. Yeats," *PY*, 48.

and outraged sense of the failure and dissolution of life in his time, his sense of literally inhabiting Apocalypse. "One thing I did not foresee, not having the courage of my own thought: the growing murderousness of the world," he wrote in his *Autobiography;*[25] and again, "After us the Savage God."[26] With study, the poem comes painfully clear both as dialectic and as apocalypse. That it moves in the ethos of tragedy is almost too clear to require mention.

The first of the poem's two stanzas is mainly a stanza of statement, moving flatly in clipped assertive clauses to fix in analytic description the landscape of an age's decay. Yeats makes here his clearest and least equivocal use of his gyre image as figure, and supports his assertions thickly with favorite images of flight and drowning, "falcon" and "blood-dimmed tide."

> *Turning and turning in the widening gyre*
> *The falcon cannot hear the falconer;*
> *Things fall apart; the center cannot hold;*
> *Mere anarchy is loosed upon the world,*
> *The blood-dimmed tide it loosed, and everywhere*
> *The ceremony of innocence is drowned;*
> *The best lack all conviction, while the worst*
> *Are full of passionate intensity.*

The climate of smothering and confusion convinces us as it convinces Yeats that this is a dissolving age awaiting some immense visitation. His first impulse is to expect the Christian revelation: "Surely some revelation is at hand;/ Surely the Second Coming is at hand." But that image fails to manifest itself. Instead of the Prince of Peace coming to announce the fullness of the Kingdom of God, what erupts out of the racial

25 Page 168.
26 Page 297.

memory, that deep cistern of symbols, is a figure of gross unreason and mindless violence:

> *The Second Coming! Hardly are those words out*
> *When a vast image out of* Spiritus Mundi
> *Troubles my sight: somewhere in sands of the desert*
> *A shape with lion body and the head of a man,*
> *A gaze blank and pitiless as the sun,*
> *Is moving its slow thighs, while all about it*
> *Reel shadows of the indignant desert birds.*

The image retreats but leaves its brutal revelation:

> *The darkness drops again; but now I know*
> *That twenty centuries of stony sleep*
> *Were vexed to nightmare by a rocking cradle,*
> *And what rough beast, its hour come round at last,*
> *Slouches towards Bethlehem to be born?*

It is a brilliant stanza, a great theme perfectly realised. Rhetoric, movement, diction, and image make that consummate fusion with meaning and feeling that we can only call inevitable. Each word rests in place both perfectly comfortable and full of potential motion, in an amazing balance of ease and stress. The stanza shows Yeats's compressed epithetical mastery at its richest yet most tersely controlled: in phrases such as "gaze blank and pitiless as the sun," "slow thighs," "indignant desert birds," and "stony sleep," the telescoped potency of his vision creates horrifying perspectives of depth and age and alien malignancy with an economy that is shocking. And Yeats's command of the right and muscular verb has never proved itself more functionally: the "reeling" of the desert birds in consternation and outrage, and that "slouches" which is the poem's brutal crown and insult, conducting the great rough beast himself to his catastrophic appointment in bitterly ironic space-time.

"The anguish of birth and that of death cry out in the same instant," says Michael Robartes early in *A Vision*. "Life is no series of emanations from divine reason . . . but an irrational bitterness, no orderly descent from level to level, no waterfall but a whirlpool, a gyre."[27] In "The Second Coming," as in a number of important later poems, what Yeats does is immensely to expand his sense of life as tragedy from the scope of the individual to the scope of the millennial, from the life of a man to the life of civilizations. In *A Vision* he symbolizes the course of a civilization in almost exactly the same figurative system which he applies to men. Civilizations are born, decay, and die in cycles of roughly two thousand years. Like men, they have their "tinctures"; each is either dominantly antithetical or dominantly primary; each fades out of its opposite at birth and fades into its opposite again at death. Thus, in Yeats's thought the Babylonian civilization is primary, the Greco-Roman antithetical, the Christian primary (at the end of which we stand, the end seen in visionary terms in "The Second Coming"), the coming civilization of the "Savage God" antithetical again. He symbolizes the motions and countermotions of epochs again by the figure of his interlocking gyres: successive eras "die each other's life, live each other's death":

> Each age unwinds the thread another age had wound, and it amuses one to remember that before Phidias, and his westward-moving art, Persia fell, and that when full moon came round again, amid eastward-moving thought, and brought Byzantine glory, Rome fell; and that at the outset of our westward-moving Renaissance Byzantium fell; all things dying each other's life, living each other's death.[28]

"A civilization is a struggle to keep self-control," he writes,

27 Page 40.
28 *A Vision*, 270–71.

"and in this it is like some great tragic person."[29] The extremes of every epoch, as one age struggles to die and another to be born, are times of violence and unreason, in which the pangs of birth and death are hardly distinguishable: "The anguish of birth and that of death cry out in the same instant." Of the period of dissolution and death, the "mere anarchy" of "The Second Coming," Yeats writes:

> The loss of control over thought comes towards the end; first a sinking in upon the moral being, then the last surrender, the irrational cry, revelation—the scream of Juno's peacock.[30]

The "blood-dimmed tide" that drowns the "ceremony of innocence" is also explained by certain images in *A Vision:*

> One knows not into how great extravagance Asia, accustomed to abase itself, may have carried what soon sent Greeks and Romans to stand naked in a Mithraic pit, moving their bodies as under a shower-bath that those bodies might receive the blood of the bull even to the last drop.[31]

> When I think of the moment before revelation I think of Salome—she, too, delicately tinted or maybe mahogany dark—dancing before Herod and receiving the Prophet's head in her indifferent hands . . . .[32]

But birth is bitter, too, whatever its tincture. Yeats quotes his own closing lines from "The Magi" in a context which shows that he means the image to describe either an "antithetical" or a "primary" birth:

> When the old *antithetical* becomes the new *primary,* moral feeling is changed into an organization of experience which must in its turn seek a unity, the whole of experience. When

29 *Ibid.,* 268.
30 *Ibid.*
31 Page 272.
32 Page 273.

> the old *primary* becomes the new *antithetical,* the old realization of an objective moral law is changed into a subconscious turbulent instinct. The world of rigid custom and law is broken up by "the uncontrollable mystery upon the bestial floor."[33]

The dialectic surrounding "The Second Coming" is, therefore, simply an aggrandizement of that surrounding "Solomon and the Witch." On the one hand Yeats establishes a rigid framework governed by an immense pessimistic determinism—adequate, if time had not already done the deed, to deal the deathblow to "nineteenth-century optimism"; within that tragic discipline of racial effort and failure, labors and fails its humanistic denial, the Prometheus of the individual will, stubbornly asserting its autonomy in the teeth of fate.

[33] Page 105.

CHAPTER SIX

Late Theory

THE GENUS PASSION

OUR INVESTIGATIONS have carried us now roughly to 1928, the date of the publication of *The Tower,* the volume of poems which ushers in Yeats's great last period occupying the eleven years remaining before his death. From now on the problem is one of embarrassing riches. Yeats had long ago forgotten how to write a bad poem. In his diary of 1909 he had said, "A good writer should be so simple that he has no faults, only sins."[1] In *The Tower* and thereafter, faults are hard to find, and if there are sins they are those of doctrine; judgment of those must be mainly matter for the individual conscience. From now on, at any rate, there is scarcely a poem upon which one would not like to attempt a comment, and scarcely one which is not either centrally or marginally relevant to our frame of tragedy.

[1] "The Death of Synge," *Dramatis Personae,* 154.

But before undertaking a reading of the poems of the last period we should seek new nourishment for the theoretical side of Yeats's practice of tragedy—collect the prose texts which seem to embody his mature definitions and create the emotional and didactic climate of the poems. Henceforth Yeats's most significant focus is upon passion—the fact and the idea. I shall examine the prose and eventually the poems under the several headings which seem to me to suggest Yeats's most significant variations on the theme of passion: Passion as Defense; Passion as Joy; Passion as Sublimation or Innocence; Passion as Transcendence or Apocalypse.

Passion as fact and idea, practice and concept, is everywhere in Yeats, as poet and man—a potency impossible to overemphasize. In the second letter of Mr. Alan Wade's collection, dated "possibly early 1887," we find Yeats writing to a former schoolmate, after having denounced George Eliot as "too reasonable": "I was once afraid of turning out reasonable myself. The only business of the head in the world is to bow a ceaseless obeisance to the heart."[2] In 1896 he writes to W. J. Horton of the limited function of intellect: "It clears the rubbish from the mouth of the sybil's cave but it is not the sybil."[3] We may recall his judgment of 1903 approving the passionate strangeness of the folk tales collected by Lady Gregory: "The imagination which remembers the proportions of life is but a long wooing, and . . . it has to forget them before it becomes the torch and the marriage-bed."[4] And toward the end of Mr. Wade's big book of his letters, we find Yeats writing to Joseph Hone of Swift, one of his great passional masters:

> There was something not himself that Swift served. He called it "freedom" but never defined it and thus has passion. Passion

[2] *Letters,* 31.
[3] *Ibid.,* 262.
[4] "Lady Gregory's Translations," *CA,* 8.

> is to me the essential. I was educated upon Balzac and Shakespeare and cannot go beyond them.[5]

All these are merely representative statements of a congenital property of temperament as well as an accumulated conviction. That passion was indeed "the essential" to Yeats is true beyond equivocation; but passion's forms and functions for Yeats need considerable explication.

PASSION AS DEFENSE

By "Passion as Defense" I mean what Yeats meant when he said that to him "the supreme aim" was "an act of faith and reason to make one rejoice in the midst of tragedy": acts of intellectual dedication and emotional commitment to make life habitable in a discipline of disaster; assertions of the human spirit in the face of tragedy; passion as a double weapon, offensive and defensive, shield and sword, against fate and time. It was his devotion to this attitude, and to this relationship between art and experience, that led Yeats in "Anima Hominis" to decry the artist's supposed need to "seek originality"; the artist's affair is with passion, Yeats said there, and if he has passion, originality will be added unto him: "It is not permitted to a man, who takes up pen or chisel, to seek originality, for passion is his only business, and he cannot but mold or sing after a new fashion because no disaster is like another."[6]

Thus disaster is the negating discipline to which passion is the pathetic yet imposing response. There is, of course, nothing original in Yeats's position; its philosophical familiarity is such that we are likely to count it among the great standard human postures, and one thinks at once of many men who have prac-

[5] *Letters,* 791.
[6] "Anima Hominis," *PASL,* 44.

ticed one or another kind of Prometheanism: Yeats himself locates it in Blake, Swift, Landor, Donne, in Timon and Lear, in his favorite mythical heroes Usheen and Cuchulain. Our job is simply to note that Yeats does commit himself stubbornly to the archetype of Prometheus, and that his attitude follows from necessities both temperamental and philosophical. "The food of the spiritual-minded is sweet," he wrote in "Synge and the Ireland of His Time," quoting "an Indian scripture," "but passionate minds love bitter food,"[7] In an interesting late letter to Olivia Shakespear he speaks in comic-ironic terms of the equation he felt between bitterness and value in his own work:

> I am in quite good spirits, impersonal, active, enjoying public admiration etc etc and so I cannot write a good letter. Presently somebody will call me names, I will remember that I am old, that "we go no more a-roaming by the light of the moon" and then I will write you beautiful letters. However, as a consolation for this hateful cheerfulness here are two stanzas from a Sophocles chorus . . . .[8]

Yeats's stance of Promethean defiance is adopted in preference to an almost equally seductive alternative way, the way of withdrawal and abstraction, of mystical dedication to "other values." This choice embodies really the greatest and most inclusive of Yeats's antinomies; in a letter to Mrs. Shakespear of 1932 he gives to the poles of this antithesis the suggestive names of "swordsman" and "saint." He has been correcting proofs of the first volume, containing all his lyric poems, of a projected limited edition of all his works; in a revealing passage he describes for Mrs. Shakespear his sensations in reviewing for the first time all his poems of forty-five years, notes the startling singleness of his themes, and goes on, with some sense

7 *CA,* 171.
8 *Letters,* 722–23.

of self-revelation, to reduce that thematic obsession to a significant formula:

> I have just finished the first volume, all my lyric poetry, and am greatly astonished at myself. As it is all speech rather than writing, I keep saying what man is this who in the course of two or three weeks—the improvisation suggests the tune—says the same thing in so many different ways. My first denunciation of old age I made in *The Wanderings of Usheen* . . . before I was twenty and the same denunciation comes in the last pages of the book. The swordsman throughout repudiates the saint, but not without vacillation. Is that perhaps the sole theme—Usheen and Patrick— "so get you gone Von Hügel though with blessings on your head"?[9]

The passage makes, I take it, a crucial repudiation of all his assorted Twilights, and whatever the quality of "belief" he gave his mystical system—that he substantially "believed" what he wrote in *A Vision* now seems to me indisputable—he sees himself as having renounced, as man and artist, for his pragmatic conduct in *this* life the way of the saint and espoused the way of Usheen, the swordsman's way: he will participate, he will fight.

Exactly what we mean by Yeats's "passion" is a complex question which admits of some simplification. Basically, as I have said, I speak of the positive vibrancy of his response to negative despair. The gist of the matter can be drawn from a few simple but potent statements of his. Thus he writes to Dorothy Wellesley two years before his death, ". . . my poetry all comes from rage or lust."[10] If we add to those great factors of rage and lust Yeats's quality of impassioned and transcendental idealism, we get something like the totality of his definition of passion. His blunt statement of ten years earlier to

[9] *Ibid.*, 798.
[10] *Letters to Dorothy Wellesley*, 120.

Olivia Shakespear drives to a conclusion uniting his fundamental motives: " . . . only two topics can be of the least interest to a serious and studious mind—sex and the dead."[11] Dogmatic and a bit posed, perhaps, but still seriously meant, and as inclusive, rightly considered, as one could wish: sex and the dead is to say life and death, the life of the body and the life of the soul. But Yeats supplies us as well the specific and formal definition we also need. It occurs in a letter to Wyndham Lewis in 1930, in which he chides Lewis for scoffing at a poet whose work he himself admires because he has found it to possess the categorical values: "passion enobled [*sic*] by intensity, by endurance, by wisdom." It is the same perfected combination of art and spirit Yeats had always felt epitomized in Swift: "We had it in one man once. He lies in St. Patrick's now under the greatest epitaph in history."[12] It is clear that passion, inclusively considered, connoted the highest values of Yeats's Pantheon: nobility, intensity, endurance, wisdom.

Not surprisingly, most of Yeats's rage in this late period is directed against one of the constant counters in the tragic configuration of being human—old age, actual or potential. The poems and the prose are full of reactions of many kinds—for the most part variously defiant—to the onset of age. Passion is his chief defense, as we will see in some sample prose references. We have already seen him in his swordsman *versus* saint passage above commenting on the fact that "denunciation of old age" had made him an early as well as a late theme. In 1926, sending Olivia Shakespear a version of section VI of "Among School Children," he wrote, "Here is a fragment of my last curse upon old age. It means that even the greatest men are owls, scarecrows, by the time their fame has come."[13]

11 *Letters,* 730.
12 *Ibid.,* 776.
13 *Ibid.,* 719.

Three years before, he had already described himself to her as "tired and in a rage at being old. I am all I ever was and much more but an enemy has bound me and twisted me so I can plan and think as I never could, but no longer achieve all I plan and think."[14] In letters to Mrs. Shakespear and others he reverts repeatedly to this bitter sense of frustration, of the leaden body dragging heels against the impassioned spirit. Thus in February, 1926, he writes to Professor H. J. C. Grierson in terms which he echoes months later to Mrs. Shakespear, and which eventually work themselves into his poetic sequence, "A Man Young and Old": "I feel constantly if I were but twenty years old and not over sixty all I ever wanted to do could be done easily. One never tires of life and at the last must die of thirst with the cup at one's lip."[15] And to Mrs. Shakespear: "One looks back to one's youth as to a cup that a mad man dying of thirst left half tasted."[16] A year and a half earlier he had described to her his simple strategy for dealing with the withering potency of age—by an act of will and imagination to deny his own chronology and to pitch his voice at the resurrected image of his own youth:

> I write for boys and girls of twenty but I am always thinking of myself at that age–the age I was when my father painted me as King Goll, tearing the strings out [of] a harp, being insane with youth, but looking very desirable . . . with dreamy eyes and a great mass of black hair.[17]

But these negatives and this strategy of factitious youthfulness are not the true center of his attitude. The center is positive, defiant, and confidently or bitterly gay. We find it in his

[14] *Ibid.*, 685.
[15] *Ibid.*, 711.
[16] *Ibid.*, 721.
[17] *Ibid.*, 705.

description of his emotion as he stands looking at his Nobel medal immediately after the presentation in 1923:

> All is over, and I am able to examine my medal, its charming, decorative, academic design, French in manner, a work of the 'nineties. It shows a young man listening to a Muse, who stands young and beautiful with a great lyre in her hand, and I think as I examine it, "I was good-looking once like that young man, but my unpractised verse was full of infirmity, my Muse old as it were; and now I am old and rheumatic, and nothing to look at, but my Muse is young. I am even persuaded that she is like those Angels in Swedenborg's vision, and moves perpetually "towards the day-spring of her youth."[18]

And we find the true center still more typically in the words of a letter to Dorothy Wellesley of December 1936:

> I had a black fortnight the result of nervous strain writing the Casement poem you have seen & another that you have not—beating the paste-board men—& some other odds & ends. I got sleepy & tired & spent my day in bed & thought of my soul. Then I noticed that every time I thought of my soul I used some second-hand phrase & knew by that that I was thinking of my soul from ambition & vanity. I said to myself "Your job is to avoid deep places & to die blaspheming" & I got well at once, went to the theatre at night & by day took the bus to Dublin.[19]

"Passion as Defense" is obviously one heading under which Yeats's late attitude to sex needs to be discussed. The passion of the body, as all have noticed, composes a major theme and strongly colors the tone of Yeats's later poems; and his violent old man's sexuality in *Last Poems,* especially with its chemical basis, so to speak, in his Steinach glandular operation of 1934, has embarrassed many of his commentators—illogically, it

18 "The Bounty of Sweden," *Dramatis Personae,* 168.
19 *Letters to Dorothy Wellesley,* 124.

seems to me. We shall have to say more of this phenomenon presently; at the moment we need only to remark his canonizing of sex as the continuation of a constant we have already established in his psychology—as central to the passional quality of the full life, hence dear to art as well as to life; and, sublimated, as kin to the workings of the aspiring spirit. The simplest reaches of his view—sex as pure joy, "nonchalant" vitality—are expressed in a letter to Dorothy Wellesley of May, 1936, in which he speaks of a randy note he has sent to Laura Riding:

> I wrote to-day to Laura Riding, with whom I carry on a slight correspondence, that her school was too thoughtful, reasonable & truthful, that poets were good liars who never forgot that the Muses were women who liked the embrace of gay warty lads. I wonder if she knows that warts are considered by the Irish peasantry a sign of sexual power?[20]

That more complex side, Yeats's view of the sexual act as a defiance of physical limitation, man's nearest approach to the transcendent state of "unity of being," which we noted earlier especially in connection with "Solomon and the Witch," is clarified newly in two letters to Olivia Shakespear about a year and a half apart. In May, 1926, he writes:

> We are at our Tower and I am writing poetry as I always do here, and as always happens, no matter how I begin, it becomes love poetry before I am finished with it. . . . One feels at moments as if one could with a touch convey a vision–that the mystic way and sexual love use the same means–opposed yet parallel existences. . . .
>
> My moods fill me with surprise and some alarm. The other day I found at Coole a reproduction of a drawing of two charming young persons in the full stream of their Saphoistic [*sic*] enthusiasm, and it got into my dreams at night and

20 *Ibid.*, 69.

> made a great racket there, and yet I feel spiritual things are very near me.[21]

And in October of 1927 he writes again to connect his notion of the union of passion and spirit with a startling experience in the occult:

> When I went to London I had just finished a poem ["Sailing to Byzantium"] in which I appeal to the saints in "the holy fire" to send death on their ecstasy. In London I went to a medium called Cooper and on the way called to my people for their especial wisdom. The medium gave me "a book test" —Third book from R bottom shelf—study—Page 48 or 84. I have only this morning looked it up. The book was the complete Dante designs of Blake. It is not numbered by pages but by plates. Plate 84 is Dante entering the Holy Fire (Purgatorio—Canto 27). Plate 48 is "The serpent attacking Vanni Fucci." When I looked this up in Dante I found that at the serpent's sting Vanni Fucci is burnt to ashes and then re-created from the ashes and that this symbolizes "the temporal Fire." The medium is the most stupid I know and certainly the knowledge was not in my head. After this and all that has gone before I must capitulate if the dark mind lets me. Certainly we suck always at the eternal dugs. How well too it puts my own mood between spiritual excitement, and the sexual torture and the knowledge that they are somehow inseparable![22]

"We suck always at the eternal dugs." Great "antithetical" natures, among whom Yeats numbered Dante and himself (both "Phase 17"), form a long continuity of passion whose Phoenix-splendor has the power almost to shake the logic of the fated cycles themselves. The weapon of passion is both shield and sword, as we said; and specifically sexual passion is

21 *Letters,* 714–15.
22 *Ibid.,* 730–31.

at once a retreat from the operations of fate and an attack upon fate's presumptive omnipotence. Sex is more than a creature comfort, more even than the mechanics of fertility; it is the means of transcendental union with what Yeats would call the deep Masters of Life.

PASSION AS JOY

The paradoxical possibility of joy within tragic experience, the reconciliation of the sufferer and his bitter destiny, that healing irony at the heart of things, the complexly simple dogma of purgation which is vital to all classical definitions of tragedy, is a basic element in the tragic system of Yeats. We have already noted it tentatively, and we need now to look at its mature expressions, confining ourselves to the most important texts of the abundance that Yeats offers in his later prose. Actually the reality of tragic joy is one of the earliest as well as the latest of Yeats's convictions, and it is nowhere pronounced more eloquently than in the rich melancholy of a speech by the poet-teacher Seanchan in Yeats's play of 1904, *The King's Threshold:*

> *What was it that the poets promised you,*
> *If it was not their sorrow?*
> . . . .
> *And I would have all know that when all falls*
> *In ruin, poetry calls out in joy,*
> *Being the scattering hand, the bursting pod,*
> *The victim's joy among the holy flame,*
> *God's laughter at the shattering of the world.*
> *And now that joy laughs out, and weeps and burns*
> *On these bare steps.*[23]

In a letter of the same year to Æ, one that is scarcely less eloquent than the play, in which he derides the "unmanly"

[23] *Collected Plays,* 75.

qualities of his early poems and plays for their "sentiment and sentimental sadness, a womanish introspection,"[24] Yeats closes a postscript with a sentence which ignores the tragic paradox but demands for joy a place in every worthy emotion: "Let us have no emotion, however abstract, in which there is not an athletic joy."[25] And in one of the last of his plays, the fantastic and beautiful *The Herne's Egg,* we find Yeats's joy fused with passion in the frenzy of transcendence which I shall later call the Passionate Apocalypse; Attracta, the maiden betrothed to the holy bird, awaits his coming with these words:

Strong sinew and soft flesh
Are foliage round the shaft
Before the arrowsmith
Has stripped it, and I pray
That I, all foliage gone,
May shoot into my joy . . . [26]

These are the bare frames of Yeats's notions of tragic joy, of passion as a kind of overarching excitement, and it remains for the poems to fill in the canvas and to show what superb art he made, as always, of doctrine. Meanwhile we may glance at a few more of the incremental prose statements. At one point in his letters Yeats pauses to admire the faculty of defensive joy, which he here calls "gaiety," as a universal in the human armory. Like so many of his most intimate and vivid letters, this one is to Olivia Shakespear. It comes late in 1927 when Yeats was recovering from his first serious illness and beguiling his convalescence with Wyndham Lewis' *Time and Western Man,* full of "admiration and envy" at its energy; he describes his symptoms and his paradoxically vital response:

24 *Letters,* 434.
25 *Ibid.,* 435.
26 *Collected Plays,* 412.

> Three days ago I spat a little red and that roused me to defy George and begin to work and now though I am better again I write verse a little every morning. . . . How strange is the subconscious gaiety that leaps up before danger or difficulty. I have not had a moment's depression—that gaiety is outside one's control, a something given by nature.[27]

Six years later, to the same correspondent, he wrote in more formal terms which show his insight into the scope of this equilibrium and a knowledge of its philosophical roots:

> We are happy when for everything inside us there is an equivalent something outside us. I think it was Goethe said this. One should add the converse. It is terrible to desire and not possess, and terrible to possess and not desire. Because of this we long for an age which has the unity which Plato somewhere defined as sorrowing and rejoicing over the same things.[28]

He is thinking again of his own phrase, "unity of being," and, very possibly, of Blake's statement which he quotes in *A Vision,* "There is a place at the bottom of the graves where contraries are equally true."[29] And one thinks again, too, of Keats's notion of "intensity," allied to his concept of "negative capability"—that intensity which is the "excellence of every art," and which is "capable of making all disagreeables evaporate from its being in close relationship with beauty and truth."[30] But Yeats is being more aesthetical than Blake and more daring than Keats. To push his idea at once to its destination, we may say that this emotionless emotion he describes is really one of the final effects of tragedy, its condition of reconstituted wholeness or reconciliation which brings the

27 *Letters,* 733.
28 *Ibid.,* 810–11.
29 Page 72.
30 Letter to George and Thomas Keats, Dec. 22, 1817, *The Letters of John Keats,* 70.

tragic sufferer and his audience to the cleansed acceptance of the bases of being, to the recognition that the spectacle of suffering and defeat is simply "life," simply "true." It helps to recall that Keats associated his version of the idea with Shakespeare, especially with *King Lear.*

These ideas of Yeats's connect themselves, clearly, with that central emotional effect he found in tragedy, and to which he gave the name of "ecstasy." So he names it again in a letter to his father, in which he refuses to say "joy" solely because he believes that an audience whom he was to address would fail to follow his thought.[31] So in the early "The Death of Synge" he had already made clear that tragic joy was to him a positive stage in the sequence of tragic emotion that follows ("the other side"—that is, beyond) and supersedes the negative emotion of "mere" grief: "The arts have nothing to give but that joy of theirs which is the other side of sorrow, that exhausting contemplation."[32]

But "that exhausting contemplation" is very close to what I am about to call "Passion as Innocence" or "Sublimation"; so it is better to turn to a passage from a late letter to Ethel Mannin which makes the crucial synopsis of all the elements in the paradox of tragic joy:

> Bitterness is more fatal to us than it is to lawyers and journalists who have nothing to do with the feminine muses. Our traditions only permit us to bless, for the arts are an extension of the beatitudes. Blessed be heroic death (Shakespeare's tragedies), blessed be heroic life (Cervantes), blessed be the wise (Balzac) . . . . I shall write it out in the style of *The Arabian Nights* (which I am reading daily). There are three very important persons (1) a man playing the flute (2) a man carving a statue (3) a man in a woman's arms.[33]

31 *Letters,* 587.
32 "The Death of Synge," *Dramatis Personae,* 126.
33 *Letters,* 831–32.

In this great mingling hate is renounced and love accepted and embodied in art, whose function becomes, whatever its means, benison and "beatitude"; all, ultimately, is in the wine cup, "and the grapes begin to stammer."

In making a slogan, a personal heraldic device, of such phrases as "bitter and gay," "tragic joy," Yeats pushes his insight into tragic truth to that last station where tragedy makes its mysterious and shocking marriage with comedy, and the two become the inextricable one flesh of the greatest art. In that exhausting contemplation where we find ourselves sorrowing and rejoicing over the same things, our academic categories turn to nonsense. Finally, it is not sleep that may be had in that deep den of all, but laughter. "Such a waggish leering as lurks in all your horribles!" says Stubb in Melville's tragicomedy; and Joyce prays, "Loud, heap miseries upon us yet entwine our arts with laughters low!" This is that "special final peripeteia, from grief to joy" that Gilbert Murray found in the "normal sequence" of tragic emotion in the classical tetralogies, carried by the fourth member, the satyr-play. Nietzsche believed that the chorus of satyrs sang and danced the assertion of "the metaphysical solace that, despite every phenomenal change, life is indestructibly joyful and powerful." It is by such encompassing logic and intuition that Yeats can assert in "Lapis Lazuli" that "Hamlet and Lear are gay;/ Gaiety transfiguring all that dread." Is the art that embodies that kind of satyr-wisdom, such "mummy-truth," tragedy or comedy? Neither and both, I suppose. What we really need to see is that in the inclusive tragic vision, comedy is a full partner.

PASSION AS INNOCENCE

One way of seeing what I call Yeats's concept of innocence is to see it as another variant of the Aristotelian doctrine of catharsis, that sense of fusion, of balance, of reconciliation, of emotional and spiritual rest and reassembly, which follows in the classical sequence of tragic emotion after the "purgation of pity and fear." Innocence, as Yeats himself names it in "Anima Mundi,"[34] might alternatively be called sublimation—a transmutation and elevation of passion into poise and peace; a state of mind outside and above both tragic sorrow and that tragic "joy which is the other side of sorrow." In explicating the doctrine here, we may rest content with a few of its major prose bases, and wait for the later verse to illustrate it and set it in effective motion.

This stage of Yeats's tragic sequence, like any late stage in a mature theory of tragedy, is an antipodal response to an original dejected bitterness; not so much an active revolt, in this case, as a snubbing, an aloofness earned by mastery not only of bitterness but of that medial state of resignation which normally follows it. And it is a condition of activity and fertility, not a mere stasis; Yeats's "innocence" is like that "mute calm" in the middle of the "tornadoed Atlantic" of Melville's being, where he did not sit but "centrally disported." A single passage from a letter to Lady Gregory gives us a tentative sketch of most of our needed elements here, and provides a further Keatsian analogy, from the "Ode on a Grecian Urn." The date is February, 1928, and Yeats is at Rapallo with the Pounds, convalescing from his serious illness of this winter:

> This is an indescribably lovely place—some little Greek town one imagines—there is a passage in Keats describing just such a town. Here I shall put off the bitterness of Irish quarrels, and write my most amiable verses. They are already, though I dare not write, crowding my head. *The Tower* astonishes me by its bitterness.[35]

Yeats's sense of shock at his own bitterness and his functional

[34] *PASL,* 93.
[35] *Letters,* 738.

resolve upon "amiability" must point us back in time to the origins of these attitudes. They have a long history, and they rest upon his original confession of the tragic facts of life, and upon a resolution to "tolerate" an insuperable limitation—the brutal foreshortening in nature of an idealist's notions of the possible: to put it simply, upon an acceptance of things as they are. The early prose shows the beginnings of that stage in Yeats's tragic process. One of the most interesting of these statements dates as far back as 1901, and thereby shows that a decision to "tolerate" had accompanied his first definitive shift to a poetry based on fact rather than dream; it had waited a long time in his mind to become a major tendency of his last period. In the essay "At Stratford-on-Avon," Yeats tries to develop a formula based upon a week's theatre-haunting at Stratford in which he has seen performances of six of the histories. "Partly because of a spirit in the place," he says, "and partly because of the way play supports play, the theatre has moved me as it has never done before."[36] He is most deeply interested in the contrast he feels between Richard II and Henry V, and his psyche at this interval is still sufficiently "twilit" so that he reacts with a softly impassioned preference for the complexly inadequate Richard, whom he sees as the type of those men

> who find themselves where men ask of them a rough energy and have nothing to give but some contemplative virtue, whether lyrical fantasy, or sweetness of temper, or dreamy dignity, or love of God, or love of His creatures.[37]

In contrast to this "vessel of porcelain" Yeats sees Henry V as Shakespeare's "vessel of clay," a man with the

> gross vices, the coarse nerves, of one who is to rule among

[36] *Ideas of Good and Evil,* 143.
[37] *Ibid.,* 159.

> violent people . . . . He is as remorseless and undistinguished as some natural force, and the finest thing in his play is the way his old companions fall out of it broken-hearted or on their way to the gallows.[38]

Then the fully developed contrast:

> Instead of that lyricism which rose out of Richard's mind like the jet of a fountain to fall again where it had risen, instead of that fantasy too enfolded in its own sincerity to make any thought the hour had need of, Shakespeare has given him a resounding rhetoric that moves men, as a leading article does today.[39]

Yeats's Shakespearean dichotomy, clearly, is an early and tentative version of his own later fundamental antinomies of "swordsman" and "saint." "The swordsman repudiates the saint," we recall his writing at the end of his life, "but not without vacillation." In this early essay, still twilit, Yeats's vacillation favors the saint, Richard, and it is the swordsman Henry who is repudiated. But what must interest us most keenly in the essay is not his special preference but his larger tolerance: his recognition, following Shakespeare's, of the reality and the validity of *both* types and their function as representing the mingling variousness that makes the paradox of man as he is, in his beautiful weakness and his ugly strength, his imposing ridiculousness. The whole conviction may simply impress one as truistic, too obvious and inescapable to confer credit; but my point is that for a man of Yeats's deep subjectivity and impassioned idealism this is an immense concession of the self to the real. At any rate we find Yeats specifically admiring just that quality Keats felt so admirable in Shakespeare and called "negative capability."[40] We see this

[38] *Ibid.*, 163.
[39] *Ibid.*
[40] Keats, Letter to George and Thomas Keats, Dec. 22, 1817, *The Letters of John Keats,* 71.

conclusively, and see explicated the quality we are trying to isolate in Yeats, in his analysis of Shakespeare's own response to his two heroes. He watched Richard, says Yeats, "with that untroubled sympathy for men as they are, as apart from all they do and seem, which is the substance of tragic irony."[41] A few pages later he concludes his analysis of Henry in a judgment interestingly different and interestingly similar:

> Shakespeare watched Henry V, not indeed as he watched the greater souls in the visionary procession, but cheerfully, as one watches some handsome spirited horse, and he spoke his tale, as he spoke all tales, with tragic irony.[42]

It is this rooted sense of life as "tragic irony" grounded on "men as they are" which underlies all the later stages in the tragic sequence. And now we must let Yeats build up slowly, in a longish passage from "Anima Mundi" of 1917, that positive state of benignity he calls "innocence," and which follows, philosophically, after the original negative bitterness and the medial passive confession of limitation:

> When I remember that Shelley calls our minds "mirrors of the fire for which all thirst," I cannot but ask the question all have asked, "What or who has cracked the mirror?" I begin to study the only self that I can know, myself, and to wind the thread upon the perne again.
>
> At certain moments, always unforeseen, I become happy, most commonly when at hazard I have opened some book of verse. Sometimes it is my own verse when, instead of discovering new technical flaws, I read with all the excitement of the first writing. Perhaps I am sitting in some crowded restaurant, the open book beside me, or closed, my excitement having over-brimmed the page. I look at the strangers near as if I had known them all my life, and it seems strange that I cannot

41 "At Stratford-on-Avon," *Ideas of Good and Evil,* 160.
42 *Ibid.,* 164.

> speak to them: everything fills me with affection, I have no longer any fears or any needs; I do not even remember that this happy mood must come to an end. . . .
>
> It may be an hour before the mood passes, but latterly I seem to understand that I enter upon it the moment I cease to hate. . . . The books say that our happiness comes from the opposite of hate, but I am not certain, for we may love unhappily. And plainly, when I have closed a book too stirred to go on reading, and in those brief intense visions of sleep, I have something about me that, though it makes me love, is more like innocence.[43]

This "innocence," which is not quite love but which is certainly the obverse of hate and rests on hate's evacuation, is a state of cleansed emptiness beyond interested passion, a state as nearly selfless as is possible for a man of Yeats's temperament—his ingrained passionateness and egotism.

Returning to the *Tower* period, we can extend the line of Yeats's thinking about this stage in the tragic emotion. Writing to Olivia Shakespear in the winter of 1928, he describes his convalescent regimen:

> Part of my cure, by the by, is to walk slowly, even turn my head slowly, that my thoughts from sympathy with my movements may slacken. If it does not I may become my own funeral pyre.[44]

His new stance of calm is physical as well as philosophical; Yeats has been talking of old age for years, but now he has had a brush with death that made death more than an academic notion: he is not the first man to take a radical new direction in those circumstances. But the shift, whatever its sources, is one to innocence and impersonality:

43 "Anima Mundi," *PASL,* 90–93.

44 *Letters,* 737.

> Once out of Irish bitterness I can find some measure of sweetness and of light, as befits old age—already new poems are floating in my head, bird songs of an old man, joy in the passing moment, emotion without the bitterness of memory.[45]

Then a statement in a letter to Mrs. Shakespear a year later shows that whereas his intention still holds, complication and irony are creeping back in (with improved health?), as they had to:

> I am writing *Twelve poems for music* . . . no[t] so much that they may be sung as that I may define their kind of emotion to myself. I want them to be all emotion and all impersonal. . . . They are the opposite of my recent work and all praise of joyous life, though in the best of them it is a dry bone on the shore that sings the praise.[46]

Almost five years later he is still writing to Mrs. Shakespear of "impersonality," but forecasting wrongly a return to the Twilight. His new impersonality is to be a very different selflessness from that early idealized emotiveness. His vignette here, as well as being doctrinally important, is one of the most touching and intimate views we ever get of Yeats:

> I think I have finished with self-expression and if I write more verse it will be impersonal, perhaps even going back to my early self. I have a longing for remote beauty. I have been reading Morris' *Sigurd* to Anne and last night when I came to the description of the birth of Sigurd and that wonderful first nursing of the child, I could hardly read for my tears. Then when Anne had gone to bed I tried to read it to George and it was just the same.[47]

But a truer definition of this impersonality, and perhaps the

45 *Ibid.*
46 *Ibid.*, 758.
47 *Ibid.*, 816.

best of all his definitions of "innocence," closes a letter of June, 1935 to Ethel Mannin:

> I want to plunge myself into impersonal poetry, to get rid of the bitterness, irritation and hatred my work in Ireland has brought into my soul. I want to make a last song, sweet and exultant, a sort of European *geeta,* or rather my *geeta,* not doctrine but song.[48]

Now, finally, he relates his "innocence" and "impersonality" to his "joy"—and, very interestingly, comes at last to phrasing which specifically echoes the Shakespeare essay of thirty-five years before. To Dorothy Wellesley he writes in December of 1936:

> A Dutch mystic [Boehme] has said "I must rejoyce, I must rejoyce without ceasing, though the whole world shudder at my joy." Joy is the salvation of the soul. You say we must love, yes but love is not pity. It does not desire to change its object. It is a form of the eternal contemplation of what is.[10]

But perhaps the last words should be pronounced by the closing sentences of the last letter collected by Mr. Wade, a fragment of a letter directed to Lady Elizabeth Pelham and written only three weeks before his death. They are sentences which honor their situation:

> I am happy, and I think full of an energy, of an energy I had despaired of. It seems to me that I have found what I wanted. When I try to put all into a phrase I say, "Man can embody truth but he cannot know it." I must embody it in the completion of my life. The abstract is not life and everywhere draws out its contradictions. You can refute Hegel but not the Saint or the Song of Sixpence.[50]

48 *Ibid.,* 836.

49 *Letters to Dorothy Wellesley,* 126.

50 *Letters,* 922.

Innocence, I take it, rests confident in refutation of logic and trusts the mystical and the primitive, in that wisdom which lives above and beneath the powers of the mind. In a sense, "swordsman" and "saint" reconcile their feud and join in one illumination in the last written words of Yeats.

PASSION AS APOCALYPSE

That part of the configuration of passion which I am calling passionate apocalypse makes up a vivid and astonishing attitude which lies, I suppose, outside any standard tragic sequence as normally recognized by criticism—though Nietzsche has notions of it, as we shall see. It is a last corner turned, a final path entered, after one has turned all normal corners and followed all the standard paths. It is much the most complex element in Yeats's configuration of passion, for it carries with it as it goes active relics of all his other passions: Defense, Joy, and Innocence. Perhaps after all it is only a composite and a heightening of these other modes; yet the heightening is such as to create a new thing, a difference in kind as well as in degree. The passionate apocalypse assumes a number of basic forms: a gay and violent sexuality; odd and extravagant themes in appropriately odd idioms; a hysterical bitterness or hysterical adoration, in which the emotion hardens under the eye into a cold and lofty rage or a sweet and lofty fusion and identification. At their most characteristic, these poems are marked by a kind of ranting extravagance in the impelling emotion and in the speech and imagery of the verse; yet all held—barely held—in equilibrium by the frantic yet whole emotion and by the intricately mastered tension of movement and form. These poems record, in Yeats's own phrase, "an old man's frenzy"—and we may helpfully recall now, as he does, "Timon and Lear"—but the frenzy of a peculiarly brilliant, intense, and masterful old man, who curses and more often blesses the life he loves and hates and is reluctantly leaving.

It is an astonishing old man's poetry, but Yeats is an astonishing old man. One is pressingly reminded of the late plays of Shakespeare, of the hyperboles and extravagances of those beautiful fantasies of bitterness and sweetness. This last response is less imposing, less unified and assured in Yeats than in Shakespeare, less slowly and less massively moving. But that is partly due to differences in form and scope—more mechanical than spiritual; Yeats's mode is still that of the brief lyric, and so his effects are less inclusive and conclusive, more tentative and dispersed, than those we feel in the big synoptic embodiments of Shakespeare's plays, where life itself seems transfixed and understood. Yeats's apocalypse is more personal, and limited by intimacy, less successfully "distanced"; we know that we are watching the lyrical last testament of one great man, not the dramatic reduction of the universe. But the achievement is the same in kind, if smaller in degree. And we should not be surprised at Yeats's ultimate art, any more than at Shakespeare's. Shakespeare's end had always been implicit in the massiveness of his vision, the depth of his pity, the healing acidity of his wit, the absoluteness of his command of speech and form. So Yeats's end had always been implicit in his romantic self-sense, in the violence of his passional nature, in his egoistic Prometheanism, and above all in his mystical idealism and humanism which held that man created reality by knowing it, and that man's divine irrationality was a power transcending mechanisms of reason and brutalities of empirical fact.

Yeats has left no very elaborate or specific rationale of his concept of Passion as Apocalypse; since the phenomenon is basically nonrational, the fact is hardly surprising. But we can isolate a sufficient number of suggestive texts to make the matter fairly clear; once again, the right explication is the poems themselves. Of course this final sane madness of Yeats's —"plunged as I am in the madness of vision"—is an extension and intensification of many attitudes contained in statements we have looked at under other headings: his aristocratic admiration for the "high, wasteful virtues";[51] the extravagance and the almost fantastic durability of his passion for Maud Gonne; the "wild old wicked men" whom he elects to his personal Pantheon, Cuchulain, Usheen, Timon and Lear, Swift, Landor, and Donne; his early definition of the "tragic ecstasy" of the Shakespearean heroes: "an ecstasy that is one half the self-surrender of sorrow, and one half the last playing and mockery of the victorious sword, before the defeated world";[52] the transcendentalism of the truest aspirations of his art and feeling. All these hyperboles point toward the multiple hyperbole of Yeats's final poems.

The Passionate Apocalypse is a complex of motives and moods; if it has a final unity, as I feel it does, it is a unity made up of likenesses of degree rather than of kind. That is, it follows from a general hyperbolic extension into ultimates of passion, of an "emotion of multitude," of modes of thought and feeling which may seem very different or even antithetical. Yeats's behavior in his later plays is perhaps the most compact demonstration of this diverse unity. Ezra Pound introduced him to the Japanese Noh plays about 1915, and the possibilities of the form strongly impressed Yeats at once. "I believe I have at last found a dramatic form that suits me," he wrote to Lady Gregory in March, 1916.[53] What Yeats coveted in the form was strictness and stark simplicity: absence of "rhetoric," the purity and directness of its embodiments of emotion, the bareness of its setting, the anonymity or impersonality of personae and

[51] "The Return of Ulysses," *Ideas of Good and Evil,* 318.
[52] "The Symbolism of Poetry," *Ideas of Good and Evil,* 245–46.
[53] *Letters,* 610.

ultimately of author; that general compactness, stripped abstractness, and functional absence of specification which spread the play's effect out like a fan from its small, tight center into transparent and universal symbolism: abundance through poverty. Yeats essayed the form often, his variants of it, and achieved with it his only full successes as playwright—such plays as *At the Hawk's Well, Calvary, The Resurrection, The King of the Great Clock Tower, The Herne's Egg,* and *Purgatory.* In these plays there is none of the sentimental self-indulgence or the mellifluous *longueurs* that overlaid and undercut the honest emotion at the centers of the early plays. Yeats accepts with a tense grace the strictness of the form. But what is most significant is the almost hysterical *emotional* density which is crammed within the formal reticence. Thus Yeats could speak of *The Herne's Egg* as "the strangest wildest thing I have ever written."[54] There we feel the precise analogy to his practice in the late lyrics. In those too we find brevity of compass, simplicity of form, an almost primer-like baldness of speech—but packed into that restraint and boldly shattering it is the same huge harshness of feeling, the same crabbed roughness of texture and movement, the same tonal violence—the superb carelessness of a poet who has mastered his art so thoroughly that he almost despises it. It is as if feeling alone matters to Yeats now, and language and form have become only unavoidable artifices to be contemptuously manhandled. This wildness within discipline forms the special paradox and so the great ragged tension of the poems of the Passionate Apocalypse: constructing a "Tower Beyond Tragedy," or an attempt at one—depending on one's nations of poetic proprieties in general and of Yeats's success or failure in the particular instance.

We can fill out the picture of Yeats's final integration of

[54] *Ibid.,* 845.

contraries of form and emotion with further passages from his letters. When he wrote to John Quinn in 1919, "It looks as if I may have a spirited old age,"[55] he made one of the most conservative of his prophecies. But the elements that made his old age almost fantastically spirited were, as I say, almost wildly mixed. On the one hand, there is the side of him to which the Noh plays appealed and which longed for classical order, strictness, reticence; we feel this in his description to Quinn of his tower home, Thoor Ballylee, as "a setting for my old age, a place to influence lawless youth, with its severity and antiquity."[56] But he came to think more characteristically of this same tower as a symbolic setting for lofty transcendental vision, for the most elaborate and excited mystical speculation; we feel this motive in the tone of his letter to Lady Gregory of January, 1918, describing his mood in response to the strange "systematic" revelations he found coming to him through the mediumship of his wife George:

> A very profound, very exciting mystical philosophy—which seems the fulfillment of many dreams and prophecies—is coming in strange ways to George and myself. . . . It is coming into my work a great deal and makes me feel that for the first time I understand human life. . . . I live with a strange sense of revelation and never know what the day will bring. You will be astonished at the change in my work, at its intricate passion.[57]

The Passionate Apocalypse is variously related to this visionary matter and to Yeats's years of work on *A Vision* itself: the emotional and intellectual excitement of the very process; his achievement there of an assured order of symbolism, both comprehensive and flexible; but above all, his sense of having

[55] *Ibid.*, 659.
[56] *Ibid.*, 651.
[57] *Ibid.*, 643–44.

laid down at last a wide and deep spiritual base from which he could roam confidently at large in art and thought—these seem to be the sources of the complex liberation of mind and feeling one senses in the late poems. Such is his own reading of the pattern. He writes to Olivia Shakespear in July, 1924, ". . . the philosophy absorbs me. But that once finished I think I shall do deeper and more passionate work than ever before."[58] Six years later he attributed his "great sense of abundance" to "George's ghosts."[59] In 1938, shortly after his publication of the revised and enlarged version of *A Vision,* he wrote to Edith Shackleton Heald, "Intensity is all. I want to be some queer man's companion."[60] A few weeks later he wrote to the same correspondent of his projected play *Purgatory* as a work which represented his own sense of the dominant qualities in his latest art:

> I have a one-act play in my head, a scene of tragic intensity . . . . My recent work has greater strangeness and I think greater intensity than anything I have done. I never remember the dream so deep.[61]

Abundance, passion, strangeness, tragic intensity, a new depth in the dream—all these are major pigments in the Passionate Apocalypse.

"All men with subjective natures move towards a possible ecstasy, all with objective natures towards a possible wisdom," Yeats wrote to Ethel Mannin in one of the last of the collected letters.[62] In attempting to characterize Yeats's last phase, ecstasy may be the truest last word—just as it was fundamental in his earliest thought. Yeats must have felt, one suspects, that with

58 *Ibid.,* 707.
59 *Ibid.,* 781.
60 *Ibid.,* 906.
61 *Ibid.,* 907.
62 *Ibid.,* 917.

A Vision he had reached his "possible wisdom"; only ecstasy was now still required of him. But we have to keep insisting that this last ecstatic mode was multiple, almost shockingly various, in content. Another of these last letters, to Dorothy Wellesley, recalls some of this variousness, the union of Yeats's visionary ecstasy with physical passion:

> In my own life I never felt so acutely the presence of a spiritual virtue and that is accompanied by intensified desire . . . . You must feel plunged as I do into the madness of vision, into a sense of the relation between separated things that you cannot explain, and that deeply disturbs emotion.[63]

We have already noticed several of these references to sexual passion in the late letters and we shall have to say much more of the phenomenon when we come to look at the late poems; it will suffice now to recall only two further such passages. In August of 1933 he writes to Olivia Shakespear:

> "Crazy Jane" poems . . . and the little group of love poems that follow are, I think, exciting and strange. Sexual abstinence fed their fire—I was ill and yet full of desire. They sometimes came out of the greatest mental excitement I am capable of.[64]

And to her he writes again a year later in his poem "Ribh at the Tomb of Baile and Aillinn" to comment on his own anachronistic sexuality with a keen sense of its irony but no shame (the image of the "conflagration" echoes a notion of Swedenborg's about the sexual intercourse of angels):

> I have another poem in my head where a monk reads his breviary at midnight upon the tomb of long-dead lovers on the anniversary of their death, for on that night they are united above the tomb, their embrace being not partial but a

[63] *Letters to Dorothy Wellesley,* 149–50.
[64] *Letters,* 814.

> conflagration of the entire body and so shedding the light he reads by.
>
> Strange that I should write these things in my old age, when if I were to offer myself for new love I could only expect to be accepted by the very young wearied by the passive embraces of the bolster.[65]

One other main element in Yeats's "ecstasy" seems on the face of it out of keeping with ecstasy in general and with passion in particular. Yeats finally names it "cold"; but he himself forces the necessary paradox by yoking the "cold" specifically with passion. Thus the progression of ideas in this letter of 1935 to Dorothy Wellesley becomes extremely revealing:

> I think that the true poetic movement of our time is towards some heroic discipline. People much occupied with morality always lose heroic ecstasy. . . . "Bitter and gay," that is the heroic mood. When there is despair, public or private, when settled order seems lost, people look for strength within or without. . . . The lasting expression of our time is . . . in a sense of something steel-like and cold within the will, something passionate and cold.[66]

Among other things, the passage gives us a useful jog back toward our main line of tragedy—with its emphasis upon the "heroic" and the "ecstatic," and this cold passion as a willed transcendence of despair. Insofar as the passage is meant to describe his own tendencies, Yeats is being, I feel, precisely accurate. His own "true poetic movement" was exactly toward something passionate and cold. There is passion in his coldness—in its weight of compressed emotion, the fullness of feeling restrained in the tension of narrow form and laconic speech; thus: "I have got the town out of my verse. It is all

65 *Ibid.*, 824–25.
66 *Letters to Dorothy Wellesley*, 8.

nonchalant verse," he writes in January, 1938, a year before his death.[67] And equally there is coldness in his passion—in its superiority to data, its anonymity, its faceless archetypal personae, in its exciting yet fundamentally unreal extravagance.

"Die blaspheming,"[68] Yeats advised himself in 1936; and proceeded to do so: the Passionate Apocalypse is one kind of gorgeous blasphemy. Yet in our final paradox it is a reverent blasphemy—heretical in its gnosticism and its almost frantic desire to love God humanistically by loving man as if he were God, and reverent in its godly human urge to spin life out to the last rich sensation of thought and feeling.

[67] *Letters,* 904.
[68] *Letters to Dorothy Wellesley,* 124.

CHAPTER SEVEN

Late Poems

"THE TOWER"

YEATS'S GREAT VOLUME of 1928 may be, for perfected achievement of theme and craft, thought and feeling, the richest single volume of English poetry of the past 150 years. The special quality of the volume is not easy to describe, and in some ways it is surprising. These poems are not, somehow, exactly the poems one would expect Yeats to write during and immediately after the psychic and intellectual experiences leading to *A Vision* and the years of labor that went into ordering the first form of that book. Except in scattered passages, the thought is not especially abstruse or difficult, and comparatively little of it points specifically at the kinds of speculation that compose *A Vision*. Basically we have here Yeats's old themes writ large. Subjects are bold and clear, the individual poems tend to stretch to greater length than earlier, and there is much of his new trick of assembling a collection of short lyrics loosely around a common theme. Yeats's established mastery of speech, movement, and tone extends itself with almost insolent ease to verse forms of new intricacy. At the same time the characteristic manners of the last poems are suggested without being fully developed. Thus *The Tower* strikes one as a kind of vivid interregnum between middle and final Yeats; one has the feeling that he has reached a watershed of spirit and of craft in which he is confidently summing up his art to date and making tentative but expert sorties into new areas. In his Introduction to *A Vision* he says, "I put *The Tower* . . . into evidence to show that my poetry has gained in self-possession and power. I owe this change to an incredible experience"[1]—the revelations coming to him through the mediumship of his wife. In this volume it is the "self-possession and power" which are most in evidence, not the philosophical manner of the "incredible experience."

Many of these poems are famous—from anthologizing and much manipulation by critics and expositors—and so they need no very elaborate analysis here. The problem is simply to place them in the context of Yeats's tragic sense of life. From that point of view one is struck most powerfully by their prevailing sadness and disenchantment: in the tragic sequence, *The Tower* is a return to the pole of negation. Looking back at these poems in the spring of 1928, Yeats himself, we remember, felt "astonished at their bitterness."[2] "Yet that bitterness gave the book its power," he went on to say, "and it is the best book I have written."[3] Yeats's "astonishment" came, apparently, from his sense of some fake staginess and over-

[1] Page 8.
[2] *Letters,* 738, 742.
[3] *Ibid.,* 742.

resonance in the dominant mood of the poems; and he resolved to mend his ways by softening and sweetening a bit and by seeking a new detachment. But the reader of the poems, though he too may be shocked by their bitterness, will likely feel no falseness in it. It is true that this bitterness has special qualities. Yeats had been bitter before and would be bitter again; but *The Tower*'s bitterness is ponderous and violent, it carries the size and pressure of philosophical premise. Perhaps it was this seeming conclusiveness that appalled Yeats in the sequel—not so much falsifying a mood as giving it a too great air of permanence. In any case, the bitterness of *The Tower* is brilliantly evoked and masterfully controlled; though one wants to see it qualified by the perspective of the whole career, there is no curse on it as art or thought, and its function in the tragic sequence proves to be organic.

The poetic tone of *The Tower* is set by a very few recurrent notes, none of them really new in Yeats. What is new, as I have remarked, is their extension in length and the added weight and philosophical seriousness which accrues thereby, and striking new intensities of passion. Basically these poems anatomize, once more, the private frustrations of age and the public frustrations of social and political violence and decay; in response, they spread out the resources of passion and art as fragments to be shored against ruins of the spirit.

"Nineteen Hundred and Nineteen" is perhaps the most absolute of the volume's negatives. There Yeats's bitterness is such that he is driven to invoke the context and the images of literal apocalypse; looking about him at the landscape of terror and vulgarity which epitomizes a failed ideal, he concludes, in terms of the apocalypse as defined by *A Vision,* that this is "the circle of the moon/ That pitches common things about"; and again,

So the Platonic Year
Whirls out new right and wrong,
Whirls in the old instead;
All men are dancers and their tread
Goes to the barbarous clangour of a gong.

Thus he makes big and doctrinal a private grief and rage; his sense of a surrounding evil is so intense that he has to relate it to cosmic norms of evil. The same tragic despair is elsewhere phrased in terms of simpler heartbreak:

But is there any comfort to be found?
Man is in love and loves what vanishes,
What more is there to say?

Centuries of hatred of England had erupted into the Easter Rebellion of 1916, promoted by radical nationalists of the Irish Republican Brotherhood, including many members of the earlier popular movements, the Gaelic League and Sinn Fein.[4] News of the Rising took Yeats by surprise, as indeed it surprised the whole nation. Yeats "fretted somewhat that he had not been consulted," according to Hone,[5] and was troubled, on the other hand, by the sense that he was perhaps obscurely responsible for the violence and death: "Did that play of mine send out/ Certain men the English shot?" The martyrdom of the Sixteen Men (including John MacBride) "lit a flame of popular resentment which assured the triumph" of Republican government for Ireland.[6] But the immediate result was the "Troubles," first occupation by the expert gunmen of the English Black and Tan constabulary and the Auxiliaries, then civil war, continuing into the twenties. The Troubles were a little war within the great war in Europe, a tragi-comic mix-

[4] Joseph Hone, *W. B. Yeats,* 319.
[5] *Ibid.*
[6] *Ibid.*

ture of *opéra-bouffe* and peculiarly intense brutality. "In 1919 the whole was vivid," T. R. Henn recalls of his own experience.[7] "In my own country, three known murderers lived within a short distance of my home; two policemen were put, alive, into a gas-furnace in a certain town; a friend was buried alive." The bridge crossing Yeats's stream at Thoor Ballylee was blown up, and there were bullet holes in the windows of his house in Dublin. The Irish "war," Henn suggests, was the last of the wars "on the Renaissance model; that is, it was deliberately planned and executed by men who had a definite object before them, and whose poetry, literature, and even religion, had been co-ordinated to that end."[8] But it was a long time before Yeats could be this philosophical about the Troubles, and their idealistic element, undoubtedly present, was buried for him in the violence and unreason of the struggle.

The specific evil that has set Yeats off is the brutality of the Black and Tan Terror; he makes that vivid enough in one unforgettable stanza:

> *Now days are dragon-ridden, the nightmare*
> *Rides upon sleep: a drunken soldiery*
> *Can leave the mother, murdered at her door,*
> *To crawl in her own blood, and go scot-free;*
> *The night can sweat with terror as before*
> *We pieced our thoughts into philosophy,*
> *And planned to bring the world under a rule,*
> *Who are but weasels fighting in a hole.*

The collapse of Yeats's Irish ideal is an evil so complete and dramatic that for the time it blots out the very possibility of good. And with the good is eclipsed the fine, all the accumulated objects of art, all the "ingenious lovely things" of the

[7] *The Lonely Tower,* 16–17.
[8] *Ibid.,* 16.

achieving spirit: "And gone are Phidias' famous ivories/ And all the golden grasshoppers and bees."

Yeats's response to these failures, seen as evidences, as I say, of cosmic decay, is a grief so intense that it swells into a nihilistic rage. He accepts the figure of "some moralist or mythological poet" who "compares the solitary soul to a swan," then sends the image on a flight of self-annihilation and insult:

> *The swan has leaped into the desolate heaven:*
> *That image can bring wildness, bring a rage*
> *To end all things, to end*
> *What my laborious life imagined, even*
> *The half-imagined, the half-written page;*
> *O but we dreamed to mend*
> *Whatever mischief seemed*
> *To afflict mankind, but now*
> *That winds of winter blow*
> *Learn that we were crack-pated*
> *when we dreamed.*

What is left in the poem is two further movements, Sections V and VI, of the bitterest disenchantment. The four terse stanzas of Section V form themselves into a liturgy of scorn—"mock at the great," "mock at the wise," "mock at the good"—and synopsize finally the hopelessness of that stance too; the last stanza scorns scorn: "Mock mockers after that/ . . . for we/ Traffic in mockery." But what is most important and most shattering in the poem is the single long stanza of Section VI, where rage and grief break all pragmatic bounds and melt into the crazed eschatology of an apocalyptic vision which telescopes time and motive, image and tone, in a brilliant anarchical irony:

> *Violence upon the roads: violence of horses;*
> *Some few have handsome riders, are garlanded*

On delicate sensitive ear or tossing mane,
But wearied running round and round in their courses
All break and vanish, and evil gathers head:
Herodias' daughters have returned again,
A sudden blast of dusty wind and after
Thunder of feet, tumult of images,
Their purpose in the labyrinth of the wind;
And should some crazy hand dare touch a daughter
All turn with amorous cries, or angry cries,
According to the wind, for all are blind.
But now wind drops, dust settles; thereupon
There lurches past, his great eyes without thought
Under the shadow of stupid straw-pale locks,
That insolent fiend Robert Artisson[9]
To whom the love-lorn Lady Kyteler brought
Bronzed peacock feathers, red combs of her cocks.

That single great stanza says more about Yeats's late passions than all my pages above on the subject. In terms of my arbitrary categories, however, it should be understood that the absolute negativism of this terrible vision is a special phenomenon, not the Passionate Apocalypse itself. The violent assertive nihilism of "Nineteen Hundred and Nineteen" comes closer, actually, to fitting my category of Passion as Defense; for Yeats's passion here is really frantic and compensatory. To what he sees as the spiritual anarchy of the cosmos he tries to oppose an equally anarchic defiance. The Passionate Apocalyse materializes in a purer form in two other capital poems of *The Tower,* in the title poem, and in "Sailing to Byzantium." These poems, like "Nineteen Hundred and Nineteen," are set going by a negative emotion, and it is the same one in both, an emotion at once more intimate and more primitive than that of "Nineteen Hundred and Nineteen"—fear, revulsion, and re-

9 Robert Artisson was the incubus of the fourteenth-century sorceress Dame Alice Kyteler (Jeffares, *W. B. Yeats,* 226).

solve attending the onset of age. Each poem announces the theme in its opening lines: in "Sailing to Byzantium" the flat declaration, "That is no country for old men"; in "The Tower" the bitter question,

> *What shall I do with this absurdity—*
> *O heart, O troubled heart—this caricature,*
> *Decrepit age that has been tied to me*
> *As to a dog's tail?*

"Sailing to Byzantium" seems to me one of Yeats's greatest poems, really a bigger thing, finally, in its intense clarity of speech and solid largeness of impact, than the later more famous "Byzantium." Here his fiction is one of purgative withdrawal, in his persona of aging poet, from that crowded kinesthetic "country" where "Fish, flesh, or fowl, commend all summer long/ Whatever is begotten, born, and dies" in that "sensual music" of pragmatic illusion; and of re-establishment in "the holy city of Byzantium," Yeats's *locus,* in old age, of achieved aspiration, "unified sensibility," "unity of being." In the confessed wreck of the body become "a paltry thing,/ A tattered coat upon a stick," the soul asserts its unbroken paradoxical wholeness by gestures of passion as defense and as joy: "Soul clap its hands and sing, and louder sing/ For every tatter in its mortal dress."

In stanzas 3 and 4 Yeats touches the notes of both innocence and apocalypse. Behind the emotion here is a despair that takes on absoluteness from the very bareness and simplicity of the statement; the despair is so complete, Yeats seems to imply, that it needs only to be named to be evoked. Body, heart, and soul desire death and obliteration, mere reunion with the abstractly beautiful design of all things:

> *Consume my heart away; sick with desire*
> *And fastened to a dying animal*

COURTESY BETTY CHANCELLOR JOHNSTON

Maud Gonne

NATIONAL PORTRAIT GALLERY, LONDON

Bust of W. B. Yeats, by Kathleen Scott

It knows not what it is; and gather me
Into the artifice of eternity.

Beyond death, however, is to lie transfiguration, a kind of selfless metempsychosis which transforms the failed being of the poet and makes himself a "monument of unaging intellect," a prophet-artifact who sings anonymously and passionlessly his perfect knowledge:

Once out of nature I shall never take
My bodily form from any natural thing,
But such a form as Grecian goldsmiths make
Of hammered gold and gold enamelling
To keep a drowsy Emperor awake;
Or set upon a golden bough to sing
To lords and ladies of Byzantium
Of what is past, or passing, or to come.

It is a most interesting apocalypse, in its embodiment of a transcendent innocence and insight, beyond life and outside personality, which asks only to be permitted to send out anonymous wisdom in an endless lofty recitative, rich and strange—"my *geeta,* not doctrine but song." The parallel prose impulse occurs in a letter to Dorothy Wellesley of April, 1936, where he quotes as a text for poets like himself the famous lines from *Richard II* (III, ii):

Let us sit upon the ground
And tell sad stories of the death of kings.

The brief question Yeats applies here is sufficient to place "Sailing to Byzantium" in the line of his tragic emotion: "Do you not feel there the wide-open eyes?"[10]

"The Tower" is one of those structures in the manner that might be called a tight-reined amble, a rhetorical structure

[10] *Letters to Dorothy Wellesley,* 65.

mingling easy, varied movement, and a strong but flexible control, firming at the end as the thought grows strict and compressed, and beautifully adapted to the impassioned rumination which is the characteristic mood of this volume. In the poem's dramatic setting, recalling that of "In Memory of Major Robert Gregory," the poet paces the battlements of his literal and symbolic tower and calls up for questioning the shades of real and fictive figures of passion. He treats their histories in a half-dozen leisurely stanzas, then draws all together in a few compact lines:

> *As I would question all, come all who can;*
> *Come old, necessitous, half-mounted man;*
> *And bring beauty's blind rambling celebrant;*
> *The red man the juggler sent*
> *Through God-forsaken meadows; Mrs. French,*
> *Gifted with so fine an ear;*
> *The man drowned in a bog's mire,*
> *When mocking Muses chose the country wench.*

His "question" is simple, clear, and ultimate:

> *Did all old men and women, rich and poor,*
> *Who trod upon these rocks or passed this door,*
> *Whether in public or in secret rage*
> *As I do now against old age?*

The answer, I take it, is a simple positive, but unspoken: "But I have found an answer in those eyes/ That are impatient to be gone." Yeats then dismisses all except his own creature Hanrahan, that "Old lecher with a love on every wind." Of him he asks a separate question, an ancient and aching one: What, once more, of Maud?

> *Does the imagination dwell the most*
> *Upon a woman won or a woman lost?*
> *If on the lost, admit you turned aside*

From a great labyrinth out of pride,
Cowardice, some silly over-subtle thought
Or anything called conscience once;
And that if memory recur, the sun's
Under eclipse and the day blotted out.

"We are at our Tower," Yeats wrote to Olivia Shakespear in May, 1926, from Thoor Ballylee, "and as always happens, no matter how I begin, it becomes love poetry before I am finished with it."[11] Love, for Yeats, till the day he died, meant first love, the old unkillable grand passion; in "The Tower" that is as alive as ever it was. The stanza above declares that fact clearly enough; and it is the most open and specific confession Yeats ever makes of his part in the failure of the great affair.

The first line of the poem's long third section, "It is time that I wrote my will," establishes the rhetorical frame of that section, and sets its shorter, tighter, three-beat measure. Inside this frame of synoptic spiritual legacy several interesting things happen. For one, Yeats exhumes his archetype of the "normal passionate man," his fisherman of 1919, and names him as his heir:

I choose upstanding men
That climb the streams until
The fountain leap, and at dawn
Drop their cast at the side
Of dripping stone . . . .

What the fisherman is to inherit is, first, Yeats's special Irish pride—grown by now, I am afraid, rather manneristic, unconvincing, and tiresome:

The pride of people that were
Bound neither to Cause nor to State,
Neither to slaves that were spat on,

[11] *Letters*, 714–15.

Nor to the tyrants that spat,
The people of Burke and of Grattan . . . .

To the fisherman he further bequeaths his "faith"—and that, while strange enough, is a great deal more imposing and interesting than his "pride." The lines embody the most categorical of all Yeats's declarations of his radical idealist humanism, crediting man himself with ultimate creativity, resting in him all significant value. Thinking of how Milton punishes that ancestral *hubris,* one shudders.

I mock Plotinus' thought
And cry in Plato's teeth,
Death and life were not
Till man made up the whole,
Made lock, stock and barrel
Out of his bitter soul,
Aye, sun and moon and star, all.
And further add to that
That, being dead, we rise,
Dream and so create
Translunar Paradise.

The poem drives to a conclusion significantly comparable to the endings of the two poems we have just been examining. The passion that closes "The Tower" is much closer to the depersonalized transcendence, a kind of superhuman innocence, of "Sailing to Byzantium" than it is to the mood and vision of apocalyptic nihilism of "Nineteen Hundred and Nineteen." Here, too, occurs apocalypse of a sort, but positive and defensive rather than annihilatory. It is not the "rage to end all things." Yeats takes in these lines the vow of the learned anchorite, and what he seeks in that office, it seems clear, is that power of "pure contemplation" which he had located on "the other side of tragedy." Learning is to endow that abstracted imperviousness of mind beyond despair which makes it possible to look upon tragic truth without madness or even tears—the "wide-open eyes." Here his bird is a less gaudy sibling of that other creature "of hammered gold and gold enamelling," and Yeats's catalogue of griefs amounts to a specification of that bird's song "of what is past, or passing, or to come." Both impulse and emotion are clearly identical in "Sailing to Byzantium" and "The Tower."

Now shall I make my soul,
Compelling it to study
In a learned school
Till the wreck of body,
Slow decay of blood,
Testy delirium
Or dull decrepitude,
Or what worse evil come—
The death of friends, or death
Of every brilliant eye
That made a catch in the breath—
Seem but the clouds of the sky
When the horizon fades;
Or a bird's sleepy cry
Among the deepening shades.

A fourth extraordinary poem in this extraordinary volume is certainly "Among School Children." This poem, too, belongs in the context of tragedy, and more simply, obviously, perhaps more centrally than those we have just been reading. Like them it is a piece of impassioned philosophical rumination, but this time Yeats acts his reverie in a more concrete and arresting dramatic scene: "I walk through the long schoolroom questioning." This is Yeats the Irish senator, conscientiously miming the Arnoldian office of inspector of schools; but it is also Yeats the lover of life, of art, and of Maud, and hater of Time "the suttle theef of youth." The negative impulsion in the poem, as has begun to seem inevitable, is the shame and grief of age; Yeats sees his own image as that of "A sixty-year-old smiling public man," and twice reinvokes his favorite figure of the scarecrow: "a comfortable kind of old scarecrow"; "Old clothes upon old sticks to scare a bird."

It is startling and most moving to see the way in which the first sight of the school children sets Yeats off immediately upon another obsessive reverie of Maud Gonne; she lies so near the top of his mind and heart that almost any random image, apparently, is enough to recall that beloved shade. "As always happens, no matter how I begin, it becomes love poetry before I am finished with it." Inevitably now he recalls her always with associations of deprivation and sorrow:

And thinking of that fit of grief or rage
I look upon one child or t'other there
And wonder if she stood so at that age–
For even daughters of the swan can share
Something of every paddler's heritage—
And had that color upon cheek or hair,
And thereupon my heart is driven wild:
She stands before me as a living child.

From the vision of Maud as a child he moves automatically to her present old-woman's image: "Did Quattrocento finger fashion it/ Hollow of cheek as though it drank the wind/ And took a mess of shadows for its meat?" Her ravaged image of course evokes his own: "There is a comfortable kind of old scarecrow."

Just as inevitably, these coupled ghosts of their youth drive the poem toward one of its main themes, the standard tragic datum of the mutability of youth and beauty. Yeats casts it in a stanza composed of a single heartbroken question:

What youthful mother, a shape upon her lap

Honey of generation had betrayed,
And that must sleep, shriek, struggle to escape
As recollection or the drug decide,
Would think her son, did she but see that shape
With sixty or more winters on its head,
A compensation for the pang of his birth,
Or the uncertainty of his setting forth?

That cruel image pushes him on immediately to another of those great vigorous stanzas which he now seems to write with the laconic ease of a finger-exercise; here the names of the archaic great are brought to serve as helpless counters of his own masterful rhetoric and confident synoptic formulae: the grandest of men are brought by tragic time into the humble lineage of the scarecrow.

Plato thought nature but a spume that plays
Upon a ghostly paradigm of things;
Solider Aristotle played the taws
Upon the bottom of a king of kings;
World-famous golden-thighed Pythagoras
Fingered upon a fiddle-stick or strings
What a star sang and careless Muses heard:
Old clothes upon old sticks to scare a bird.

After the specification and intimacy of all this, the logical relationship of the closing stanza is not at first clear; it seems tactically odd and disjunct:

Labor is blossoming or dancing where
The body is not bruised to pleasure soul,
Nor beauty born out of its own despair,
Nor blear-eyed wisdom out of midnight oil.
O chestnut-tree, great-rooted blossomer,
Are you the leaf, the blossom or the bole?
O body swayed to music, O brightening glance,
How can we know the dancer from the dance?

But what Yeats is doing, it seems to me, is pointing out more fragments to be shored against ruins. The governing sequence of the poem's images begins with the figure of the child, with its beauty and wholeness, moves to the coming of grief, then to the coming of age and its grotesquerie and, implicitly, death. He has confessed evanescence, the fragility of all images, the omnipotence of time—he accepts those as "the given" for man, the unshakable discipline of his human condition; then asks, what next? That pattern fixed, all man can do is live well in his allotted space: unite his means and ends, live "existentially," illuminate all with beauty and passion, convert life into high art, incarnate in the spirit's unified being "monuments of its own magnificence."

The source of both the closing images is to be found, I suspect, in a cryptic passage in *A Vision;* where, in an interesting way, he telescopes the tree (as "flower") and the dancer in a single figure. Yeats speaks there of the most mysterious and difficult of all his ideas, that of the "Thirteenth Cone," which is a phaseless phase outside his dialectical antinomies; he calls it the place (or time) of "deliverance from birth and death."[12] "The *Thirteenth Cone* is a sphere because sufficient to itself," he writes; "but as seen by Man it is a cone. It becomes even conscious of itself as so seen, like some great dancer, the perfect flower of modern culture, dancing some primitive dance and conscious of his or her own life and of the dance."[13]

What both the poetic stanza and the prose passage really seek is "unity of being," release from the tragical dialectic of life, "deliverance from birth and death." This becomes still clearer if we bring in evidence yet another image that is almost certainly in Yeats's mind as he writes, that of the beautiful girl Iseult Gonne singing on the Normandy coast, "words and music of her own composition":

[12] *A Vision,* 240. [13] *Ibid.*

> She thought herself alone, stood barefooted between sea and sand; sang with lifted head of the civilizations that there had come and gone, ending every verse with the cry: "O Lord, let something remain."[14]

The poem itself begs for union of body and soul, beauty and suffering, wisdom and labor, tree and fruit, artist and art: in short, for perfected being. But perfected being, according to *A Vision*—according, also, to Yeats's and everybody else's common sense—is "an ideal or supernatural incarnation."[15] That is the tragic sense of life, "common knowledge," "general to Man," who is "bound to birth and death."[16] What we do, then, is the familiar Promethean thing: assert the absurd, pretend our omnipotence, advance our imperfection as far as we can upon the perfect, and let the splendor of the attempt answer for the achievement—Passion as Defense and as Joy.

We may legitimately take leave of *The Tower* with a brief look at only one other poem, the "Two Songs from a Play." The volume contains other wonderful poems, notably the famous sonnet "Leda and the Swan" and the gnomic "All Souls' Night," epilogue poem to *A Vision,* with its "mummy truths" and its testimony to the fascination and power of mystical speculation that could make Yeats forget even tragedy in its spell: "I need no other thing,/ Wound in mind's wandering/ As mummies in the mummy-cloth are wound." But those poems lie outside our frame. And it is really only the last stanza[17] of "Two Songs from a Play" that needs to occupy us, and that very simply. The first three stanzas are magnificent poetry, formally very different from the poems we have been examining—wholly visionary in setting and imagery, regular

[14] *Ibid.,* 220.

[15] *Ibid.,* 82.

[16] *Ibid.,* 240.

[17] This stanza was not actually added until 1931. See Richard Ellmann, *The Identity of Yeats,* 250.

in prosody, brutal and brilliant in speech; but their cryptic difficulty vanishes once we catch the key that they apply Yeats's gyre metaphor to the cycles of history, and their very abstractness and largeness of scope virtually removes them from the tragic frame. What does remain fundamental for us is the last stanza's reduction of the whole immense abstraction to an affirmation of man's continuing tragic function: he is to reduce tragic fact to irrelevancy by the simple power of passion; his defense against time and decay and empirical helplessness is his testimony of absolute commitment, his dedication of his "resinous heart." This may be Yeats's grandest as well as his most succinct affirmation of Passion as Defense:

Everything that man esteems
Endures a moment or a day.
Love's pleasure drives his love away,
The painter's brush consumes his dreams;
The herald's cry, the soldier's tread
Exhaust his glory and his might:
Whatever flames upon the night
Man's own resinous heart has fed.

Like "The Second Coming" and "Leda and the Swan," "Two Songs from a Play" is a poem of violent Annunciation or Epiphany, dramatizing in this case the First Coming, that of Christ, who "walked that room and issued thence/ In Galilean turbulence." The poem presents another of those climactic intervals within the cycles of history when "the anguish of birth and that of death cry out in the same instant." In the words of the second stanza,

The Roman Empire stood appalled:
It dropped the reins of peace and war
When that fierce virgin and her Star
Out of the fabulous darkness called.

The anti-Christian animus behind that image is revealed in the prose of *A Vision:*

> The world became Christian, "that fabulous formless darkness" as it seemed to a philosopher of the fourth century, blotted out "every beautiful thing," not through the conversion of crowds or general change of opinion, or through any pressure from below . . . but by an act of power.[18]

But it is the closing stanza that helps us to get close to Yeats's understanding of human tragedy. There the other stanzas' theme of cosmic mutability is made small and brought near: evanescence is a root fact of every man's condition; the process of experience and the process of decay are remorselessly coterminous. Earlier he had put the mummy-truth more gently in "Nineteen Hundred and Nineteen": "Man is in love and loves what vanishes,/ What more is there to say?" Now he presents the harsh particulars in a series of flat, end-stopped, stoical clauses. But the last word is had by the defensive passion. "Whatever flames upon the night" carries a double meaning; the flames are the ensign of destruction, but they are also the ensign of splendid beauty, the light and the warmth which rise out of man's commitment of his "resinous heart."

"THE WINDING STAIR AND OTHER POEMS"

The new freedom and confidence Yeats felt after completing *A Vision* really begins to bring in its harvest in his volume of 1933, *The Winding Stair and Other Poems.* It is the longest of his volumes, and though for sustained excellence it does not quite match *The Tower,* it contains magnificent single poems and is intensely interesting throughout for various reasons. The themes thrown up by the thought of *A Vision* begin to get formal treatment here; the philosophical resolution reached

[18] *A Vision,* 278.

there liberates Yeats for an affirmative tragic vision more confident and conclusive than ever before; and establishment of the "system" frees him for a simplified return upon passion which uses the system for a firm base—while mocking it and every other system that hopes to explain or control the spirit of man. There is less of the lengthy rumination, the massive indecisiveness, the open-ended effect that marked the great poems of *The Tower;* the new poems tend to be shorter, crisper, cockier. This poet is so sure of where he is that he can afford to be anywhere, and so he roams at large, especially in mood and tone. This is a volume of many moods, but all passionate and all convinced. The special brassy atonality which is a hallmark of the late poems appears often here, especially in the brief, undecorated, gnomic lyrics which come to be the dominant form in his last three volumes. Oddly, the thematic range is, if anything, narrower than that of *The Tower.* Virtually all the poems treat one or more of three basic themes: a few poems continue his nihilistic rage to end all things; but the great majority treat that theme of conflicting philosophical attitudes which he names in the *Letters* Swordsman *versus* Saint—with balance tipped toward the Swordsman; or the great theme of the Lion and the Honeycomb—sweetness in decay, triumph in tragedy. Whatever the theme, passion is "the essential." Everywhere we feel Yeats's new muscularity of spirit; he has decided to maunder no longer over the pathos of old age and to vaunt its wit, its prescience, and its power of feeling. He is becoming the "wild old wicked man" prepared to "die blaspheming." But, to remind us once more that this "old man's frenzy" really only elaborates a congenital condition, we have a stanza from, "Remorse for Intemperate Speech," of 1931:

Out of Ireland have we come.
Great hatred, little room,

Maimed us at the start.
I carry from my mother's womb
A fanatic heart.

Yeats's nihilism has cooled, thickened, and saddened since *The Tower*. In *The Winding Stair* his rage is intermittent, and when it comes it is less ranting, more pitying and more elegiac, and thereby differently impressive. It is the elegiac note which dominates his reveries in "Coole Park and Ballylee, 1931." Though he promises violence early in the poem—"For Nature's pulled her tragic buskin on/ And all the rant's a mirror of my mood"—his actual tone is disciplined by a sense of the grief and grandeur of Lady Gregory's approaching end; it is her stick he hears restless overhead as he thinks and writes: "Sound of a stick upon the floor, a sound/ From somebody that toils from chair to chair." She stands to Yeats as always for indomitable aristocracy, depth of tradition, and a spiritual richness above factionalism; her imminent passing can only move him to confession of the decay of that whole side of his programmatic dream—"that high horse riderless":

We were the last romantics—chose for theme
Traditional sanctity and loveliness;
Whatever's written in what poets name
The book of the people; whatever most can bless
The mind of man or elevate a rhyme;
But all is changed, that high horse riderless,
Though mounted in that saddle Homer rode
Where the swan drifts upon a darkening flood.

Yeats's poem of sad tribute to the Gore-Booth sisters, friends of his youth and relics and casualties of the radical politics he had briefly shared with them, is really more genuinely moving and a more considerable poem, because his relation to the subject is native rather than adopted, both broader and more intimate, a relation which lets this poem escape the subtle faking and theatricality which seems to me to creep into all Yeats's poems asserting his own kinship to aristocracy. In the vivid and intricately rhythmical opening lines, Yeats evokes in a flash the girls in their grace of youth and security, then projects their bitter present:

The light of evening, Lissadell,
Great windows open to the south,
Two girls in silk kimonos, both
Beautiful, one a gazelle.
But a raving autumn shears
Blossom from the summer's wreath . . . .

A dozen lines later he presents his brooding, apocalyptic conclusion on the lesson of the "raving autumn." Inside the annihilatory urge, one feels the continuing pressure of Yeats's own guilt; he never quite forgave himself for his withdrawal, abstractly right though he believed it, from the processes and consequences of "the great gazebo":

Dear shadows, now you know it all,
All the folly of a fight
With a common wrong or right.
The innocent and the beautiful
Have no enemy but time;
Arise and bid me strike a match
And strike another till time catch;
Should the conflagration climb,
Run till all the sages know.
We the great gazebo built,
They convicted us of guilt;
Bid me strike a match and blow.

Yeats's complicated and important poem "Vacillation" may

be read as an anti-Christian testament, or as a paradoxical Christian affirmation, as Virginia Moore is inclined to read it;[19] yet it seems to me the poem's real thematic center is less theological than philosophical, and Yeats is in fact exploring again his own great dichotomy of Swordsman and Saint. In the process, he sets forth what I have called the third major theme of this volume, that of the Lion and the Honeycomb. This theme inevitably overlaps that of Swordsman *versus* Saint, often virtually fuses with it, and perhaps it is not especially profitable to try to keep the two formally apart. Certainly they coalesce in the multiple affirmations of passion in all Yeats's late poetry. In terms of my categories, "Vacillation" seems to celebrate Passion as Defense and as Joy. The poem is not perfectly realized, it is blurred in tone and in expression in its first three stanzas; but basically Yeats is counterposing here his old antinomies of "primary" and "antithetical" in their simplest connotations of active and passive, pragmatically dynamic and spiritually withdrawing. But what is especially significant in this poem is that he refuses a crudely absolute separation and accepts a marked cross-fertilization of values; the Swordsman triumphs, but not without concessions and not without fruitful mimicry—"not without vacillation," as he had put it in his letter to Olivia Shakespear.[20] And the upshot of this unavoidable and productive vacillation is Joy:

And he that Attis' image hangs between
That staring fury and the blind lush leaf
May know not what he knows, but knows not grief.

This Joy is various. In Part III of the poem it is the triumphant emotion accompanying tragic reconciliation:

19 Virginia Moore, *The Unicorn: William Butler Yeats' Search for Reality,* 403–406.

20 *Letters,* 798.

No longer in Lethean foliage caught
Begin the preparation for your death
And from the fortieth winter by that thought
Test every work of intellect or faith,
And everything that your own hands have wrought,
And call those works extravagance of breath
That are not suited for such men as come
Proud, open-eyed and laughing to the tomb.

The stanza lays down, very clearly, a personal Testament directing the behavior of the mature poet and man; and the Testament is composed, phrase by phrase, of the basic texts of the tragic sense of life.

In Part IV the Joy is that dramatic but vaguer and softer phenomenon of mystical beatitude:

My fiftieth year had come and gone,
I sat, a solitary man,
In a crowded London shop,
An open book and empty cup
On the marble table-top.

While on the shop and street I gazed
My body of a sudden blazed;
And twenty minutes more or less
It seemed, so great my happiness,
That I was blessed and could bless.

These phrases have a familiar ring, and we recall now that they are recollected from an experience of many years before and set down in *Per Amica Silentia Lunae*.[21] There Yeats had traced this sense of the mystical inflowing of beatitude to liberation from partisan passion, from hatred, opening an entrance to love: ". . . latterly I seem to understand that I enter upon it the moment I cease to hate."[22]

21 "Anima Mundi," *PASL,* 91–93.
22 *Ibid.*, 92.

"Vacillation" turns specifically theological in its last two sections, VII and VIII. In Part VIII, Yeats reverts interestingly to his old dialogue form and presents a tender disputation between the two parts of man, Soul and Heart, or Saint and Swordsman: one pointing inward to the reflective spirit and upward to God, the other outward to the arena of the passions. Both are parts of Yeats, but his stronger allegiance is to the Heart, and he brings that organ to victory and the last word by calling up an archetype of Passion, Homer, in an irrefutable *argumentum ad hominem,* and equipping him with the weapons of the beloved enemy:

> THE SOUL. *Seek out reality, leave things that seem.*
> THE HEART. *What, be a singer born and lack a theme?*
> THE SOUL. *Isaiah's coal, what more can man desire?*
> THE HEART. *Struck dumb in the simplicity of fire!*
> THE SOUL. *Look on that fire, salvation walks within.*
> THE HEART. *What theme had Homer but original sin?*

The last section elaborates Heart's triumph by turning the address against an orthodox Catholic theologian, Von Hügel (whose works were part of Yeats's concentrated philosophical studies after he finished *A Vision),* and by further manipulation of his archetype of passion. Yeats again pre-empts weapons of the enemy, mysticism and miracle, even mines the Old Testament for his key metaphor, accepts, in fact, everything except Christianity's exclusive systematic embodiment of belief; but there his pagan humanism draws him up, he feels possessed of a vision actually larger and more satisfying than the Christian:

> *Must we part, Von Hügel, though much alike, for we*
> *Accept the miracles of the saints and honor sanctity?*
> *The body of Saint Teresa lies undecayed in tomb,*
> *Bathed in miraculous oil, sweet odors from it come,*

Healing from its lettered slab. Those self-same hands perchance
Eternalized the body of a modern saint that once
Had scooped out Pharaoh's mummy. I—though heart might find relief
Did I become a Christian man and choose for my belief
What seems most welcome in the tomb—play a predestined part.
Homer is my example and his unchristened heart.
The lion and the honeycomb, what has Scripture said?
So get you gone, Von Hügel, though with blessings on your head,

The implication seems clear: Yeats's humanism includes Christianity, but Christianity is not large enough to contain him. Yeats's spiritual arrogance is not less than total: only the breezy brilliance of his dismissal of a great theology makes it possible to choke down that arrogance. How much ignorance and how much of a vivid stupidity enter into Yeats's theology is a problem outside my province and my competence; but somebody ought to deal with the problem at length. Virginia Moore has made the most conscientious attempt to date, in her chapter, "Was Yeats a Christian?"[23] But her partisanship, I feel, has led her to impose some oversimplifications on her data. Her argument is long, learned, ingenious, and interesting, but I leave it unconvinced. The whole question is a vexed one, and too complicated to enter into at length here. Yeats behaved with a special ambivalence toward Christ and the Church, and Virginia Moore keeps him vaguely a Christian largely by separating Christ and the Church. Yeats was proud of his family's long tradition as members of the Anglo-Irish gentry and of the Church of Ireland; he insisted to his wife that

[23] *The Unicorn*, 384–431.

his children be brought up strictly in that church;[24] and numerous speeches and actions show a lingering affection for the ritual and theology of the church. But the contrary evidence of the poems and of *A Vision* seems to me to overbalance his leanings, or rather "yearnings," toward Christianity. In the long run his loyalty goes unmistakably to another tradition, the mystical-magical gnostic and hermetic one. Austin Warren's summary seems to me precisely accurate: "In Yeats, religion returns to its pre-Christian and indeed pre-monotheistic character, becoming the search for knowledge of the unseen and for gnostic power."[25]

We have seen his assent to the description of Christianity as a "fabulous formless darkness," "blotting out every beautiful thing," and we may take time to glance at a few of the other anti-Christian texts of *A Vision*. Certain pages of Yeats's great visionary last chapter, "Dove or Swan," show conclusively that a number of basic Christian dogmas were wholly unacceptable to him. Among them are its notion of its own exclusiveness, its possession of the "one truth"; its emphasis upon "revelation" of a rigid corporate truth, conceived outside man and conditionally granted unto him; its notions of the "one life," denying multiple incarnations, and defining the after-life as a single existence designed and directed by God; its complex quietism, minimizing the passional and the aesthetic, minimizing ego, emphasizing service and selflessness. More than anything else, it is Yeats's hubristic humanism which is outraged by the Christian pattern with its remorseless diminutions of man's notions of his own powers and perquisites. The great and astonishing lines of the title poem of *The Tower* are the work of an anti-Christian as well as an anti-Platonic thinker:

24 Moore, *The Unicorn,* 384.
25 "William Butler Yeats: The Religion of a Poet," *PY,* 236.

I mock Plotinus' thought
And cry in Plato's teeth,
Death and life were not
Till man made up the whole,
Made lock, stock and barrel
Out of his bitter soul,
Aye, sun and moon and star, all.
And further add to that
That, being dead, we rise,
Dream and so create
Translunar Paradise.

The identification of Christ and Plato is made again in *A Vision,* and they are charged with the same crime: both formularize truth and so put an end to dynamic creativity, truth as constantly recreated by man's violent trial and error:

> Aristotle and Plato end creative system—to die into the truth is still to die–and formula begins. Yet even the truth into which Plato dies is a form of death, for when he separates the Eternal Ideas from Nature and shows them self-sustained he prepares the Christian desert and the Stoic suicide.[26]

Even before Plato, the Christian crimes of revelation and monotheism had been prepared by Anaxagoras

> when he declared that thought and not the warring opposites created the world. At that sentence the heroic life, passionate fragmentary man, all that had been imagined by great poets and sculptors began to pass away, and instead of seeking noble antagonists, imagination moved towards divine man and the ridiculous devil. Now must sages lure men away from the arms of women, because in those arms man becomes a fragment; and all is ready for revelation.[27]

The "passionate fragmentary man," we must remember, was

[26] Page 271.
[27] *Ibid.,* 272–73.

for Yeats an ideal man. He creates life and beauty in his search for personal wholeness; but he is a singularly unchristian man: "Fragment delights in fragment and seeks possession, not service."[28] But the full motions of Yeats's humanism can only be felt in a long passage such as the following, with its detailing of the Christian indignities:

> God is now conceived of as something outside man and man's handiwork, and it follows that it must be idolatry to worship that which Phidias and Scopas made, and seeing that He is a Father in Heaven, that Heaven will be found presently in the Thebaid, where the world is changed into a featureless dust and can be run through the fingers; and these things are testified to from books that are outside human genius, being miraculous, and by a miraculous Church, and this Church, as the gyre sweeps wider, will make man also featureless as clay or dust. Night will fall upon man's wisdom now that man has been taught that he is nothing. He had discovered, or half-discovered, that the world is round and one of many like it, but now he must believe that the sky is but a tent spread above a level floor, and that he may be stirred into a frenzy of anxiety and so to moral transformation, blot out the knowledge or half-knowledge that he has lived many times, and think that all eternity depends upon a moment's decision. Heaven itself, transformation finished, must appear so vague and motionless that it seems but a concession to human weakness. It is even essential to this faith to declare that God's messengers, those beings who show His will in dreams or announce it in visionary speech, were never men. The Greeks thought them great men of the past, but now that concession to mankind is forbidden. All must be narrowed into the sun's image cast out of a burning-glass and man be ignorant of all but the image.[29]

28 *Ibid.*, 275.

29 *Ibid.*, 273–74.

Such a passage as this, it seems to me, is impossible to rationalize away. If Yeats believes what he has written here, then he does not believe in Christian dogma. The point is, of course, of general interest in any study of Yeats, and it is especially useful to us if it proves, as I think it does, that he systematically examined and rejected a theology which would have injected a supernatural and other-worldly palliative into his conception of life as tragedy. Our incarnation is remorselessly tragic, Yeats believed; and so, as we shall see when we examine "Byzantium," is our "discarnate state" after death. I suspect that he would have agreed completely with I. A. Richards' radical statement,

> Tragedy is only possible to a mind which is for the moment agnostic or Manichean. The least touch of any theology which has a compensating Heaven to offer the tragic hero is fatal.[30]

To revert to "Vacillation." My interest in the poem, of course, lies principally in its elevation of human passion to the level of transcendent value, embodied in Homer and that magnificent phrase, "his unchristened heart." "Non-Christian" is only a small part of the basic meaning of "unchristened" here; its more fundamental meanings draw an equation to that "resinous heart" and "fanatic heart" we have met in other poems. Above all, the crucial induction of the great paradoxical figure of the lion and the honeycomb offers us a truly central image in the tragic configuration. That *multum in parvo* Yeats submits as a cardinal text in the "predestined part" he understands as his office. That sense of triumph in disaster, figured in the bees and honey rich and alive in the body of the dead carnivore, gives this poem its philosophical center. And Yeats's amazing mastery of tone in the closing stanzas, his ar-

30 *Op. cit.*, 246.

rogant joy, his patronizing heart-wholeness, underscores the confidence that comes from his certainty that he has arrived at an oblique eminence "the other side of tragedy."

"Byzantium" is technically a far more perfect poem than "Vacillation," but I doubt that it is as important philosophically. It is thickly esoteric, and that fact, plus its undeniable beauty and brilliance as a lyric, has made it an almost overpopular subject for exegesis. So we may safely confine ourselves to noting its simple and perhaps unexpected relevance to our context of tragic passion. "Byzantium" is set in Yeats's otherworld and dramatizes the "dreaming back" of the transported spirits who, in his vision, "unwind the winding path" of their earthly lives. The "systematic" reference of all this has its own fascination, and "Byzantium" is exciting poetry both as esoterica and as public communication; yet what interests me most is the violent dynamism which informs Yeats's visionary landscape. He cannot see even Paradise as a quietistic retreat; it continues the moil and heat of the earthly life. The poem's final effect is the reverse of elegiac; we feel the compulsive activity of conflict in the "unwinding" spirits, but more especially in the image of the souls in passage, the very violence of whose transition recreates the kinesthesia of earthly struggle:

> *Astraddle on the dolphin's mire and blood,*
> *Spirit after spirit! The smithies break the flood,*
> *The golden smithies of the Emperor!*
> *Marbles of the dancing floor*
> *Break bitter furies of complexity,*
> *Those images that yet*
> *Fresh images beget,*
> *That dolphin-torn, that gong-tormented sea.*

This same fantastic microcosm will reappear even more overtly in the later satirical "News For the Delphic Oracle." Passion dies hard.

Yeats's notions of the soul's experience after death, or "between death and birth," as he preferred to say,[31] fill a complicated chapter, "The Soul in Judgment," in *A Vision*. Briefly he envisioned a sequence of six "discarnate states," which he named "The Vision of the Blood Kindred"; the "Meditation" or "Dreaming Back" or " Return" or "Phantasmagoria" (all stages within the "second state"); the "Shiftings"; the "Marriage" or "Beatitude"; the "Purification"; and the "Foreknowledge." The interrelationships of these "discarnate states," and their relations to the wheel of the "Four Principles" (which moves "at right angles" to the wheel of the "Four Faculties"[32]), are too impossibly complicated to enter into here. Suffice it to say that they make the period "between death and birth" a fiercely active interregnum (of varying lengths, perhaps several generations[33]) in which the spirit seeks "freedom"[34] before reincarnation; and in which it is "compelled to live over and over again the events that had most moved it"—first in order of "intensity of passion" and then in order of occurrence.[35] Thus the after-life, or the between-lives, of the soul, as Yeats sees it, is a state the obverse of peace and passivity; he makes that perfectly clear:

> Neither the *Phantasmagoria,* nor the *Purification,* nor any other state between death and birth should be considered as a reward or paradise. Neither between death and birth nor between birth and death can the soul find more than momentary happiness.[36]

And so he has defined the whole of imaginable existence as tragic dynamism.

31 *A Vision,* 223.
32 *Ibid.*
33 *Ibid.,* 236.
34 *Ibid.,* 226.
35 *Ibid.*
36 *Ibid.,* 236.

Yeats's apotheosizing of passion, his elevation of Swordsman over Saint, his heartbroken and heart-whole admiration of *Saeva Indignatio,* is everyhere in *The Winding Stair;* it will be sufficient to cite briefly only two appearances of the theme as it rises out of and supports Yeats's fierce affection for the four great Irishmen he saw as examples of the passionately committed spirit, Swift, Goldsmith, Burke, and Berkeley. In "The Seven Sages" these four appear as spiritual heroes whose impassioned humility "understood that wisdom comes of beggary," and whose humanistic scorn made them haters of that cold and niggling meliorism that Yeats names "Whiggery":

> *Whether they knew or not,*
> *Goldsmith and Burke, Swift and the Bishop of Cloyne*
> *All hated Whiggery; but what is Whiggery?*
> *A levelling, rancorous, rational sort of mind . . .*

And yet more imposingly, the same admiration impels the almost hysterical rhetoric of "Blood and the Moon":

> *I declare this tower is my symbol; I declare*
> *This winding, gyring, spiring treadmill of a stair is my*
> *ancestral stair;*
> *That Goldsmith and the Dean, Berkeley and Burke have*
> *travelled there.*
>
> *Swift beating on his breast in sibylline frenzy blind*
> *Because the heart in his blood-sodden breast had dragged him*
> *down into mankind,*
> *Goldsmith deliberately sipping at the honey-pot of his mind,*
>
> *And haughtier-headed Burke that proved the State a tree,*
> *That this unconquerable labyrinth of the birds, century after*
> *century,*
> *Cast but dead leaves to mathematical equality;*
>
> *And God-appointed Berkeley that proved all things a dream,*

That this pragmatical, preposterous pig of a world, its farrow that so solid seem,
Must vanish on the instant if the mind but change its theme,...

As we have noted, the theme of the Lion and the Honeycomb, which is basically the theme of tragic joy, appears in its fused form with the theme of Swordsman *versus* Saint in "Vacillation." The two themes coalesce again in another poem of kindred structure, "A Dialogue of Self and Soul," which is still more revealingly, because more concretely, autobiographical. This time "Self," containing, clearly, definitive Yeats, replaces "Heart" as opponent of "Soul." Soul summons, as before, to the "darkness" of withdrawn contemplation, to a willed mystical apartness that will transcend the human condition:

I summon to the winding ancient stair;
Set all your mind upon the steep ascent,
Upon the broken, crumbling battlement,
Upon the breathless starlit air,
Upon the star that marks the hidden pole;
Fix every wandering thought upon
That quarter where all thought is done:
Who can distinguish darkness from the soul?

But in this poem Yeats as Self is literally and adequately the Swordsman. In the poem's dramatic fiction he bears on his knees the five-hundred-year-old sword given him in 1920, in a ceremonial gesture that had moved him deeply, by his Japanese admirer Sato.[37] This "consecrated blade" and its housing of wood and of flowered embroidery he flourishes as symbols of vitality and commitment, rather than withdrawal:

Montashigi, third of his family, fashioned it
Five hundred years ago, about it lie
Flowers from I know not what embroidery—

[37] Yeats, *Letters*, 662.

Heart's purple—and all these I set
For emblems of the day against the tower
Emblematical of the night,
And claim as by a soldier's right
A charter to commit the crime once more.

Establishment of this dialectic occupies the poem's first section of five stanzas; but then Soul is brushed aside and Self, who is quintessential Yeats, delivers an eloquently simple peroration extending to four stanzas which amounts to an impassioned definition of tragic reconciliation as developed in the life of the poet. The first stanza of this section summarizes both the tragic data and the acceptance:

A living man is blind and drinks his drop.
What matter if the ditches are impure?
What matter if I live it all once more?
Endure that toil of growing up;
The ignominy of boyhood; the distress
Of boyhood changing into man;
The unfinished man and his pain
Brought face to face with his own clumsiness . . .

"I am content to live it all again/ And yet again," says the affirming Self, "if it be life . . . ." That is the crucial clause: "if it be life." Reconciliation to the tragic facts of life makes welcome even

that most fecund ditch of all,
The folly that man does
Or must suffer, if he woos
A proud woman not kindred of his soul.

Maud again.

The closing stanza draws up the poem's summation. There Yeats lays claim to a beatitude more inclusive and durable than that of "Vacillation." This beatitude is not a psychological matter of mood but a condition of philosophical conviction that depends in turn upon a fundamental spiritual recognition—the leveling and mingling of contraries as they take on the existential uniformity of being equally "life." In its intimate, personal, romantic way, this recognition is basically that of tragic reconciliation; and the emotion it endows is Passionate Joy and Innocence, the legacy of paradox of the Lion and the Honeycomb: "Out of the eater came forth meat, and out of the strong came forth sweetness."

I am content to follow to its source
Every event in action or in thought;
Measure the lot; forgive myself the lot!
When such as I cast out remorse
So great a sweetness flows into the breast
We must laugh and we must sing,
We are blest by everything,
Everything we look upon is blest.

The rather precise echo of Browning—probably quite unconscious—is interesting, and, following the reference to Maud—Yeats's Lucrezia—significant. But what is more deeply interesting is how pallid and unconvincing seems Andrea's reverie, moving as it is in its own context, when set against the denser environment of Yeats's accumulated passion.

The most characteristic emblems of this volume—the tower, Sato's sword and its elegant housing, Yeats's beautiful young wife, himself in his office of "foolish passionate man"—are all assembled midway in a little poem of three cryptic couplets candidly called "Symbols":

A storm-beaten old watch-tower,
A blind hermit rings the hour.

All-destroying sword-blade still
Carried by the wandering fool.

> *Gold-sewn silk on the sword-blade,*
> *Beauty and fool together laid.*

This has some of the genuine apocalyptic tone, "all emotion and all impersonal," which is coming increasingly to dominate these late poems. This "impersonal" emotion sets the governing tone of the twenty-five brief lyrics of the sequence "Words for Music Perhaps" and of the eleven lyrics of the sequence "A Woman Young and Old." Their theme, basically, is Lion and Honeycomb, existential affirmation, joy beyond tragedy. We can afford time for only a glance at a very few of these poems, and our best examples will come from the "Crazy Jane" group. We can only notice in passing, too, Yeats's habit here and here after of counterpointing his lyrical-dramatic stanzas against a refrain of a line or two, variously extravagant—sometimes intensely bitter, sometimes pointedly enigmatic, sometimes merely noncommittally lyrical; a habit which is itself a symptom of the general apocalyptic impulse: "All things remain in God," "Love is like the lion's tooth," "Prove that I lie," "A bone wave-whitened and dried in the wind," "Mad as the mist and snow," "I carry the sun in a golden cup,/ The moon in a silver bag," "Tall dames go walking in grass-green Avalon."

The seven "Crazy Jane" poems belong, I think, in the list of Yeats's great poems. What is most striking in them is their achievement of a kind of dense limpidity, an astonishing weight of meaning and feeling compressed inside their strict measure and almost monosyllabic speech. They are little masterpieces painted, as it were, entirely in primary colors. "Crazy Jane on God," despite its title and its refrain, is an existential poem locating joy exclusively in passional experience; moral consequence is irrelevant, value lies in the act itself:

> *I had wild Jack for a lover;*
> *Though like a road*

That men pass over
My body makes no moan
But sings on:
All things remain in God.

"Crazy Jane Grown Old Looks at the Dancers" appears more complex in theme, but essentially it says the same thing in a richer idiom. In the first two stanzas "old" Jane recalls semi-visionary scenes of a passionate dance in which the partners had seemed to threaten each other with murder; she closes the second stanza with the line, "They had all that had their hate," thereby reasserting Yeats's ambiguity of passion that rests value not in consequence but in quantity of feeling, and underscoring that duality in the refrain, *"Love is like the lion's tooth."* The tight third stanza restates the duality and insists again upon passion itself as the only true residence of significant value, of the real:

Did he die or did she die?
Seemed to die or died they both?
God be with the times when I
Cared not a thraneen for what chanced
So that I had the limbs to try
Such a dance as there was danced—
Love is like the lion's tooth.

The richest of these poems, "Crazy Jane Talks with the Bishop," is short enough to quote entire. Here all the passional paradoxes are knit in the great third stanza: the truth of the physiological and psychological association of beauty and filth, the literal neighborliness of the organs of excretion and love, the ambivalence of love and rage, the necessity of decay to life. It is really this sort of thing that Mr. Eric Bentley had in mind when he spoke of the "dung of passion" in Yeats.[38] The figure

[38] "Yeats as a Playwright," *PY*, 247.

the poem makes is that of the Biblical metaphor, the Lion and the Honeycomb; in our frame, it asserts the association of suffering and salvation, the purgative power of disaster, the fullness of joy that comes only with the fullness of grief:

> *I met the Bishop on the road*
> *And much said he and I.*
> *"Those breasts are flat and fallen now,*
> *Those veins must soon be dry;*
> *Live in a heavenly mansion,*
> *Not in some foul sty."*
>
> *"Fair and foul are near of kin,*
> *And fair needs foul," I cried.*
> *"My friends are gone, but that's a truth*
> *Nor grave nor bed denied,*
> *Learned in bodily lowliness*
> *And in the heart's pride.*
>
> *"A woman can be proud and stiff*
> *When on love intent;*
> *But Love has pitched his mansion in*
> *The place of excrement;*
> *For nothing can be sole or whole*
> *That has not been rent."*

"LAST POEMS"

In dealing with Yeats's *Last Poems* of 1936–39, it seems best to let the poems have their say approximately in the order in which they lie in the volume, with only informal attempts at classification. But we shall have need of all our established headings from time to time, in trying to order these brilliant and variegated poems within the frame of tragedy. For Yeats talks here upon all his basic tragic themes, and talks for the most part with special terseness and compression. The result is a grand and strange volume, one that crowns a lyrical career of grandeur and strangeness with a quite extraordinary and moving adequacy. We must say once more that no other poet in English ever wrote poems of such range and quality at Yeats's age of more than seventy.

We must preface our examination of the *Last Poems* with a brief look at the only poem of the preceding volume, *A Full Moon in March,* which requires special notice, the small lyric "A Prayer for Old Age." Short and simple as it is, it is doctrinaire and important Yeats—not only "old" Yeats but the Yeats of every period except the earliest. His secular "prayer," we see, is for continued passion and "irrational" wisdom, the kind of blood-wisdom rooted in absolute faith in feeling, and making mock of "mere" abstract thought. The first stanza prays for this fusion of sense and sensibility by violently dislocating the seat of thought:

> *God guard me from those thoughts men think*
> *In the mind alone;*
> *He that sings a lasting song*
> *Thinks in a marrow-bone.*

The second stanza scorns conventionally admirable wisdom and scorns that egoism which would prefer its own public dignity to the creative embarrassment of truer art:

> *From all that makes a wise old man*
> *That can be praised of all;*
> *O what am I that I should not seem*
> *For the song's sake a fool?*

Then the last stanza takes its positive stand in favor of a paradoxical dignity composed of "foolishness" illuminated by passion and thereby marrow-bone wisdom:

COURTESY DENIS JOHNSTON

W. B. Yeats with the Abbey Theatre Company on the eve of their departure for a tour of America in September, 1931. *Seated, l. to r.: Maureen Delaney, W. B. Yeats, Eileen Crowe, Kate Curling, Mac Shields, May Craig. Standing, l. to r.: Shelah Richards, Lennox Robinson, Michael Dolan, F. J. McCormick, Denis O'Dea, Arthur Shields, Fred Johnson, P. J. Carolan, Barry Fitzgerald.*

NEW YORK PUBLIC LIBRARY PICTURE COLLECTION

W. B. Yeats in 1933

From a photograph by Edward Steichen.

I pray—for fashion's word is out
And prayer comes round again—
That I may seem, though I die old,
A foolish, passionate man.

The kind of "foolishness" Yeats has in mind is clearly of the order of that "tragical mirth," the tragi-comic prescience and bitter gaiety of the Shakespearean fool. Aside from its obvious canonizing of passion, what we should particularly notice in this little poem is Yeats's centering of value in the art object itself, ignoring "for the song's sake" any ignoble special pleading of the ego. The two motives conjoined show that Yeats is working now in accordance with the program announced in his letter of 1929 to Olivia Shakespear: "I want them to be all emotion and all impersonal."[39] But the poem has little need for commentary. In its line of thought and its simplicity and candor, it will serve us well as a text for reading the *Last Poems*.

"The Gyres," which stands first in the volume, is for our purpose an important poem. For not only does it activate the Yeatsian concept I have called Passion as Joy, it also provides another basic piece of evidence in support of my belief that Yeats's tragic vision ultimately dominates the deterministic bias of his mystical "system"—that alternative passionate conviction of his. The poem is one of the most formally doctrinal of those poems of a sort of desperate gaiety which rise out of a negative tragic vision of things—negative vision and positive response, once more. In the first of the poem's three eight-line stanzas, Yeats presents another of those apocalyptic or pseudo-apocalyptic situations of violent cultural stress, apparently not of the finality of that in "The Second Coming" but certainly of one of those circles of the moon "that pitches common things about," wherein all that he finds spiritually dear reels in a gyre of confusion and ignominy. "The Gyres! The

[39] *Letters*, 758.

gyres!" he begins excitedly. To the spectacle he summons one he names "Old Rocky Face"; "Old Rocky Face, look forth." The identity of this enigmatic personage is a question of some interest. Mr. Jeffares identifies him as Shelley's Jew, Ahasuerus,[40] and Virginia Moore believes he is Blake's Urizen.[41] To me he more explicitly recalls Yeats's own earlier "mask" in "Ego Dominus Tuus" of Dante—"the gaunt Dante of the *Divine Comedy,*"[42] as he is called in *A Vision:*

> *I think he fashioned from his opposite*
> *An image that might have been a stony face*
> *Staring upon a Bedouin's horse-hair roof*
> *From doored and windowed cliff. . . .*

As such, he would represent Yeats's ideal "antithetical" man, making productivity of the stresses of the most exacting disciplinary oppositions, and as such, also, obviously, a persona of Yeats himself. The subsequent text of the poem, especially of the third stanza, and the general setting of the theme in the dynamism of creative oppositions—the deepest of all Yeats's convictions—seem to me to support this identification rather conclusively. The spectacle to which Old Rocky Face is invited, at any rate, is familiar Yeatsian end-of-the-world landscape. But what must interest us most keenly here is not setting but response—that attitude of committed detachment which Yeats now names, unequivocally, "tragic joy":

> *The gyres! The gyres! Old Rocky Face, look forth;*
> *Things thought too long can be no longer thought,*
> *For beauty dies of beauty, worth of worth,*
> *And ancient lineaments are blotted out.*
> *Irrational streams of blood are staining earth;*
> *Empedocles has thrown all things about;*

[40] *W. B. Yeats: Man and Poet,* 289.
[41] *The Unicorn,* 420.
[42] Page 141.

Hector is dead and there's a light in Troy;
We that look on but laugh in tragic joy.

The weaker second stanza makes clear that what Yeats mourns most keenly is the dissolution of ancient grace and splendor under the rising pressure of modern vulgarity—the decay of what he calls in a later poem in this volume "beautiful lofty things," and what he here names "a greater, a more gracious time." But again the response concerns us more than does the negative stimulus, and again the response is the positive one of imperative tragic joy: "What matter? Out of cavern comes a voice,/ And all it knows is that one word 'Rejoice!' " The rationale of that imperative is worked out in the third stanza, where Yeats makes clear his conviction that "foolish, passionate" men like himself and Rocky Face retain their phoenix-powers of creative deprivation, fertility in decay, their ability to revitalize the ruins of "any rich, dark nothing"; thus to set moving again, doomed but splendid, the aristocracy of spirit and passion he calls with laconic bitterness "that unfashionable gyre":

Conduct and work grow coarse, and coarse the soul,
What matter? Those that Rocky Face holds dear,
Lovers of horses and of women, shall,
From marble of a broken sepulchre,
Or dark betwixt the polecat and the owl,
Or any rich, dark nothing disinter
The workman, noble and saint, and all things run
On that unfashionable gyre again.

"Lapis Lazuli," the poem which immediately follows "The Gyres," seems to me certainly one of the great lyrics of this century and unquestionably one of Yeats's half-dozen finest poems. It is heartening, too, in a sense, to see that it is a poem entirely independent in theme and imagery of his esoteric system—making the point that Yeats is a great poet quite apart from the equivocal business of *A Vision*. The poem stands, as I suggested at the outset of this study, squarely at the tragic center of Yeats's view of man, of art, and of history. In "Lapis Lazuli," Yeats touches and brilliantly animates most of the major beliefs composing his tragic vision: he confesses the conventional negative tragic facts of man's condition, then scoffs at those who are satisfied to find that negative conclusive; he virtually redefines dramatic tragedy, at least to his own satisfaction, by his overmastering extension of tragic reconciliation into a kind of triumphant hilarity; finally, he passionately reasserts the humanistic immunity of man to destiny. The poem is thus an imposing and deeply moving demonstration, as well as an assertion, of Yeats's notions of the immense potency of art and of the human spirit. Fittingly, it is the specific poem Yeats had in mind when he spoke of "an act of faith and reason to make one rejoice in the midst of tragedy."

Aside from all this philosophical weight, the poem is one of the most purely pleasurable of all Yeats's poems of any period. It has a delightful limpidity of thematic statement, a felicity of selection and clarity of outline in the images, and a dignified simplicity of speech which show Yeats's absolute command of his mood and his medium, coupled with an openness of structure and texture and an easy fluency of movement that are rare in these late poems. Yeats was quite right to call "Lapis Lazuli" "almost the best I have made of recent years."[43]

The first of the poem's five stanzas of varying length is an ironic salute to those—he limits them to "hysterical women"—who are "sick of the palette and fiddle-bow,/ Of poets that are always gay," and who insist that the poet confine himself to celebrating the admittedly malign face of things. Yeats does not pause to reason with these folk. Instead his anger and dis-

[43] *Letters to Dorothy Wellesley*, 91.

gust send him off, in the second stanza, on an oblique and magnificently effective rebuttal; he sails into his redefinition of tragedy: what is it, after all? Not, he concludes, the crushed submission of man to malignancy but his defiant spiritual transmutation of dread into triumph. The stanza is one of the great things in Yeats, in its philosophical obduracy, the heat of its conviction, the brilliant specification of its argument, and the vivid aliveness of its speech:

All perform their tragic play,
There struts Hamlet, there is Lear,
That's Ophelia, that Cordelia;
Yet they, should the last scene be there,
The great stage curtain about to drop,
If worthy their prominent part in the play,
Do not break up their lines to weep.
They know that Hamlet and Lear are gay;
Gaiety transfiguring all that dread.
All men have aimed at, found and lost;
Black out; Heaven blazing into the head:
Tragedy wrought to its uttermost.
Though Hamlet rambles and Lear rages,
And all the drop-scenes drop at once
Upon a hundred thousand stages,
It cannot grow by an inch or an ounce.

In the rush of his hyperbole Yeats has redefined not only the vulgar notion of tragedy as "the common lot"; but also, let us recognize, by turning it romantically extravagant and hubristic, he has redefined accepted academic conceptions of the term: those admit a "reconciliation" between man and destiny far short of Yeats's excited humanism. I mean to impugn neither Yeats's definition nor the "academic" one, but merely to point out a basic distinction between them which is at root theological: Yeats's gnostic humanism is not really content with "reconciliation," it drives him on to assert that man is not only spiritually equal to his fate and able to bear it unbroken, he is spiritually superior to his fate and able to bear it essentially untouched.

The stanzas which follow are equally but differently fine. Technically the whole movement of the poem from this point is dazzling. There occurs a kind of geometrical shrinking of all the poem's elements at the same pace: tension gradually relaxes, movement gradually slows, images gradually diminish in frequency and size, and at the end the poem glides away into a sweetly solemn elegiac silence, its point made once and for all. The third stanza, again ignoring mechanical transitions, sets Yeats's conclusion drawn from dramatic tragedy in the context of explicit human history. The opening lines continue but reduce the hyperbole of the preceding stanza in a stately panorama of congenital disaster, accepted simply as fact:

On their own feet they came, or on shipboard,
Camel-back, horse-back, ass-back, mule-back,
Old civilizations put to the sword.
Then they and their wisdom went to rack.

Then the theme of mutability is trusted to one man, Callimachus, whose art is allowed to stand for all fine utterances of the aspiring spirit:

No handiwork of Callimachus,
Who handled marble as if it were bronze,
Made draperies that seemed to rise
When sea-wind swept the corner, stands;
His long lamp-chimney shaped like the stem
Of a slender palm, stood but a day.

Then once again the original unblinking assertions: disaster is inevitable, disaster is irrelevant:

All things fall and are built again,
And those that build them again are gay.

The next to last stanza unveils at last the rich little object which gave the poem its impulse, its title, its theme, and its final synoptic symbol:

Two Chinamen, behind them a third,
Are carved in lapis lazuli,
Over them flies a long-legged bird,
A symbol of longevity;
The third, doubtless a serving-man,
Carries a musical instrument.

The final stanza elaborates that image. Yeats has made all his passionate assertions, his fine ranting is done; now he needs only to point to their simple symbolic equivalents, and this he does with exquisite grace and calm. Now each detail takes on its automatic philosophical weight. Avalanche, snow, fruit trees, art, performer, age, and gaiety all settle into a stylized pantomime in which the happy conclusion of the most absolute of conflicts is such a certainty that the conflict itself comes to seem only sweetly formal and balletic:

Every discoloration of the stone,
Every accidental crack or dent,
Seems a water-course or an avalanche,
Or lofty slope where it still snows
Though doubtless plum or cherry-branch
Sweetens the little half-way house
Those Chinamen climb towards, and I
Delight to imagine them seated there;
There, on the mountain and the sky,
On all the tragic scene they stare.
One asks for mournful melodies;
Accomplished fingers begin to play.

Their eyes mid many wrinkles, their eyes,
Their ancient, glittering eyes, are gay.

It seems to me an unforgettable poem, the kind of absolute achievement which leaves one no opening for quarrels—unless they be philosophical ones.

With a far greater naturalness and propriety than in the poems of his middle age—where the habit had something of the pathetic air of menopause—Yeats writes often, variously, and movingly in *Last Poems* of old age and its dilemmas, some of them standard, some of them peculiar to his special psyche. His simplest expression of both the standard and the special tension of old age occurs in the poem "The Apparitions." There he speaks with self-knowing but unrepentant irony of his mystical studies, the ridicule and the satisfaction those have brought him, pictures the calm gratification he has found in intellectual maturity and in leisure long-sought and soundly earned, declares the general "deepening" of his joy, then quietly brings all this accumulated depth and calm to confront the Great Enemy. And counterpointing the confident images of each of the three stanzas is the understated horror of the folk-symbol of death, the chief "apparition" of the title, "a coat upon a coat-hanger." I quote the second and third stanzas:

I have found nothing half so good
As my long-planned half solitude,
Where I can sit up half the night
With some friend that has the wit
Not to allow his looks to tell
When I am unintelligible.
Fifteen apparitions have I seen;
The worst a coat upon a coat-hanger.

When a man grows old his joy
Grows more deep day after day,

His empty heart is full at length,
But he has need of all that strength
Because of the increasing Night
That opens her mystery and fright.
Fifteen apparitions have I seen;
The worst a coat upon a coat-hanger.

But this calm resolution in the face of old age and death, convincing as it is in passing, is hardly the most characteristic Yeats. He makes other more native responses. "Why Should Not Old Men Be Mad?" is one of the most important of these, and a good deal closer to the center of his true emotion. This is one of the relatively rare instances in which Yeats's bitterness is unbroken and unrelieved, a remorseless detailing of the data of disappointment and decay, the utter negative pole of his tragic dualism. In his first four lines he reconstitutes his favorite persona of human obduracy, the fishermen, in obviously specific reference to a man I am unable to identify:

Why should not old men be mad?
Some have known a likely lad
That had a sound fly-fisher's wrist
Turn to a drunken journalist . . . .

The next couplet scoffs bitterly at Maud's daughter, Iseult Gonne, who after refusing Yeats himself married a man he held in contempt (later he radically revised his low opinion of Francis Stuart: "If luck comes to his aid he will be our great writer"[44]):

A girl that knew all Dante once
Live to bear children to a dunce . . . .

The couplet that follows forms one of the grossest of his insults to Maud and her betrayal of himself and her own basic femininity:

[44] *Letters,* 799–800.

A Helen of social welfare dream,
Climb on a wagonette to scream.

Having established his three cases of representative human ignominy, Yeats goes on in the remaining lines to set them in the inclusive frame of ineluctable despair:

Some think it a matter of course that chance
Should starve good men and bad advance,
That if their neighbors figured plain,
As though upon a lighted screen,
No single story would they find
Of an unbroken happy mind,
A finish worthy of the start.
Young men know nothing of this sort.
Observant old men know it well;
And when they know what old books tell,
And that no better can be had,
Know why an old man should be mad.

But a still more truly characteristic motive impels a better poem which is also deeper Yeats. This is "An Acre of Grass," from which we have already had occasion to borrow a text. "An Acre of Grass" is one of the capital poems on the theme of the "foolish, passionate man" and one that convincingly represents our category of Passion as Defence. Here Yeats spends the first two stanzas in quiet evocation of old age's typical climate of passive mediocrity, that dull neutrality from which he will ask passion to defend him:

Picture and book remain,
An acre of green grass
For air and exercise,
Now strength of body goes;
Midnight, an old house
Where nothing stirs but a mouse.

My temptation is quiet.
Here at life's end
Neither loose imagination,
Nor the mill of the mind
Consuming its rag and bone,
Can make the truth known.

But there, midway, the poem breaks sharply in tone, movement, and theme, and Yeats's energy flows into an imperative plea that he may find strength to reconstitute himself as a worthy follower of those "foolish, passionate" artists and tragic personages whose declared disciple he had been all his life, and never more than now when the end of all things approaches. The result is two of the greatest of all Yeats's many remarkable short stanzas, dense with meaning and feeling. This is his theme of defensive and creative passion, "the fanatic heart" in its pure state:

Grant me an old man's frenzy,
Myself must I remake
Till I am Timon and Lear
Or that William Blake
Who beat upon the wall
Till Truth obeyed his call;

A mind Michael Angelo knew
That can pierce the clouds,
Or inspired by frenzy
Shake the dead in their shrouds;
Forgotten else by mankind,
An old man's eagle mind.

All these are testamentary poems in that they try to draw up the balance-sheet of a life and dispose in one way or another of an old man's spiritual remains. In fact, it might be argued that virtually all the poems in this volume have something of that air and that function. "The Man and the Echo," for example, is a poem in which the testamentary urge is explicit and interesting, though inconclusive. Yeats presents himself here in a rather uncommon posture of shaky querulousness; he is "old and ill" and troubled by a kind of cloudy guilt, wondering if "words of mine" had actually led to violence and bloodshed:

All that I have said and done,
Now that I am old and ill,
Turns into a question till
I lie awake night after night
And never get the answers right.

Confusion and disaster seem for the time so absolute that he "Sleepless would lie down and die." The sepulchral "Echo" sends back the refrain, "Lie down and die." In the next stanza the "Man" rejects the chance to "shirk" in death, then goes on to picture first the weak irresolution of typical old age and then his desired ideal resolution in which he will be able to order and systematize a lifetime's warring urges into a final spiritual peace before death:

While man can still his body keep
Wine or love drug him to sleep,
Waking he thanks the Lord that he
Has body and its stupidity,
But body gone he sleeps no more,
And till his intellect grows sure
That all's arranged in one clear view,
Pursues the thoughts that I pursue,
Then stands in judgment on his soul,
And, all work done, dismisses all
Out of intellect and sight
And sinks at last into the night.

But "Echo" answers hollowly, "Into the night." Although the

stanza which follows is interesting, "Echo's" resonant irony is the poem's effectual close. Yeats leaves the end open and neutral, in essence. "O Rocky Voice," he asks of Mystery, "Shall we in that great night rejoice?" But then he dares not answer his own great question. Instead he shifts his ground radically to the merely empirical world of passion and sense:

> *But hush, for I have lost the theme,*
> *Its joy or night seem but a dream;*
> *Up there some hawk or owl has struck,*
> *Dropping out of sky or rock,*
> *A stricken rabbit is crying out,*
> *And its cry distracts my thought.*

The effect of "The Man and the Echo" is not one of Yeats's most impressive; but the end of the poem does dramatize, though rather factitiously and so unsatisfactorily, a tactic with a genuine philosophical base: his need to confess the final submission—at any rate, the repeated submission—of his mysticism to passional reality.

We may note only briefly before passing on to more fundamental themes two further poems which we may call testamentary. His "Beautiful Lofty Things" is simply a short but vivid catalog of figures that have stayed with Yeats all his life as supreme images of the aristocracy of the indomitable spirit: "All the Olympians," he names them in the last line of the single stanza, "a thing never known again." He lists five of these heroes, O'Leary and O'Grady, his own father, "his beautiful mischievous head thrown back," Lady Gregory defying an assassin at the age of eighty, and finally, of course, Maud Gonne under the aspect of divinity: "Pallas Athene in that straight back and arrogant head." "Arrogant," I am afraid, is a truly germane word for Yeats, and the fact is probably the hardest thing to forgive in him—really harder to forgive than his desire to "die blaspheming": that, at least, is metaphorical.

But we can set the impulse to arrogance for the time being in a gentling context with a quick look at "The Municipal Gallery Revisited." It is a poem which recalls, in some ways, a greater poem, "In Memory of Major Robert Gregory." Like that, it is a tributory poem, cast in a dramatic structure, and like that it is seized midway by a single powerful image and emotion which then commands the whole poem and forcibly unifies what had been loosely agglomerated ideas. Yeats presents himself in the gallery in the opening line, "Around me the images of thirty years." At first he is moved only to a kind of shallow wonder at the romantic unreality of the images of Ireland about him on the walls: " 'This is not,' I say/ 'The dead Ireland of my youth, but an Ireland/ The poets have imagined, terrible and gay.' " But then he begins to focus more closely on the portraits and sees images—of Lady Gregory, her son Robert Gregory, her nephew Hugh Lane, Hazel Lavery, John Synge—of persons who have had for him the most intimate and intense human meaning; and abruptly his casual tourist's exercise turns into a heart-breaking spiritual pilgrimage in which he is shaken by a flood of feelings: the rich significance of these persons to his own mind and art, the fact that they hang here as dead ghosts of dead days of which he is himself a lingering relic, the sense of his own old age and infallibly imminent death:

> *Heart-smitten with emotion I sink down,*
> *My heart recovering with covered eyes;*
> *Wherever I had looked I had looked upon*
> *My permanent or impermanent images . . . .*

But it is Lady Gregory's image which grips him most cruelly, that linked with Synge's and his own in the triumvirate of the arduous adventure of the Abbey Theatre. It is his view of

Lady Gregory that softens his "arrogance" for us, by mingling it with "humility" and turning it functional with the quality of ideal behavior—"the old high way," "that high horse riderless":

> *But where is the brush that could show anything*
> *Of all that pride and that humility?*
> *And I am in despair that time may bring*
> *Approved patterns of women or of men*
> *But not that selfsame excellence again.*

In the sixth stanza his summation of the Abbey ideal softens the arrogance further, as Yeats makes the ideal available, at least in theory, to both "the noble and the beggar-man," and pictures the whole program as based in a kind of primitive-aristocratic agrarianism: "All that we did, all that we said or sang/ Must come from contact with the soil, from that/ Contact everything Antaeus-like grew strong." And the final stanza seems to me to destroy most of what remains of the curse as Yeats shifts, gracefully but convincingly and touchingly, the whole credit for his own eminence from himself to his friends:

> *You that would judge me, do not judge alone*
> *This book or that, come to this hallowed place*
> *Where my friends' portraits hang and look thereon;*
> *Ireland's history in their lineaments trace;*
> *Think where man's glory most begins and ends,*
> *And say my glory was I had such friends.*

The gesture has not destroyed, I suppose, our apprehension of an arrogant pride in Yeats's composition; but it has qualified it by showing its alloys of gratitude and loyalty and serious notions of service to an ideal higher than the ego. Yeats is full of all kinds of pride—social, spiritual, intellectual; and his ego is immense and sometimes it fakes its way. But his seems to me for the most part a functional and forgivable arrogance because it aims at a general as well as a personal eminence, rather a true shared eminence of spirit than a merely personal vanity.

It is time now to pay some attention to that other more famous phenomenon of Yeats's late poems, his notorious senescent sexuality. The theme is everywhere, but it grows less shocking with a closer look, and less overbearing as one reads these poems in the neighborhood of related poems; I hope, in any case, to have prepared the way for a saner acceptance by showing how Yeats's theme of sex finds a solid doctrinal accommodation in that general canonizing of passion in which it is an important but not exclusive motive. I mean that his old-man's sexuality "makes sense" philosophically. How much sense it makes physiologically is not really our problem.

The purely personal side of the matter has been considerably exaggerated, I think. It is not insignificant, but it is not finally the dominant consideration. That the sexuality in these late poems is in important part Yeats's sexuality is unquestionable. Possibly there is something embarrassingly wish-fulfilling in such an ironic little lyric as "Politics," with its epigraph from Thomas Mann, "In our time the destiny of man presents its meaning in political terms"; not so, obviously, for the moment for Yeats:

> *How can I, that girl standing there,*
> *My attention fix*
> *On Roman or on Russian*
> *Or on Spanish politics?*

And in his famous quatrain "The Spur" he seems to present the case as candidly as poetic speech can make it:

> *You think it horrible that lust and rage*
> *Should dance attention upon my old age;*

> *They were not such a plague when I was young;*
> *What else have I to spur me into song?*

But Yeats is really being a bit consciously provoking and a bit disingenuous in such poems. The "plague" was not new, he had been saying for a long time that his poetry "all came from rage or lust"; the impulse was not merely an aberration of old age, as he well knew. If we sublimate Yeats's terms slightly, in any case, we will come to cover most of the lyrical motives of most poets. But what we really need to do with these terms, to understand Yeats more truly, is to let them coalesce and turn abstract; then we see that what Yeats means by his bravado is really only the bases of that inclusive concept "passion" we have been talking about for a long time. It is that general truth which makes the whole matter philosophically important. Yeats's personal sexuality, as an element in his poetry, is fundamentally one piece with his established general conviction that "passion is the essential," and his specific old man's conviction that an old poet should go on testifying vividly to his continuing commitment to the passional values of life. He must not resign passion by default and so capitulate to fate and time; rather he must "die blaspheming"—must defiantly covet just such aberrations as this anachronistic sexuality we are tempted to find embarrassing. His job is to die flourishing the "resinous heart" of the "foolish, passionate man." That Yeats is willing to suffer his own personal embarrassment by flaunting his personal as well as his impersonal and doctrinal involvement testifies, if nothing else, to his full seriousness.

Undoubtedly the merely personal, the physiological or psychological motives in the pattern were extremely important to Yeats; but what matters most for our special argument is doctrine and its poetic vestment. According to doctrine, these poems are meant to be part of a body of final poems designed to be "all emotion and all impersonal." That sought paradox is worth insisting on. For it is their variegated and complex "impersonality" which gives to some of the most characteristic late poems their strange functional abstractness, their wide and deep limpidity, their range of application, and much of the special poignancy with which they move a reader. Further, their impersonality defines these poems' place on the tragic scale: these are, basically, those poems which rise from that ground of sublimation, tense peace, and "contemplation" on "the other side of tragedy." And this impersonality is a crucial element of poetic attitude and poetic method in the expression of all Yeats's late themes; of those, lust is only one.

But the sexual theme is our current concern, and we may look first at the poem "The Wild Old Wicked Man"; it is an especially interesting case in that it shows us this very transformation of motivation from personal to impersonal. For the most part it is quite literally true here that there is no objective reason to suppose that the speaker in the poem is Yeats himself rather than an abstract dramatic projection of motive. We make the identification with Yeats, I suppose, out of our stubborn habit of associating each of any poet's speakers, especially first-person speakers, with the poet himself, and of course because we have heard Yeats speak similarly before in *propria persona.* But now the identification is unnecessary and indeed unfortunate, because it tends to falsify theme. That theme of indomitable passion, generalized and impersonal, a sort of universal good, is evoked, we find, as much by the suggestive refrain, "Daybreak and a candle-end," as by the dramatic argument from stanza to stanza.

The "wild old wicked man/ Who travels where God wills" makes his plea to a coy mistress, "Kind are all your words, my dear,/ Do not the rest withhold," and goes on to boast not only of his potency but of the special seductions of his experience and his eloquence:

> *"I have what no young man can have*
> *Because he loves too much.*
> *Words I have that can pierce the heart,*
> *But what can he do but touch?"*
> Daybreak and a candle-end.

The reluctant lady, who speaks only once, refuses him on grounds of religion:

> *"Love to give or to withhold*
> *Is not at my command.*
> *I gave it all to an older man:*
> *That old man in the skies.*
> *Hands that are busy with His beads*
> *Can never close those eyes."*
> Daybreak and a candle-end.

(The probability that it is Maud Gonne's conversion to Catholicism which lingers in Yeats's mind here makes this the only "personal" reference in the poem.) Seeing the hopelessness of his suit, the old man dismisses the lady at once and turns to more susceptible quarry:

> *"Go your ways, O go your ways,*
> *I choose another mark,*
> *Girls down on the seashore*
> *Who understand the dark;*
> *Bawdy talk for the fishermen;*
> *A dance for the fisher-lads;*
> *When dark hangs upon the water*
> *They turn down their beds."*
> Daybreak and a candle-end.

Then, after a stanza which reasserts the old man's virility and his wit, the poem closes with two stanzas of rowdy philosophy which first confess universal tragedy then undercut it, or try to, pragmatically with the "second-best," Passion as Defense:

> *"All men live in suffering,*
> *I know as few can know,*
> *Whether they take the upper road*
> *Or stay content on the low,*
> *Rower bent in his row-boat*
> *Or weaver bent at his loom,*
> *Horseman erect upon horseback*
> *Or child hid in the womb."*
> Daybreak and a candle-end.

> *"That some stream of lightning*
> *From the old man in the skies*
> *Can burn out that suffering*
> *No right-taught man denies.*
> *But a coarse old man am I,*
> *I choose the second-best*
> *I forget it all awhile,*
> *Upon a woman's breast."*
> Daybreak and a candle-end.

Yeats carries this impersonality, or abstract passion, or willed detachment from his own passional argument, yet further in others of his "sex" poems, by simple and efficient devices. Sometimes, as in "The Wild Old Wicked Man," he affects a careful anonymity; sometimes, as in "The Three Bushes," he designates persons noncommittally by station or office: "lady," "lover," "chambermaid"; sometimes, as in the "Crazy Jane" sequence or in "Malachi Stilt-Jack" of "High Talk," he consciously names his persons tragi-comically; in "Supernatural Songs" he reverts to favorite personae of Celtic myth; or he may simply choose good generic Irish names, as in "John Kinsella's Lament for Mrs. Mary Moore." His purpose is obvious and important: he aims to assert that this is not his own passion, not an old man's pathetic sexuality, it is man's passion, Everyman's—hence the faceless anonymity. But his management of tone in these poems is, of course, a good deal more fundamental than such devices in his achievement of "impersonality"; and that is not a matter to be explained in a phrase or two, or perhaps, to be explained at all. Every reader must accept it from the poems themselves.

The intricate tragi-comic balance of many of these poems is probably best caught in the last-named poem above. I suppose it is crudely possible to classify "John Kinsella's Lament" as "light verse," as one anthologist has done.[45] But it is clearly a poem of heartbreak, a good deal heavier than light; and whatever its deliberate boozy rowdiness, it is, as much as any other of Yeats's poems, "an act of faith and reason to make one rejoice in the midst of tragedy." The poem is a true lament, and it begins by impugning Death's bad taste in choosing the valuable one, John Kinsella's "old bawd":

> *He might have had my sister,*
> *My cousins by the score,*
> *But nothing satisfied the fool*
> *But my dear Mary Moore,*
> *None other knows what pleasures man*
> *At table or in bed.*
> What shall I do for pretty girls
> Now my old bawd is dead?

The last stanza will be enough to evoke the poem's fine posture of defiance of every value but the true one, the emotional:

> *The priests have got a book that says*
> *But for Adam's sin*
> *Eden's garden would be there*
> *And I there within.*

[45] Oscar Williams, ed., *A Little Treasury of Modern Poetry* (New York, Charles Scribner's Sons, 1950).

No expectation fails there,
No pleasing habit ends,
No man grows old, no girl grows cold,
But friends walk by friends.
Who quarrels over halfpennies
That plucks the trees for bread?
What shall I do for pretty girls
Now my old bawd is dead?

It is Passion as Defense, obviously, but in the scornful grace of its ballad measure and in the pleasure it takes in its own defiant incongruities, the "lament" rises as well into an affirmative Joy.

But perhaps the strangest and most exciting of all these "wild old wicked man" poems is "News for the Delphic Oracle." Its excitement is of a different quality from that of all Yeats's other "sex" poems, and it moves one very differently than does the intimate pathos of "John Kinsella's Lament." The poem may easily strike some readers as decidedly unpleasant. There is an air of almost gloating savagery about it, and Yeats's leer here comes closer to being genuinely salacious than in any other poem. The nearly brutal irony which informs the poem from the title to the last word of the text comes, I think, from Yeats's arrogant assurance of the rightness and necessity of his view of passion and his cocky desire to state that view under the most overbearing figure he can conceive. "News for the Delphic Oracle" is his sardonic commentary upon the following sweetly florid reassurance given by the Cumaean Sibyl to Amelius, disciple of Plotinus, who had asked her of the fate of Plotinus's soul:

> Celestial! Man at first, but nearing now the lot of the divine! The bonds of human fate are loosed for you, and, strong of heart, you beat your eager way from out the roaring tumult of this fleshly life to the shores of that wavewashed coast free

from the thronging of the guilty, thence to take the grateful path of the sinless soul. Where glows the splendor of God, where Right is throned in the stainless place, far from the wrong that mocks at law, where all is unison and winning tenderness and guileless joy. Where dwell the just Aeacus, and Plato, consecrated power, and fair Pythagoras and all else that form the choir of Immortal Love; there where the heart is ever lifted in joyous festival. O Blessed One, you have fought your many fights, now, crowned with unfading life, your days are with the Ever-Holy![46]

Yeats takes, obviously, the keenest pleasure in acidifying all this lush prophecy into a brilliantly bitter panorama of lust invading the precincts of the Ever-Holy and transforming it into an anarchic bacchanalia: lust survives even death itself and mocks Paradise in its own power. The poem is almost oppressively dazzling. In its mastery of sardonic tone, economy of ironic image, and easy manipulation of a kind of synoptic chaos, it is one of Yeats's great technical triumphs. The poem has clear affinities to the earlier "Byzantium"—in its presentation of a scene of "dreaming back" after death, its setting in the mystic exoticism of the Yeatsian otherworld, its images of souls in passage, and so on—and it is a revealing exercise to set the two poems side by side. Nothing will show more clearly the radical shifts of Yeats's last poems into new reaches of strangeness in tone, tempo, and theme. Having said this much, it is probably enough now simply to leave the poem to make its own points without analysis of detail:

I

There all the golden codgers lay,
There the silver dew,
And the great water sighed for love,

46 Kimon Friar and John Malcolm Brinnin, eds., *Modern Poetry,* (New York, Appleton-Century-Crofts, 1951), 551.

And the wind sighed too.
Man-picker Niamh leant and sighed
By Oisin on the grass;
There sighed amid his choir of love
Tall Pythagoras.
Plotinus came and looked about,
The salt-flakes on his breast,
And having stretched and yawned awhile
Lay sighing like the rest.

II

Straddling each a dolphin's back
And steadied by a fin,
Those Innocents re-live their death,
Their wounds open again.
The ecstatic waters laugh because
Their cries are sweet and strange,
Through their ancestral patterns dance,
And the brute dolphins plunge
Until, in some cliff-sheltered bay
Where wades the choir of love
Proffering its sacred laurel crowns,
They pitch their burdens off.

III

Slim adolescence that a nymph has stripped,
Peleus on Thetis stares.
Her limbs are delicate as an eyelid,
Love has blinded him with tears;
But Thetis' belly listens.
Down the mountain walls
From where Pan's cavern is
Intolerable music falls.
Foul goat-head, brutal arm appear,
Belly, shoulder, bum,
Flash fishlike; nymphs and satyrs
Copulate in the foam.

Clearly this carries us beyond the plane of the simply real and into the neighborhood of that phenomenon I have called Passion as Apocalypse. I have meant by that term, chiefly, a kind of hyperbolic or fantastic utterance, a studiously oblique abstraction carefully separated from its physical and emotional bases; a way of making ironic commentary upon thought or feeling for which a plainer intellectual approach seems to Yeats inadequate. It involves a kind of disembodiment, and yet results in a special luminous transparency. It is another of those postures "the other side of tragedy," adopted when the basic tragic cycle of disaster, suffering, reconciliation, and joy has been run through and, so to speak, "mastered." It declares its mastery by its defiant independence of logical and empirical roots; it is essentially a gaudy demonstration of the bloody-unbowed spirit, a little bit mad perhaps; "You can kill me but you can't eat me."

"News for the Delphic Oracle" is such a flourish, and could have been cited under the heading of Passion as Apocalypse if we had chosen to handle it so. A good many other poems we have examined had some similar traits, "Byzantium," for example, and "Nineteen Hundred and Nineteen"; and most of Yeats's late plays have this strange apocalyptic excitement and logical dislocation.

I should like to look now at only three poems from his last volume which seem to me to belong fully in this category: "The Statesman's Holiday," "The Circus Animals' Desertion," and "High Talk." The very titles of the poems perhaps define the mode more efficiently than my attempted explication above. These three poems have been scarcely noticed at all by commentators on Yeats, but I feel they need to be seen as among the most comprehensively significant of all his lyrics.

In "The Statesman's Holiday" he has at least implicitly in mind, I suspect, his own late years as senator of Ireland, and he makes bittersweet ironic metaphor with his half-comic sense of himself in that toga as his point of abstract departure. The poem is made of three rough twelve-line stanzas with one of his most gaudily lovely refrains, "Tall dames go walking in grass-green Avalon." It is an undistinguished poem until about midway, when it takes on its essential nature and stature. The first stanza details the familiar Yeatsian disgust with the ignoble dullness and mediocrity of public life in his time, and ends with the standard Yeatsian resolve: "So I have picked a better trade/ And night and morning sing:/ *Tall dames go walking in grass-green Avalon.*" In the second stanza he lists the public figures with whom he might be ironically confused, then explodes, "Ach, call me what you please!" At this point the poem comes to life, not violently but lyrically. Yeats will be none of the things he has scorned, but a pastoral bard of the utmost simplicity and abstract loveliness; when the sophisticated values have all turned corrupt, he will make his functional return to the primitive sources of beauty:

Here's a Montenegrin lute,
And its old sole string
Makes me sweet music
And I delight to sing:
Tall dames go walking in grass-green Avalon.

The third stanza extends the abstraction into a kind of primer-imagery of vivid nonsense. The nonsense, of course, makes the most crucial sense: ultimately only the heart's passion is true, "passion to me is the essential." Return, as Bitter Fool, to innocence, return to rags, to crime, to the keenness of the animals, return to pride, to gauds and jingles, return to comedy and to dirt, he says, and be renewed in passion:

With boys and girls about him,
With any sort of clothes,

With a hat out of fashion,
With old patched shoes,
With a ragged bandit cloak,
With an eye like a hawk,
With a stiff straight back,
With a strutting turkey walk,
With a bag full of pennies,
With a monkey on a chain,
With a great cock's feather,
With an old foul tune.
Tall dames go walking in grass-green Avalon.

We sense, once more, Maud's contribution to the imagery: she is the model for the tall dames, and hers is the hawk and the "stiff straight back."

"The Circus Animals' Desertion" needs a rather more detailed reading, not because it is a difficult poem but because it is much fuller and more specific in content. It is an important and revealing poem to read now as we near the end of this examination of Yeats in his frame of tragedy; for it too is a "testamentary" poem, almost the last of those roll-calling poems in which Yeats sought to survey his own career. In this one he reveals a crucial truth about his own sense of himself. The poem is made of five stanzas in Yeats's favorite ottava rima form, grouped in three sections. The first and last stanzas frame the poem by stating the theme candidly, though differently.

Stanza 1 presents the old poet seeking a theme and failing to find it. "Maybe at last," he concludes, "being but a broken man,/ I must be satisfied with my heart." Deserted by inspiration and fancy, he may be driven to revert to the raw material, the primitive tissue of emotion. At the moment he says nothing of that organ other than that it is an old man's needy retreat. Laconically, then, picking up the extravagant figure of the title, Yeats leads in the gaudy caravan of the themes of his prime of poetic life:

Winter and summer till old age began
My circus animals were all on show,
Those stilted boys, that burnished chariot,
Lion and woman and the Lord knows what.

Each of the three stanzas of the second section recalls the central theme of one of his major works, and in each case Yeats tries to make clear his own personal relation to the theme, the work in which it was embodied, and the emotion which gave it rise. The tone is what it should be, that of a mature, ruminative mind in conversation with itself. The verse movement is masterfully easy yet closely controlled. "What can I do but enumerate old themes?" asks the first line of this section, and the stanza goes on to recall "that sea-rider Oisin led by the nose/ Through three enchanted islands, allegorical dreams,/ Vain gaiety, vain battle, vain repose." All this he judges as "Themes of the embittered heart, or so it seems,/ That might adorn old songs or courtly shows." The bitterness was not his, Yeats implies; what had moved him was his own vaguely but avidly necessitous heart, creating a surrogate romantic passion: "But what cared I that set him on to ride./ I, starved for the bosom of his faery bride?" Yeats then turns to the "counter-truth" of *The Countess Cathleen.* And all its fantastic ironic tale, he makes clear, was nothing more than elaborate metaphor, a figurative premonitory construction of his fears for Maud's fanatic heart: "I thought my dear must her own soul destroy,/ So did fanaticism and hate enslave it." "This brought forth a dream," he goes on. The "dream" is in one sense the art-object, the play itself, but by extension the "dream" of Irish nationalism, the Celtic Renaissance, of course the Abbey Theatre especially. But the important line is the one which closes the stanza, making Yeats's crucial emotional identification with the created thing: "This dream itself had all my thought and love." The next stanza makes this identification a good deal more specific. It speaks of his early play "On Baile's Strand": "When the Fool and Blind Man stole the bread/ Cuchulain fought the ungovernable sea." "Heart-mysteries there," he says, as he had said of his tale of Oisin. But again he maintains that it was not the "mysteries" themselves which held him so much as their corporate image:

> *Heart-mysteries there, and yet when all is said*
> *It was the dream itself enchanted me:*
> *Character isolated by a deed*
> *To engross the present and dominate memory.*
> *Players and painted stage took all my love,*
> *And not those things that they were emblems of.*

"Not those things that they were emblems of" is the key line of the poem's developing argument, and it signalizes a fundamental conclusion in Yeats's understanding of himself: important as has been his whole philosophizing tendency, at its deepest and truest level his imagination is a dramatizing and sensate one, concretizing and image-making. And what animates and fertilizes the true dream is the heart and the heart's emotion. This is made movingly clear in the poem's last stanza, another of Yeats's great stanzas, I think. It is the tone, imagery, and theme of this particular stanza which lead me to classify what is otherwise a relatively sober reflective poem among the poems of Passionate Apocalypse. Yeats makes here one of the most moving and conclusive of all his assertions of the elemental primacy of passion for him, passion as the real primitive tissue out of which rise all the "ladders" of art and philosophy, and without whose fertile vulgarity and uninstructed fanatic emotion they are nothing:

> *Those masterful images because complete*
> *Grew in pure mind, but out of what began?*
> *A mound of refuse or the sweepings of a street,*

Old kettles, old bottles, and a broken can,
Old Iron, old bones, old rags, that raving slut
Who keeps the till. Now that my ladder's gone,
I must lie down where all the ladders start,
In the foul rag-and-bone shop of the heart.

It is the great tragic recognition of Crazy Jane again, the figure of the Lion and the Honeycomb:

But love has pitched his mansion in
The place of excrement;
For nothing can be sole or whole
That has not been rent.

"High Talk" also bears a title of involuted irony, and wildly figurative, yet it is also the one right descriptive title for the content of the poem. It seems to me an astonishingly brilliant poem, a perfected fantastic realization unlike anybody else's poem and unlike anything else in Yeats. In its creation of an extravagant unreality, it is closest, I suppose, to the last stanza of "Nineteen Hundred and Nineteen" and to "News for the Delphic Oracle." It is the kind of absolute poem about which it is extremely difficult, and probably unprofitable, to talk at length. It makes its own devastatingly adequate commentary upon itself. I set it down here complete so that it may speak for itself undisturbed, and then I will go on to say what seems unavoidable:

Processions that lack high stilts have nothing that catches
the eye.
What if my great-granddad had a pair that were twenty foot
high,
And mine were but fifteen foot, no modern stalks upon higher,
Some rogue of the world stole them to patch up a fence or a fire.
Because piebald ponies, led bears, caged lions, make but poor
shows,

Because children demand Daddy-long-legs upon his timber toes,
Because women in the upper storeys demand a face at the pane,
That patching old heels they may shriek, I take to chisel and plane.

Malachi Stilt-Jack am I, whatever I learned has run wild,
From collar to collar, from stilt to stilt, from father to child.
All metaphor, Malachi, stilts and all. A barnacle goose
Far up in the stretches of night; night splits and the dawn breaks loose;
I, through the terrible novelty of light, stalk on, stalk on;
Those great sea-horses bare their teeth and laugh at the dawn.

One hardly knows where to begin. It is a highly excited and deeply exciting poem. "All metaphor, Malachi, stilts and all." Yeats seldom stays with any metaphor so long as he stays with this one. That he develops this one so intricately, so long and grandly, in such mad speech, suggests that it satisfied him rarely and specially. "Malachi Stilt-Jack," "Daddy-long-legs upon his timber toes," must be, certainly, Yeats himself; he has found the one great metaphor for himself which we could never have predicted and for which we had no right to hope. In its insane way, the poem says the same things as "The Statesman's Holiday" and "The Circus Animals' Desertion." It is a poem "elevating" passion in an inspired hyperbole; it mocks conventional values by a dislocation of proportion and perspective which asserts the categorical virtue of extravagance. What matters most is the stretching of passion until it dominates fate and creates its own world. If I am right about the poem's meaning, it embodies in the most powerful single figure Yeats ever conceived the ultimate of all his humanistic presumptions. This figure rises on shafts of its own creation until it faces the shrouding element, dominates and alters it, then presses on in a new overbearing reality imposed upon the cosmos itself:

". . . night splits and the dawn breaks loose;/ I, through the terrible novelty of light, stalk on, stalk on."

The poem is a massive piece of the Yeatsian Apocalypse. The very length and sweep of the lines bespeak his confident joy in the size of his vision. The poem's place in the system of tragedy is easier to feel than to describe. But as I see it, all this loftiness, this surreal hyperbole, this grand stiff movement, this potent muscularity, collect themselves into the reconstituted total of the parts of the shattered spirit. The poem asserts the power of the will to reassemble itself, reanimate itself, and to create for the self-reconstituted man a joyously habitable environment. The creation of that "terrible novelty of light," the light of passion illuminating its own asserted universe, had been the goal of all Yeats's last poems.

"No modern stalks upon higher." That is the point at which one would prefer to take leave of Yeats. But he almost forces one to conclude with "Under Ben Bulben" by depositing his own epitaph there. Yet that seems to me a lesser poem than those we have just read, and it sinks anticlimactically if we are carrying those in mind. Yeats makes a formal and on the whole deplorable return upon his own self-conscious Celticism in "Under Ben Bulben," and that had always been really the phoniest side of him: "Irish poets, learn your trade . . . ." Yeats was after all too big a man to bother with that sort of special pleading; he was a world-poet, not an Irish poet. And the famous epitaph,

Cast a cold eye
On life, on death.
Horseman, pass by!

that, too, falsifies Yeats. He had never really known how to cast a cold eye either on life or on death. His eye was one of the warmest ever granted a man by God. He was a man like his own Cuchulain, "A man that had six mortal wounds," all of them earned in conflict with tragic reality, and none of them quite sufficient to kill him—"a man violent and famous." One may, I suppose, find something abstract, possibly even something "cold," in a Montenegrin lute with "its old sole string," or in the heart conceived as a "foul rag-and-bone shop," or in a Malachi Stilt-Jack "stalking on"; but the "terrible novelty of light" in which those images move is cold only in the sense that it is high. It is the high cold light of achieved revelation.

CHAPTER EIGHT

Conclusions

Early in his "Excursus on the Ritual Forms Preserved in Greek Tragedy," Gilbert Murray outlined a "normal sequence" of the successive movements of the "original Dionysus Mystery," the primitive Eniautos-celebrations, which follow the "normal pattern for the fate of the Year-Daimon" or Year-Spirit: "Agon, Pathos, Messenger, Threnos, Theophany, or, we might say, Anagnorisis and Theophany."[1] At the end of his essay Murray anglicized his "normal sequence" as "Contest, Tearing-Asunder, Messenger, Lamentation, Discovery, Recognition, and Resurrection."[2] The sequence is a figurative dramatization of brute facts of life, and an effort to control those facts by group practice of mimetic magic: life is sustained

1 In Jane Harrison's *Themis,* 344.
2 *Ibid.,* 362.

by the fertility of the earth, which is in turn subject to the cyclical flux of the seasons, waxing and waning—"Keeping his seasons and rages," to adapt a perfectly harmonious phrase of Eliot's from "The Dry Salvages." The center of the ritual symbolism is the analogy between the four-part division of the year, Spring, Summer, Autumn, Winter, and, wishfully, Spring again, and the "seasons" of man's life, youth, maturity, old age, death, and, wishfully, rebirth. Just as the twenty-four-hour day-night performs in microcosm the rhythm of the year, so the life of one man performs in microcosm the rhythm of the life of the race.

I would suggest the thesis that the poems of W. B. Yeats, taken as a whole, draw a design substantially identical to the design of the Dionysus-mystery which is the primitive original of tragedy; and two hypotheses: first, that the original tragic design is still the governing design of "systematic" tragedy—the codified dramatic form and literary concept; second, that any fully serious order of thought or of art, not utterly idealistic or utterly fatalistic, will likewise almost helplessly reproduce the ideological configuration expressed in the "normal sequence" of archetypal tragic ritual—thus that this ritual ordains the great "normative" pattern of serious human thought at least in the Western World.

My thesis I hope to demonstrate. My two hypotheses I have no hope of proving, and I throw them out as matters of personal conviction and grounds for argument. The first of them is quite unoriginal, and has been developed by Murray and Herbert Weisinger, among others. The second may or may not be original, and it is probably undemonstrable. I almost hope so; for, like Murray's suspicions as to the innate limitation of tragic subject matter,[3] it strikes me as a "terrifying" hypothesis—implying our helpless lack of originality in

[3] "Hamlet and Orestes," *The Classical Tradition in Poetry,* 226.

thought, and our helpless incapacity to "do" anything about the conduct of life. Still, it seems to me "indicated," though probably undemonstrable, and certainly horrible.

One thing which is certain, in any case, is the interrelationship of "systematic" or formal tragedy and "generic" tragedy, the philosophical or "sub-philosophical" sense of life. The first is a sophistication, a tailoring and projection, of the second; in the amalgam of "systematic" tragedy, "generic" tragedy supplies the subject matter to be subjected to the plastic ordering of drama. I note with some sense of shock, as a small instance of our helpless philosophical mimicry, that my own antithesis-synthesis comes to the same thing as the formula of Nietzsche: "Tragedy is the Apollonian embodiment of Dionysiac insights and powers."[4] He speaks of what I am calling "systematic" tragedy—Apollonian systematizing of Dionysiac or "generic" intuitions. But the "generic" tragic sense of life gets itself uttered in art forms other than the dramatic; and that is where Yeats and his lyrics come in. And yet the Yeatsian "generic" tragedy proves to fall into patterns notably like those of dramatic tragedy; and this leads us to the interesting multiple union: the ritual-generic, the systematic-dramatic, and the Yeatsian-lyrical all appear to roll themselves up into a ball—particolored, but still one ball—of philosophical significance.

Murray has proved the detailed survival of the primitive ritual elements in the Greek tragic plays, and the very familiarity of the names he gives to the stages in the ritual sequence makes the point, too. Seeing the plays in the context of the ritual order reminds us, as we tend to forget, that the typical Greek tragic ending was relatively "soft." Only relatively; but, judging by the single plays of Euripides, the *Oedipus at Colonus* of Sophocles, and by the ending of the *Oresteia* of Aeschylus, the only extant complete trilogy, it does appear that

[4] Nietzsche, *op. cit.,* 56–57.

the Greek tragedians habitually lightened their tragic actions somewhat with a Theophany at the end, promising either the restored benevolence of the gods, or, as in the case of Oedipus, the actual apotheosis of the tragic hero.[5]

If we accept Shakespeare as the norm, as he certainly is the giant, of "modern" tragedy, the case is different, and harsher. The general ritual resemblance continues, but what Shakespeare does is to adopt the logic but to telescope the units of the Eniautos-sequence. Of the primitive Greek order of Contest, Tearing-Asunder, Messenger, Lamentation, Discovery, Recognition, and Resurrection, the Messenger and the Lamentation (the least organic of the Greek elements) tend to disappear as formal members of the Shakespearean sequence. The Contest and the Tearing-Asunder remain to compose the bulk of the tragic action. The Resurrection disappears in its Greek sense of a supernatural manifestation of power and benevolence. But it reappears, reduced and secularized, to join with the Discovery (of tragic truth) and the Recognition (of tragic guilt and error) in the final complex cathartic effect of the great Shakespearean endings: the effect we commonly call "Reconciliation." The Reconciliation, I take it, involves the humble confession of fallibility, the admission of inadequacy and of the wrongness of pride, submission to the rightness and power of a "moral order," or "secret cause," or, perhaps, "a divinity that shapes our ends"—though Reconciliation certainly does not occur in Shakespeare in any simple *mea culpa,* take-me-to-heaven sense. When Horatio says, at the end of *Hamlet,* "Good night, sweet prince,/ And flights of angels sing thee to thy rest!" nobody understands the speech literally. Hamlet, Lear, Othello, Macbeth, Brutus, Antony, are all "Dead, dead, dead!" and we know the fact is tragic and not

[5] "Excursus on the Ritual Forms Preserved in Greek Tragedy," in Jane Harrison's *Themis,* 347–54.

to be salvaged by any thought of apotheosis. They are "reconciled" and "reconstituted"—too late—before death, but not "resurrected," not other than fatally dead.

But neither in the Greeks, nor, certainly, in modern tragedy can we find a true equivalent survival of that important "special final peripeteia, from grief to joy" of the ritual, the disappearance of which puzzled Murray, and which he finally decided must have been embodied in the satyr-play, the fourth member of the early Greek tragic tetralogies.[6] I am going to suggest that in the poems of Yeats we can find just such a peripeteia, "from grief to joy," that his last poems—with their sensuality, and all those emotional and technical hyperboles which we can group and call apocalyptic passion—have to be seen as a quite literal lyric equivalent of the satyr-play. But I have maintained that the total design of Yeats's generic-tragic lyrics reproduces the total design of primitive tragedy, and of that systematic tragedy which follows the basic sequence of the ritual. We must first demonstrate this large general resemblance, and then fit the satyr-element into the big picture.

The main lines of the argument are suggested by my categories of Yeatsian passion: Defense, Joy, Innocence, Apocalypse; or by a cardinal prose text such as, "To me the supreme aim is an act of faith and reason to make one rejoice in the midst of tragedy";[7] or by a cardinal poetic text such as, "All things fall and are built again,/ And those that build them again are gay." The Yeatsian version of the tragic sequence includes Agon, Pathos, Threnos, Anagnorisis, and Theophany—except that the god who manifests himself is man. In more familiar terms, it includes Suffering, Opposition, Reconciliation, Transmutation, and Transcendence. To "rejoice in the midst of tragedy" is to transmute tragic fact into its opposite.

[6] *Ibid.*, 344–45.
[7] *Letters to Dorothy Wellesley*, 13.

"All things fall" confesses tragic fact; "and are built again" asserts transmutation of tragic fact, man's adequacy to it; "those that build them again are gay" asserts transcendence of tragic fact, man's superiority to it. We may try to recall and redistribute in their significant sequence those statements from Yeats's prose and poetry which will show most compactly the logic of his thought about tragedy.

Everything begins with the negative pole of the tragic antinomy: the confession of *lacrimae rerum,* the immanence of suffering, the strict equation drawn between tragedy and "life" —life *is* tragedy. This recognition follows hard upon the corollary rejection of the "dream" of happiness and well-being and the perfectibility of things, as a normative or even possible condition:

> Children play at being great and wonderful people, at the ambitions they will put away for one reason or another before they grow into ordinary men and women. Mankind as a whole had a like dream once; everybody and nobody built up the dream bit by bit, and the ancient story-tellers are there to make us remember what mankind would have been like, had not fear and the failing will and the laws of nature tripped up its heels.[8]

The true condition of life is very different:

> We seek reality with the slow toil of our weakness and are smitten from the boundless and the unforeseen. Only when we are saint or sage, and renounce Experience itself, can we, in the language of the Christian Caballa, leave the sudden lightning and the path of the serpent and become the bowman who aims his arrow at the center of the sun.[9]

We begin fairly, in the confidence of strength and beauty,

[8] "Lady Gregory's Translations," *CA,* 20–21.
[9] "Anima Hominis," *PASL,* 45–47.

But a raving autumn shears
Blossom from the summer's wreath.

Life is "disaster," a discipline of constantly new disaster, and merely following the rhythm of disastrous events is enough to make an artist constantly "original":

> It is not permitted to a man, who takes up pen or chisel, to seek originality, for passion is his only business, and he cannot but mold or sing after a new fashion because no disaster is like another.[10]

Only a sentimental and dishonest art can deny these facts of life: all "happy art" expresses the "hollow image of fulfilled desire";[11] though it is true that if we abstract ourselves sufficiently from the brute processes of being, we can sustain the illusion of beneficence: "The food of the spiritual-minded is sweet, but passionate minds love bitter food."[12]

Acceptance of the discipline of disaster constitutes initiation into tragic maturity—the only true maturity: "We begin to live when we have conceived life as tragedy."[13] Initiated tragic man now turns about and begins to feed upon the tragic fact which tries to devour him. As he counters all that would deprive him, he becomes for the first time fully alive, and that creative abrasion sharpens his edge and polishes his metal. One recalls Hopkins'

sheer plod makes plow down sillion
Shine, and blue-bleak embers, ah my dear,
Fall, gall themselves, and gash gold-vermillion.

More prosaically, Yeats puts it,

[10] *Ibid.*, 44.
[11] *Ibid.*, 25–26.
[12] "Synge and the Ireland of His Time," *CA*, 171.
[13] *Autobiography*, 165.

> The poet finds his mask in disappointment, the hero in defeat. The desire that is satisfied is not a great desire, nor has the shoulder used all its might that an unbreakable gate has never strained.[14]

Tragic man begins to feel an actual hunger for "harsh facts, for ugly surprising things, for all that defies our hope."[15] And gradually he acquires an active distaste for the "sweet food" of the sentimentalists and rhetoricians of shorter vision: "this hateful cheerfulness."[16]

He comes to see the pattern of all experience, even love, as "tragic war."[17] He opposes that remorseless dialectic with all the resources of human passion: "passion ennobled by in tensity, by endurance, by wisdom";[18] thus, by violent activity, by rocky obduracy, by attempts to pierce the mystery of the "Mothers of Being, whose names are Wish, Will, Woe."[19] By turns he practices the passionate intensity of the Swordsman, Usheen or Cuchulain, countering the retreat from reality of the Saint; the endurance of the Fisherman, or Landor or Swift; the mystical insights of Blake, or Robartes or Ribh. He resolves to "die blaspheming,"[20] flourishing his indomitable will. Such comfort as he has comes from the sense of splendid commitment of the "fanatic heart":

> *Whatever flames upon the night*
> *Man's own resinous heart has fed.*

His heart, like Gloucester's, "bursts smilingly." Yeats draws up a full program of behavior for the tragic initiate, one that

14 "Anima Hominis," *PASL,* 40–41.
15 "Preface to the First Edition of *The Well of the Saints,*" *CA,* 143.
16 *Letters,* 722–23.
17 Yeats, "Ego Dominus Tuus," *Collected Poems,* 157.
18 *Letters,* 776.
19 Nietzsche, *op. cit.,* 124.
20 *Letters to Dorothy Wellesley,* 124.

will carry him out of the childhood of sentiment, through the life of creative conflict, to death in the free air, destroyed but not defeated:

> *No longer in Lethean foliage caught,*
> *Begin the preparation for your death*
> *And from the fortieth winter by that thought*
> *Test every work of intellect or faith,*
> *And everything that your own hands have wrought,*
> *And call those works extravagance of breath*
> *That are not suited for such men as come*
> *Proud, open-eyed and laughing to the tomb.*

Now the passion gradually calms and cools. The opposition continues, but it is differently based and more temperately expressed. The tragic initiate moves toward poise and peace. He has reached both resignation to tragic fact and a new sort of confidence, a sense of personal adequacy, as he sees he has not been spiritually killed by either the deprivation or the conflict. He is ready for his reconciliation. This is the cathartic state, purged of pity and fear, the effectual end of most systematic tragedy. This state of cleansed emptiness comes with the confession of nothingness:

> I shall find the dark grow luminous, the void fruitful when I understand I have nothing, that the ringers in the tower have appointed for the hymen of the soul a passing bell.[21]

It is an empty state, but not a quiescent one; the purification of suffering has cleared an entrance to new creativity:

> He only can create the greatest imaginable beauty who has endured all imaginable pangs, for only when we have seen and foreseen what we dread shall we be rewarded by that dazzling unforeseen wing-footed wanderer.[22]

21 "Anima Hominis," *PASL,* 29–32.
22 *Ibid.*

Yeats, as tragic initiate, "reconciled" to tragic truth, now makes a return upon reality, newly seen. He posits a kind of folk-truth, or blood wisdom, higher than logic, and running so deeply in the long racial underground of "emotional continuity" as to be out of reach even of tragic fatalism. "We suck always at the eternal dugs."[23]

> The abstract is not life and everywhere draws out the contradictions. You can refute Hegel but not the Saint or the Song of Sixpence.[24]

doubtless plum or cherry-branch
Sweetens the little half-way house
Those Chinamen climb towards, and I
Delight to imagine them seated there;
There, on the mountain and the sky,
On all the tragic scene they stare.
One asks for mournful melodies
Accomplished fingers begin to play.
Their eyes mid many wrinkles, their eyes,
Their ancient, glittering eyes, are gay.

This deep peace rests upon the greatest anagnorisis of all, the recognition that beauty is defined, made real, brought into being, only by the shocking contact with the ugly—the great paradox of joy out of suffering, fertility out of decay, the Lion and the Honeycomb:

"Fair and foul are near of kin,
And fair needs foul," I cried.
"My friends are gone, but that's a truth
Nor grave nor bed denied,
Learned in bodily lowliness
And in the heart's pride.

[23] *Letters*, 731.
[24] *Ibid.*, 922.

"A woman can be proud and stiff
When on love intent;
But Love has pitched his mansion in
The place of excrement;
For nothing can be sole or whole
That has not been rent."

So says Crazy Jane to the Bishop. With a requisite "intensity," Keats wrote, "All disagreeables evaporate from their being in close relationship with Beauty and Truth."[25] So in Yeats's thought fair and foul, loss and gain, take on the sadly beautiful unanimity of being simply "true," simply "life." One accepts them equally with a clean satisfaction beyond bitterness: "What matter if the ditches are impure?/ What matter if I live it all once more?" "I am content to live it all again/ And yet again, if it be life."

I had wild Jack for a lover;
Though like a road
That men pass over
My body makes no moan
But sings on:
All things remain in God.

But this purgative state, which is the pinnacle of systematic tragedy, serves Yeats as a plateau, a place of rest and reconstitution, more than passive, potentially fertile, looking toward that "joy which is the other side of sorrow."[26] "That shaping joy has kept the sorrow pure."[27]

Thus far in the Yeatsian sequence, all energy has been defensive energy, spent in patching against the tide of negative energies washing out from *lacrimae rerum*. In the phase of reconciliation, positive and negative energies stand off in vir-

[25] *Letters,* 70.
[26] "The Death of Synge," *Dramatis Personae,* 126.
[27] "Poetry and Tradition," *CA,* 128–31.

tual equilibrium; now the "shaping joy" which purifies sorrow tips the balance, the defensive energy turns to attack, and the process of transmutation, which will come to triumph in the phase of transcendence, has begun. Having survived the tragic discipline, the initiate starts up excitedly from his purgation and begins actively to impose his will on life. He has learned how to sublimate and how, variously, to "master" the processes of being. His "mastery" is the assertion of an absurdity, and deep inside he knows that too. He practices the absurdity because psychically it "works"—keeps him sane, makes life possible. The illusion of mastery is a powerful one, capable, in all but the darkest nights of the soul, of concealing its own falseness.

Yeats's tragic joy laughs in a variety of tones. Rarely, it speaks a kind of nihilistic abnegation, hollow and sardonic, as in

> *Irrational streams of blood are staining earth;*
> *Empedocles has thrown all things about;*
> *Hector is dead and there's a light in Troy;*
> *We that look on but laugh in tragic joy.*

Also rarely, it is an egotistic cackle, absconding from the contest or asserting the imperviousness of his own aesthetic fabrications, the superiority of art to life:

> *What's riches to him*
> *That has made a great peacock*
> *With the pride of his eye?*
>
> . . . .
>
> *Live he or die*
> *Amid wet rocks and heather,*
> *His ghost will be gay*
> *Adding feather to feather*
> *For the pride of his eye.*

It may express only a stoical obduracy:

> *Bred to a harder thing*
> *Than Triumph, turn away*
> *And like a laughing string*
> *Whereon mad fingers play*
> *Amid a place of stone,*
> *Be secret and exult,*
> *Because of all things known*
> *That is most difficult.*

More often and more deeply, his joy is a dynamic, transforming emotion, a gaiety "transfiguring all that dread." Synge's fine "astringent joy"[28] is of that essence, associated with "strength" and "hardness," but heightening or lightening those adamants, and setting them to the attack.

Tragic man shows his wounds as emblems of victory, not of defeat:

> *Soul clap its hands and sing, and louder sing*
> *For every tatter in its mortal dress.*

This is the basic tragic joy, the resurrection of the free-standing spirit from the ground of disaster:

> *And I would have all know that when all falls*
> *In ruin, poetry calls out in joy,*
> *Being the scattering hand, the bursting pod,*
> *The victim's joy among the holy flame.*

Yeats speaks in the ancient phoenix-imagery of overmastering fertility and rejuvenation. This spiritual transmutation of empirical disaster accumulates, ultimately and paradoxically, a humility and selflessness that is toughened by a reasserted egotism more racial than personal, braving the worst that fate can offer. Yeats himself locates this spiritual complex in the

[28] "Preface to the First Edition of *The Well of the Saints*," *CA*, 139–40.

ends of Shakespeare's tragedies; and Bradley, too, felt there an extra-Aristotelian emotion and called it "exultation."[29] It is an affirmation beyond the relative neutrality of catharsis. Perhaps we do have to list this among the great standard emotions of "systematic" tragedy, though to me it seems much more typically Shakespearean than Greek:

> Shakespeare's persons, when the last darkness has gathered about them, speak out of the ecstasy that is one half the self-surrender of sorrow, and one half the last playing and mockery of the victorious sword, before the defeated world. . . . Timon of Athens contemplates his own end, and orders his tomb by the beachy margent of the flood, and Cleopatra sets the asp to her bosom, and their words move us because their sorrow is not their own at tomb or asp, but for all men's fate. That shaping joy has kept the sorrow pure . . . .[30]

Yeats's location of the roots of this emotion in "generic" tragedy, in one's very sense of life, of "all men's fate," is expressed in this passage generalizing on the evidence of Synge:

> . . . he contemplates even his own death as it were another's and finds in his own destiny but as it were a projection through a burning glass of that general to men. There is in the creative joy an acceptance of what life brings, because we have understood the beauty of what it brings, or a hatred of death for what it takes away, which arouses within us, through some sympathy perhaps with all other men, an energy so noble, so powerful, that we laugh aloud and mock, in the terror or the sweetness of our exaltation, at death and oblivion.[31]

Finally, the transcendental impulse of the Yeatsian tragic joy is caught in the sexual-philosophical metaphor of the late play *The Herne's Egg:*

[29] "Hegel's Theory of Tragedy," *Criticism,* 61.
[30] "Poetry and Tradition," *CA,* 128–31.
[31] "Synge and the Ireland of His Time," *CA,* 162–64.

Strong sinew and soft flesh
Are foliage round the shaft
Before the arrowsmith
Has stripped it, and I pray
That I, all foliage gone,
May shoot into my joy.

Yeats's extra-tragic phase of transcendence, like his phase of joy, continues the affirmative counterattack upon life; and like his joy, it appears in many forms. Once his joy reaches that elevation he calls "ecstatic," it behaves variously: it may be very calm or very excited. When calm it lives in the condition of "innocence"; in its state of excitement it develops the Yeatsian equivalent of the satyr-play which is the raffish and extravagant *coda* of the tragic tetralogy.

Yeats found that he entered the state which was not quite love, but "more like innocence," when he "ceased to hate."[32] This variety of transcendence must be called a kind of emotionless emotion, "beyond tears and laughter," of evacuated motives, beyond the self, "the other side of tragedy"; poems of such mood he called in a letter "all emotion and all impersonal."[33] The metaphor of his own which best catches the state of transcendent innocence is his comment on the passage in Richard II,

Let us sit upon the ground
And tell sad stories of the death of kings;

"Do you not feel there the wide-open eyes"?[34] he asks. The tragic initiate is carried "beyond grief into pure contemplation,"[35] into a state Yeats does finally call, inclusively, "love,"

32 "Anima Hominis," *PASL,* 40–43.

33 *Letters,* 758.

34 *Letters to Dorothy Wellesley,* 65.

35 "The Tragic Theatre," *CA,* 197.

"a form of the eternal contemplation of what is."[36] The condition may approach "trance":

> Tragic art, passionate art, the drowner of dykes, the confounder of understanding, moves us by setting us to reverie, by alluring us almost to the intensity of trance. The persons upon the stage . . . greaten till they are humanity itself. We feel our minds expand convulsively or spread out slowly like some moon-brightened, image-crowded sea. That which is before our eyes perpetually vanishes and returns again in the midst of the excitement it creates, and the more enthralling it is, the more do we forget it.[37]

In that condition, "passion becomes wisdom."[38] "What is" is still brutally paradoxical: "Love has pitched his mansion in/ The place of excrement"; and still infallibly tragic: "that discourtesy of death." But the great ineluctable tragic evidences have taken on an air of distance and unreality, muted and blurred in the great fusions of "life" and "truth":

> *Till the wreck of body,*
> *Slow decay of blood,*
> *Testy delirium*
> *Or dull decrepitude,*
> *Or what worse evil come—*
> *The death of friends, or death*
> *Of every brilliant eye*
> *That made a catch in the breath—*
> *Seem but the clouds of the sky*
> *When the horizon fades;*
> *Or a bird's sleepy cry*
> *Among the deepening shades.*

"Our traditions only permit us to bless," now says the tragic

[36] *Letters to Dorothy Wellesley*, 126.
[37] "The Tragic Theatre," *CA*, 207.
[38] *Ibid.*, 198.

initiate, artist or Everyman, "for the arts are an extension of the beatitudes."[39] He concludes that there is only one possible ultimate emotion, "the emotion of multitude": "We are blest by everything." At the end all that is required of him is song; he becomes an anonymous voice "set upon a golden bough to sing." He may sing the crazy anthem of the old hermit:

> *While he'd rummaged rags and hair,*
> *Caught and cracked his flea, the third*
> *Giddy with his hundredth year,*
> *Sang unnoticed like a bird.*

On his dignity, his song will be "bird songs of an old man, joy in the passing moment, emotion without the bitterness of memory,"[40] "a last song, sweet and exultant, a sort of . . . *geeta,* not doctrine but song."[41] (*The Tempest* was Shakespeare's *geeta.*) What he sings of, out of "the artifice of eternity," to "lords and ladies of Byzantium," is transmuted and transcended actuality—"what is past, or passing, or to come."

This "wide-eyed," entranced, depersonalized, passionless "contemplation of what is" is one of the three last reaches of Yeats's mode of tragic transcendence. The other two, his rowdy sensuality and the complex of his apocalyptic hyperboles—of theme, image, speech, and music—are passionate indeed; and they compose the Yeatsian satyr-play, Murray's "special final peripeteia" in the tragic sequence, asserting the resurrection of the human spirit in renewed wholeness, ready to "live it all again." It is a return, with a sense of deep identification and in a mood of high excitement, to the oldest bases of being. Again we have to think of the primitive Dionysiac component in Nietzsche's synthesis, which speaks the first and last word in formal tragedy, and submits only medially and grudgingly to

39 *Letters,* 831–32.
40 *Ibid.,* 737.
41 *Ibid.,* 836.

the Apollonian plasticizing, in order that it may find an intelligible idiom; after which it "seeks to escape back into primordial reality."[42] So with these last great wild satyr-play poems of Yeats. In their fertility ritual, "an old man's frenzy," but splendid and imposing, the primordial reality to which return is made is the heart, for Yeats the seed-bed of passion, creativity and courage.

> *I sought a theme and sought for it in vain,*
> *I sought it daily for six weeks or so.*
> *Maybe at last, being but a broken man,*
> *I must be satisfied with my heart . . . .*

The return is to the "dung of passion,"[43] but dung in its archetypal duality of decay and fertility:

> *Now that my ladder's gone,*
> *I must lie down where all the ladders start,*
> *In the foul rag-and-bone shop of the heart.*

The note of pathos those passages sound is relevant but not central. The Dionysiac chorus of satyrs, says, Nietzsche, sang and danced "the metaphysical solace that, despite every phenomenal change, life is indestructibly joyful and powerful."[44] So, again, with the satyr-lyrics of Yeats. They may sing "an old, foul tune," celebrating the athletic sexuality of the "gay, warty lads":[45]

> *Down the mountain walls*
> *From where Pan's cavern is*
> *Intolerable music falls.*
> *Foul goat-head, brutal arm appear,*
> *Belly, shoulder, bum,*

[42] *Op. cit.,* 132.
[43] Eric Bentley, "Yeats as a Playwright," *PY,* 247.
[44] *Op. cit.,* 50.
[45] *Letters to Dorothy Wellesley,* 69.

Flash fishlike; nymphs and satyrs
Copulate in the foam.

But the foul tune is actually primitive-religious, aiming to dramatize the metaphysical solace of indestructible fertility and joy. And it carries with it the elevating conviction that in some mysterious way the lust of the body and the lust of the soul are deeply kin:

> One feels at moments as if one could with a touch convey a vision—that the mystic way and sexual love use the same means—opposed yet parallel existences.[46]

The satyr-poems speak a marrow-bone wisdom, cruder and tougher and more ancient than the cerebral:

God guard me from the thoughts men think
In the mind alone;
He that sings a lasting song
Thinks in a marrow-bone.

Its speech is extravagant, the images strange, the music cacophonous and wild; when "all is in the wine cup," the grapes do "begin to stammer":[47]

this pragmatical, preposterous pig of a world,
its farrow that so solid seem,
Must vanish on the instant if the mind but change its theme.

Malachi Stilt-Jack am I, whatever I learned has run wild,
From collar to collar, from stilt to stilt, from father to child.
All metaphor, Malachi, stilts and all. A barnacle goose
Far up in the stretches of night; night splits and the dawn breaks loose;

46 *Letters,* 714–15.
47 "Discoveries," *CA,* 91–93.

I, through the terrible novelty of light, stalk on, stalk on;
Those great sea-horses bare their teeth and laugh at the dawn.

Stephen Spender, who reacts, like Auden, ambivalently to Yeats—scornful of his philosophy but grateful for his technical poetic instruction—makes the outright charge that

> Yeats's poetry is devoid of any unifying moral subject, and it develops in a perpetual search for one. Although he has much wisdom, he offers no philosophy of life, but, as a substitute, a magical system, which, where it does not seem rhetorical, is psycho-analytic, but not socially constructive.[48]

In his evaluation of *Words for Music Perhaps*, especially of the lyrical sequences of Crazy Jane and Tom the Lunatic, Walter E. Houghton picks up these judgments of Spender as a focus for his own commentary. The force of Spender's attack, he concludes, is "vitiated by overstatement"; but, if the criticism is distorted, "it is the distortion of a truth, for *Words for Music Perhaps* is indeed devoid of any unifying moral subject, and for that reason it is not socially constructive."[49] The ground of Houghton's agreement with Spender is made clear in this paragraph:

> For all his citation of Sophocles and Shakespeare, Yeats produces a very different tragic effect. Because the hero is not at war with evil, within or without, we cannot feel that profound sense of pity and terror which comes from witnessing a world of moral disorder. On the contrary we "*rejoice* in every happiness that comes to him, and *sorrow* at his death as if it were our own." This is hardly the mood of tragic catharsis. It is the mood which Yeats, in 1938, rightly defines as the mood of his plays, "tragic ecstasy."[50]

48 "Yeats as a Realist," *PY*, 190.
49 "Yeats and Crazy Jane: The Hero in Old Age," *PY*, 385.
50 *Ibid.*

I do not wholly understand the judgments of these two men, and insofar as I do understand them, I mainly disagree with them. Not without gratitude: Mr. Houghton's essay, especially, is one of the most intelligent and helpful of all the published studies of Yeats; but I do feel moved to dispute some of these premises, hoping thereby to come closer to understanding and evaluating Yeats and his practice of tragedy.

Whether Spender is writing in 1934 from his specifically Marxist base makes little difference; it is accurate enough if we say he attacks Yeats on vaguely Christian-Socialist or "humane" grounds. The basic equation he draws is between "morality" and "social-constructivism." Yeats has no philosophy of life and no unifying morality because his system is not "socially constructive." Houghton's argument is allied but a good deal more complicated. He is wrong, to my way of thinking, because he thinks too narrowly here about both morality and tragedy. Implicitly, he posits a *proper* tragic subject, tragic conflict, and tragic emotion: "a world of moral disorder," a "war with evil," a "mood of tragic catharsis." Yeats is at fault, morally at fault, in his handling of all three elements, subject, conflict, and emotion. It is by quarreling with their definitions that I would hope to refute both Spender and Houghton.

Spender argues that that only is moral which is socially constructive—to which we must agree; but he further implies that only that which works progammatically at large-scale social amelioration is socially constructive. Looked at from that strict point of view, Yeats's thought may indeed appear cold, abstracted, idiosyncratic, egotistic, inhumane. But the key to the rebuttal of those charges is to be found in the falseness of Spender's dichotomy, "psycho-analytic, but not socially constructive." If we can agree that psychoanalysis is antisocial, or non-social, then Yeats is guilty as charged; but that case seems to me absurd. Of course psychoanalysis aims to be socially constructive: it aims to understand and reconstitute the sick individual and send him back, healed, into society, to clean and strengthen the social fabric by cleaning and strengthening the individuals who compose it. And Yeats's personalized, individuated, and admittedly highly eccentric approach to man and society has the same implicit program.

I suspect that Yeats differs from Spender, not morally, but practically: in the quantity of his hope—his far lesser optimism—and on grounds of ways and means. Unquestionably there was in Yeats a taint of the snob and the egoist. But these were not his deepest dye, which was humanistic and idealistic—ambitious for the race, not merely for the ego. "The persons upon the stage," he writes, "greaten till they are humanity itself."[51] He was concerned with "all men's fate,"[52] with the problems "general to men,"[53] and believed that the noblest personal energy rose out of "sympathy with all other men."[54] Yeats did, after all, try passionately to understand man and history. Doubtless he falsified both; any "systematizing" does so. You do not really understand man by "classifying" him, even if you cut your two "tinctures" into twenty-eight "phases" and churn those with four whirling "faculties"—but neither do you degrade and insult him. I should say Yeats's attempt is less crude than most, it is full of valuable insight, and it is certainly not *morally* culpable; whatever its eccentricities, they are humanistic rather than egoistic.

In shifting from the Aristotelian base, according to Mr. Houghton, Yeats produces "a very different tragic effect." Implicitly in Houghton's view Yeats's very different tragedy is inferior and explicitly it is "amoral." In Yeatsian tragedy, "the hero is not at war with evil;" rather the tragic subject is that of

51 "The Tragic Theatre," *CA,* 207.
52 "Poetry and Tradition," *CA,* 128–31.
53 "Synge and the Ireland of His Time," *CA,* 162–64.
54 *Ibid.*

the "heroic psychology of self-surrender and self-assertion."[55] Because the subject is not that of the universal moral warfare, the Yeatsian tragic emotion is not true catharsis, but a more intimate and lesser sentimental involvement and identification. At only one period, says Houghton, does Yeats show a "full awareness of evil"[56]—the nightmare period of the Great War and the Irish Revolution, roughly 1915–22, when he wrote such poems as "The Second Coming," "Meditations in Time of Civil War," and "Nineteen Hundred and Nineteen." These poems, Houghton agrees, are "great tragic odes," but their pity and terror is not "purified" because there is no "counteraffirmation."

> "The growing murderousness of the world" stands unchallenged; no hero faces "the Savage God" . . . Overwhelmed by this nightmare vision, Yeats could only revolt with a "rage to end all things." Had he come through this period of despair, and, with renewed faith in the heroism latent in man, still held fast to the moral problem, he would have created a tragic art in the same kind as Shakespeare's; but after the recoil toward mysticism he returned to the earlier mode of heroic art, however deepened and widened . . . . What he did find was an amoral faith in the heroic man.[57]

The argument is persuasive, but it rests upon assumptions with which we are not bound to agree. Certainly it would have shocked Yeats as a description of himself. If Yeats's "amoral" philosophy was what Houghton says it was, then it was not what Yeats thought it was. It was Yeats who posited a "Vision of Evil," and made the vision a criterion of greatness in art. He wrote of Shelley in *A Vision,*

> He lacked the Vision of Evil, could not conceive of the world

55 "Yeats and Crazy Jane: The Hero in Old Age," *PY,* 386.

56 *Ibid.* 57 *Ibid.,* 386–87.

> as a continual conflict, so, though great poet he certainly was, he was not of the greatest kind.[58]

Yeats and Houghton are operating with different definitions of evil, and so Yeats thinks he has the vision, and Houghton thinks he has it not.

What Houghton means by evil he does not make plain, and he seems to assume that we will understand him. I take it he means evil in the Christian sense of sin and wrongdoing, contrary to the laws of God, perpetrated by individuals or groups. Yeats recognized evil in that sense, and occasionally, as in "Nineteen Hundred and Nineteen," it formed his tragic subject—as Houghton says. But the evil of "The Second Coming," the evil of "The blood-dimmed tide is loosed, and everywhere/ The ceremony of innocence is drowned," symbolized by the great "rough beast" surrounded by the "indignant desert birds" of that fable—that is a different essence, and closer to what he means by the Vision of Evil. This is cosmic evil, that of "irrational streams of blood staining earth," of what W. M. Dixon called the "moral offensiveness" of the organization of things,[59] and Nietzsche called "the antagonism at the heart of the world";[60] in Yeats's words, that in the cosmic order which "defies our hope."[61] It was this cosmic enmity to man which defined full evil for Yeats. It is what he meant by "the world as a continual conflict" in the sentence on Shelley; Shelley, a "Godwin perfectibility man,"[62] to adapt Keats's description of their friend Dilke, had not grown up to that tragic truth.

This Yeatsian evil is not Christian, and I suppose one could say, technically, in that it is not subject to a right-wrong code

58 Page 144.
59 *Tragedy,* 140.
60 *Ibid.,* 71.
61 "Preface to the First Edition of *The Well of the Saints,*" *CA,* 143.
62 Keats, *Letters,* 234.

of conduct, that it is not a "moral" concept. But surely it is as fatal as any other evil, and is as genuinely philosophical, if not so familiarly theological. And to say that Yeatsian tragedy is "amoral" because it does not conduct the "war with evil" in standard terms, seems to me to emasculate both tragedy and morality. The true distinguishing fact again is Yeats's eccentric humanism: he wrote a humanist tragedy about a humanist evil rooted in a humanist morality.

Mr. Houghton's statements that Yeats offers "no counteraffirmation"; that " 'the growing murderousness of the world' stands unchallenged; no hero faces 'the Savage God' "; that he "could only revolt with a 'rage to end all things' "—all these seem to me to make errors of fact that need to be challenged. Yeats revolted in many ways other than that of nihilistic rage—in a great variety of counteraffirmations: in varieties of acceptance, the "eternal contemplation of what is," the "bird songs of an old man," his *geeta,* "sweet and sorrowful," all his "beatitudes"; in varieties of defiance, his "old man's frenzy," his Fisherman's toughness and his Swordsman's dynamic violence, his indomitable willingness to "live it all again, if it be life"; in varieties of transcendence, all those "ladders" rising out of the "foul rag-and-bone shop of the heart," all those "praises of joyous life," the poems of "tragic joy" in which "soul clap its hands and sing, and louder sing/ For every tatter in its mortal dress," all the yea-saying satyr-poems of the "wild old wicked man" and of Crazy Jane and John Kinsella, in all the extravagances of spirit and of craft in the poems of passionate apocalypse. The "rage to end all things" does not begin to contain the counteraffirmations of Yeats to tragic negation. His final emotion is not rage but joy, a complex joy which has looked into the heart of disaster and survived to praise life. So Keats wrote in his letters,

> Until we are sick, we understand not;—in fine, as Byron says, "Knowledge is Sorrow"; and I go on to say that "Sorrow is Wisdom"—and further for aught we can know for certainty "Wisdom is folly"![63]

And so Melville wrote, almost as if by echo:

> There is a wisdom that is woe; but there is a woe that is madness. And there is a Catskill eagle in some souls that can alike dive down into the blackest gorges, and soar out of them again and become invisible in the sunny spaces. And even if he for ever flies within the gorge, that gorge is in the mountains.[64]

These are the same essence as Yeats's "counteraffirmative" tragic joy, a thing larger than rage and larger than despair.

Mr. Houghton does seem to equate "a moral basis" and Christianity, "moral faith" with the sense of a "Divine Presence."[65] Having failed to find a moral faith, he says, Yeats ended up with an "amoral faith in the heroic man." Again the question and the conclusion seem to me less than fair. Yeats is not a Christian, he is a humanist: "Homer is my example, and his unchristened heart." He would come very close to accepting the shocking dictum of Protagoras, "Man is the measure of all things."

> *Death and life were not*
> *Till man made up the whole,*
> *Made lock, stock and barrel*
> *Out of his bitter soul,*
> *Aye, sun and moon and star, all.*
> *And further add to that*

63 *Ibid.*, 141.

64 *Moby Dick* (New York, Oxford University Press, 1947), 398–99.

65 "Yeats and Crazy Jane: The Hero in Old Age," *PY,* 387.

That, being dead, we rise,
Dream and so create
Translunar Paradise.

Is humanism by definition amoral? Perhaps so; but only if so, is Yeats's faith amoral. Of his Homer with "his unchristened heart" Yeats asks, "What theme had Homer but original sin?" Morality is not the property of a single theology, though a single theology may embody it most greatly. Mr. Houghton says that Yeats falls back from a social morality to a "faith in the heroic man." What makes that statement misleading is the definite article: Yeats's faith is in "heroic man," not "the heroic man." He is not talking about exceptional isolated humanist heroes, the lone Prometheus, but of a heroism "general to men," racial Prometheanism. The concept may be foolish but it is not amoral. The "I" of Yeats, as of Whitman, is a "generic I." No other induction is really possible from such poems as the Crazy Jane poems Mr. Houghton uses as his instance: their hero is Everyman. Yeats himself, at least, placed his idea of heroism in very respectable company. Near the end of his life he wrote to Ethel Mannin, "Blessed be heroic death (Shakespeare's tragedies), blessed be heroic life (Cervantes), blessed be the wise (Balzac)."[66]

The faith of Yeats in heroic man is not the weakness of his tragic vision, but the very center of its strangeness and its strength. Yeats is a very great heretic; his spiritual arrogance is complete. His respect for man is so absolute that he leaves him alone with tragedy. Stripped of all supernatural reference, man stands naked before tragic fact; his destiny is his own to make. Every man is newly primitive man in an alien universe: the situation of generic tragedy. Yeats's tragic fable is a fable without a solution except that resident in the spirit of man.

[66] *Letters,* 832.

"The east has its solutions always and therefore knows nothing of tragedy. It is we, not the east, that must raise the heroic cry." If man performs well in the tragic action, he is permitted to walk on at the end in his own absurd and splendid Theophany. As a sense of man, of art, and of life, it seems to me superbly arrogant and intensely exciting. Yeatsian tragedy has the greater richness of being a way of life as well as of art: "We begin to live when we have conceived life as tragedy." Yeats would like to take his tragic man through the course of the systematic tragic discipline, then send him back into life, instructed and chastened, but equipped with new powers of transcendence, and ready, like Malachi Stilt-Jack, to stalk on through the terrible novelty of light.

Index

William Butler Yeats: The Lyric of Tragedy has been set on the Linotype in eleven-point Baskerville, with two points of leading between lines. Linotype Baskerville is a recent revival of the mid-eighteenth century design by John Baskerville, whose type was the first English roman of the "transitional" family.

Norman

University of Oklahoma Press

92
30
122

JOSÉ

ARMANDO PALACIO VALDÉS

TRANSLATION AND INTRODUCTION

BY HARRIET DE ONÍS

BARRON'S EDUCATIONAL SERIES, INC.
GREAT NECK NEW YORK

PRINTED IN THE UNITED STATES OF AMERICA

Library of Congress Catalogue Card No. 61-8199

ARMANDO PALACIO VALDÉS
(1853-1938)

José, one of the most popular and widely translated of Palacio Valdés's many novels, is here presented in a new English version. It is the moving account of the lives of simple fisher folk in a village on the Cantabrian coast of Asturias. This was a way of life which the author knew at first-hand, for as a child he had spent his summers in just such surroundings with his mother's family in Avilés, near Cape Peñas, one of the best harbors of the region. He began to go out to sea with the fishermen when he was but a boy. He himself has said: "The little coastal village which serves as the setting of this novel was a paradise to me in my boyhood years. There I enjoyed, as nowhere else, the charms of the sea, for it was then my passion. I have never been happier than at that time. Those brave and simple fishermen received me with so much cordiality that they awoke in me the desire to share their life and their work. For one summer I was just a fisherman . . . there I became acquainted with José, with Gaspar, and with Bernardo; all were my friends . . . I regarded it as a great compliment when one of the fishermen said to me at leave-taking: 'What a pity, Don Armando, you would have made a good sailor.' "

The Bay of Biscay, where the story unfolds, is generally conceded by seamen to be the most treacherous body of water on the Atlantic Coast. It is a saying that anything can happen there and usually does. Violent storms may arise in a moment, endangering the lives of those who go down to the sea in ships. The risk to the fishermen's lives mentioned again and again in *José* is real and constant. Small wonder that Palacio Valdés felt immense respect for the courage of the men who get their meager living from these treacherous waters, many of them knowing that "full fathom five" their fathers lie.

Armando Palacio Valdés came of a distinguished family of Asturias, that northern region of Spain, which has had a marked personality of its own since the days when Spain first appeared on the stage of history. It held out stubbornly against conquest by the legions of Rome, the finest soldiers of the empire, who were amazed at the bravery of the "Astures," who went to their death defiantly singing their war songs. Asturians are characterized to this day by that same bravery, combined with a great practical sense, industry, balance, tolerance, and ironic humor. All these traits are to be found in Palacio Valdés, for he was the embodiment of the spirit and character of his native region.

A portrait of the artist as a young man reveals to us a finely-modelled face, large, mild eyes, a short nose, and a calm, broad brow. He looks out on the world with the gentle wonder of a well-bred youth. At the time of this photograph he was still a fledgling lawyer, who had received his preparation at the University of Oviedo in Asturias and later at the University of Madrid. But his literery inclinations were already manifesting themselves, for at the age of twenty-two he was the editor of *La Revista Europea,* Spain's leading scientific journal at the time. He described his change from law to literature as one of those "whimsical turns of fortune."

His entry into literature began with articles on philosophic and literary subjects. He prepared a series of sketches of orators, novelists, and poets which were published in the magazine of which he was the editor. After several volumes of literary criticism, he turned to the writing of fiction, and in 1881 published his first novel, *El señorito Octavio*. Although it was well received, it did not satisfy the author, who realized that he lacked the maturity and experience of life that would have given its theme of illicit love and adultery verisimilitude. The publication in 1883 of *Marta y María,* a novel whose two main characters bear the names of the Biblical sisters of Lazarus, and who resemble them in many ways, launched him on his life work, which he followed almost uninterruptedly until his death. In addition to his long list of novels, he was the author of many short stories, some of which are among the finest of the period. Like his novels, they are unpretentious, direct, graceful, humorous, and related with such consummate art that they remain engraved upon our memory.

His literary life spans half a century, and may be

divided into two sharply differentiated epochs: that of naturalistic positivism, representing the final development of the realistic novel, which had flourished abundantly in all Europe; and that of idealistic subjectivism, represented by the triumph of the movement known in Spain as "modernism," around 1892. During the first epoch Palacio Valdés was the contemporary of such Spanish writers as Valera, Pereda, Pérez Galdós, and doña Emilia Pardo Bazán; in the second, of those known as "the generation of 1898," men like Valle-Inclán, Unamuno, Azorín and Baroja. Among those of the earlier generation, he was young; among those of the second, old. But the period to which a man belongs does not depend wholly on his age. Palacio Valdés had the characteristics of both periods, and yet does not belong entirely to either. For that reason, throughout his long creative life, he fitted in with the change of taste, and was able to produce work after work, his inspiration unexhausted, never losing touch with his public and preserving to the end of his life his freshness and vitality.

During the earlier period, when realism was the norm of the novel, Palacio Valdés was completely at home. His approach and his procedures were realistic; his novels were regional and contemporary, and his creations and the world against which they were set were taken from living reality, and were the fruit of his observation of it. None of the authors of his day was more faithful to reality. It might seem that Palacio Valdés had invented nothing, that he had limited himself to copying what he had seen, the persons he had known, the places where he had lived, the surroundings his eyes had rested upon. Nevertheless, Palacio Valdés viewed and interpreted reality in a manner which differed radically from the methods of realism. This, especially in its later development, to which the term Naturalism was applied, presented life as though it were the product solely of physical and mechanical forces over which man had no control, and of which he was the helpless, hapless toy.

It must be borne in mind, however, that Naturalism, as it existed in other European literatures, especially in France, never put down deep roots in Spain. Cold, detached scientific observation does not suit the Spanish temperament. It is not that the Spaniard lacks a penetrating eye for the somber, the cruel side of life, but he brings to his vision a personalized emotion. Spanish writers see man, not in the abstract, or as the puppet of deterministic forces, but as an individual, with his weaknesses, but also with his strength, with his triumphs as well as his defeats. As Don Quixote said: "The wicked enchanters may rob me of success, but nobody can take from me my heart and my courage." The Spanish ideal of beauty is characterized by the ability to look upon life unflinchingly and still accept it, and to see and convey this beauty in even the lowliest, the most abject of beings by virtue of the honesty and understanding with which they are portrayed. This is what was done by Cervantes and Velázquez, the most realistic and at the same time the most idealistic of Spanish artists, each in his own field.

Palacio Valdés is never pessimistic, however tragic the facts he deals with may be, nor does he ignore the role played by the spiritual forces in life. Not that he is unaware of its darker side, its sufferings, sorrows, and disappointments, but these are always redeemed and ennobled by kindliness and compassion. His own personal traits, his nobility of soul, his tenderness, his humor, color the reality he depicts and give his novels their enduring charm.

With the triumph of "modernism," Palacio Valdés could continue to be himself without difficulties of adjustment. He had only to intensify the personal element, which had always been present in his work, and his ideological and religious preoccupations in order to meet the requirements of the new canons of literature, and thus he was able to hold the public's esteem and popularity which, with the change of taste, many of his earlier contemporaries lost, at least temporarily.

Throughout his long career his art was characterized by two fundamental qualities, his humor and compassion, which set him apart from his fellow writers, with the exception of Pérez Galdós, and which have made him more accessible to foreign readers. It is not that he artificially selects the pleasanter aspects of life; there is no lack of suffering, pain, and tragedy in his world. Yet the ugliness and sorrow he depicts never make us turn aside with revulsion or horror, but rather inspire pity and tenderness toward those beings whose sufferings we share. As the great critic Azorín has said of him: "In his literary art he achieved the supreme art: unpretentiousness, simplicity of expression, the evocation of a delicate, ineffable, ideal reality which is above the violent and vulgar reality which is apparent to all eyes." And Palacio Valdés himself wrote that the greatest satisfaction his literary labors had brought him was ". . . knowing that some of my pages have brought smiles to the lips, and others tears to the eyes; and the comforting certainty that nobody has gone away from the reading of my novels less pure or less noble than he was."

In spite of the fact that his traits and qualities were those of his native region, Asturias, which was the setting of many of his novels, Palacio Valdés was not a regional novelist. The regional writer's theme is the region itself; his object is to describe the local life of a given area; the interest lies in the fidelity with which he portrays something that is unique by reason of its difference. But in his case the regional elements are the lyrical expression of the author's own emotions, or form the setting against which the action of the novel is played out. *José*, which is set with such accuracy of observation against the background of the author's youthful experiences, is one of his most idealistic works, in which there is a wealth of that tenderness and humor so characteristic of the author himself.

Some of his best works, such as *La Hermana San Sulpicio* (1889), *Los majos de Cadiz* (1896) and *La alegria del capitán Ribot* (1899) completely forsake this regional setting, and have as their background Andalusia and eastern Spain, than which no sharper contrast to

Asturias could be imagined. Yet it is the personality of Palacio Valdés which sets their tone, and lends them the charm of his northern humor, less brilliant but deeper than that of the South.

As George T. Northrup has observed of Palacio Valdés in his *Introduction to Spanish Literature*, "although Spain has produced greater novelists, she has given the world few more delightful." This is clear throughout *José*, which is not only a gripping story, whose interest never flags, but also embodies its author's unpretentious philosophy. Faced with the eternal problem of the meaning of life and man's destiny on earth, Palacio Valdés took refuge in the only possible solution to this insoluble problem, which is the simple doctrine of faith, hope and charity. In the face of seemingly insurmountable adversities, José found strength and finally happiness in the power of love, kindliness of heart toward those who had done him harm, and overcame evil and despair by his moral and ethical courage.

Palacio Valdés's last published work, which appeared in 1929, was his *Testamento literario*, a work of self-appraisal, and the summing-up by a modest man, pleased but never blinded by the success and fame he had enjoyed. On one occasion he said, "I can say with Goethe: my entire life is to be found in my works." Aside from what we know of him in this way, there is little else of importance. He lived, he enjoyed happiness, he had his share of suffering, which he bore with resignation and humility, and he triumphed in the work he loved. He always kept aloof from the hurly-burly of life, devoted to his family, his friends, his writing. He was a hard-working, upright, methodical person, who sought primarily neither gain nor applause; he wrote for his own satisfaction, and received his rewards when they came with gentle and humorous self-depreciation. "My days," he wrote, "have glided by, gentle, serene, perfumed by the aroma of love and friendship, beclouded only by the departure of beings I have loved to a higher realm." A whole and wholesome man.

"The most admirable feature of Palacio Valdés's work," Federico de Onís has written, "is the unity of tone and the unwavering level he has maintained throughout his writings with serene and restrained assurance, which is reflected in his simple and natural style, equidistant from the vulgarities of realism and the preciosity of 'modernism,' and of which, like our daily bread, we never weary."

HARRIET DE ONÍS

fond to his family, his friends, his writing. He was a hard-working, painstaking [illegible] person, [illegible] primarily [illegible] [illegible] his own [illegible] and [illegible] his readers with [illegible] [illegible] self-depreciation. [illegible] [illegible]: "They [illegible] by [illegible] serene, permeated by the [illegible] of love and [illegible] [illegible] the [illegible] of [illegible] [illegible] to a higher [illegible] whole and [illegible] man."

"The most admirable feature of [illegible] work," [illegible] has written, "is the universal tone and the unwavering level he has maintained throughout his writings with serene and restrained sincerity. [illegible] is reflected in the simple and natural style, [illegible] from the [illegible] of [illegible] and the [illegible] of [illegible], and of which, like our daily bread, [illegible] never weary."

[illegible]

If one day you should come to the province of Asturias, don't leave without taking a glance at Rodillero. It is the oddest, most singular village in the province, if not the most beautiful. Yet even in point of beauty, I think it compares well with any other, although perhaps that's not the general opinion. In speaking of Rodillero, most people smile pityingly as they do when mention is made in conversation of a cripple or hunchback or some other creature grotesquely marked by the hand of God. That is unfair. I confess that Rodillero is in no wise elegant, but—what is more important—it is magnificent.

Imagine yourself traveling along a high coastal upland, picturesque and pleasant like the rest of the countryside. You will keep coming upon white villages scattered over the mesa, half hidden among the foliage of the trees, and little farms in whose orchards rose-cheeked yellow apples hang in clusters over the road. A clear stream makes its serpentine way through the center, shedding coolness and delight. You have before you the great blue spread of the ocean; behind you, the distant peaks of mountains forming a dark and abrupt cordon around the broad and level stretch of arable land. Now as you near the sea, you begin rapidly to descend, following the stream, toward a dark and gloomy ravine. Rodillero lies in its depths. This ravine has been carved in the shape of a sickle; hence it offers a good many windings and levels before losing itself in the ocean. On both sides of it, the cottages comprising the village are studded into the cliff itself, for the high walls enclosing it make room only for the creek and a narrow street that skirts it. Street and stream follow a series of S-curves, so that sometimes you find yourself facing the mountain, hearing the murmur of the sea behind it, and not knowing where to turn to see it; but the stream will keep telling you. Beyond that spot, you will pass by another tier of houses set one above the other like a stone staircase, and once more you come up against the cliff, closing off your way. The sound of the sea grows louder, the street wider. Here you come upon a boat being careened, yonder some nets spread out in the sun. You will catch the nauseating odor of rotting fish remains; the creek runs dirtier and more sluggish, with a few boats floating on it. Finally, upon rounding a headland, you find yourself face to face with the sea. As the tide penetrates the dark throat of the creek, the stream fattens. As it ebbs, it leaves bare a beach not of sand but of shale. There is no jetty, nor any other structure to shelter the boats. When the sailors come back from their fishing, they are obliged to drag their boats up high and dry.

Rodillero is a fisherman's village. As a rule, the houses are small and poor, with a view only to the front; to the back, the rock face shuts them off. Some, less poor, are owned by the few outstanding inhabitants who have made their money, for the most part, by the trade in pickled fish. Behind the houses there is usually a garden which may be entered from the second floor and which is cut into the mountain itself. Three or four vacant, half-ruined big houses are the property of old, titled families. Long ago, the gentry who dwelt in them fled from the somber and monotonous life of that strange village. When you visit it, you will admit they were right. It must be sad indeed to live in the depths of that dark ravine where the noises of the sea and the wind resound as in a sea shell.

Yet no one in Rodillero is bored. There is no time for that. The hard, ceaseless struggle that must be maintained against the ocean in order to feed themselves absorbs this handful of humanity to such a degree that none of the pleasures of the great cities are missed. The men put out to sea in the morning or at midnight, according to the season, and return in the afternoon. The women keep busy, delivering the fish to the nearby villages or dressing them in the processing plants, weaving or mending nets, sewing sails, and carrying on their domestic tasks. Extraordinary differences may be observed between the two sexes, in character and mental capacity. The men as a rule are sober, taciturn, long-suffering, limited in intelligence, and stout of heart. One notes that in school the boys are high-spirited and sharp-witted; but as the years go by, these qualities little by little grow dim. This can be attributed solely to the exclusively materialistic life they lead almost from the time they start earning their living. From the sea to the tavern; from the tavern home;

from home to the sea again, and so on, day after day, until they die or grow useless. Nevertheless, there remains in the depths of their souls a spark of spirituality which is never extinguished, for their faith keeps it alive. The people of Rodillero are deeply religious. The constant danger to their lives moves them to place their thoughts and their hopes in God. Every day the fisherman yields himself to the sea, to the unknown; every day he goes out to lose himself in that blue infinity of air and water, never knowing whether he will return. And, indeed, some of them never return. Few years ever pass without Rodillero paying its living tribute to the Ocean. At times the tribute is terrible. In the winter of 1852, eighty men perished, a third of the able-bodied population. Little by little this life molds their spirit, freeing them of material interests, making them generous, serene, and tender to their families. Misers, schemers, and cheats do not abound among seamen as they do among landsmen.

The women are different. They possess the qualities their husbands lack, along with the defects. They are intelligent, with a lively and enterprising turn of mind; they are astute and able, hence almost always the managers of the family. On the other hand, they are likely to be avaricious, gossipy, and quarrelsome. All this in the moral terrain. In the physical, we may as well grant immediately that in Asturias, probably in all Spain, no others can stand comparison with these women. Tall, slender, with firm, rosy flesh, heavy black hair, large eyes, black too, whose gaze has the severity of Greek goddesses; a straight or slightly aquiline nose, joined to the forehead in a delicate line, ends in slightly flaring and extraordinarily mobile nostrils which indicate an impetuous and passionate nature. The mouth is fresh, in vivid red contrast with the whiteness of the teeth. They walk with majesty like women of Rome; they speak rapidly with a musical intonation which brings them immediate recognition wherever they go. They seldom smile and when they do, it is with a kind of Olympic disdain. I doubt that a more beautiful collection of women can be found in any other region of Spain.

In this corner of the earth, as in all others, comedies and dramas play themselves out, less complicated than in the cities, owing to the simpler customs, but perhaps no less interesting. One of these begs to be told. It is the plain story of a poor seaman. Listen to it, those of you who love the humble truth, for it is to you I dedicate it.

I

It was two o'clock in the afternoon. The sun was gleaming brightly, sparkling over the sea. The breeze had barely enough strength to swell the sails of the fishing boats cleaving the ocean at random. Seen from a distance, the jutting cliffs along the coast and the mountains inland seemed swathed in the thinnest of blue gauze. The coastal hamlets shone like white dots in the depths of the coves. All was silence, the solemn, infinite silence of the sea in calm. Most of the fishermen were sleeping or dozing in varied and haphazard positions. Some lay face down, some face up on the gunwale, some supine, some prone on the bottom panels or planking. In their right hands, they all held fishlines which streaked the water behind the launch in parallel stripes. Force of habit kept them from letting go even in the deepest slumber. Thirty or forty boats were moving within sight of one another, forming a kind of square, gliding so slowly over the smooth and shining surface of the water that at times they appeared motionless. Occasionally the canvas flapped against the masts with a soft sound inviting sleep. The heat was suffocating and sticky, as rarely happens on the sea.

The master of one of the vessels let go the tiller

for a moment, took out his handkerchief and wiped the sweat from his forehead. Then he grasped the tiller again and sent a searching glance along the horizon, noting that a boat had moved away to a considerable distance.

Soon he resumed his careless pose, staring at his sleeping companions with absent eyes. He was young, blonde, blue-eyed, and though his face was weathered and deeply burned, it was handsome nonetheless. His beard, full and abundant; his dress, like that of all sailors, white cap above blue cotton trousers and jacket, yet somewhat neater and finer.

At last one of the sailors raised his head from the gunwale; rubbing his eyes, he muttered thickly in a bad humor:

"Devil take me if we don't stay becalmed all day!"

"Don't you believe it," said the master, again scanning the horizon. "Before an hour's up we'll have a fresh breeze out of the west; the signs are coming from there. Tomás has already tacked to go and meet it."

"Where is Tomás?" asked the sailor, staring at the sea, his hand like a sun-shield above his eyes.

"You can't see him now."

"Has he made a catch?"

"It didn't seem so to me . . . ; but he'll get something . . . and we'll all make a haul. We won't go home today without bonito."

"Well, we'll see," grunted the sailor, again lying face down.

Again the master was the only man on the boat awake. Tired of looking at the faces, the sea, and the boats, he fixed his eyes on an old sailor asleep on his back beneath the seats, an alarming expression of ferocity upon his face. But the master, far from showing fear, smiled with pleasure.

"Hey, Bernardo," he said, touching the shoulder of the sailor who had just been talking. "Look at the ugly face the old Pirate puts on when he goes to sleep."

The sailor raised his head again and smiled mockingly.

"Wait a minute, José; let's play a joke on him . . . Hand me that rock . . ."

Instantly comprehending, the master picked up a big stone which served as ballast in the stern and silently brought it to his shipmate. The latter was slowly and carefully drawing the Pirate's fishing line out of the water. When he came to the hook, he wrapped the line tightly around the stone and let it slip very delicately into the water. Then with all speed he flung himself down on the gunwale in the attitude of sleep.

"Oh, Holy Mother!" shouted the startled sailor, feeling the strong pull on his line. He got up in such haste that he hit his head on the seat, but he made no complaint.

His mates all awoke and leaned over the port side where the Pirate was starting proudly to haul in his line.

Bernardo also raised his head, exclaiming ill-humoredly:

"So the Pirate's got a bite! As long as there's a single fish in the sea, this double-damned rascal will latch on to it!"

Thus speaking, he winked at one of the sailors, who nudged another, and he another, until in an instant almost all of them were brought in on the joke.

"Is it a big one, Pirate?" went on Bernardo.

"Big? . . . Come here and feel; you'll see how she pulls."

The sailor took the line the other held out to him, and making faces of astonishment to his companions, he exclaimed in a solemn tone:

"Sure enough! I'll be damned if she doesn't go to thirty pounds. She'll be the biggest catch of the season."

Meanwhile the Pirate, trembling, smiling, bubbling over with pride, was hauling in the line vigorously, but delicately, taking care to pay out from time to time so that his catch might not get away from him. Hard put to contain their mirth, the fishermen bent their heads over the water.

"Now what kind of charm or devil's magic can this highway robber carry around with him to help him hook fish even when he's asleep?" Bernardo kept exclaiming as he made increasingly grotesque faces.

The Pirate had noticed that the bonito, contrary to custom, kept pulling toward the bottom, but he paid no heed and kept hauling on the line until the stone could be plainly seen through the water.

Then the cat was out of the bag! All at once the fishermen loosed the rein on their laughter, as they sorely needed to do; bursting into shouts of joy, they hugged their sides and rolled on the seats, helpless to control the flood of their guffaws.

"Haul it aboard, Pirate, it's close enough!"

"It isn't bonito, but it's a fish prized for its tenderness."

"Especially with oil and vinegar and a dash of red pepper."

"What'll you bet it weighs thirty pounds, as I said."

Chagrined, scowling, and in a foul humor, the Pirate brought the stone to the side, untied it, and cast his line into the water. Then he threw his mates a terrible look and muttered:

"Pigs! If you'd ever been in the fixes I have, you wouldn't be so fond of joking."

Mumbling fierce oaths, he stretched himself out again. His companions' laughter went on unchecked for a good while, bursting out again at some jesting remark when it had almost died away. Nevertheless, it came to a halt at last, or rather, it turned into gay chatter, and finally lethargy and slumber.

The breeze had begun to freshen. The flapping of the canvas against the masts yielded to the whisper of water under the keel.

Without losing sight of the boats, the master raised his head and sniffed the wind—which meant a catch—with delight. He took a look at the fishing lines to make sure they had not fouled, luffed a little, sheeted home, and got under way. The vessel responded to these maneuvers, heeled over and picked up speed. The sharp eyes of the helmsman noted that a boat had just dropped anchor.

"We're over the bonito now," he called loudly, but no one awakened.

A moment later, the sailor nearest the bow shouted, "Oh, Holy Mother!"

The master slackened the sheet to stop the boat. Before starting to haul in his line, the sailor paused, struck by the memory of the earlier joke, and casting a wary eye at his mates, said:

"Is this a stone, too?"

"Pull, you lubber!" shouted José, fearing the fish might get away.

The bonito had run out almost all the line by now. The seaman began to draw in with all his strength. For every few fathoms of line he hove into the boat, he paid out again, for the fish was running it very taut and it could easily snap. Thus hauling in and paying out, he could soon make out a dark form, struggling furiously and sending out gleams of silver. The nearer the fish came to the surface of the water, the greater and more furious his struggles to turn around and escape. At times when the line was paid out, he seemed to succeed, in some degree mimicking the man who fancies himself liberated by flight from his fatal destiny. At other times, spiritless and yielding, he let himself be dragged docilely to his death. As he was wrested from his native element and hauled aboard, he splashed water over the whole crew with his leaping and twisting. When they pulled the hook out of his mouth, he lay motionless a moment as if feigning death. But soon he began to struggle beneath the seats with such violence and fury that he came very near throwing himself into the water again. But no one was any longer paying any attention to him. Two other bonitos had struck at almost the same time and the fishermen were busy heaving them over the side.

The catch was abundant. In a matter of three or four hours' work, a hundred and two bonitos were stowed away.

"How many?" came the call from a boat passing nearby.

"A hundred and two. And you?"

"Sixty."

"What did I tell you!" exclaimed Bernardo, speaking to his mates. "You'll see they won't take home eighty at the most. When a man wants to marry, he gets sharp enough to cut himself."

All faces turned smilingly to the master, on whose lips a smile also appeared, making his face still handsomer.

"When are you going to be married, José?" asked one of the sailors.

"Tomás and Manuel have hauled their tackle aboard to make for land," he announced, not answering the question. "Loose that halyard, Ramón; we're going to come about."

When the maneuver had been carried out, Bernardo said:

"You were asking when José is going to be married . . . ?"

"Well, that's plain enough . . . As soon as the boat is launched."

"When will it be tarred?"

"Very soon. The caulker told me it would be ready in less than two weeks," replied Bernardo.

"There'll be bacon and ham on that day, eh, José?"

"And the best Rueda wine," said another.

"And Havana cigars," added a third.

"I'll give all that up," said Bernardo, "if he takes us to the play at Sarrió on the day of the wedding."

"That's impossible! Don't you realize José can't stay up late that night?"

"All right, then. Let him give us the money to go and he can stay home."

The master listened to it all without a word, the same benign smile on his lips.

"What play could be better than to go to sleep with the teacher's daughter?" cried one.

"Now, now! Be careful what you say," declared José, half smiling, half angry.

His crew enjoyed the vulgarity as if it were the most refined wit, and they kept on with their joking and teasing as the wind, which had begun to die down, drove them gently toward land.

II

Dusk was falling when the boats entered the cove of Rodillero. A crowd composed almost entirely of women and children was waiting on the beach, shouting, laughing, arguing. The old men kept a little apart, seated calmly on the gunwale of some boat which slumbered on the gravel waiting to be careened. The upper and middle class people watched the homecoming of the boats from stone benches in front of the houses nearest the beach. From lifelong experience, the crowd along the waterfront knew before the loaded boats arrived that they were bringing in bonito. And as always at such times, this news was reflected in smiles on their faces. The women held big baskets ready to receive the catch, and they rolled up their sleeves with a kind of voluptuous satisfaction. The children climbed the nearest rocks to find out as soon as possible what lay waiting in the bottom of the boats. The vessels slowly drew nearer. The sober-faced, silent fishermen let the oars fall lazily in the water.

One after another they beached their boats on the gravel. The sailors left them with a broad jump to avoid wetting themselves. Some remained on board to unload the fish which they hurled one by one on the beach. The women seized them, beheaded and gutted them with incredible speed, piled them in the baskets, and hitching up their skirts, went a few steps into the water to wash them. A good portion of the shallows and the pebbles at its edge were soon stained with blood.

Immediately upon jumping to land, the masters grouped together and fixed the price of the catch. The owners of the pickling plants and the women who dealt in fresh fish were awaiting the results of the parley with suspicion.

One women, more decently dressed than the others—aged, wrinkled, sharp-nosed, with sunken black eyes—went to José and anxiously asked him:

"How much?"

"A *real*[1] and a half."

"A *real* and a half!" she exclaimed in an angry voice. "And when do you intend to come down on it? Do you think we're going to go on paying the same price when there's a lot as when there's a little?"

"Don't hold it against me, Señora Isabel," answered José, shamefaced. "I didn't open my mouth. The others set the price, I didn't."

"But you should have told them," answered the old woman in the same irritable tone," that it's not fair; we're going broke; and we simply can't go on this way."

"Now don't be angry, señora . . . I'll do what I can to bring it down tomorrow. Besides, you know . . ."

[1] A *real* was worth about five cents, the American nickel.

"What?"

"That you can pay me my two shares of the profit for the boat and myself whenever you wish."

"I wasn't talking about that," declared Señora Isabel, suddenly softening. "But you know very well we're losing money; the man from Astorgas will turn back our barrels if this goes on . . . Look, Elisa is over there at the weighing. I can see you're more anxious to have a chat with her than with me."

José smiled, and saying good-bye, moved on a few steps.

"Listen, José," cried Señora Isabel, coaxing him with a smile, "how much will you let me have them for?"

"For whatever you want to pay; I already told you that."

"No, no. It's up to you to decide."

"Would a *real* and a quarter be too high?" he asked diffidently.

"That's high," replied the old woman, still with her coaxing smile. "Come now, to avoid any more argument, let's make it a *real*. What do you say?"

José shrugged his shoulders to indicate resigned acceptance, and strode toward one of the various establishments which, under the pompous name of factories, surrounded the beach. In the doorway stood a young girl, tall, fresh, rosy like many of her neighbors, though with finer and more regular features than most of them. She was dressed in the same fashion as they, but with more care and neatness. Her kerchief, tied at the back, was not of percale, but of wool; her shoes of fine kid, her stockings white and clean. Her arms were bare, and truly they were as beautiful and delicately molded as arms could be. She was absorbed, attentive to the operation of weighing the bonito in her presence. This was being done by three or four women aided by a sailor. Sometimes she took part, holding the fish in her hands.

When she heard José's step, she raised her head and her big, lustrous eyes smiled sweetly.

"Hello, José. Are you all through with your business?"

"We still have to haul up the boats. Have they brought all the fish?"

"Yes, it's all here now. Tell me," she went on, going up to José, "what price have you set?"

"A *real* and a half, but I set it at a *real* for your mother."

Elisa's face suddenly reddened.

"Did she ask you to?"

"No."

"Yes, yes. Don't deny it. I know her very well . . ."

"Come now, don't get cross . . . I offered it to her at that price because I know she can't make any money otherwise . . ."

"She does make money, José. Yes, she does," answered the girl sadly. "The thing is that she wants to make more . . . To her money is everything."

"Pshaw! I won't go broke on that account."

"Poor José!" she exclaimed after a pause, as she placed an affectionate hand on his shoulder. "You're so good! . . . Luckily, those stingy actions of hers that embarrass me will soon come to an end. When are you planning to launch the boat?"

"We'll see if it can be done on St. John's Day." [2]

"Then why don't you speak to my mother now? That was the date set; it would be a good thing to remind her of it."

"Do you think I should?"

"Of course. Time is going by and she acts as if she doesn't remember it."

"Then I'll speak to her right away, as soon as we beach the boat . . . That is, if I dare," he added somewhat shyly.

"José, faint heart never won fair lady."

"Shall I speak to your stepfather, too?"

"It doesn't matter. In any case, it'll be what she wants."

"So long, then."

"Good-bye. Don't be long, so we won't be having supper when you come."

José went back to the beach where the sailors were starting to haul the boat up high and dry, no easy task. The twilight was ending and the night beginning. The women and children were helping their husbands and fathers in that exhausting daily chore. The long-drawn chant of the men could be heard as they pushed in unison. And among the deepening shadows, their

---

[2] June 24.

silhouettes stood out, forming a tight group around each vessel. The boats were moving, their progress impeded by the dry upper beach where they had to force them across the gravel. At a safe distance from the water, the men left them to go about gathering up the fishing gear they had scattered over the beach, and after casting a final look at the sea, now dark and motionless, they left the spot and went in small groups into the town.

After issuing the necessary orders for the following day, José also turned his steps toward the village. Rapidly he traversed its single street, fairly well lighted at that time of night by the large number of open taverns. A rumble of voices and laughter issued from them. Ignoring the friends who shouted an offer of a drink, he came nearly to the end of the village and entered a shop whose bright lights gaily broke the darkness of the street. In that narrow little store, low-ceilinged as the cabin of a ship, everything was sold: dried codfish, hats, matches, bacon, the Catechism, and ballads. Nevertheless, fishing tackle and other maritime gear occupied first place. Three or four huge spools of cable were lying on the floor, serving as stools; strings of fishhooks hung from a beam running from wall to wall, and some half-full cans of caulking compound spread through the place a penetrating aroma which made everyone unaccustomed to it slightly dizzy. But the noses of the habitual hangers-on at the store were never offended by the odor. Perhaps they didn't even notice the presence of those stench-pots.

Seated behind the pine plank which served as a counter was Señora Isabel. Her husband, Don Claudio, the teacher of the beginning grades (and the last ones, too, for there were no others in Rodillero) was standing to one side, gravely cutting a slab of soap into slices. The long cutaway coat he was wearing at the time was adorned with muslin over-sleeves tied to his arms with strings, and the rare erudition and high-flown language he glorified in did not divert him from his lowly task. Ten years ago he had married the widow of the late Vega, a storekeeper and fish pickler. During all that time Don Claudio had learned how to bestow equal attention nobly and without suffering thereby on both the exalted labors of teaching and the humbler ones of trade, paying equal homage, as he used to say, to Minerva and to Mercury. He was fifty years old, more or less, with a yellowish skin, wide nose, sparse hair, and eyes that protruded in an unchanging expression of fright or surprise, as though he were constantly witnessing some tragic scene which only he could see. He was of a benign and peaceable temperament except in school, where he punished the small boys unmercifully, not through inclination, but by virtue of the teaching doctrine deeply rooted in his soul. The canings, the blows on the palm of the hand, the ear-twistings, the cuffs on the head were to Don Claudio an integral part of the learning process, just as were reading, writing, and reckoning. The whole thing was comprised under the generic name of punishment. Don Claudio always pronounced this word with reverence. Soaring to the peaks of metaphysics, he considered punishment not an evil but one of the most delectable and pleasurable gifts man owed to God's providence. According to this theory, he who chastises should be considered a guardian angel, like him who staunches blood from a wound. He tried to surround his chastisements with formality, in order to achieve fairness and exemplary behavior; never did he inflict them hastily or impetuously. First he acquainted himself thoroughly with the offense committed, and after weighing it carefully in the scales of justice, he wrote down the verdict on a piece of paper and passed sentence on the culprit. The condemned went to join the other malefactors in a corner of the schoolroom where they awaited the fateful hour with spasms of salutary terror. When the lessons were done, Don Claudio scanned the list of punishments and, with it in front of him, he began to carry out the sentences in the chronological order of their occurrence, before the whole school. Once his accounts were closed, he would deal out fatherly pats on the tear-stained cheeks of the boys who had been flogged, saying affectionately:

"Go home, my sons, go on home now. Some day you'll thank me for the tannings I've given you."

In the town he was generally esteemed and was received everywhere with that good will, not devoid of contempt, which the world accords the inoffensive. All the townspeople knew that at home Don Claudio was in chains; that his wife could wrap him around her finger, not only because his humble and pusillanimous disposition lent itself to that, but also because in the conjugal partnership he was the poor one and his wife the rich one. Señora Isabel's wealth was only temporary, to be sure, for it came from the deceased Vega. In time everything would revert to Elisa. But as long as she had it (and it would be hers to manage for a long time yet since Elisa was only twelve years old at the death of her father) Don Claudio had thought to make a good match by marrying the widow. At least that was the unanimous opinion of the village. Hence they had no sympathy for his domestic troubles, as they should have; instead the goodwives of the town used to say in ironic tones:

"He wanted a rich wife, didn't he? Well, now he's got her."

III

"A good haul today, eh, José?"

"At the last moment. I was sure we wouldn't bring home twenty pounds."

"How much did the catch weigh?"

"I don't know . . . ; there's Señora Isabel."

She, who must have known perfectly, turned her eyes to Elisa and asked:

"How many pounds, Elisa?"

"Eleven hundred forty."

"Then, if it's at a *real* and a half, you must have made about twenty *duros*[3] today," remarked the first speaker, no less a personage than the Justice of the Peace of Rodillero.

Elisa blushed brightly again on hearing these words. José lowered his head somewhat shyly and said between his teeth:

"Not that much, not that much."

Señora Isabel went on sewing impassively.

"What do you mean not that much?" burst out Don Claudio, strongly accenting the syllables as was his custom: "It seems to me the Judge has figured it short.

[3] A *duro* is approximately a dollar.

Nothing could be easier than to calculate exactly what is coming to you. It is the simplest of problems in elementary arithmetic. Wait a moment," he added, going to a shelf and pulling out a piece of paper and a quill pen.

Señora Isabel fixed him with a sharp and icy stare that would have annihilated him if he had not had his back to her at that moment. He took a horn ink bottle from his pocket and unscrewed the top, not without difficulty.

"Now let's see. This is the problem. One thousand one hundred and forty pounds of bonito at a *real* and a half a pound, how many *reales* does that give us? We have to multiply one thousand one hundred and forty by one and one half. This is multiplication of a whole number by a mixed number. We must reduce the mixed number to a common denominator . . . ; one times two is two. We now have two halves plus one half. They have a common denominator; we now add the numerators. Two and one is three. Three halves. Now we multiply the whole number by the fraction. Three times zero is zero; three times four is twelve, carry one . . ."

"Will you please not bother us, darling?" interrupted Señora Isabel, hard put to it to restrain her anger. "We're tired of listening to you carry and lug around so many broken numbers and fractions to no purpose."

"My dear woman . . . are you implying that I count on my fingers? . . . Knowledge . . ."

"Nonsense! . . . You're not in the schoolroom now. Be good enough to keep still."

Don Claudio grimaced with resignation, screwed the top on the bottle again, put it in the pocket of his frock coat, and went back to cutting up the soap.

After a pause, the judge smoothed over the rebuff to Don Claudio with a well-rounded defense of arithmetic. To him there were no sciences but the exact sciences. But Don Claudio, though grateful for the helping hand, set himself against the Law's arguments and entered upon a discussion of the order and the dignity of the sciences.

The Justice of the Peace of Rodillero was an infantry captain, long since retired. He was residing—or vegetating—in his native village on the scanty stipend tardily and grudgingly paid him by the Government. A sister, older than he, took care of his house and garden. He was a taciturn man, a worrier, extremely touchy, and well known for his scrupulousness and impartiality. Extreme rigidity of character and an invincible attachment to his own opinions were considered his shortcomings.

At his side was an elderly gentleman with noble and regular features, long white mustaches, and a beard which hung down to his chest. His hair was also long and unkempt, his eyes black and burning, his gaze haughty, and his smile scornful. His meager, bent body was a pedestal unworthy of that beautiful head. Moreover, the combination of a dirty, rumpled frock coat, trousers of coarse cloth, and the hob-nailed boots of a laborer all helped to diminish his stately presence. His name was Don Fernando de Meira. He was a member of an old and noble family of Rodillero, long since completely ruined. The sons of this family had scattered over the world in search of a living. The only one who had stayed, attached to the old crumbling mansion like an oyster to its shell, was Don Fernando, whose training as a lawyer had been of no use to him in earning a livelihood, either because he lacked the necessary aptitude, or because this noble scion of the House of Meira felt utter contempt for any occupation that was not hunting or fishing. He lived in one of the least dilapidated rooms of his house, which had begun long ago to collapse in one place after another. The mice, openly skirmishing and fighting pitched battles all around him, served him as companions, together with the timid little lizards that nested in the crevices and the walls, and a multitude of bats flying about at night with an eerie noise. No one knew of any property or income he could derive a living from, and in the village it was taken as an article of faith that the old man had stared hunger in the face many a time.

When he was younger, he used to hunt and usually brought home abundant game, for he was the most skillful marksman in the region. As his strength failed, he concentrated on fishing. On days when the sea was calm, Señor de Meira used to go out in his boat for squid, horse mackerel, ocean perch, or mullet, according to the time of year and the condition of the water. He showed himself as expert at this as at hunting. Whatever fish he could not use he would give away to the people of Rodillero, for Don Fernando would have starved to death before selling even one fish caught by his own hand. But these gifts inspired others in return, and thanks to them, the gentleman could meet the most pressing needs of his kitchen in the way of food, firewood, oil, eggs, and so on, and even permit himself a little excess at times. He himself prepared the food he ate, and not without skill, according to the village. An extraordinary stew of his, made as no other cook could make it, was highly praised. But there came a day when the village learned with surprise that Señor de Meira had sold his boat to a merchant from Sarrió. Everyone guessed the reason, however much he tried to hide it by saying he had got rid of it in order to buy a better one. From then on, he used to fish from the shore with a pole, or, which is the same thing, he used to wait patiently for the fish, seated on some solitary rock, instead of going out to get them. When none came, the neighbors noticed that no smoke rose from the chimney of the de Meira house.

"Mother, why don't you settle your accounts with José? . . . It's time for supper," said Elisa to Señora Isabel.

"Are you hungry?" replied the latter, a false smile rising to her lips. "Well, wait a while, my child, for I must finish what I have in my hands."

From the moment José came into the store, Elisa had kept making covert signs to him, encouraging him to call her mother aside and tell her what they had agreed upon. The sailor seemed hesitant and shy. He indicated to his sweetheart, also by signs, that he was waiting for the regulars to go home. She replied that they wouldn't go until the very moment that supper was ready. José could not make up his mind. Finally the girl, tired of her fiancé's indecision, undertook to suggest to her mother what we have just heard, beckoning toward the back of the store, there to broach the conversation they were hungering for. Señora Isabel's response left them downcast and thoughtful.

Three or four seamen had come into the store after our José, one of them Bernardo. As usual, the conversation turned on money; who had more, who less. They were speaking of a prominent man in the province who had just acquired some nearby land.

"Is this count very rich?" asked one of the sailors.

Don Fernando solemnly raised a hand and said:

"My cousin, the Count of La Mata has over six thousand acres of income-producing land in Pilona which he inherited from his mother; he must have inherited very little from his father. The estate of the Velascos never amounted to much, and my uncle has wasted a good deal of it."

"The five hundred acres he bought in Riofontán," said the Judge, "are the best in the region. It was cheap at twenty-two thousand *duros*."

"Don Anacleto was in need of funds. His son had spent a fortune in Madrid, so they say," remarked Don Claudio.

"He probably got the land cheap when he bought it years ago," observed one of the seamen.

"Whom did he buy from?"

Don Fernando raised his hand again with the same majesty, saying:

"From my cousin the Marquis de las Quintanas . . . But he did not need the money; he sold the land in order to transfer his income to Andalusia."

"Is that gentleman your cousin, too?" asked Bernardo, lifting his head with a comical grimace which made the others smile.

Don Fernando shot him an angry glance.

"Yes, sir. He's my cousin . . . And what of it?"

"Nothing, nothing," said Bernardo with feigned stupidity. "It just struck me that you're away ahead in the cousin sweepstakes."

"Well, let me tell you," cried Don Fernando loftily, "that my house is two centuries older than his. When the Quintanas were a good-for-nothing, poverty-stricken lot of petty squirelings in Andalusia, the lords of Meira had already raised their standard in Asturias and founded their collegiate church, and set up their gibbet in the lands now owned by Pepe Llanos. A Quintana considered it a great honor to come asking for the hand of a lady of the Meira house . . . There were ample dowries in my family then for every female who was married . . . Dowries for the house of Miranda, for the Peñalta house, for the Santa Cruz, the Guzmán, all came from my house . . ."

"Well," said Bernardo, grinning, "no wonder you're so poor."

Don Fernando's eyes flashed angrily at hearing those hateful words.

"See here you, you swine, you clown, have I ever asked you for anything? What business is it of yours whether I'm rich or poor? Just remember that you and I weren't nursed on the same milk, you jackass . . ."

"Don Fernando, calm yourself," said Don Claudio. "Anger is a poor counsellor."

"Pay no attention to him, Don Fernando," said Señora Isabel.

"Peace, peace, peace, gentlemen," cried the judge, raising his hands authoritatively.

Bernardo was laughing to himself, seemingly paying no heed to the insults heaped upon him by Señor de Meira. Scenes like this were frequent between those two. The light-hearted seaman delighted in teasing the old man and getting him worked up. Later, he would repent of what he had said and they would make their peace until the next time. The aged nobleman was incapable of holding a grudge against anyone; his fits of anger were like spray in the wind.

"Mother, it's time to have supper now," said Elisa, taking advantage of the silence which followed the wrangle. "José must want to go home."

Señora Isabel made no reply. Some while ago, her sharp eye had noted that Don Fernando was attempting to have a private word with her husband. At the moment of Elisa's reiteration of her theme, her mother observed Señor de Meira giving a furtive pull to Don Claudio's coat, then going to the door as though about to look at the weather. The schoolmaster was following him.

Before they could start tc talk, Señora Isabel said:

"Claudio, reach me that packet of pearl buttons that's been started."

Don Claudio turned on his heel, went to the row of shelves, and reaching up as high as he could, took the buttons down from the top shelf. As he handed them to her, his wife said to him, speaking peremptorily in a low voice:

"Go upstairs."

The schoolmaster opened his big, bulging eyes uncomprehendingly.

"Get out of here!" said his wife, giving his sleeve a jerk.

Without asking for an explanation, Don Claudio hastened to obey. He went through the door which led to the hall and on up the stairway into the house.

"Señor de Meira needs a few pennies," said Bernardo into the ear of the sailor nearest him. "Did you see how smartly Señora Isabel scented what was going on? If she hadn't been so nippy about getting the teacher out! . . ."

The sailor grinned, glancing at the gentleman standing in the door waiting for Don Claudio.

"Gentlemen, will you stay to supper?" asked Señora Isabel, rising from her chair.

The regulars got up also.

"José, you'll come upstairs with us, won't you?"

"Whatever you wish. If tomorrow would be a better time to take care of that . . ."

"All right, if that's what you wish . . ."

Elisa could not repress a gesture of displeasure, and she said abruptly:

"Mother, tomorrow is a bad day, you know that . . . We have to seal a lot of barrels, and then there's mass which always delays us a little . . ."

"Never mind, girl . . . never mind . . . ; we'll settle the whole thing now," replied Señora Isabel, fixing her daughter with a cold, searching stare which disconcerted her.

Saying good night, the regulars left. Señora Isabel barred the door, picked up the lamp, and went up the stairs, followed by Elisa and José.

The living room they entered was tiny, in keeping with the store. Thanks to Elisa's care, it was pleasingly arranged and attractive. The furniture was old, but it shone. A small gilt-framed mirror was covered with white gauze to protect it from the flies; on the table rested two big sea shells, and between them was a rudely executed glass model of a bark. Such maritime mementos usually adorned the decent parlors in Rodillero. Some bad prints representing the Conquest of Mexico were hanging on the walls in black frames. Scenes between Hernán Cortés and Doña Marina held the preferred spots. Beneath the mirror were some photographs, also framed, wherein Señora Isabel and the late Vega were shown soon after they were united in the bonds of matrimony. Half a dozen chairs and a sofa with a linen cover completed the furnishings.

As they entered the parlor, Don Claudio, who had been standing bemused in the hallway, went away and left the room to them. Señora Isabel moved to the alcove in search of a dog-eared notebook, coming apart at the seams, in which she kept an account of all her business. Elisa seized that moment to say quickly to her sweetheart:

"Don't fail to speak to her."

José made an affirmative sign, although he made clear the fear and turmoil the situation aroused in him. The girl also went out when her mother came back into the parlor.

"Sunday, three hundred seven pounds," said Señora Isabel, setting the lamp on the table and opening the notebook, "at a *real* and a quarter. Monday, a thousand and forty, at a *real;* Tuesday, two thousand two hundred, at half a *real.* Wednesday you didn't go out. Thursday, two hundred thirty-five, at two *reales;* Friday, nothing; today, eleven hundred forty, at a *real* and a half . . . Isn't that right, José?"

"Whatever you say, señora . . . I don't keep an account."

"I'm going to figure it out."

The old woman began to multiply. The scratching of her pen was the only sound in the room. José awaited the result of the operation, turning his beret in his hand. At that moment his mind was empty of the interest or the desire to know how much money he was to be paid. His whole being was in turmoil and suspense at the idea of discussing the business of his wedding. Frantically he sought some clever way to broach the subject once the accounting had been made.

"That's four thousand seven hundred and three *reales* and three quarters," said Señora Isabel, raising her head.

José's silence gave assent. There came a pause.

"We'll have to subtract from that the reduction you made me on your share of the profit and the boat," declared the old woman, her voice softening a little. "Sunday you made it a *real;* Monday, three quarters; Tuesday there was no rebate because the price was low; Thursday, a *real* and a half, and today a *real.* Isn't that right?"

"Yes, señora."

"This is a hard thing to figure . . . Would you like me to call it three quarters, to avoid any mistakes? . . . It seems to me I'm losing money on this . . ."

José agreed without stopping to think whether he was making or losing money. The old woman started to write down new figures on the piece of paper, and José to rack his brains anew for a way out of that difficult situation.

At last Señora Isabel was finished. José approved his own spoliation, and a handful of gold passed from her to him to be divided the next day among his crew. After he had put the money into a leather purse and stuck it into the folds of his sash, he returned to twirling his beret in trembling hands. The critical moment when he must speak had come. José had never been an eloquent talker. Just then he felt bereft as never before of the talents which make for eloquence. A rush of blood rose to his throat and stuck there. He was barely able to reply in monosyllables to the questions Señora Isabel put to him concerning the events of the catch and his expectations for the next trip. After sucking his blood, the old woman was making an effort to be amiable. But in spite of that, the conversation died without the sailor's having succeeded in putting his thoughts into words. And now Señora Isabel was about to indicate that it was at an end by getting up from her chair when Elisa suddenly opened the door and came in on the pretext of getting some scissors she needed. As she left, she sent him signals and made faces behind her mother's back, all to the end of forcing him to keep his promise. They were so final and so imperative that the poor sailor, screwing up his courage and making a supreme effort, ventured to say:

"Señora Isabel . . ."

The unnaturalness of his voice startled and surprised the old woman.

"What did you say, dear?"

The look accompanying this question made him lower his head. A few moments of suspense and embarrassment ensued. Finally, without raising his eyes, he said in a hoarse voice:

"Señora Isabel, I'm planning to launch my boat on St. John's day . . ."

Contrary to his expectations, the old woman uttered not a single word in argument. She continued to stare at him fixedly.

"I don't know whether you remember that last winter you told me . . ."

Señora Isabel remained silent.

"I wouldn't want to inconvenience you . . . but as time is going by, and there's no real reason . . . and besides, people keep asking one when . . . and I've made arrangements for the house . . . It seems to me it would be best to finish the business before the winter's upon us . . ."

Not a word. The señora did not open her lips. José was growing more and more perturbed. He stared earnestly at the floor, perhaps in the hope that it would open up.

At long last the old woman deigned to exclaim gaily:

"What a fright you gave me, dear! Seeing you so confused, I thought you were about to tell me some bad news, but it turns out you were talking about what is nearest my heart."

The seaman's face suddenly lit up.

"How wonderful, señora! I was afraid . . ."

"Why? Don't you know I want it as much as you do? . . . José, you're a good boy, hard-working, clever, without a single bad habit. What more could I ask for my daughter? Ever since you started to court her, I've looked upon you with favor, for I'm sure you'll make her happy. Up to now I've done whatever lay within my power for you both, and God willing, I intend to continue doing it. I'm always mulling things over, trying to see in what way we can bring about this fortunate match soon . . . But you young people are so impatient and you can spoil things with your haste . . . Why are you in such a hurry? Both you and Elisa are young, and although, thank God, you have enough to live on, tomorrow or some other fine day, if you have a lot of children, perhaps you won't be able to say the same . . . Have a little patience. Work as hard as you can so there'll never be any fear of hunger, and the rest will come in good time."

José's face clouded over again.

"Meanwhile," went on the old woman, "don't worry as far as Elisa is concerned. I'll watch out to see that her love doesn't grow less, and that she'll be as good and industrious as she's always been up to now . . . Come, don't feel sad. There's no happier time than the time of an engagement. Launch your boat soon to take advantage of the bonito season. When it's over, then we'll talk, if it's been a good one."

Upon saying this, she got up. José did likewise, without raising his eyes from the floor; so sad and downcast was he that he awakened pity. Señora Isabel gave him a few affectionate pats on the shoulder, at the same time pushing him toward the door.

"Come, dear, we're going to have supper now; you must want yours and so do we. Elisa," she added, raising her voice, "light José's way out; he's going. Go now; good night, until tomorrow . . ."

"Rest well, señora," replied José, his voice faint.

Elisa went down the stairs with him and opened the door. They gazed at each other dejectedly.

"Your mother's not willing," he said.

"I heard the whole thing."

They stood silent a moment; he outside the doorway, she inside with the lamp in one hand, the other bracing her in the angle of the door.

"Last night," said the girl, "I dreamed about shoes . . . that's lucky, and that's why I was so anxious for you to speak."

"You see," he answered with a mournful smile, "you can't place your trust in dreams."

After another moment's silence, they held out their hands to each other and pressed them tightly, saying almost in the same breath:

"Good-bye, Elisa."

"Good-bye, José."

IV

When the fish runs were scanty along the coast of the Bay of Biscay, some boats from that region used to come to fish the waters near Santander and Asturias. Their crews chose the port they liked best and there they spent the bonito season which lasted approximately from June to September. While they stayed in the harbor of their choice, they led the same life as the local sailors; they went out to sea with them and returned with them at the same hour. The only difference was that the Biscayans ate and slept on their boats where they threw together a rough kind of shelter for the night, covering it with tarpaulins and hanging it with old sails so they could sleep, while the natives went contentedly home to bed in their own houses. There were no rivalries or friction between them. The Biscayans are peaceful and good-tempered by nature; the Asturians, livelier and shrewder, but generous and hospitable. At sea, they helped one another and cordially reported their luck back and forth. After they had landed, they repaired together to the taverns to argue amiably over a few drinks of wine. The Biscayans are more abstemious than the Asturians; they seldom get drunk. The latter, like the Southern people, are given to salty jokes and pithy sayings, and they teased the others about their virtue.

José's father was one of those Biscayans. When he came one summer to fish with the others, José's mother was a beautiful young woman, a widow with two small daughters, willing, indeed obliged, to support them by working as a fryer in a fish-packing plant. José's father established relations with her and seduced her with the promise of marriage. In vain the beautiful Teresa waited for him. Within a few months it became known that he had married another woman in his own region while José was already quick within her.

Teresa was of an impetuous and ardent temperament, passionate in both her loves and hates, quick to anger over trifles, unruly as a wild mare, and bad-tempered. She had the stupid self-love of the ignorant, and she lacked the counterpoise of good sense which common people usually possess. Her quarrels with her neighbors were known to all; she had made herself feared for her tongue and her fists. When anger took hold of her, she was transformed into a fury. Her beautiful big black eyes took on a ferocious expression and all her features were distorted. Hearing her screaming in the streets, the inhabitants of Rodillero used to shake their heads with disgust, saying: "That crazy woman of Ramón de la Puente's" (that was the name of her dead husband) "is at it again."

The treachery of her lover made her sick with rage. Nothing less than a bloody revenge would have satisfied her. For a time her poor daughters paid for the seducer's crime. She never spoke to them except in shouts which terrified them; their slightest fault cost them cruel whippings. All day long nothing but blows and cries could be heard from the dark shop where the widow lived.

It was under such auguries that our José first saw the light of day. Teresa neither could nor would take care of him. She turned him over to a village woman who consented to do it for a few *reales,* while she went back to the hard work of her job. When after two years the foster mother brought him back to her, she did not know what to do with him; she left him to the care of his little sisters, who in turn abandoned him to go and play. The poor child used to cry for hours on end, lying on the hard-packed earth of the store without the comfort of a single caress. When the girls dragged him out into the street with them, it was only to seat him there, half-dressed, and in danger of being trampled by draft-animals or run over by a cart. If, out of charity, some neighbor picked him up, Teresa, instead of thanking her for it when she came home, would berate her for "sticking her nose in other people's business."

As José grew a little older, this aversion was plainly manifested in the ill-treatment she made him suffer. If she had always been fierce and terrible to her legitimate daughters, it is easy to imagine how she would be toward that boy, the son of a man she loathed, a living testament to her weakness. During his childhood, José was a martyr. Never a day went by without his feeling the violence of the maternal hand. When he inadvertently committed the slightest misdeed, the poor child began to tremble and ran to hide in any corner of the village. All in vain. Teresa, burning with anger, a broomstick in her hand, prowled the streets looking for him, spitting threats, dishevelled like one of the Furies, followed by a train of those urchins who always enjoy tragic spectacles, until she found her child and dragged him home. If some good-hearted neighbor scolded her from his doorway for her cruelty, you should have heard the insults and abuse which poured scalding and sharp from the widow's lips! As a rule, the imprudent critic found himself obliged to retire, bested and shamed.

For a brief time the boy went to school where he showed a quick and lucid intelligence, soon dimmed by the rough labor of fishing. When he was twelve years old his mother put him to work as a boat boy, so that with the half-share given him at the distribution of earnings, he was able to help support the household. He found the change welcome. It was better to spend the day on the sea than in the schoolroom submitting to the chastisements of the teacher. The boat master very seldom struck him; the sailors treated him almost like one of themselves. Most days he went to bed without having been dealt a single blow; although when it was time to get up, his mother used to rouse him with a punch or two in the face. Moreover, he was proud to be earning his own bread.

At sixteen, he was a robust boy, with regular features somewhat marred by exposure to weather, slow in his movements like all seafaring men. He spoke seldom and smiled sadly, still under the maternal thumb as much as when he was seven years old. At sea he proved so diligent and courageous that he began to earn full pay sooner than others. Persuaded by a ship's captain, he left off fishing when he was nineteen to sail on a frigate running to America. Only then could he enjoy complete independence, though he voluntarily sent a portion of his pay to his mother. But affection for his village, memories of his childhood companions, and, however strange it may seem, love for his family, all were strong enough to cause him to leave the overseas run and take up the work of a fisherman again. Nevertheless, he would go out with only the best stores and gear. During his voyages, he had made some money from the goods he was allowed to bring in, and with it he bought a boat. From then on, his fortunes changed markedly. In a place as poor as Rodillero, the owner of a boat plays an important role. He was almost a personage among the sea men who combined respect for his position with appreciation for his courage and skill. His work began to reward him well. In a matter of two years, he had saved enough to build another boat, for his own needs were not great.

During this time he set his heart on Elisa, a beauty among the beauties of Rodillero, good, modest, hard working, and reputed to be rich. If he had not noticed her himself, he would have been forced to do so by the words of his friends and the advice of the goodwives of the village. "José, why don't you court the teacher's daughter? No girl in Rodillero could suit you better. José, you ought to marry the teacher's daughter; she's as good as gold, and quiet; don't be a fool, speak to her. The best match for you, José, would be the teacher's daughter . . ." They repeated it so often that at last he began to want her to be his. For her part, she was hearing identical suggestions regarding the sailor wherever she went. The women never wearied of commending his handsome presence, his diligence, and his conduct.

But José was excessively shy, and grew more so with the realization that he was in love. For a long while, his only manifestation of the tender feeling inspired in him by Elisa was to follow her closely with his eyes wherever he met her. Yet he still avoided an opportunity to meet her face to face. None of this kept the girl from knowing almost at once what was going on in the fisherman's heart. And, returning it measure for measure, she began to send him those lightning-swift glances which girls employ to set aflame the hearts of men in love with them. José felt them; he enjoyed them; but he dared not take a step to bring himself nearer her. One day he confessed his amorous yearnings and his keen desire to talk with the teacher's daughter to his friend Bernardo. The latter laughed heartily at his shyness and strongly urged him to overcome it; but however much he tried, he accomplished nothing.

Time went by, but matters remained at a standstill, to the visible chagrin of the girl, who had grown mistrustful of ever seeing them reach a satisfactory outcome. Bernardo, seeing his friend sadder and more shamefaced by the day, decided to rescue him from his plight. On the afternoon of a picnic, both men were walking a little apart from the rest of the company in the meadow when they saw coming toward them a group of girls also out walking. Elisa was among them. Inspired, the light-hearted sailor smiled mischievously. He engaged in maneuvers which brought them close to the girls, and when the opportunity came, he gave his friend a strong shove which made him collide with Elisa, at the same time saying, "Elisa, here is José." Then he ran away. Blushing and confused, José stood face to face with the beautiful girl, also blushing and confused. "Good afternoon," he finally managed to say. "Good afternoon," she replied. And so the die was cast.

Love takes a firm hold on reflective, silent, and virtuous men. José's passion, the first and only one in his life, quickly sent down deep roots. Elisa repaid his love in full. The shrewd mother herself appeared to look upon them with favor. The neighbors watched with pleasure. Everything smiled on the lovers in the beginning.

But when the sailor was at the harbor's mouth, so to speak, when his hand was almost on his prize, the boat began to leak. His heart told him the obstacle was not small, but serious. As he felt at his back the closing of Elisa's door, leaving him in the darkness of the street, a great sadness, like despair, took possession of his spirit. Many presentiments crossed his mind. He felt an oppression in his chest, and although he had not been running, he paused a moment to catch his breath. Later, as he walked along, he made vain efforts to drive away his sadness by sensible reasoning. All was not yet lost; Señora

Isabel had not opposed the wedding, merely postponed it. If worse came to worst, it could be brought about without her consent.

Deep in his brooding, he failed to see a man coming along the street until he had collided with him.

"Good evening, Don Fernando," he said, recognizing the gentleman.

"Hello, José. I'm glad I met you. You may be able to tell me the best way to get to Robledal . . . or rather, to the house of Don Eugenio Soliva."

"The best way is the Sarrió road to Antromero; there you take the Nueva road, running past the church. It's a little longer; but it's dangerous to go along the beach at night . . . But, why are you taking such a long trip at this hour? It's nearly twelve miles."

"I have some business . . . to discuss with Don Eugenio," said Señor de Meira with a mysterious air.

The seaman's lips twitched in a slight smile.

"I'm going into the tavern to have something to eat. Would you like to come with me before starting your trip, Don Fernando?"

"Thank you, José. I accept the invitation to prove again my esteem for you," replied the Señor de Meira, placing a tutelary hand on the sailor's shoulder.

The two men entered the nearest tavern and seated themselves in a far corner. José ordered bread, cheese, and wine. Señor de Meira ate and drank with remarkable appetite. When they had finished, they went out into the street again, saying good night to each other like good friends. The fisherman stared after the gentleman for a moment and murmured:

"Poor Don Fernando, he was hungry!"

The old man's figure melted into the shadows of the night. As on many other occasions, he was going to borrow money. Everyone in the village was aware of these secret excursions to the neighboring towns. Sometimes his forays took him to the most distant points in the province, always by night and by stealth. Unfortunately, Señor de Meira almost always returned as he had gone, with empty pockets, but always stiff-necked and with the courage to undertake another campaign.

José went on his way to his house, only a few minutes' walk away. He found his mother in the kitchen with his two sisters. Seeing them all together, his face darkened. These sisters, older than he, had long since married; one of them had six children. Each lived in her own house. The seaman knew from experience that every time they got together with their mother, whose disposition and tongue they had inherited, it boded trouble for him. This witches' sabbath at an unusual hour seemed a bad omen. And he, who faced the wrath of the ocean daily, began to tremble before those three women gathered like a tribunal. Before the threatened storm could break, he tried to go to bed, simulating fatigue.

"Aren't you having supper, José?" asked his mother.

"I'm not hungry, I had something to eat at the tavern."

"Have you settled your accounts with Señora Isabel?"

This question was the first muttering of the thunder. José heard it with terror, yet he answered in a tone of indifference:

"Yes, we've done that."

"And how much was your share from this catch?" the mother questioned him again, poking the fire and affecting absent-mindedness.

The second roll of thunder sounded much nearer.

"I don't know," replied José, again feigning indifference.

"Haven't you got the money with you?"

"Yes, señora. But until I've settled up with the crew tomorrow, I don't know exactly what my share amounts to."

A long pause ensued. Although the seaman kept his eyes on the floor, he felt the inquisitorial stare of his sisters who hadn't opened their mouths up to now. His mother went on poking at the fire.

"And what was the price you set for the bonito today?" she said at last.

"What it was bound to be set at, Mother . . . don't you know?" replied José, stammering.

"No, I don't know," replied Teresa, laying the poker on the hearthstone and lifting her head with resolution.

The sailor lowered his head and muttered rather than spoke:

"At the going price . . . , a *real* and a half . . ."

"You're lying! You're lying!" she screamed, advancing a step and fixing him with her burning eyes.

"You're lying! You're lying!" cried his sisters almost in the same breath.

José kept still, not daring to defend himself.

"We know the whole thing! . . . All of it!" went on Teresa in the same tone. "We know you've deceived me, cheated me since the run began, you rascal; that you're giving away the bonito to that rogue of a woman while your mother works like a dog after sweating all her life to support you . . ."

"You work because you want to; you know that very well," said the seaman humbly.

"And all for what!" went on Teresa, refusing to listen to her son. "So that shameless woman can laugh at you, can rob you blind, throwing her daughter at you as bait so she can slam the door in your face in the end . . ."

These words wounded José in his most sensitive spot.

"Mother," he exclaimed agitatedly, "I don't know why you hold such a grudge against Elisa and her mother. Even if I do marry, I'm not going to abandon you on that account. The boat I have now will be yours . . . and if you need more, you'll have more . . ."

"Do you think you're going to get married, you simpleton?" said one of the sisters, smiling sarcastically.

"This is none of your business," replied the seaman, turning on her angrily.

"Your sister is right. You're a fool, a fool!" screamed the mother. "Can't you see you're the laughingstock of the village? Can't you see that witch is deceiving you so she can suck your blood?"

Poor José, so cruelly tormented, could no longer maintain the humble attitude he usually showed toward his mother, and, raising his head with dignity, he answered:

"What is mine is mine to give to whom I choose. You, Mother, have no reason whatever to complain . . . Up to now what I've earned has been yours . . ."

"So you're throwing that in my face, you knave?" she shouted, more and more furious. "That's all I needed . . . After having worked so hard to bring you up; after scorching my face over the kettles, dragging myself around day and night to bring home a crust of bread for you and your sisters, you insult me like this?"

Here Teresa flung herself into a chair and began to sob loudly.

"I'd rather die than have my son insult me so!" she went on, between tears and groans. "Let me die! . . . Why am I still in this world if my only son throws the crust of bread I eat in my face!"

She went on in that vein, pouring out complaints and laments, tossing her head in desperation, and raising her hands to heaven.

All solicitude, the daughters rushed to console her. Frightened by the effect of his words, José was at a loss to know what to do. He had no heart to answer his sisters, who turned on him while consoling their mother, excoriating him:

"Get out, you unnatural son! You ought to be

ashamed of yourself! Do you want to kill your mother? Some day God will punish you . . ."

He weathered the squall with resignation, and when he saw that his mother was a little calmer, went silently to his room. His heart was so heavy he could not fall asleep for a long time.

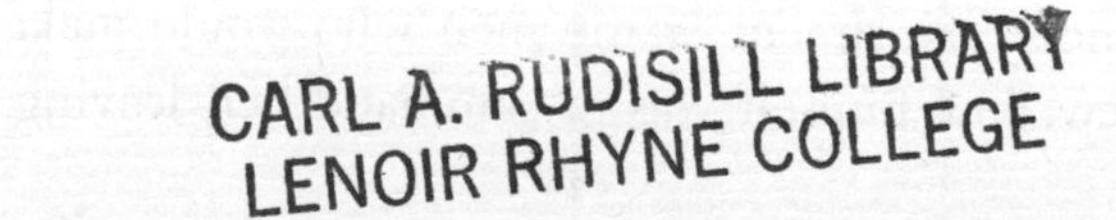

V

With the coming of a new day, José's depression waned. He convinced himself there was no reason for so much anxiety. In the light of the sun, the obstacles which had seemed insuperable at night, seemed to him trifling. Hope flooded his heart again and he felt full of the courage to overcome them.

Indeed, it appeared that events justified this sudden rebound from sadness to gayety. On the succeeding days he found Señora Isabel more amiable than ever, strongly encouraging the lovers, demonstrating to him with deeds, if not words, that sooner or later he would be Elisa's husband. The girl likewise gained confidence and began to make roseate plans for the future, hoping to overcome her mother's resistance and shorten the period of the engagement.

As for José, fortune continued to smile on him. On St. John's day, he launched the new boat as he had planned, and it began to dance free and light over the waves, promising him many good days of fishing. The priest came to bless it, and later the tavern rang to the usual noisy merriment of the men who would make up the crew. José himself was to command her, leaving the old boat to another skipper. On the following day, he put her to work fishing for bonito. Rarely had such an abundant run been seen—so much so that our seaman was on the way to growing rich in spite of Señora Isabel's bloodsucking at every settlement of their accounts.

What a lucky summer that was! By dint of constant pressure, Elisa succeeded in dragging from her mother permission to be married at the end of the run, that is to say in the month of October. Innocently lulled by this promise, the sweethearts basked in the promise of their forthcoming union. They had entered upon that interval in life, happy as none other, when heaven offers nothing but smiles to lovers, and the earth its blossoms. To both of them, work was a shower of blessings. Every bonito that took José's hook and came plunging over the side of the boat seemed a herald announcing his wedding. On the day when he turned home with two hundred fish floundering on the planking, he thought what a giant stride he had taken toward Elisa. She, in the processing plant, had no thought of resting; all day she was busy supervising the operations of weighing, cutting up, salting, frying, and packing the fish. By nightfall, she could hardly stand up; but she would let herself fall on the bed with a smile on her lips as she said to herself: "We've got to work hard; we'll have children some day . . ." Elisa's happiest hour was the one just before supper. Then José would come to the shop where there was a pleasant group which made it possible for them to be together, exchanging words and glances. They seldom used the dialogue of love; they did not need to. To those who love deeply, any word is drenched with it. Apart from that hour, their happiest moments were those when they said good-bye; she with the candle in her hand as we saw her on the night we met her; he outside the door, leaning against the frame. During those few moments, they would exchange a little of that which overflowed their hearts, their lips trembling, until Señora Isabel rudely broke the enchantment by summoning her daughter.

The girl could delight in still another happy hour during the day. That was during the siesta. While her mother was lying down for a short time after dinner, Elisa would go out of the house and climb one of the hills around the village, there to bask in the sight and coolness of the sea. At that time of day the heat in Rodillero was stifling during the months of July and August. The breeze from the sea could not penetrate beyond the first windings of the ravine, which left most of the place breathless among the enfolding mountains. The girl would climb slowly along a wide path that cut through the pines to the chapel of San Esteban, perched on the mountain top, and there she would sit down in the shade. From that spot she could look out upon a vast expanse of ocean upon which the burning sun beat down. Near the land, the sky was a deep blue; above the sea it was paler, turning to a grayish tone at the horizon. White dumpling clouds were piled up toward the east, above the peak of Peñas, the highest on the Cantabrian coast. It and other distant promontories were scarcely visible against the gray sash of the horizon. But the nearest, San Antonio, behind which lay the Bay of Sarrió, received the full rays of the sun and stood out in a vivid orange hue. Elisa's eyes sharpened as she scanned the far reaches of the sea looking for the fishing boats. Usually they stayed in line with the entrance to Rodillero, a long distance off, almost lost in the light haze hanging above the horizon. Eagerly she would count those white dots and fondly make the effort to determine which of them was her sweetheart's boat. "That one to the left that's moving away a little, that must be his; you can tell by the whiter sail, because it's new! Besides, he always likes to go off by himself a little and lay to on his spare rigging . . . There's no one who can smell out the fish as he can." And hugging her illusion, she would zealously follow the maneuvers of that boat until it either moved so far away as to be lost to sight, or came nearer. Sometimes she would notice them all making for the home port. Then she would make a wry face, exclaiming: "No good! There's not much bonito today." But joy fought with disappointment in her heart, for she would see her lover all the sooner. She would wait a while longer to see them emerge little by little into the realm of light from the grayish haze which enfolded them. With shortened sails, they looked like phantoms gliding smoothly over the water. As if obeying the signal of an invisible hand, they would begin to draw together, and in a few minutes they would be lined up like a small squadron. When she could see them close at hand, she would rush down to the village. Nobody, not even

José, knew about those happy moments she spent in the solitude of San Esteban's mountain.

Time was slipping by, not as rapidly as our lovers wished, but certainly much faster than suited Señora Isabel. She could not think of Elisa marrying without tremors of anger and fear, for with the wedding ceremony, she would be obliged to turn over to her daughter the shop and the other property of her late husband. And although she was resolved in any case to oppose the wedding with all her might, still she was reluctant to be forced to show her hand, for she feared that love might lead Elisa to some act of rebellion. Therefore, with her head chock full of iniquity, she searched tirelessly for some way to break that bond and go back on the promise they had dragged out of her. At last she thought she had found an infallible means, through a certain base machination doubtless suggested to her by the devil as she lay wakeful in her bed.

In the village there was a boy reputed to be foolish or feeble-minded, the son of the sacristan of the parish. He had reached the age of at least twenty but could neither read nor write, nor was he fit to work at anything but ringing the church bells—with masterly art to be sure—and to wander along the edge of the sea, gathering crabs, sea-snails, and octopi among the rocks. At this he was also a master. The boys used to make fun of him and often they would chase him through the streets with shrill cries. What most used to vex poor Rufo (that was his name) was to be told that his house was falling down. This would cut him to the quick, and the little boys never tired of it. Wherever he went he would hear a childish voice calling to him from near or far away, but usually far away: "It fell down, Rufo, it fell down." Hearing this, the unfortunate creature would become distraught as though some grievous injury had been inflicted on him; his eyes would roll and his mouth foam, and in this state he would run like a wild beast after the children, who took good care to put distance between them immediately—the more distance the better. At times his accesses of rage caused him to fall unconscious to the ground. The villagers felt sorry for him, and when they witnessed such scenes they never failed to scold the boys sharply for their cruelty.

It was known in the village that Rufo cherished in his heart a lively and ardent passion for the teacher's daughter. This, too, served as a pretext to make fun of him, although grown men were the ones who delighted in doing this. Whenever he passed a group of sailors, they would call him to give him some news about Elisa. Once they told him she had been married that morning, news that left the poor idiot stricken; another time they advised him to ask Señora Isabel for the girl's hand because they had had it on good authority that she was secretly in love with him, or, should the mother refuse to make them happy, to kidnap her. They also brought José's name into these jokes. They would speak ill of him, calling him ugly, a schemer, and a poor fisherman. This would make the poor fool laugh and jump up and down with joy, and, in comparing him with José, they would assure him very seriously that he was incomparably the more dashing, and that though he caught fewer fish, he rang the bells better. Thus, in proportion as love for Elisa grew in the breast of the idiot, hatred for José also grew. Rufo considered the man his mortal enemy, to such a degree that every time he met José he would cast angry looks at him and mutter insulting words, all of which caused the lucky seaman to laugh, as was only natural.

Elisa, too, laughed at this love which flattered her womanly vanity nonetheless. For admiration is welcome even when it comes from fools. On meeting Rufo in the street, she would assume an amiable expression and speak to him in the tender protective tone used for children. She enjoyed the grimaces and the fawnings with which Rufo groveled before her like a faithful dog. She solemnly promised to marry him, provided he obeyed his father and stayed his hand from hitting the children. With an expression of longing, Rufo would ask: "When?" "I don't know, my friend," she would reply. "Ask Our Lord and see what He says." The poor creature spent whole hours on his knees in the church, asking the famous Christ of Rodillero when the wedding would take place, but no answer ever came to him. "He doesn't want us to marry yet," Elisa told him. "Be patient and good, so He will relent."

Señora Isabel had hit upon the idea of making use of the passion of this unfortunate to break up—or at least postpone—the union of her daughter and José. One day she went out walking along the shore where she knew Rufo used to go to catch crabs, and she met him as if by chance.

"Hello, Rufo, are you getting anything?"

The idiot raised his head and smiled upon seeing Elisa's mother.

"Tide's out, don't bite," he answered in the broken phrases peculiar to him.

"Come, come, there's quite a few," answered Señora Isabel, drawing near and casting a glance at the hand-basket where his catch lay. "Your father's lucky to have you; every day you take a basket of crabs home to him."

"Father don't like crabs . . . he throws them all out into the street . . . and he hits Rufo with a stick . . ."

"He hits you because you catch crabs?"

"Yes, Señora Isabel."

"Well, your father hasn't much taste; crabs are very good. See here, when your father doesn't want them, bring them to me. Elisa likes them very much."

The sad, weak face of the idiot suddenly lighted up at hearing Elisa's name.

"Elisa likes crabs?"

"Very much."

"All, Elisa; all, Elisa," he said emphatically, spreading his arms to compass the edge of the sea.

"Thank you, Rufo, thank you. You love Elisa very much, don't you?"

"Yes, Señora Isabel, I much love Elisa."

"You'd be glad to marry her?"

The fool grinned from ear to ear. Confused and abashed, he stared at Señora Isabel without daring to reply.

"Come, speak up. Wouldn't you marry her?"

"You don't want me," he said at last, timidly.

"I don't want you to? Who told you that?"

"You want José."

"Bah! If José were poor I wouldn't want him. I like you better; you're handsomer, and there's no one in Rodillero who can ring the bells like you."

"José doesn't know how," said the idiot in a triumphant tone, displaying a great joy.

"Of course he doesn't! All José knows is how to fish for bonito and hake . . ."

"And bass . . ." Rufo pointed out, passing suddenly from joy to sadness.

"All right, bass, too. What of it? On the other hand, you catch crabs and octopus . . . and limpets . . . and sea-snails . . . and sea-urchins . . . and oysters . . . Besides, you fish alone, without anyone to help you, while José needs his friends to help him. How much do you think José would catch if he didn't have a boat?"

"He's got two," Rufo again pointed out sadly.

"All right. But the old one isn't much good . . . If it weren't for the new one, I wouldn't let him have Elisa, did you know that?"

The dull, light-colored eyes of the idiot glinted with a fleeting expression of anger.

"I sink new boat," he exclaimed, striking the tongs he held in his hand against a rock.

"Because José has obligations to take care of," went on the old woman as if she had not heard those words. "He has to feed his mother who'll have to stop working soon, but you're free. Your father makes enough to keep himself. Besides, you have a rich brother in Havana . . ."

"He's got watch," said Rufo, interrupting her.

"Yes, I know."

"And gold chain that hangs down, Señora Isabel."

"I know, I know. You'll have one, too, if you marry my daughter. You'd be the owner of a store, and you'd make a lot of money . . . and you could buy a horse to take Elisa to the picnics with her in front and you behind, like the priest of Armedo and his housekeeper . . . And you'd have riding boots like Don Casimiro's son."

The old woman was painting a picture of innocent happiness, not forgetting a single detail however nonsensical, to encourage the fool. He listened to her with wonder and suspense, smiling beatifically as though he saw before his eyes a celestial vision. When Señora Isabel had completed her description, a period of silence ensued.

Finally with a sorrowful shake of her head, she said:

"If only it weren't for José!" And she stood staring reflectively out at the sea.

Rufo started as if someone had pinched him; his

face clouded over, and he also stared fixedly at the horizon.

"Well, Rufo, I'm going home, for Elisa will be waiting for me. So long."

"Good-bye," said the idiot without turning his head.

Señora Isabel moved slowly away. When she had gone a long distance, she turned around to stare at him. He was still standing as she had left him, motionless, his eyes fixed upon the sea.

VI

That year, as every other year, the same thing happened: the large number of Biscayan boats caused some ill-feeling in Rodillero at the end of the bonito season. So many boats congregated in the shoal water every afternoon that the fishermen could not beach them all. However high up the first ones were pulled, the last ones had no room left and their masters were obliged to leave them lashed together at the mercy of the sea. This caused certain quarrels and hard words. There was a good deal of grumbling, and from time to time there were sharp complaints to the harbor master. But this did not prevent the Biscayans from staying on in the port, as long as the authorities in Sarrió did not order them to leave. The clashes were not so many nor so sharp as might be expected, however, owing to the peaceful temperament of both the natives and the outsiders.

As long as the weather was propitious, as it almost always is there during the months of June, July, and August, everything went along fairly well. But when September came, the discords and the mutterings grew in proportion to the danger to the boats which remained afloat. Though the sky may look serene during these months and the breeze may not stiffen, a heavy surf is often whipped up by storms gathering in distant regions. These rough seas, which prevail for a great part of the autumn along that coast, were a worry to the owners of vessels, who feared the moorings on the boats might part at any moment and one would ram another's beam. Merely to go down to the beach at night was enough to ascertain that such fears were well-founded. The seas would set the boats dancing; they would slam into one another and creak as though protesting against the blows, producing a rumble like that of an excited crowd in the silence and darkness. Sometimes the noise was like a pleasant chat about the various events of their hazardous life; at other times like a heated dispute in which all of them wanted to take part at once and to state their opinions; again it was a serious and angry fight which would cost some of them their lives.

An unlucky event came at last to justify those who were most worried and who most insistently demanded the departure of the Biscayans.

One dark—though calm—night of the aforementioned month, the chattering of the boats grew very animated toward the early hours of the morning. Soon it degenerated into a dispute which grew sharper by the moment. At one o'clock in the morning, a real and monstrous battle was joined, like nothing ever seen before. The Biscayans, who were sleeping on board their boats, found they had to get up in a hurry and maneuver skillfully to prevent heavy damage. For an hour they worked like beavers to avoid the ruin of many boats and the abandonment of others, their own as well as those of Rodillero, for the shocks were severe and the cables in danger of parting. Finally the fury of the seas increased so much that, judging themselves helpless to avert a catastrophe, they ran through the village shouting an alarm. Most of the men and many of the women responded instantly. When they arrived on the scene, some boats had already broken loose from the force of the prolonged pounding. A Biscayan knocked violently on José's door:

"José, get up at once; your boat is loose."

The seaman leaped from his bed aghast, pulled on his trousers and jacket in all haste, and with a crowd of others ran bare-headed and barefooted to the edge of the water. His trained ear noted a dry and ill-omened sound above the roar of the seas. The confused spectacle before his eyes stopped him in his tracks.

The sea was extremely rough. The pitching of the boats that had remained afloat was dizzying. Repeatedly they cannoned into one another. Above the roar of the breakers that dry noise, like the rubbing together of bones, could be plainly heard. To this loud clamor was added the shouts of the men working together to save their boats, their silhouettes vivid among the shadows. They kept blaming one another for not preventing the collision of the launches. At all costs, they tried to get them apart and keep them separate. The women were screaming, more fearful for the lives of their men than for the ruin of the boats. The men answered their cries with terrible oaths. All this created an infernal din, inspiring fear and distress. The darkness was not so great as to make it impossible to distinguish objects. Many people had brought lanterns which darted swiftly from side to side like falling stars.

When José had recovered from his amazement, he ran to the spot where he had left his new boat, the one in danger, for the old one was high and dry. Yet his fear was not great, for he had had the good luck to arrive in port in time to anchor behind a huge rock which projected into the sea forming a natural pier. He leaped on the vessel nearest the shore and moved from one to another until he reached the spot where he had left his. But when he arrived, he found that it had disappeared. In vain he scanned the area with his eyes; in vain he questioned his companions. No one had noticed it. Finally a man carrying a lantern shouted to him from the beach:

"José, a while ago I saw a boat go adrift. I don't know if it was yours."

Poor José felt a clutching sensation in his heart. It could be no other, for all the rest were there.

"If it's yours, it couldn't get very far," said a sailor beside him. "What little wind there is, is on-shore; the seas will have driven it right back."

These words were spoken solely with the intent to offer consolation. The man who uttered them knew full well that with that night's undertow, it could as easily be driven out to sea as to land.

Nevertheless, José took heart.

"Gaspar, lend me the lantern," he shouted toward the land.

"Where are you going?"

"Along the shore to see if I can find her."

Moved by pity, the seaman who had consoled him said:

"I'll go with you, José."

The man with the lantern said he would, too. Together the three of them hastened away from the beach at Rodillero and followed the shore line, scrupulously searching every spot where they thought the boat might have run aground. After a mile of walking among the big rocks, they came out on a wide, sandy beach. That was where José had set his hopes. If the boat had gone aground there, she was safe. But though they paced it all slowly, they saw nothing.

"It seems to me it's useless to go any farther, José," said Gaspar. "The road among the rocks must be under water now; it's still rising."

José insisted on going ahead. He hoped he might find his boat in the little bay of Los Angeles. But the beach there was under water, and however closely they hugged the mountain, they were splashed by the incoming seas, one of which finally washed completely over José and put out the lantern. The sailors firmly refused then to go another step. No one carried matches to light it again. To travel in the dark was to run the risk of a broken head, or at least a leg, among the rocks. José told them to turn back, but he refused to go with them.

He was alone in the darkness between the mountain which reared its peak above his head and the boiling and furious sea, whose breakers seemed enormous dark gullets hungry to swallow him. But our sailor refused to be terrified by the seas and the darkness. Leaping from rock to rock and utilizing the moments of calm to follow the most difficult passages, he succeeded in reaching the Bay of Los Angeles at a late hour. He saw nothing there either, even though he ranged widely, exploring one by one the big rocks enclosing the bay. Finally, worn out and exhausted, his feet cut, soaking wet, and despairing, he turned toward home.

By the time he reached the broad beach near Rodillero, it was daylight. The sun was shining above the horizon and starting to climb majestically into a blue sky. The water which beat against the coast was roiled as always after the bottom had been stirred up by a heavy surf, and it curled angrily against the rocks on the shore and pounded them with crashing blows. Sometimes it covered them completely in a white mantle of spray; again it climbed them furiously only to fall back spent before reaching the top; sometimes it contented itself with entering every hollow and concavity in battle array to see if some enemy were hidden there and do him to death. And finding no one on whom to vent its fury, it fell back growling and muttering threats, to renew the charge yet more violently. The seas broke in serried ranks upon the broad sandy beach, ceaselessly renewing themselves. They came in line of battle, high and menacing, tossing their manes of spume;

they would advance majestically over the field of the cloth of gold, hoping to encounter resistance, but upon finding only emptiness, they let themselves fall back lazily, conquered not by an adversary, but by their own weight and strength. And behind these came others, and hard upon them still others, and later others, and so forever, with no end and no repose. And still out there in the distance, infinite legions could be seen gathering angrily together, rising up from all the corners of the earth to succor their companions.

The immense agitation of the ocean, lashed into motion for some mysterious reason, that confused heaving which stretched to the broken line of the horizon, offered a strange contrast to the laughing serenity of the sky. José stood still for a moment, facing the sea, and contemplated the panorama with the never-ending wonder of the seaman. Neither anger nor despair was in his face. Accustomed to yielding their lives and property to the might of the sea and to being bested in their struggles against it, fishermen bear its inclemencies with resignation, and respect its fury as they would that of an angry and omnipotent God. At that moment he was more concerned about a boat he could descry battling the seas on the line of the horizon than about his own boat. After following its maneuvers closely for some time with knowledgeable eyes, he went on his way to the village. When the first houses came into view, he was seized by a gloomy thought: the loss of his boat was going to thwart his approaching marriage again. As if only then aware that he was half-dressed and soaking wet, he began to shiver.

VII

The damage done in Rodillero by that great "tidal wave" (as the fishermen called a high sea) was very considerable: four or five boats broken up, and a great many others damaged. The Biscayans, the supposed cause of it all (and they actually were, though in an innocent manner) went about abashed and ashamed. As soon as the sea had calmed, some two days after the event, they hoisted sail for their own land, leaving the port less obstructed and the town quiet.

José's boat had been the only one carried away by the sea, a fact which caused a good deal of comment, for the moorings to the land had not parted but had gone intact with the boat. Supposing, as was logical, that the lines were secured, this was not easily explained. When during low tide, José hove the four-fluked anchor which the boats used, he was astounded to see that the cable had not been parted by a heavy pull but by a knife. In vain he tried to explain to himself that strange phenomenon by natural means, but it was useless to cudgel his brains in the face of what lay before his eyes. Finally, to his sorrow, the suspicion that a mischievous hand had been at work could not be denied. But this caused him even greater surprise. Whose hand could it be? Only an enemy's, and he had no enemies. To his knowledge, there was no one in the village capable of such villainy. And to avoid slandering anyone, even in his own mind, he determined, with his usual loyalty, to think no more about it, and not to broadcast his shocking discovery. He buried it in the depths of his spirit, doing everything possible to forget it completely. The loss of his boat discouraged him not at all; but the consequences which that loss brought with it filled him with bitterness.

Señora Isabel pretended to sympathize deeply with him in his trouble; she outdid herself in plaints and laments; she burst forth in violent imprecations against the Biscayans. Nevertheless she made clear in all her words that she considered the mischance very serious.

"Isn't it a shame that those good-for-nothing outsiders should be the cause of the ruin of the people who belong in Rodillero?"

And speaking directly to José:

"Don't worry, dear, don't worry about being ruined . . . God will not fail you as He has never yet failed you . . . . Work in good faith, for as long as you're young, there's always the hope of bettering your luck."

These words of consolation left our seaman deeply distressed, for they told him unmistakably that there was to be no talk of marrying for the time being. And indeed he let the time go by without uttering a word concerning it, either to the schoolmaster's wife, or alone with his sweetheart. But his sadness, reflected in his face, proclaimed openly the weight which lay heavy on his heart. He made the effort to appear serene and smiling in the schoolmaster's store, and tried to take a merry part in the conversation, but suddenly his face would fall and he would rub his forehead in discouragement. Something similar was happening to Elisa. She also knew it was useless to talk to her mother about the wedding, and she tried in vain to hide her disappointment. During the brief conversations she held with José, neither dared raise the subject at all; but in their faltering voices, the long, sad looks they exchanged, and the slight tremor of their hands as they took leave of each other, they showed without need for explanation that the same thought was making them both miserable. The worst of it was that they could not yet guess when their anxieties might have an end. To consider all the scrimping that José must do to buy another boat was tantamount to postponing their union for several years.

While the lovers were suffering thus, the word that the loss of the boat had not been accidental, but intentional, began to run through the village. No one knew who started it. The circumstance that the mooring lines had been carried away intact lent much color to this speculation. Moreover, it also became known that the anchor cable had not parted, but had been cut. Teresa was one of the first to pick up the rumor. And with the peculiar lucidity of women, especially those of a fiery temperament, she instantly put her finger on the heart of the matter.

"Elisa's mother's hand was at work here!"

In vain her women cronies tried to insinuate the

idea that there were people in the village envious of José's good fortune. She refused to listen to them.

"No one wishes harm to my son. Even though there may be someone who envies him, no one is capable of doing him harm."

Nothing could change her mind. She was running over with virulence toward her enemy. During those first days, no one dared speak a word to her. She grew thin and yellow and she spent her time rampaging around the house like a hungry beast. Finally, one day, she planted herself in front of José, her arms akimbo, and said:

"What will you bet I'm going to grab your sweetheart's mother by the neck and wring it?"

José halted in terror.

"Why, Mother?" he asked in a quaking voice.

"Just because. Because I've taken the notion to . . . What have you got to say about that?" she replied, fixing him with a haughty stare.

The seaman lowered his head and made no answer. Knowing his mother, he waited for her to unburden herself.

Seeing that he would not reply, Teresa went on, passing abruptly from apparent calm to a furious exaltation:

"Yes. Some day I'll grab her by her few remaining hairs and drag her down the beach . . . That trollop! That sow! . . . That shameless hussy! . . ."

She ran hot-temperedly through the whole catalog

of insults. José remained mute during the hailstorm. When it began to taper off, he asked again:

"But why, Mother?"

"Why? Why? Because it was she, that jade, who made you lose your boat . . ."

"How do you know that?" asked the fisherman calmly.

Teresa did not know it, far from it; but anger made her insist just then that she did know it, of her certain knowledge, and having neither facts nor reasons to marshal in support of her statement, she made up for them with shouts, insults, and threats.

José tried hard to dissuade her, pointing out the grave sin she was committing by imputing such wrongdoing to anyone without being certain of it; but the widow refused to listen. With growing fury, she went on uttering threats. Whereupon the sailor, deeply troubled, began to think that if his mother carried out what she was threatening, his relations with Elisa would be severed permanently. He exclaimed anxiously:

"Mother, I beg you, for God's sake, not to ruin me!"

The tone in which he spoke was so full of pain that it touched Teresa's heart, for she was not ungovernable except when anger blinded her. She stopped for a moment, then muttered darkly. Finally she let herself be softened and promised to keep still. But within three or four days, in a fit of bad temper, she again burst out in threats against her enemy. This left José depressed and apprehensive, expecting any moment that she would kick up a scandalous disturbance that would finish off his wavering courtship.

Nor was Teresa idle; she was seeking at any cost to convert into certainty the suspicions gnawing at her. She prowled the streets of the village, questioning her friends, carrying on her investigations with greater dexterity and ingenuity than an experienced police agent. Finally she found out that several days before the event, Señora Isabel had had a long talk with Rufo, the imbecile, on the seashore. This fact bathed the whole shadowy subject with light. There could no longer be any doubt. The schoolmaster's wife was the intelligence and Rufo the arm which had committed the crime. Then to obtain proof of it, Teresa availed herself of a means as appropriate to her nature as it was opportune. She went immediately in search of Rufo. She found him on the strand, surrounded by several seamen who were amusing themselves by teasing him, and she flew straight at him, her eyes blazing with anger, as she said:

"So it was you, you overgrown rascal, who cut the cables on my son's boat so it would be lost? You're going to die at my hands right now!"

The idiot, taken by surprise, fell into the trap. He took several steps backward, turned very pale, and clasping his hands in abject fear, he said:

" 'Scuse me, Señora Telesa . . . 'Scuse me, Señora Telesa! . . ."

Then she gave herself away. Instead of going on in

that angry and threatening tone, she let a smile of triumph break over her face.

"Aha! So it really was you! . . . But this trick was never your own idea . . . you're too stupid . . . Someone put it into your head . . . The schoolmaster's wife put you up to it, didn't she?"

Recovered from his fright and warned by that smile, the fool had enough cunning not to compromise his idol's mother.

"No, señola; no, señola; it was only me . . ."

Teresa did her best to drag the secret out of him; but in vain. Rufo would not be moved. The sailors, tired of the contest, exclaimed:

"Go on, leave him alone, Señora Teresa; you won't get any more sense out of him."

The widow, persuaded beyond doubt that the author of her misfortune was Señora Isabel, enraged and infuriated because she had been unable to drag it physically out of the idiot, ran straight to the other woman's house. The latter was sitting at the door of her shop, sewing. Teresa saw her from afar and screeched in a waggish tone:

"Hello, Señora Isabel! So you're sewing! I'm going to help you a bit."

We cannot know what Señora Isabel found unusual in that tone, nor what she saw in the widow's eyes when she raised her head. The fact is that she rose abruptly from her chair, took it inside with her, and barred the door, all with such speed that however fast Teresa ran, she could not get there in time. Seeing herself cheated, she pounded furiously on the door, screaming:

"So you're trying to hide, you hussy? So you're trying to hide . . . ?"

But Señora Isabel appeared immediately in the window, saying with affected calm:

"I'm not hiding, no. Here I am."

"Come down a minute, señora," answered Teresa, disguising the threatening tenor of her words with a smile.

"Why do you want me to come down? To get a better look at that old hag's face of yours?"

This terrible insult was spoken in a calm, almost friendly tone. Teresa reared wildly, feeling the spur, and shaking her fists at the window, she shouted:

"To tear out that serpent's tongue and throw it to the dogs, you vicious woman!"

Some passersby were now surrounding the widow; heads began to appear at the windows of neighboring houses, waiting with visible satisfaction for the tragicomic spectacle to begin. Quarrels between women are very frequent in Rodillero. It's logical, given the lively and excitable disposition of most of them. Lack of education and the absence of urbanity, both common to the masses, not only make for frequent quarrels, but always give them a gross and repugnant aspect. Moreover, in Rodillero, there is something traditional and unique in the quarreling. Since ancient times, the wrangles among the women of this village have been famed throughout Asturias, and it is recognized that when they break out, none are more hideous and disgraceful. Hence, all the women, accustomed from childhood to witnessing them and often taking part, are accomplished in the art of quarreling, and some become finished artists. This distinction never lies hidden; for example, it is said: "Fulana quarrels well; Zutana flies off the handle too soon; Mengana screeches but doesn't say anything," as in Madrid the endowments of important orators are discussed and assessed. Not so very long ago in Rodillero there was a person who eclipsed all the women jousters and routed them as soon as they entered the lists. This was a man, although he had a good deal of the woman in him, judging by his gestures and tastes. His name was, or is, Pedro Regalado, but no one there knew him by any other name than Don Cándido the old woman. Although Teresa had engaged in numberless quarrels, she had never reached the pitch of perfection demanded by her colleagues. Owing to her native impetuosity, she lacked that ability to conceal her wounds in order to injure the adversary without exposing herself, that opportune raising and lowering of the voice, that persuasive gesturing of the hands, that ironical smile, that retreating with majesty and suddenly attacking again with a new insult in the mouth. Señora Isabel, because of her somewhat higher station, seldom descended to the arena of the street, but she was generally feared for her shrewdness and malevolence.

"You went to the dogs a long time ago, you poor thing," she said, unmoved by Teresa's terrible threat.

"That's what you'd like to do, throw me to the

dogs! But first you want to make me beg alms by taking the food out of my mouth."

"What did I take of yours?"

"My son's boat, you slut!"

"So I ate up your son's fishing smack? I didn't think I had such a big gullet."

The bystanders laughed. Teresa, burning with fury, screamed:

"Laugh, you hussy, laugh! Everyone in town knows you were the one who cajoled the sacristan's idiot into cutting the boat's cables."

The schoolmaster's wife turned pale, and for an instant she froze; but recovering herself quickly, she said:

"What everyone in town knows is that you ought to be locked up for a madwoman."

"You'll be locked up, and soon too, in jail. I'll have you dragged off to jail or I'm not the woman I think I am."

"Shut up, fool, shut up," said the schoolmaster's wife, letting a smile play around her mouth, "Can't you see they're all laughing at you?"

"To jail! To jail!" repeated the widow loudly and turning to those around her, she demanded emphatically, "Have you ever seen such a vicious woman? . . . Her mother died of a blow this hussy gave her with a frying pan, well you know it . . . She threw her brother out of the house, and he was forced to enlist . . . As for her husband, a good man, she let him die like a dog without a doctor or medicine so she wouldn't have to part with a few pennies . . . which weren't hers in the first place. And if she hasn't killed the one she's got now, it's because he's so weak and soft he doesn't bother her with anything."

At this moment, Don Claudio, who was standing behind his wife, not daring to intervene in the talking-match, stuck out his ill-favored face, made even more ugly by the indignation it reflected, and said:

"Be still, foul-mouth; get out of here or I'll call the justice of the peace right now."

But his wife, who had been reining in her anger with a great effort, found a means to relieve her feelings without compromising herself, and lifting her arm, she dealt him a superb back-handed punch in the face. The poor pedagogue, seeing himself so unexpectedly maltreated, had only enough spirit left to exclaim as he lifted his hands to the injured part:

"Woman! Why are you punishing me?"

Teresa was so carried away by her enumeration of her enemy's evil doings that she did not notice that comic incident, but went on declaiming to the crowd around her:

"Now she's robbing her daughter of the money her dead husband had from his parents, and she won't let her get married so she won't have to give up her prize . . . She'd rather keep her teeth in it!"

Señora Isabel uttered a strident laugh.

"So now it's out! You're offended because I don't want my daughter to marry one of your ilk, aren't you? You'd like to get your claws on my money and play ducks and drakes with it, wouldn't you? Lick yourself, you poor thing, lick yourself, your mouth is greasy."

The widow turned red as fire.

"Neither my son nor I need your money. All we want is not to be robbed by you. Thief! Thief! Thief! Thief! . . ."

The fury that possessed her made her repeat this over and over, thus making herself liable to arrest. The schoolmaster's wife aimed at the kind of invective that could be voiced with impunity.

"What have I stolen from you, you poor wretch? Nobody remembers when what you had was stolen from you."

"Thief! Thief! Thief!" screamed the widow, choking with rage.

"Be still, fool, be still," said Señora Isabel, her smile never leaving her lips. "Come, it looks as if you want me to call you *that thing* . . ."

"You'll wind up on the gallows, you fiend!"

"Don't worry about my calling you *that word*, because I don't want to." Then turning to the bystanders, she exclaimed jocularly: "Isn't that woman stubborn, she's determined that I shall call her *that word!* . . . And I don't want to!"

On saying this, she spread her arms with such amusing deliberation that it excited the laughter of the watchers. Teresa's fury had reached its peak. The insults pouring from her mouth became increasingly gross and frightful.

However great may be our love for the truth, however keen our wish to paint faithfully such a striking scene, our respect for our readers forces us to call a halt. Their own imagination will readily fill in the rest of the picture. The tongue-lashings went on for some time in the same vein; that is, Señora Isabel fencing with mockery and sarcasm, Teresa laying about her with every imaginable insult. She was accompanying her violent words with action. She moved back and forth with amazing celerity; she would spin around like a top; she would wave her arms in all directions; she jerked off the kerchief at her throat which was smothering her; her whole body shook as if in contact with an electric current. A hundred times she left the spot and as often came back to hurl a new insult in her enemy's face with a voice grown hoarse.

Exhausted at last by so much exertion, her voice almost gone, she went away for the last time. The onlookers lost sight of her in the windings of the street. Señora Isabel, the victor, shouted after her from the window:

"Go on, go on! Go home and take some linden and orange-flower tea if you don't want to get the palsy and burst!"

Teresa did in fact have heart trouble, and after she had suffered some setback, she would feel it. As soon as she came home she collapsed with such a serious attack that the local doctor had to be called in all haste.

VIII

When José came home from the sea in the afternoon and was told what had happened, he felt the most acute suffering of his whole life. He could give no thought to it, however, until his mother had come out of her attack. The care she demanded and the anxiety she had aroused did much to make him forget his own misfortune. But when she had recovered after two or three days, he felt the blow to his heart so keenly and so cruelly that he was almost sick. In spite of this, he never let fall from his lips one word of recrimination. He buried his troubles within his breast and went about his daily tasks with his usual apparent calm. But when he returned from the sea in the afternoons, instead of going to the schoolmaster's store or even spending a while in the tavern with his friends as he used to do, he went home as soon as the business connected with the catch had been finished, and did not go out again until sailing time the next day.

This resignation bothered Teresa more than an hourly quarrel would have done. She went about quiet and ashamed. Her maternal heart smote her as she saw the mute, sombre sadness of her son. Although that would not have sufficed by any means to snuff out the flame of her anger, and though she longed frantically to wreak total revenge on Señora Isabel, she began to feel something akin to remorse. But this did not deter her from filing a legal claim against the sacristan for damages caused by his son Rufo who, as an imbecile, was not responsible in the eyes of the law. And as the facts were proved by the evidence, the judge of Sarrió sentenced the sacristan to keep the idiot shut up indoors and to indemnify José for the value of the boat. The first requirement was complied with at once; but the second was not so easily carried out. The sacristan lived on the scanty perquisites paid him by the priest, and was not known to have any other worldly goods. When the clerk of the court went to attach his property, he was obliged to take the furniture, the kitchen fixtures, and the bed clothes, none of which brought much money, old and worn out as they were. But the sacristan's wife must have thought them worth their weight in gold or marble, judging by the weeping and sighing it cost her to part with them. This woman had the reputation in the village of being a witch. The mothers regarded her with terror and took good care not to let her kiss their little ones; the men sometimes consulted her before a long voyage to ascertain its outcome. Instead of trying to correct this opinion, she encouraged it by her conduct, in much the same way as did some of the unfortunate women whom the Inquisition sent to the stake long ago. To such lengths can feminine vanity be carried. She told fortunes with cards or by the lines in the palm; she took the curse off those who were unable to enjoy marriage; she dispensed unguents and powders to awaken love in the desired person, and bore herself with an air of competency and a show of mystery which greatly excited the superstition of the poor fishermen.

Watching her house being stripped of its furnishings, she burst out in such terrible curses on Teresa and her son that she horrified the curious who had followed the clerk of the court and the constable, as they always do in such cases.

"God grant that trollop may have to beg alms in the streets and be hanged for a thief! God grant that everything she eats may turn to poison! God grant that her son may one day go to sea and not come back!"

While the officers of the law were carrying out their duties, she never ceased invoking heaven and hell against her enemies. The neighbors present left in terror.

"I wouldn't want to be in the shoes of José, the widow's son, for the sake of all Don Anacleto has," an old seaman was saying to those walking beside him. "That woman's curses are to be feared."

"They won't amount to much," replied another, younger and lighter of heart.

"I tell you they will. You're a boy and you can't remember; but Casimiro and Juan here know very well what happened to me years ago because of her . . . I was on my way to the beach one afternoon to go out after hake when she called me to ask me to take her Rufo with me and make him my boat boy. Of course I refused to do it, because that poor fool has never been good for anything. Then she turned against me like a mad dog; she heaped insults and curses on me. I kept on my way, paying her no heed, and went aboard. We reached the beach about nine o'clock, and had our lines out until daybreak. Would you believe that I caught only three hake? All the other boats came in with eighty, a hundred, and one even had a hundred and thirty. The next day the same thing happened to me more or less, and the next day, and the next! . . . Finally, my boy, there was nothing for me to do but go to her house and beg her for God's sake to take the curse off me . . ."

The old seamen supported what their shipmate had said. When the other villagers learned of the tremendous maledictions uttered by the sacristan's wife, they also pitied José sincerely. Teresa herself, on hearing of it, felt frightened, however much her pride forced her to conceal her fear.

At the dinner hour, Señora Isabel, who had heard the news in the street, passed it on to her daughter with great relish.

"Have you heard the news, Elisa?"

"What?"

"That they went to attach the furniture belonging to Eugenia, the sacristan's wife, on account of what her son, Rufo, had done to José's boat . . . But I wouldn't care to be in José's shoes or his mother's! . . . The curses that woman put on them won't bear repeating . . . I heard they were terrifying . . ."

Elisa, whose impressionable and superstitious turn of mind was well known to her mother, turned pale.

"According to what they say, those curses were frightful," went on the old woman, inwardly licking her lips, "that she would see them begging alms in the streets . . . that José might have to steal to eat, and that she might later see him hanging from a gibbet . . . that he might go out to sea some day and not come back . . ."

Elisa's hand trembled as she lifted her spoon to her mouth, while her mother, with refined cruelty, repeated one by one the maledictions uttered by the sacristan's wife that morning. Finally tears fell from the girl's beautiful eyes. On seeing them, the mother waxed very indignant.

"What are you crying about, you fool? Is there a girl in the world any stupider? . . . Wait and I'll give you something to cry about!"

And getting up from her chair she administered a couple of hard slaps in the face which reddened the girl's pale cheeks.

As these events were taking place in Rodillero, the bonito season was coming to an end; more accurately, it had completely ended. This was during the last days of October. The weather was calm. The sea rippled lightly all along its expanse at the passing of the cold autumn winds. The sky looked pale and pellucid toward dusk; violet clouds hung suspended above the horizon. Owing to the purity of the atmosphere, the headlands along the coast seemed nearer. When the wind came in gusts, chill tremors ran over the surface of the sea as if the monster had goose flesh.

The time had now come for sardine fishing, more relaxed and less dangerous than for the bonito. Unfortunately, there were few sardines along the coast that year. The boats went out morning and afternoon, and came back most days with less on the planking than the value of the fish cast as bait. How different was that year from the preceding one when the men could catch enough in an hour to be able to go home satisfied; when the gulls wheeled in flocks above the ships to feed on the scraps from the booty; when the boys, perched on the rocks, saw the sardines gleaming like huge piles of silver ingots in the bottom of the boats.

And since there were no sardines, neither was there bait to go out for congers and hake, nor to fish off shore for sea bass, sole, red mullet, and other delicious fish. Hence hunger was soon to make itself felt in Rodillero, for fishermen generally live from day to day with no thought for the morrow. Some, however, fought against poverty by continuing to go out for bonito, although it, too, was scarce, and this late in the season, such fishing entailed a great risk. At this time of the year, the sea can kick up very suddenly. The wind may veer abruptly to come from another quarter, and the boats have to go far out to find the bonito. José was one of those daring seamen, but finally he heeded the warnings of the old men and the counsel of his own experience, and decided to give up the bonito fishing and concentrate on sardines, though with scant hope of a good yield.

Before starting the sardine fishing, he journeyed by land to Sarrió one morning with the object of buying bait. The day had dawned serene. The sea was the color of milk. The sun was wrapped in a thin white mist for a considerable time and the capes in a transparent bluish haze. Above the smooth expanse of the sea, the sky was streaked with violet and rose-mottled clouds, and the wind was starting to blow up fresh from the northeast. By one o'clock in the afternoon, the breeze was dying down; toward the land some little white clouds appeared like tufts of wool. A change to foul weather was taking place. Within a half-hour, that was clearly evident. The west wind had won out over its enemy and had begun to blow hard, but without yet giving cause for concern. However, it kept rising little by little, so that by three o'clock it was at gale force.

The seamen who had stayed in the village were all gathered on the shore. From then on, the southeast gale kept increasing in force. A stir of fear began to make itself felt in the village—a confused, low rumble arising from the comings and goings of the people, from the questions they asked one another. The women left their housework and went to the doors and windows, staring at one another worriedly and asking with eyes and tongues:

"Have the boats come in?"

"Are the boats outside?"

One after another, those whose men were on the sea directed their steps toward the shore, gathering in groups and exchanging fears. But before they had reached the beach, the wind began to rage with a violence seldom seen. Within a few moments, it had reached hurricane force. As it funneled through the narrow ravine of Rodillero with a hellish roar, it beat furiously at the doors of the houses, tore off window gratings, and flung handfuls of filth in the villagers' eyes. The women, terror-stricken, stopped talking and ran distractedly to the beach. The other villagers—men, women, and children, who had no relatives on the sea—also left their homes to follow. The one cry heard in the streets was: "The boats! The boats!"

As the crowd debouched on the shore, the sea offered a beautiful rather than an awe-inspiring sight. The sudden gales had not yet brought with them any great stirring of the waters, only a swift surface swell. Hence the vast smooth plain was only lightly ruffled. All along its expanse, infinite numbers of white dots gleamed, alternately appearing and disappearing with a magic sparkle. But the hundreds of eyes fixed anxiously on the horizon could see no sign of a boat. Then a voice cried: "Let's go to San Esteban! To San Esteban!" Everyone left the beach to climb the mountain which overlooked an immense expanse of water. Most of them went running to the road behind the village which led to the church; but the children and the poor women whose husbands and brothers were on the sea set about climbing its face. Impatience, terror, anxiety lent them the strength to surmount the sharp rocks and brambles.

When they had reached the top and scanned the great plain of the ocean, they could see three or four white dots on the line of the horizon. Those were the boats. Later several others appeared one after another, standing out with increasing definition.

"They're all making for land under nothing but the foresail," said one of the seamen who had just arrived.

"Making for land, yes. But they're trying to reach the nearest shelter. They're headed for Peñascosa," replied another.

The group of spectators gathered on the mountain top was being rapidly swelled by those still scrambling up. The wind whipped the women's kerchiefs and forced the men wearing hats to hold them on. An anxious silence reigned among that handful of humanity. The hurricane howled in their ears until it dazed and deafened them. All eyes were fastened on those white specks which seemed to hang motionless out there on the horizon. From time to time, the seamen exchanged quick observations:

"The choppy sea must be hampering them."

"Pshaw! . . . That doesn't matter. Right now the sea isn't giving them the slightest trouble. If they can make shelter, there's nothing to worry about."

"They'll have to luff a good deal."

"Of course. They'll have to beat to windward . . . even so, I don't know if they'll be able to put in behind the cape."

At last the boats were lining up one behind another out where the seaman was pointing.

The group breathed again. But this respite began to give way to anxiety in proportion as time went by and the boats failed to appear above the point of land nearest Rodillero, called The Horn.

Half an hour passed. The group of villagers kept their eyes on the cape with an expression of painful uneasiness. The wind kept rising ever higher and more violent.

"They're taking a long time," said one seaman in the ear of another.

"Maybe they put in to the bay at Peñascosa," replied the other.

"Or they're jogging on and off and can't make land."

The first one was right. After a long wait, a boat appeared off The Horn under topsail close-reefed.

"It's Nicolás de la Tejera's boat!" cried several voices.

"Praise be to God! Blessed be the Most Holy Virgin! Our beloved Christ has saved them!" cried the wives and mothers of the crew almost with one breath.

And they went running down to the beach to wait for their men.

In a few minutes another appeared.

"It's Dorotea's Manuel," they cried immediately.

The same blessings and shouts of joy were heard. Another throng of women and children detached itself and ran toward the shore.

Then came another, and another, and thus the boats made their appearance one by one. The group on Mount San Esteban was dwindling little by little as the boats entered the cove of Rodillero. Soon only a handful of people were left. One boat was missing. On the beach it was already known that that boat would never arrive, for it had foundered; but no one dared climb San Esteban to give the news. The poor women there kept on waiting with their little children in their arms, silent, motionless, sensing their tragedy and making every effort to drive the terrible thought from their minds.

Now the sun was setting in crimson splendor. The wind was still blowing furiously. The ocean's waters had stopped curling, and were swelling arrogantly. Still the wives and mothers stayed on, their eyes fixed on the sea, waiting for their men to appear. Not one of them spoke a word either of fear or consolation; but, without their knowing it, tears rose to their eyes. The wind promptly dried them.

While all this was going on in Rodillero, José was hurrying homeward by the Sarrió road. As an experienced seaman, he knew at the first sign of foul weather that a dangerous gale was in the making. As he noted the unusual violence of the gusts, he said to himself sadly: "Some misfortune is bound to happen in Rodillero today." He quickened his pace as much as he could. From time to time he stopped for a moment to climb some headland near the road and scan the horizon in search of the boats. When the hurricane reached its peak force he could hardly contain his impatience. He gave the barrel of bait he had bought to another traveler he met by chance, and began to run like a deer until he was out of breath.

By the time he came to the first houses in the village, it was nearing dark. A group of children was playing ninepins in the outskirts. As he passed in front of them, one said:

"José, Tomás's boat was lost."

Shocked, the seaman stopped and asked:

"The one my brother-in-law, Nicasio, was on?"

The boy, frightened now and sorry he had spoken, lowered his head and made no reply.

José turned pale. He took off his beret and began to pull at his hair, uttering moans and broken phrases. Escorted by the children, and others who kept gathering, he went on his way to the village and entered it. "Here's José; here's the widow's José," the villagers said as they went to doors and windows to watch him pass, white-faced, beret in hand. As he came to a tavern, three or four voices called to him; several seamen came out to stop him, and they made him go in. One of them was Bernardo, another, the Pirate.

"They've just told me that Tomás's boat was lost . . . Wasn't anyone saved?" he asked unsteadily as he set foot in the tavern.

None of the sailors grouped about the room would answer him. After a few moments' silence, one of them finally said:

"Come on, José, have a glass of wine and pull yourself together. It could happen to any of us."

José let himself drop onto the bench nearest the counter, and buried his face in his hands, ignoring the glass his companion placed in front of him. After a pause, however, he raised a hand to it and drained it avidly.

"What can we do! It's all in God's hands!" he said, replacing the glass on the counter. And wiping away a few tears with his cap, he asked in his normal voice: "How did it happen?"

"Well, boy, they went down because they wanted to," answered one of the men. "While all the rest of us were putting back to shore under close-reefed foresails, on the watch every minute and scared almost out of our wits, we saw Tomás hoisting his foresail . . . It looked to me as if he hadn't even made it fast when, bang, the boat turned turtle . . . capsized!"

"Didn't anyone come up?" asked José.

"Yes. We saw three or four."

"And why didn't you pick them up?"

"Because we were a long way from them . . . Joaquín de la Nota was coming behind us, well to the weather side . . . We thought he would pick them up."

"You thought! You thought!" exclaimed Bernardo indignantly. "What I think is that you ought to have been marched off to jail by the civil guard the minute you hit the beach."

"Why, you mule, why?" asked the other angrily. "What could we do, passing a couple of gun-shots' distance away from them? Did you want us all to drown to save them?"

"You drown! You drown! . . . Too bad you didn't!

. . . And why didn't you lower the sail to the floor timbers and row to them?"

"Shut up, you fool, shut up! Do you think that was a sea you could fool with?"

"The sea was fine! . . . a little choppy, no more than that."

"What do you know about what's happening on the sea when you were on land, scratching your belly?"

"The sea was fine, I tell you . . . And besides, why didn't you at least drop anchor, as a last resort, and wait for them to come up with you?"

While Bernardo and the other sailor were arguing, José remained silent, his head in his hands in an attitude of profound dejection. He was thinking of his sister, left with six children, the eldest eleven years old, and no protection other than the canopy of heaven. And despite the fact that his sisters had never been kind to him and had often tormented him, he still felt a great affection for them. The tavern-keeper's wife, a fat, sluggish woman, was staring at him pityingly and making efforts to console him, now and then offering him a glass of wine. He would reach out his arm absent-mindedly to pick it up and drink it to the dregs without being entirely aware of what he was doing.

When the argument between Bernardo and his shipmate was at its height, loud cries were heard in the street, and almost at the same moment our seaman's sister burst into the tavern, the sister who had just been widowed, her hair in witch locks, her face distraught, and surrounded by her children. She rushed to José and threw herself into his arms, bursting into shrill lamentations that silenced and sobered all the seamen. He received her with tears of his own. When they broke apart, the woman gathered her children around her, and shoving them toward José, said with a theatrical air which repelled the bystanders who were aware of all that José had suffered at her hands:

"My children, you have no one to take care of you any more. Get down on your knees in front of your uncle and ask him to be a father to you. He, who is so good, may take care of you."

The generous-hearted sailor was not aware, as the others were, of his sister's hypocrisy. He embraced the children, saying:

"Don't worry, you poor little things. As long as I have a crust of bread, it shall be yours and your mother's."

He wiped his eyes and said to his sister:

"Go on, take them home, it's late now."

As soon as the mother and children left the tavern, the argument over the afternoon's accident broke out anew. All the sailors were gradually drawn into it, until no one could make himself heard.

José stood silently beside the counter, drinking occasionally from the wineglass which the tavern-owner's wife kept filling for him. Finally he had drunk so much without noticing it that he passed out and had to be carried home completely drunk.

IX

He did in fact take the widow and her children into his house and kept them as well as his scanty resources would permit. But these were dwindling rather than increasing. The sardine season remained unlucky to the end. There was a scarcity of congers and hake. When the sea-bream season came around, in the months of December and January, José was in debt for more than a thousand *reales,* and he still lacked the money to pay for four barrels of bait, which amounted to a sizable sum. Finding himself dogged by his creditors, he got rid of his boat, which being old and hurriedly sold, brought him very little. Once his boat was gone, he had no choice but to sign on another as ordinary seaman, earning a wage which, like all the others, was very small that year.

These calamities were aggravated by the absence of peace in his house. His mother did not bear her reverses patiently; she rebelled against fortune, bursting at the slightest excuse into a clamor which could be heard by everyone to the farthest corners of the village. Inside the house, her daughter, grandchildren, and José himself when he was home from the sea, were the victims of the rage which had pervaded her whole body and was choking her. Moreover, the married sister was far from pleased to see the widow and her children eating their mother out of house and home and impoverishing her, while she herself had not got so much as a straw mattress from her (those were her words); and she never failed to throw it in her sister's face as often as she could, thus giving rise to disgusting quarrels which turned the house into a veritable hell.

To get away from it for a while, and to drown his sorrows, our hapless seaman used to go to the tavern occasionally to spend several hours talking and drinking with his shipmates. Little by little the vice of drink, which he had loathed, was taking a hold on him. And if it failed to master him, as it did others, and to make him forget his obligations, it was still strong enough so that the word was going around the village that "he was turning into a drunk." Señora Isabel hastened to publish this news among her cronies.

Neither poverty, toil, nor domestic discord would have sufficed to depress the fisherman's spirit if loneliness of heart and disillusionment had not been added to them. Having grown up in unhappiness, having suffered the blows of mischance since birth, having struggled against the ferocity of the sea and the no less ferocious temperaments of his mother and sisters, he would not have minded one more lash from fortune's whip if his life had not been lighted for a short while by the sun of happiness. But he had stumbled upon love in his monotonous life, and at the same time upon prosperity. Suddenly both prosperity and love had fled. The beam of sunlight had gone out. He was left engulfed in the shadows of poverty and loneliness. And if it is true that there is no greater unhappiness than to recall bygone felicity in times of misfortune, no wonder poor José sought a respite from his family and a momentary forgetfulness of his troubles in the artificial gayety lent by wine.

He had not spoken to Elisa since his mother's quarrel with Señora Isabel, nor had he seen her except from afar. As soon as he descried her figure (which was infrequently, for he spent the entire day on the sea) he would hurry away or lose himself in a group to avoid meeting her, or he would seek refuge in the nearest tavern. He was driven by shame and fear in the beginning. He was afraid that Elisa might be offended and would not want to speak to him. Later, gossip, never idle in such cases, brought to his ears the word that the girl was inclined to despise him, that her mother had talked her around to that, and that she was soon to marry a pilot from Sarrió. Then he took care to avoid meeting her, out of dignity. The reverses he later suffered also helped to estrange him from her. He thought, and not without reason, that a ruined man with as many obligations as he had, was no match for any girl, least of all for one as sought-after as the schoolteacher's daughter.

Things stood like this when his mother suggested to him one day when the boats remained in port for lack of wind that he go to Peñascosa with her, only a little more than half a league from Rodillero. Teresa had a sister there who had offered potatoes and other vegetables from her garden. In their poverty, it was a very acceptable gift. They decided to go in the afternoon and come back after dark so José would not have to go loaded down through the village in the middle of the day. Although there was no highway to Peñascosa, the people of that village and of Rodillero habitually used a path cut along the edge of the sea unless they were going by cart or on horseback. It was this path which mother and son were following as the sun was getting low.

It was a cold clear day in the month of February. The sea was a dark blue. As the path was not wide enough for two people to walk abreast, the mother went ahead and the son was following her. They went along in a sad silence. Gayety had long since fled their hearts. When they were about half way, in a passage where the path left the rocks along the coast and entered a broad and pleasant stretch of country, they saw two people in the distance coming toward them. Teresa paid no attention to them; but José, accustomed to scanning great expanses, was soon able to make out that the two were Señora Isabel and her daughter. His heart gave a bound as he thought that they must unavoidably meet face to face. Then what would happen! He dared not say anything to his mother; he let her go along absent-mindedly with her eyes on the ground; but finally she raised her head and, noticing the two distant figures, she turned around and asked him:

"Listen, José, doesn't it look to you as if those two women are Señora Isabel and Elisa?"

"I think so," answered the seaman quietly.

"Ah!" cried Teresa with fierce relish, and without a word she quickened her pace, doubtless fearing that her son would try to prevent the plan suddenly born in her imagination.

José followed her with an anxious heart, not venturing to say anything to her. Nevertheless, after they had walked on a few paces his fear of a violent and scandalous scene overcame his filial respect, and he undertook to say sternly:

"Mother, for God's sake, please don't make trouble for yourself or me."

But Teresa kept going ahead without a word, as if she wanted to escape being reasoned with.

A little farther along, he said again, even more sternly:

"Think carefully before you do anything, Mother!"

The same silence on Teresa's part. By that time those coming from Peñascosa had drawn near to those going there. When they were a stone's throw apart, Señora Isabel stopped and hesitated a moment whether to go on or retreat, for she had noticed the far from peaceful purposefulness with which Teresa was coming toward her. Finally she chose the middle course of standing still. Teresa came on swiftly; but at a distance of twenty or thirty paces, she also stood still and, putting her hands on her hips, she began to question her enemy in the sarcastic tone that anger always made her adopt:

"Hello, señora! . . . How are you, señora? . . . Are you well . . . And your husband, too? . . . I haven't had the pleasure of seeing you for quite some time . . ."

"José, look out for your mother, she's crazy!" shrieked Sénora Isabel, her face paling.

"Ah, señora! So, after making him beg for his bread and laughing at him, you're still asking him to protect you?"

Suddenly, her ironical expression changing to one of fierce rage, she sprang like a tiger across the distance which separated her from her enemy and threw herself upon her, screaming:

"You've driven me crazy, you trollop! . . . But now you're going to pay me back for everything."

The fight was as furious as it was repugnant. The widow, stronger and more mettlesome, at once succeeded in knocking Señora Isabel down; but the latter, summoning every means of defense, seized her enemy's earrings and tore them from her ears, which bled copiously.

José on one side and Elisa on the other had thrown themselves into the fray to pull their mothers apart, struggling in vain to accomplish it. Elisa's face was covered with tears; José was pale and shaken. At one of the crucial moments of the fight, their hands met by chance. And in a common impulse, they raised their heads and looked lovingly at each other as they tenderly clasped hands.

Finally José caught his mother around the middle, lifted her in the air, and went to set her down several steps away. Elisa helped hers to get up. Both parties went on their way. Each mother went away muttering endless threats. The son and daughter frequently turned their heads to look back until they lost sight of each other.

X

Two months after the events we have just related, Don Fernando, of the great house of Meira, was walking around the huge feudal hall of his family mansion one night. Anyone might have missed the artistic bronze lamp, suitably proportioned to the majestic breadth of the room, or the handsome silver candelabra of a later period. The stone flooring was not level, smooth, and intact as in former centuries. Here and there it exhibited holes which, even though worn by the noble tread of the feet of the lords of Meira, hence worthy of veneration, were yet open enemies to the entirety and soundness of the limbs, whether seignorial or plebeian. But Don Fernando was well acquainted with the holes and skirted them without having to look as he strode with rapid step from one end of the hall to the other, enveloped in darkness.

His footsteps echoed hollow and deep through the crumbling mansion. But the mice, long accustomed to hearing them, showed not the slightest alarm, and tranquilly went on with their work of destruction, breaking the silence of the night with a light, continuous gnawing. The bats, with even less concern, flew about in their fantastic dance above the head of the old man with a dry and muffled flutter.

At that moment, Don Fernando would willingly have been metamorphosed into a mouse, even perhaps, into a bat. However poor a thing it might be to gnaw on wood, buried in a sullen hole, or to hang lethargically through the day from the cornice of a door so as to be able to fly during the lugubrious hours of the night, was it any worse, perhaps, than to be deprived of an exit into the sunlight and of a walk in free air after having known the delights of both? This was, in fact, what had happened to the noble scion of the house of Meira nearly a month ago. And why? All for such a trifle as the lack of a shirt.

For some time now, Don Fernando had had but one; yet it had enabled him to keep up a front. When it was dirty, he used to wash it with his own hands; he would hang it in a patio behind the house; when it was dry, he ironed it carefully and put it on. One morning, however, while the shirt was hanging in the sun and the Señor de Meira was waiting indoors for it to dry, a donkey belonging to a neighbor succeeded in entering the courtyard through one of the many breaches in its walls. Señor de Meira saw it go up to the shirt, but he suspected nothing untoward. He saw it sniff the shirt and still failed to guess its intentions. Only upon beholding it in the donkey's teeth did he become aware of his lack of foresight, and he felt a rent in his heart like that in the shirt. Thenceforth, Don Fernando would no longer set foot in the street during the daylight hours. It would have been most repugnant, and rightly so, to his lofty feudal sensibilities to appear without such an indispensable garment before the sons of those former vassals over whom his forefathers used to exercise their right of physical punishment and other privileges equally despotic if less violent.

Among the sons of those vassals, the word was soon getting about that Don Fernando was "having a hell of a bad time." And though hunger was hovering like a voracious eagle over the heads of most of the villagers in Rodillero, there were people whose hearts were filled with pity and who tried to succor the gentleman without offending his extreme and very touchy pride. Our José was the one who most distinguished himself in this generous undertaking. He employed a thousand subterfuges and deceptions to oblige Señor de Meira to accept his aid. Sometimes he would go to him and make mention of an old debt his mother owed the House of Meira; often he sent him a gift of fish; or, carrying food in a basket, he would go to sup with the old man in pleasant companionship. Don Fernando, aware of the seaman's precarious situation, would heroically refuse such longed for help, and José could talk him into accepting it only after a long argument, and would turn his head in order not to see the tears of gratitude. There were days when no one appeared at the forlorn mansion, and it was then that Don Fernando went through "a hell of a hard time," as the voice of the people expressed it.

Now he was going through worse and more cruel

times than ever. For twenty-four hours no food whatever had entered his stomach. And it might be inferred that nothing would pass his lips for several more hours, for it was midnight and all the villagers were abed. With every hour that passed, his misery increased. His step was not so quick. From time to time he would wipe his brow, where drops of cold sweat had gathered, and breathe sighs which died sadly on the air without reaching the corners of the murky room. The last of the noble and powerful house of Meira was about to faint. Without being well aware of what he was doing, moved no doubt by the simple instinct of self-preservation, he left the room rapidly, went down the crumbling stairs in a few bounds, and rushed out into the street. Once there, he stood still, not knowing where to turn.

It was a warm, dark night in spring. Heavy clouds completely hid the stars. Don Fernando looked around him with a pitiful expression of anxiety. After hesitating for a few moments, he began to move slowly along the street in the direction of the outskirts of the village. As he passed in front of the houses, he paused, uncertain, considering whether he should call for help; but a keen sense of shame dominated him as he was about to approach a door, and he went on. He kept walking, convinced, however, that he would soon collapse with hunger. He began to feel dizzy and noticed that he could not see clearly. When he reached the front of Señora Isabel's house, one of the last in the village, he stopped . . . Where was he to turn? Was he to die like a dog in the empty street? Then he stared around him again and saw at his left the whitely gleaming wall of the schoolmaster's garden. It was a lush, prolific garden, full of fruits and vegetables; the best in the village, or more accurately, the only good one. The criminal impulse to enter that garden and take some vegetables assailed the good gentleman. Instantly he rejected it. It assailed him again. Again he rejected it. Finally, after a hard but unequal struggle, sin won the day. Don Fernando said to himself in an attempt to whitewash his plan to steal: "Well, am I going to let myself starve to death, then? A few potatoes more or less wouldn't mean a thing to the schoolteacher's wife. She has plenty . . . ill-got at the expense of the poor fishermen . . ."

And thus hunger suddenly made a socialist of the last scion of the great House of Meira.

He followed the edge of the wall, turned to the left, and sought behind the house the most accessible spot to enter. The wall was not so high there, and was broken and had fallen in several places. Using the holes as footholds, Don Fernando managed to climb it. Once up, he seized the branches of an apple tree and lowered himself to the ground by them slowly and with great caution. After standing motionless for a few minutes to make sure no one had heard him, he moved very slowly into the garden. The first thing he did when he found himself among the rows of vegetables was to pull up an onion and eat it. No sooner had he swallowed it almost intact than he pulled up three or four more and put them in his pockets. Then he turned on cat feet toward the wall. But before he had reached it, he discovered with terror that the branches of the apple tree into which he had jumped were moving, and by the very scant light of the night he saw the bulk of a man moving among them. This man dropped to the ground, as Don Fernando had done. The old man stood as if turned to stone. And his fear and shame increased as the other man took a few steps into the garden and came toward him. The first thing that occurred to the nobleman was to throw himself to the ground. The man brushed right by him. It was José.

"Has he, too, come to steal?" thought Don Fernando. But José gave a long whistle and the Señor de Meira guessed that it was a matter of a love tryst, something that surprised him a good deal, for he had believed, like everyone else in the village, that relations between Elisa and the seaman had been broken off a long time ago. Shortly after the whistle, another figure appeared at the side of the house, and the lovers went to each other and began to talk in tones so low that Don Fernando could hear no more than a faint whispering. The gentleman's situation was difficult. If the young people should take it into their heads to stroll about the garden or to stay in it until daybreak, and if they should see him, what shame! To avert this danger, he crawled slowly and soundlessly to the apple tree and hid among the brambles which grew around its base, to wait for José to climb the tree again and go home. But soon after he had settled himself there, a few large drops of rain began to fall. The lovers also came to take shelter under the apple tree, one of the few dense and leafy trees in the garden and the farthest from the house. Don Fernando gave himself up for lost and began to sweat with fear. He dared not move a finger. Elisa and José sat down on the ground, close to each other, with their backs to the gentleman, all unaware of his presence.

"And why do you think your mother is suspicious?" said José in a low voice.

"I scarcely know how to tell you. But for several days now she's been staring at me a great deal and she never leaves me alone for a moment. The other day while I was sweeping the parlor, I started to sing. She came upstairs immediately and said: 'It seems you're very happy, Elisa! It's been a long time since you raised your voice in song.' She said it in such a way and with such a false smile that I blushed and said nothing."

"Come, you're imagining it!" replied the seaman.

After this exclamation, however, he was thoughtful, and after a time, he said:

"It's a good thing to be forewarned. Be careful that she doesn't catch you."

"That would go hard with me! It would be better if I'd never been born," replied the girl with terror in her voice.

They were both quiet again. Elisa was playing with the grass, her head down and her manner preoccupied. José shyly stretched forth his hand, and pretending to play with the grass also, he managed to stroke his sweetheart's fingers gently. The rain, coming down harder now drummed on the leaves of the apple tree with a sad and monotonous beat. The garden breathed forth a pervasive scent of damp earth.

"Are you planning to go out on the sea in the morning?" asked Elisa after a pause, raising her beautiful lustrous eyes to the seaman.

"I don't think so," he replied. "What's the use?" he added bitterly. "For the past week we haven't brought in five dollars' worth of fish."

"I know, I know. This year there's no hake in the sea."

"This year there's no anything!" cried José angrily.

They were silent again. Elisa kept on playing with the short blades of grass. The seaman had caught one of her fingers in his and was softly pressing it, not venturing to take her hand. After a while, Elisa began to speak in a low, tremulous voice, without raising her head:

"José, I think the cause of all that is happening to us is the curse the sacristan's wife put on you. Why don't you go to her and ask her to lift it? . . . Ever since that woman cursed you, nothing has gone right for you."

"Nor before either," José remarked with a melancholy smile.

"A lot of people have done it," the girl went on, paying no heed to her lover's observation. "Listen, you know what Pedro, Matiella's boy, used to be like, so thin and yellow you could hardly bear to look at him . . . Everyone thought he was going to die. As soon as she begged Eugenia's pardon, he began to improve and you can see how well he is now."

"Don't you believe in that kind of witchcraft, Elisa," said the seaman with an inflection which betrayed that he was not far from believing it, too.

Elisa made no reply; instead she clutched his arm with a gesture of terror.

"Did you hear that?"

"Hear what?"

"Right here in the blackberries."

"I haven't heard a thing."

"I thought I could hear someone breathing."

They both froze for a moment, listening intently.

"You scare easily, Elisa!" said the seaman, laughing. "It's the noise of the rain falling through the leaves to the ground."

"It seemed to me like breathing! . . ." answered the girl, not taking her eyes from the brambles where Señor de Meira was hiding, but loosing her hold on her sweetheart's arm.

Meanwhile, the old man was sweating copiously, afraid José might come to search the blackberry bushes. Luckily, that did not happen. Elisa soon grew calm, and seeing her lover downcast and with bowed head, she changed the subject, hoping to cheer him.

"When are you going to start going out for bonito? . . . I'm anxious for the run to begin . . . I feel in my heart that it's going to be a good one . . ."

"We'll see," replied José, shaking his head doubtfully. "I think we'll start going out in about fifteen or twenty days . . . What else can we do? . . ."

"The good weather is coming along . . . and the pilgrimages will be starting soon . . . What fun! . . . The one to Our Lady of Light is a month from tomorrow," said Elisa, forcing herself to seem gay.

"What does it matter when the pilgrimages begin if I can't go to them with you!" exclaimed the seaman in a gloomy tone.

"Don't lose your courage, José. Everything will come out all right . . . You must put your trust in God . . . I pray to our beloved Christ every day for your good fortune and ask Him to touch my mother's heart . . ."

"It's hard, Elisa . . . very hard . . . If she didn't like me when I had a few pennies, how is she going to like me now that I'm poor and have so many relatives on my back?"

Elisa saw the truth of this remark; but with the sublime obstinacy that love gives to women, she replied:

"It doesn't matter . . . I believe she's going to soften. Let's have faith in our Beloved Christ of Rodillero, who has worked greater miracles . . ."

The rain was coming down very hard; so much so that the tree no longer protected the lovers. The leaves were bent back with the weight of the water and were pouring it down on their heads. But they were hardly aware of it, entirely absorbed as they were in the delight of being together; their hands entwined, their eyes meeting in ecstasy.

Elisa finally succeeded in dispelling her sweetheart's melancholy. Their conversation took a happy turn. They recalled to each other incidents which had taken place on past pilgrimages, and remembering them, they laughed heartily.

"Do you remember when Nicolás invited us to the San Pedro outing? . . . You whispered to me: 'We'll have to drink up all the wine he brings out . . .' "

"Because I could see right away that the old skinflint wanted to make a splash at any cost."

"It was hard work for me to down the whole glass in one swallow! You drank yours before you could say Jack Robinson . . . and Ramona didn't do so badly either. Whenever I think of the poor man's face when he saw us draining the glasses, I have to laugh like mad, even if I'm all alone . . ."

They both laughed, trying not to make any noise.

"Of course," Elisa went on, feigning severity, "you got a little bit gay later, and you kissed my cousin Ramona."

"I don't remember."

"No, you don't remember because you don't want to remember."

"Anyway, no one knows what he's doing when he's drunk."

"It wouldn't occur to you, however, to go jump in the water."

"Of course not!"

"But it does occur to you to kiss the girls."

"Never, unless I'm drunk," said José firmly.

"Good heavens, I hope I'll have as many little angels around my head when I'm dying as the number of kisses you've given!"

"You'll go to heaven alone!" replied the seaman, laughing.

The chat became a merry argument. The lovers were drunk on that innocent conversation, finding everything they said to each other so funny that they could not help bursting into laughter which they smothered behind their hands. The dark, rainy night could not have been fairer nor more pleasant.

But Elisa thought again that she could catch the sound of breathing which had frightened her earlier. For a moment or two she was quiet and absent-minded. Then, not wanting to mention anything to José, lest he again call her easily frightened, she decided they should separate.

"It must be very late by now, José," she said, getting to her feet. "Besides, it's raining cats and dogs."

The seaman also got up, although reluctantly.

"How quickly the times passes with you, Elisa!" he said shyly.

The girl gave him a sweet smile on hearing that declaration which the seaman had never before ventured to utter, and blushing a little, she held out her hand to him.

"Until tomorrow, José."

José took her hand, pressed it long and tenderly, and answered sadly:

"Until tomorrow."

But he would not let her hand go. Elisa had to say to him again:

"Until tomorrow, José."

She pulled herself away from him and went rapidly toward the house. The seaman made no move until he guessed that she was inside. Then he cautiously climbed the garden wall, straddled it, and disappeared over the other side.

A few moments later, Señor de Meira emerged from his hiding place, wet to the skin.

"Poor young things!" he exclaimed, forgetting his own misery, and mounted into the apple tree with difficulty. Once in the street, he directed his steps toward his feudal mansion, mulling over in his mind a plan as noble as it was singular.

XI

A few days later, Don Fernando de Meira presented himself at José's house very early, before the latter had gone down to the sea.

"José, I must speak to you in private. Come and take a walk with me."

The seaman thought the old man had come for help, although he had never before asked it directly. When hunger pinched him hardest, he used to come saying:

"José, the bread is all gone at Sinforoso, and I wouldn't like to change bakers . . . If you could lend me a loaf . . ."

But before he would go even that far, the gentleman had to be very hard pressed. Otherwise, he would not humble himself to ask for anything, directly or indirectly. Nevertheless, José came to his own conclusions, for it was not easy to think anything else. And picking up a handful of pennies and putting them in his pocket, he went out into the street with the old man.

Don Fernando led him out of the village. When they had gone some distance from it, near to the broad sandy beach, he broke the silence, saying:

"Let's see now, José. You must be a little pinched for money, aren't you?"

José believed this confirmed what he had been thinking; but the protective tone in which the gentleman asked the question surprised him a little.

"Well . . . so-so, Don Fernando. I'm not very flush . . . but after all, as long as I'm young and able to work, I can usually earn a crust of bread."

"A crust of bread isn't very much . . . Man does not live by bread alone," declared Señor de Meira sententiously. And after walking along for a few moments in silence, he suddenly stopped short, and facing the sailor, he asked him:

"You'd be very happy to marry Elisa, wouldn't you?"

José stood still, silent and confused.

"I? . . . I don't have anything to do with Elisa any more . . . Everyone knows that . . ."

"Then everyone knows a lie, for you're courting Elisa; I'm certain of that," declared the gentleman firmly.

José stared at him in alarm and began to stammer another denial, when Don Fernando stopped him, saying:

"Don't bother to deny it, just tell me frankly if you would gladly be married."

"I should say so!" said the mariner, lowering his head.

"Then you shall be married," said Señor de Meira,

making his voice as deep and resonant as possible, and extending both his hands.

José quickly raised his head and looked at him fixedly, thinking that he had gone mad. Then, lowering his eyes again, he said:

"It's impossible, Don Fernando . . . Let's not think about it."

"Nothing is impossible to the House of Meira," replied the gentleman with greater solemnity.

José shook his head, venturing to doubt the potency of that illustrious house.

"There is nothing impossible," said Don Fernando again, sending him a haughty stare, worthy of a warrior of the reconquest of Spain from the Moors.

José smiled tolerantly.

"Listen a minute to me," went on the gentleman. "During the past century, one of my forbears, Don Álvaro de Meira, was mayor of Oviedo. There was a house belonging to the priest there that obstructed the public street, and the mayor determined to have it torn down. Immediately he ran into opposition from the bishop and the chapter of the cathedral, all of whom indicated that he must not think of attempting it, under pain of excommunication. But the mayor, paying no heed to threats, ordered a squad of police to go there and they began to tear it down. The bishop was notified of the happenings. His Grace was vexed; he convoked the chapter and they decided to put on their vestments to excommunicate anyone who dared to touch the house. My great-grandfather learned of that, and what did he do then? He ordered the public executioner to go there and read a proclamation which stated that any policeman who got down off the roof would be punished with a hundred lashes . . . Not a single one came down, my boy! And the house was razed to the ground."

With an energetic movement of his hand, Don Fernando toppled the priestly edifice with one blow. José appeared to be completely insensitive to the prowess of the Meiras. He kept on gazing sadly at the ground, perhaps reflecting that it was a pity the power to punish by whipping was no longer a perquisite of the lords of Meira, otherwise it might not be impossible that he himself would request a few lashes for Señora Isabel.

"When a Meira takes anything into his head," went on the gentleman, "it's time to beware and to tremble! . . . Here," he added, taking a packet out of his pocket and offering it to José. "Here's ten thousand *reales*. Buy yourself a boat and credit me with whatever is left over."

The mariner stood there stupefied, not venturing to stretch forth his hand. He was thinking that this was a mad notion of Señor de Meira's whom many already believed to be of unsound mind.

"Take it, I tell you. Buy yourself a boat . . . and get to work."

José took the package, unwrapped it, and grew even more bewildered when he saw that it contained gold coins. Smiling proudly, Don Fernando went on:

"Let's get to another matter now. Tell me, how old is Elisa?"

"Twenty."

"Has she had her birthday yet?"

"No, sir. It seems to me her birthday is next month."

"Very well. Next month I shall tell you what you are to do. Meanwhile, try to make sure that no one learns of your trysts . . . Look sharp, and be wise."

Don Fernando spoke with such authority, and he raised his eyebrows so high that despite his meager and twisted little figure, he succeeded in arousing the respect of the seaman. José almost came to believe in the mysterious and invincible might of the House of Meira.

"Another thing . . . Can you have the use of the boat tonight?"

"What boat? My skipper's?"

"Yes."

"To go where?"

"To take a ride."

"If it's only for that . . ."

"At twelve tonight, then, come to my house ready to put out to sea. I need your help for something you'll soon know about . . . Now go back home and start the negotiations for buying your boat. Go to Sarrió for it, or have it built here; whichever seems best to you."

Bewildered and highly perplexed, our fisherman took leave of Señor de Meira. He pondered the whole thing again as he was returning to his house. How could the ruined nobleman have got his hands on that money? José decided not to make use of it until he could find out.

Puzzles, especially puzzles about money, last only a short while in villages. Two hours had not gone by before it became known that Don Fernando had sold his house the preceding day to Don Anacleto, who wanted to turn it into a fish-packing plant, and that alone, for it was in truth uninhabitable. Señor de Meira had mortgaged it long ago to a business man in peñascosa for nine thousand *reales*. Don Anacleto paid this sum off, and gave him fourteen thousand over and above that. In view of all this, José decided to return the money to the generous nobleman as soon as he could see him. It seemed to him indecent to accept money its owner needed so badly, even in the form of a loan.

Nevertheless, he kept thinking about that mysterious night engagement, and was impatiently awaiting the hour to see what it was about. A little before the clock on the Town Hall struck twelve, he turned his steps toward the de Meira castle. He knocked on the worm-eaten door, and before long Don Fernando himself opened it.

"You're punctual, José. Have you got the boat in the water?"

"Certainly, sir."

"Very well. Come here and help me carry this to it."

Don Fernando pointed to a package resting in the vestibule of the house in the lantern light. It was wrapped in a piece of canvas and tied up with cords.

"I warn you it's very heavy."

In truth, when José tried to move it, he knew it

was evidently almost impossible to carry on their shoulders. He believed it was an iron chest.

"We can't carry it on our shoulders, Don Fernando. Wouldn't it be better to drag it little by little toward the beach?"

"Whatever seems best to you."

They did actually drag the package outside the house. Don Fernando put out the lantern, closed the door, and they slowly worked the massive object toward the boat, not without difficulty, by moving it end over end. Señor de Meira was taciturn and melancholy, never opening his lips. José's mood matched his. But at the same time he was curious enough to want to find out what that extremely heavy case contained.

They had to lay two planks between the boat and the beach, and thanks to them, they could roll the chest along them until it was loaded on board. Then they got in, and in the deepest silence, began to pull away from the other vessels.

It was a clear, beautiful, moonlit night. The sea was tranquil, sleeping like a lake. The atmosphere was mild as summer. José grasped both oars, against the wishes of the gentleman, who attempted to take one of them, and they were borne smoothly over the water, away from the land.

Señor de Meira was seated in the stern, as silent and reserved as when he left the house. José, pulling evenly on the oars, was studying him attentively. When they were about two miles out from Rodillero, after rounding the Horn, Don Fernando stood up.

The seaman shipped his oars.

"Help me throw this package into the water."

Jose hastened to help him; but ever more eager to solve the mystery, he ventured to ask with a smile:

"I assume it won't be money you're throwing overboard, Don Fernando?"

The old man, squatting to make ready to lift the load, paused, stood up, and said:

"No, it's not money . . . It's something worth more than money. I was forgetting that you have a right to know what it is, since you've done me the favor of helping me."

"I didn't ask you for that reason, Don Fernando. What's inside it is no business of mine at all."

"Untie it."

"Certainly not, Don Fernando. I don't want you to think . . ."

"Untie it, I tell you!" repeated Señor de Meira in a tone which brooked no argument.

José obeyed, and after unwinding the canvas wrappings that covered it in several layers, he finally disclosed the object. It was nothing but a slab of stone, rudely carved.

"What is this?" he asked in astonishment.

Don Fernando answered in slow, hollow tones:

"The escutcheon of the House of Meira."

An embarrassed silence fell. José stared closely at the old gentleman, unable to shake off his astonishment and awaiting some explanation; but Don Fernando was in no hurry to give it. With his arms crossed over his chest and his head bent, he was staring unblinkingly at the stone which he had just openly displayed. At last he spoke in a low, tremulous voice:

"I have sold my house to Don Anacleto . . . for some day I shall die, and what difference does it make whether it falls into the hands of strangers before or after? . . . But I sold it on the condition that I could remove the escutcheon from the house . . . For several days now I've been working through the night to get the stone off the wall . . . Finally I managed it . . ."

Since Don Fernando fell silent after pronouncing those words, José thought it permissible to ask him:

"And why are you throwing it into the water?"

The aged nobleman gave him an indignant glance.

"Idiot! Would you like to see the escutcheon of the great House of Meira above a fish-processing establishment?"

But he soon softened and added:

"Look at that coat of arms . . . Observe it carefully . . . Since the fifteenth century it has stood above the door of the House of Meira . . . not this same stone, for as our family has allied itself with other great houses, the stone had to be changed and new quarterings added to the coat of arms, but it was another like this . . . During the past century at the time that the Meiras and the Mirandas were united, it became definitively fixed . . . There are five quarterings. The one in the center is the Meiras' . . . it is placed at what is called in heraldry the *point of honor* . . . Its arms are: azure, a bend argent, with wyverns or; a bordure argent, with eight ermines sable . . . You will ask," added Don Fernando with an indulgent smile, "where are those colors? . . . It's a very natural question, since you have no notion of heraldry . . . The tinctures on the stone are represented by conventional symbols. The gold, look at it here in this quartering, is represented by means of little dots traced with a burin; the silver by a smooth, uniform background; the azure by thin horizontal lines; the gules, by perpendicular lines, and so on . . . ; it would take a long time to explain it all . . . The Meiras were first united with the Viedmas. Here is their coat of arms in this first quartering, of gules, a bridge argent with three arches, through which runs a mighty river, and a tower or, ascendent in the middle of the bridge; a bordure argent and eight plain crosses azure . . . Later they married the Carrascos. And here on the left, we have their quartering, equally divided into two parts: the first argent, a lion rampant sable; the second or, a tree issuent from a mound and in foliage, with a bird set above the cope, and a dog baying at the foot of the trunk . . . Neither bird nor dog can be plainly seen, for weather has obliterated them . . . but here they are . . . Later the Meiras were united with the Angulos: their quartering is argent, five ravens sable in saltire . . . The ravens can't be seen very well either . . . Finally, they were joined with the Mirandas, whose quartering is or, a castle gules in fosse, surmounted by a knight armed with halberd emerging from the battlements, accompanied by five bezants vert and argent, placed two on each side, and one on the point . . . The whole escutcheon, as you see, is crowned with a steel helmet burnished with five grilles."

The sailor understood not a word of Señor Meira's discourse. He stared at him in amazement. The sea rocked the boat softly.

"In every period of history," went on Don Fernando in an emphatic voice, "illustrious sons have come from the House of Meira, very eminent men . . . You must know very well that in the fifteenth century, Don Pedro de Meira was Knight Commander of Villaplana, of the Order of Santiago, and that Don Francisco was the magistrate of Seville and solicitor in the parliament of Toro. You must also know that another son of our family was President of the Council for Italy; his name was Don Rodrigo. Another, called Don Diego, was a justice of the Royal Tribunal of Mexico City, and later presided over the one in Guadalajara. In the past century, Don Álvaro de Meira was mayor of Oviedo and founded a collegiate church and an elementary Latin school; you must know it very well."

José knew absolutely nothing about all that; but he nodded his head to please the decayed gentleman. Suddenly the old man fell silent and sat motionless for a good while until, lowering his voice, he began to speak again in a sad tone:

"My older brother, Pepe, was a lost soul . . . you must often have heard about it . . ."

That was, in fact, the only thing José knew about the de Meira family.

"A dancer ruined him . . . The little bit that had

been left to me was taken by him, under the threat that he would marry her if I refused to give him what I had . . . To save the honor of my house, I gave it to him . . . Don't you think I did right?"

José again agreed.

"How I have suffered since then, José! . . . How I've suffered!"

The nobleman rubbed his forehead in discouragement.

"The great House of Meira dies with me . . . But it will not die dishonored, José; I swear that!"

After having taken this vow, he fell silent again in an attitude of melancholy. The sea kept gently rocking the boat. The pale light of the moon shimmered on the water.

After a long pause, Don Fernando emerged from his meditations, and, his eyes glittering with tears, he turned toward José who gazed at him sadly, and said as he breathed a sigh:

"Let's get on with it . . . Lower the stone over that side, I'll guide it on this side . . ."

Between them, they managed to balance the escutcheon on the gunwale. Then Don Fernando gave it a strong shove. The coat of arms of the House of Meira broke the surface of the water with a loud noise and sank into its dark depths. The bitter drops splashed upward on the old man's face, and mingled with the no less bitter tears he was shedding.

For a moment he remained motionless, his body bent over the gunwale, staring at the spot where the stone had disappeared. Then, straightening himself, he said quietly:

"Row for land, José."

He went back to the stern and sat down. The seaman began to move the oars without a word. Although he failed to understand completely the sorrow of the nobleman, and was not far from believing, like all the rest of the villagers, that the old man was not entirely of sound mind, he felt a profound pity at seeing him weep; he would not have thought of intruding upon that heartsick withdrawal. But the determination to return the money to the old man never left his mind. He could plainly see that, in Don Fernando's circumstances, such a favor was a definite mental aberration. He earnestly desired to bring up the subject, but did not know how to begin. Three or four times it was on the tip of his tongue, but each time he suppressed it, for his words seemed inadequate. Finally, seeing they were close to land, he could find no better means of freeing himself from the pressure than to take the ten thousand *reales* out of his pocket and tender them to the old gentleman, saying with some embarrassment:

"Don Fernando . . . From what I can see, you're not very flush . . . I'm more than grateful for what you've tried to do for me; but I ought not to take this money when you need it . . ."

Don Fernando, losing his temper, his eyes flashing with indignation, interrupted with a shout:

"Scoundrel! Idiot! After I've done you the honor of confessing my ruin to you, you insult me! Put that money away this very second, or I'll throw it in the sea!"

José realized he had no choice but to take it back. And after begging the gentleman's pardon for the alleged insult, he did so. Nevertheless, he resolved he would see to it that the old man should lack for nothing and that he would return the money at the first favorable moment.

They jumped ashore and parted like good friends.

XII

José kept secret all that had taken place, as Don Fernando had urged him to do. The old man again promised him that he would be able to marry Elisa provided he carried out to the letter everything he told him to do, and he convinced the young man that the success of the project depended entirely upon the secrecy with which it was carried out.

The good gentleman found lodging for the price of six *reales* a day; if it was not appropriate to the antiquity and nobility of his ancestry, at least it was sufficient to keep him from starving to death, as we know he had been not far from doing. Strangely enough, as soon as he had a few pennies in his pocket, his aristocratic pride rose a few handbreadths higher. He strolled through the village with chin up, step measured and firm, casting at the villagers glances far more suited to the Middle Ages than to our own day, greeting the girls with a gallant and patronal smile, as if he might still exercise his seignorial rights.

Whenever the occasion arose, he would treat his male vassals to a glass of wine and the female vassals to sweets from the confectionery. But it must be stated, in the interests of truth, that the men and women vassals failed to accept Don Fernando's favors with that respect and submissiveness displayed by their forefathers of old upon receiving the feudal prodigality of the great House of Meira. Rather it seemed that they condescended to drink his wine and accept his sweets solely to avoid wounding the nobleman's delicate sensibilities. And even a certain smile of compassion could be observed on their lips, which if they could have seen it, would have made all the sons of that illustrious house—the Knight Commander of Villaplana, the solicitor for the parliament of Toros, the President of the Council for Italy, and so on, and so on, turn over in their graves. And as if that pitying smile were not sufficient to tarnish the prestige of his lineage, the comments made behind the old gentleman's back would have been even more humiliating: "This poor Don Fernando figures that fourteen thousand *reales* will never come to an end. How much better off he'd be if he would open a little store and get an income from it! But no, he's going to spend it all in a week, and then we'll have to take care of him."

Elisa, one of the most beautiful of Señor de Meira's vassals in Rodillero, was likewise one of the most rebellious. The noble gentleman tried in vain to extend his patronage to her every time he met her; in vain he offered again and again a small bag of almonds bought just for her in Sarrió; in vain he displayed toward her all the resources of the most refined gallantry, reminiscent of the glorious days of the Hapsburgs. The pretty girl received his encomiums with a sweet and benevolent smile, showing no trace of admiration or awe. Sometimes when the ceremonious advances and the mellifluous phrases reached their peak, a certain trace of ridicule might even be glimpsed behind her soft, wistful eyes. The truth of the matter was that Nature had done nothing whatsoever to second Don Fernando's feudal inclinations. To see him with his little stoop-shouldered figure standing before the tall, slender Elisa, even the most active and fantastically inventive imagination would not have been capable of recognizing in him the lord of the castle facing a timid vassal.

On two or three occasions, he had suddenly broken the thread of his old-fashioned gallantries to ask her:

"How old are you?"

"Twenty."

The last time, he said to her:

"Have you your baptismal certificate?"

"I think so, sir."

"Then bring it to me tomorrow. But be careful that no one knows about it. I have made up my mind that you and José shall be married without further delay."

That benevolent and compassionate smile we have mentioned came again to Elisa's lips upon hearing these words, and when she left the old gentleman after a chat with him, she could not help murmuring:

"Poor Don Fernando! He's stark mad!"

However, on the advice of José, who had some (although not much) confidence in the power of the

House of Meira, she brought the old man the document the next day. She had nothing to lose by it, and it would please the good gentleman. The girl who, unlike her sweetheart, had no reason to place any faith in Don Fernando's power, took the whole matter as a joke.

What she did take more seriously, however, was the curse of the sacristan's wife—more seriously every day. Superstition had sunk deep roots into her ingenuous soul. As she now saw the implacable constancy with which fortune insisted upon thwarting her happiness, it was natural that she should attribute it to an occult and mysterious power which, when all was said and done, could be nothing but the curse of that witch. To undo or offset its potency, she often used to have recourse to prayer in the little shrine of the Beloved Christ of Rodillero, a famous image found in the sea several centuries earlier by some fishermen.

But it was in vain that within a short period of time she had burned more than a dozen candles and recited more than a million paternosters; in vain also that she offered to spend a whole day in the shrine without food or drink, and carried out her promise. The Beloved Christ either did not hear her, or wished to try her courage still further. Her love affair was growing more hopeless by the day. She could even tell herself that it was over and done with, if she thought about it calmly. José was being constantly lashed harder by misfortune. She herself was coming more and more under the heavy yoke of her mother, not daring to move without permission, nor answer back a word.

In such a bad situation, she began to consider the idea of mollifying the sacristan's wife, and thus overcome the evil influence the other woman might be exerting over her life. Her first thought was that José ought to beg to have the curse lifted. Time and again she insistently advised him to do it. But seeing that he resolutely refused, and knowing his stubborn and determined nature, she made up her mind to humble herself.

During the siesta hour one afternoon, she slipped out of the house, went into the street without being seen, and turned her steps toward the steep road leading to the sacristan's house near the church; both buildings were somewhat apart from the village upon a little plateau about halfway up the mountain. As she was going along so worried and bemused, she failed to see Jose's mother cutting furze for the stove not far from the road. Teresa raised her head and said to herself in surprise:

"Goodness! Where can Elisa be going at this hour of the day?"

First she followed the girl with her eyes, and then, full of curiosity, she began to walk behind her, keeping her in sight. She saw her stop at the door of the sacristan's house, knock, and enter.

"Oh, what a hussy!" she said sharply. "So you're hand in glove with the sacristan's wife! It always seemed to me that you couldn't be as good as you look, with that face like a plaster saint . . . I'll fix you, my girl, I'll fix you!"

Elisa was hand in glove with the sacristan's wife merely because she went into her house. This lack of logic had always been characteristic of Teresa. Anger would completely obscure the scanty judgment God had given her. She pretended to despise the curse of the sacristan's wife; her savage pride drove her to burst forth in insults whenever the woman was mentioned. But the truth was that no one in Rodillero believed more blindly in such witchcraft than she.

Eugenia came out to receive the girl and was greatly surprised at her visit; but when she learned the object of it, she displayed considerable satisfaction and triumph. Elisa explained, blushing and stammering. Eugenia, swelling up like a toad, refused to grant her pardon as long as Teresa and José themselves had not come to ask it. In vain Elisa entreated her with tears in her eyes; in vain she threw herself at the woman's feet with clasped hands, and begged for mercy. It was of no avail. The sacristan's wife, gloating over her humiliation and almost believing in the supernatural power the simple fisherfolk attributed to her, kept repeating arrogantly:

"There'll be no pardon as long as Teresa herself doesn't come and beg it on bended knee . . . just as you're doing now."

Elisa went away, her soul in distress. She knew very well that it was out of the question for her sweetheart's mother to take such a step. And since the sacristan's wife refused to lift the curse, she believed in it even more firmly than before.

She was walking along with a lagging step, her eyes on the ground, thinking of the bad luck which had always dogged her love. Judging by the obstacles He had piled up in its way in a short space of time, God undoubtedly did not favor it. The road she was going down was winding and steep. Occasionally it offered some flat stretches like staircase landings.

As she came to one of those, Teresa suddenly appeared before her. Since José's mother had never shown her any antipathy despite the rupture between the two families, Elisa smiled at her; but Teresa flew at her and answered the greeting with a hard blow in the face.

Poor Elisa was overcome at such unexpected maltreatment. Instead of defending herself, she put her hands up to her eyes and began to cry brokenheartedly.

Astounded, Teresa stood still, at odds with herself after this savage act. Elisa's humble and resigned attitude took her by surprise. And to justify to herself her unworthy deed, or perhaps to work herself up and thus escape remorse, she began to scream insults at her victim, as she always did:

"Go on, you trollop, go on back to the sacristan's wife! Are you taking lessons in witchcraft? I'll give you a broomstick. Look at her, look at her, the little hypocrite! And how bold she's getting! I should think you wouldn't have to leave home to learn witchcraft!"

These unjustified insults, following the blow, had such an effect upon the unfortunate girl that she was overcome by emotion and fell fainting to the ground. This was all that was needed to disconcert the widow completely. And with a change of heart, typical of her passionate nature, she went suddenly from anger to compassion, and running to lift Elisa in her arms, she began to croon to her:

"Poor little thing! Poor little thing! Pay no attention to me, darling! . . . I hurt you, didn't I? . . . I'm crazy! My poor little girl! To hit you, when you're so good and so lovely! What will my José say when he hears about it!"

Seeing that Elisa was not coming to, she began to pull her own hair desperately.

"Animal, animal! No woman is more of an animal than I am! Dear blessed Christ, help me, and heal this child! . . . Elisa, dear little Elisa, come to, darling, for God's sake!"

But the girl's swoon persisted. Teresa stared around her, seeking water to throw in her face. Not seeing any, and not daring to leave Elisa alone, she finally undertook to lift her in her strong arms and carry her on her back toward a fountain a little way down the slope. When she had bathed the girl's temples with water, she brought her to. The widow hastened to kiss her and ask her pardon; but those sudden rough caresses surprised the girl so much they almost made her faint again instead of reassuring her. Finally, between sobs and tears, she managed to say:

"Thank you . . . You're very kind . . ."

"Me kind! You call me kind!" interrupted Teresa vehemently. "I'm stark raving mad . . . You're the kind one, my little dove . . . Are you all right? . . .

Did I hurt you very much? . . . What will my José say when he finds out about this!"

"I went to the sacristan's house to ask her to lift the curse . . ."

When she heard this, Teresa began to pull at her hair again.

"What a fool I am! I'm a crazy woman! People are right when they say I ought to be tied up . . . To think of hitting this child when she was doing me a kindness!"

It was Elisa's turn to console her. Only after repeated assurances that she had suffered no harm whatsoever, that she was no longer frightened, and that she would forgive her and love her, was she able to calm Teresa.

Meanwhile, the girl had got up off the ground. Teresa brushed her clothes carefully, dried her tears on her own apron, and embracing and kissing her effusively over and over again, she went with her down the road from the church, her arm around the girl's waist, until they came to the village. Along the way they talked about José. What other subject could those two talk about with greater pleasure? Elisa told Teresa that either she would marry her son, or no one. Teresa showed herself completely mollified and flattered by this demonstration of affection. They exchanged confidences and secrets; they promised each other to work with might and main to bring about that marriage, and finally, when they reached the village, they said good-bye very affectionately. Teresa, still ashamed of what she had done, asked the girl before they parted:

"Elisa, you do really forgive me from your heart, don't you?"

"But if you hit me, it's because you have a right to . . . Am I not your daughter now?" the girl replied with a sweet and gracious smile.

Teresa embraced her again, weeping.

XIII

The happy outcome of the preceding events, which might very well have undone the somewhat vague schemes of the House of Meira with regard to the fortunes of Elisa and José, served in the end to further them. From that time forward, a firm friendship was established between Elisa and her sweetheart's mother, a friendship both took pains to conceal. They met secretly, rapidly exchanging news and messages from and to José. The girl's trysts with the young man during the quietest hours of the night were still going on. All three minds were pondering ways to achieve the marriage they desired against the wishes of the schoolmaster's wife, for by now they were all convinced that they could get nowhere with her. It was entirely clear to Elisa that the cause of that fierce opposition was nothing but avarice, the refusal to relinquish the property which had belonged to her dead father. But not only did she not admit this to anyone, she made every effort not to believe it herself and to drive such a thought from her mind. She even made frequent promises to herself that when the time came, she would give up her possessions in order to spare her mother distress.

But though such an intention might have been in her thoughts and in José's, she was unable to take a step to put it into effect. The poor seaman's lack of education and the abject ignorance of the two women did not permit them to glimpse a ray of light in the matter. On this occasion, as on many others during the Middle Ages, the lord of the manor was obliged to go to the rescue of the common folk. The House of Meira was silently at work on their behalf without their knowing it, much less anyone else in Rodillero, maneuvering with the mystery and the diplomatic zeal that has always characterized the great families: the Atrides,[4] the Medici,[5] the House of Austria.[6] Don Fernando had journed to Sarrió more than half a dozen times and had come back without anyone's guessing the true nature of the business which took him there. One time it was to buy fishing tackle, another to order some shoes, another to see a sick relative, and so on and so on—subtly lying and deceiving everyone with truly Florentine finesse. Neither Teresa nor Elisa had failed to notice that the shadow of the noble liege lord was hovering protectively over them; there were clear indications of this. When he passed by them he would shoot them glances of profound complicity, at times accompanied by inexplicable winks, or he would mutter some mysterious word, such as "Hope"; "Your friends are watching over you"; "Silence and a

---

[4] Sons of Atreus, i.e.: Menelaus and Agamemnon, leaders in the Trojan War.

[5] The famous ruling family of Florence during the Renaissance.

[6] The Hapsburg dynasty.

close mouth"; and various others in the same vein aimed at startling and impressing them. But most of the time they gave no sign of understanding, either because they actually failed to comprehend them, or because they did not attribute to the gentleman's diplomatic maneuvers all the importance they really possessed. José alone was privy to them to some degree, although he had little faith in their efficacy.

One day Don Fernando summoned José to his lodging; handing him a paper, he said:

"Elisa will have to sign this document."

"But, how . . . ?"

"Carry it to her in your pocket. Have a horn inkwell handy and a pen . . . and the first time you have the opportunity . . . do you understand?"

"Yes, sir."

"Let's leave it like that then."

When after several days, José returned the paper with her signature, the gentleman said to him:

"You'll have to ask Elisa if she's prepared to do anything; to disobey her mother, and to live for a few months away from her home in order to marry you."

This commission was a much greater undertaking and presented the seaman with far more formidable difficulties. Elisa could not make up her mind to take such a daring step. The fear of committing a sin and of failing in her filial duty held her back. But the priest, to whom she made confession, was aware that the opposition of her parents was irrational unless based solely upon self-interest, and that she was within her rights in disobeying. Nevertheless, she had always been so much under her mother's thumb, she was so terrified of the old woman's cold, cruel wrath, that the idea of openly rebelling against her was overwhelming. A considerable time had to elapse; José had to entreat her over and over again, even with tears in his eyes; and she had to persuade herself that there was absolutely no other recourse or means of extricating herself from that intolerable situation and of attaining what she so ardently desired, before she could finally bring herself to consent to it.

Señor de Meira having been informed that she had given in, said to José in the imperious tone appropriate to his station:

"Come for me this afternoon; we have something to do together."

José bowed his head to signify his obedience.

"Are you prepared for anything?"

The same gesture of respect.

"Very well, then. You are not unworthy of the high opinion I have formed of you. When one is undertaking something arduous, diplomacy and valor must go hand in hand; bear that in mind. My family has always been characterized by such traits; prudence and decisiveness. Don Alfonso, the governor of Rebollar, one of my ancestors on the distaff side, was known during his time and during the American wars of conquest as a consummate diplomat; and yet this in no wise detracted from his courage which, on occasion, verged on temerity."

"And what time do you want us to go for Elisa?" asked José, fearing, not unreasonably, that the gentleman was as crack-brained as he was reputed to be.

"After dinner . . . at one o'clock."

"Well, with your permission, Don Fernando . . . I have to mend a net . . ."

"All right, all right; so long, then."

At the appointed hour the seaman went to Señor de Meira's lodging. Soon afterward, they left together and turned their steps down toward the beach. Before they had reached it, Don Fernando stopped in front of a house somewhat more decent than its neighbors.

"Stop. We're going in here."

"Into Don Cipriano's house?"

"Into Don Cipriano's house."

Señor de Meira knocked at the door and asked if he might see the local judge. The old woman who came to the door, the sister of the judge, told them he was taking his siesta. Don Fernando was insistent; it was an urgent matter. Grumbling and out of patience, for she was far from ready to concede any lordly rights to Señor de Meira, the old woman finally went off to arouse her brother.

Don Cipriano, whom we have already had the honor of meeting when we saw him in the shop run by the schoolmaster's wife, received them affably, though he was obviously surprised.

"What's new, Don Fernando?"

The old man took a paper out of the pocket of his

threadbare frock-coat, unfolded it with the deliberation of a pedant, and gravely presented it to the judge.

"What is this?"

"A petition by Doña Elisa de Vega to be removed from her mother's custody and placed where the law may provide, so that she may freely manifest her will to contract a marriage."

Don Cipriano took a quick step backward.

"What? . . . Elisita . . . the daughter of the schoolmaster's wife?"

Don Fernando nodded his head in assent.

The justice of the peace snatched his silver-rimmed eyeglasses from the table and put them on in order to read the document.

It was a long process, for in his approach to the written word, Don Cipriano had moved on leaden feet all his life. While this was going on, José kept his eyes anxiously fixed on the judge's face.

Señor de Meira was absent-mindedly stroking his long white beard.

"I had no suspicion of this!" exclaimed the judge, finally raising his head. "And in truth I can't help admitting that I'm sorry . . . After all, Señora Isabel and her husband are friends of mine . . . and there's going to be a lot of hard feeling . . . Did you draw up this petition, Don Fernando?"

"Is it in order, Judge?" replied the other gravely.

"Yes, sir."

"That's enough then; nothing else is necessary."

Don Cipriano turned white, then red. No man

in the world was more abnormally sensitive than he. A look could wound him, a single word upset him badly. He believed now that Don Fernando was trying to teach him a lesson in tact, and his expression changed.

"Señor, Don Fernando—I was not trying to . . . The way you spoke . . . It seems to me . . ."

"It was not my intention to offend you, Judge. My only desire was to affirm my right to be silent before you as an official . . . Moreover, you've been my friend for a long time, and I've always taken great pleasure in extending my hand to you. The fact that you were a member of His Majesty's armed forces is enough to earn you the highest possible consideration from all well-born men."

The tone and attitude accompanying these words of Don Fernando's must have been very like those of the nobles of days long ago in speaking to some member of the commons when they took counsel together on the business of government. But Don Cipriano, unfamiliar with such purely historical deportment, was instantly mollified instead of being further insulted.

"Thank you, Don Fernando; thank you very much. Since I am so fond of that family . . ."

"I esteem them, too. But let's get down to cases. Elisa wants to marry this boy. Her mother has been impeding it for no reason whatsoever . . . perhaps because he's poor . . . or perhaps (I won't swear to this, I merely state it as an hypothesis) to avoid turning over the legacy from the late Vega which she uses to do business with and profits from. There's no other recourse than to ask the protection of the law; and the girl has done so."

"Very well. Now the next step is for me to go and ask the child to ratify what is petitioned herein. If she affirms it, we shall proceed to the matter of the custody."

"And when will that be?"

"Today . . . This afternoon, if you wish."

"If it's in the afternoon," José pointed out, "the whole town will know about it and there'll be a lot of gossip . . . If you would agree to leave it until later, after dark . . ."

"As you wish. It's all the same to me. But I warn you that the presence of the Town Clerk will be needed, and he's in Peñascosa today."

"Don Telesforo will be here by dusk," said Señor de Meira.

"Then I have no further objections. I'll expect you both by dark."

"Now, Don Cipriano," said Señor de Meira, bowing gravely, "I trust that no one will learn what has gone on here . . ."

"What do you mean by that, Don Fernando?" asked the judge, again turning pale.

Don Fernando smiled benevolently.

"Nothing that might offend you, Judge . . . You're an honorable man and there's no need to recommend secrecy in affairs which demand secrecy. I mean only that in this matter we must all exercise the greatest care. We must let no one suspect what is afoot, nor let anything whatsoever be inferred about it."

"That's something else," replied Don Cipriano, mollified.

"We're all agreed, then, that after nightfall you'll be waiting for us, isn't that correct?"

"Yes, sir."

"Until then."

The grandee offered his hand to the member of the third estate.

"Good-bye, Don Fernando; good-bye, José."

As soon as it was dark, on a warm and starry August night, Don Fernando, Don Telesforo (who had arrived opportunely a few minutes earlier), and José walked to the judge's house again. Only Don Telesforo went in. The nobleman and the seaman waited at the door. Within a minute or two Don Cipriano came out, closely accompanied by his remarkable cane with tassels and a gold head, and somewhat more distantly by the Town Clerk. After exchanging friendly greetings in high, unnatural voices, they went up the street toward the schoolmaster's house in silence.

As always at that hour of the night, the taverns were open and crowded. Light and the confused and unpleasant rumble of voices and oaths escaped through the open doors. Our friends gave them a wide berth in order to avoid being noticed. Poor José was trembling with fear. Calm and brave as he was in the face of the hazards of the sea, he felt his heart shrink and his knees buckle at the thought of what would happen when Señora Isabel saw that she had been outwitted. More than twenty times he was on the point of fleeing, leaving the other gentlemen to carry out their task alone; but the thought that Elisa was going to need him there to give her courage stopped him every time. How would the poor girl feel when the time came? As he asked himself this question, José took courage himself and went along quietly behind the three old men.

In front of the schoolmaster's house, the judge stopped and said to them in a low tone:

"Now I'm going in with Don Telesforo alone. You, Don Fernando, can stay near the door with José, in case you may be needed to encourage the girl."

The seaman agreed with all his heart, for at that moment a hair would have been rope enough to hang him. Don Cipriano and Don Telesforo left them. The light from the store shone on them briefly. They went in. A shiver of pure fright shook José.

XIV

A number of seamen and a group of women had congregated early in the store as usual, to pay homage to the wealth and importance of Señora Isabel. The harbor master and a man from Astorgas who dealt in pickled fish were also there. The gathering was silent, hanging on the words of the venerable Don Claudio who was seated behind the counter on an old cowhide chair, reading aloud by lamplight from a soiled, dog-eared book.

It was the custom of that company to relax in the reading of some novel. The women particularly enjoyed following the dolorous twists of the plot. For it was always a very sad tale that was told; anything else would have bored the listeners. A wife abandoned by her husband who, by dint of patience and sweetness, succeeds in winning him back to her arms; the adventures of an abandoned child who turns out in the end to be the son of a duke or some such thing; the travails of two lovers whom fate has cruelly persecuted for years. There were two or three dozen of these novels in Rodillero which had made the rounds of the village several times, always with the same flattering success, and each time with slightly greasier pages. Always there was the "happy ending": it was the indispensable requisite. Don Claudio was greatly affected by the mischances narrated, and he used to weep over them. When he was all choked up he never failed to suggest that someone else read until he could clear his head a little.

The novel now in hand was entitled *Maclovia and Federico, or, The Tyrolean Mines.* It was a touching account of the trials of two lovers who, born of distinguished lineage, were forced to earn their living with their own hands, owing to parental severity. Federico and Maclovia were married in secret. The girl's father, a very bad-tempered prince, pursues them. They flee, and Federico goes to work as a day-laborer in a mine. With admirable courage, his young wife follows him. They have a son; they suffer a thousand sorrows and injustices. Finally the prince relents and rescues them from all that misfortune, carrying them off in triumph to his palace. The women, and even the men, were deeply absorbed, and dying to find out how it all ended. Occasionally one of them would exclaim in a tone of pity:

"Ah, the poor little girl; everything happened to her!"

Their pity was always for the feminine element in the book.

Señora Isabel, as usual, was sewing behind the counter, at the side of her faithful husband. The troubles of the young lovers seemed to leave her cold. Elisa was also sewing; but she frequently got up from her chair, under various pretexts, displaying a restlessness which had immediately attracted her shrewd mother's attention.

"You've got quicksilver in your veins today, girl!"

It was not quicksilver but fear, and very great fear, the girl had. How many times had she repented of yielding to José's pleas! Chills ran up and down her back whenever she thought of what was going to take place that night. Her heart was dancing about in her chest with such intensity that she was surprised the others failed to notice it. She had prayed to every saint in heaven, and had promised them a thousand sacrifices if they would extricate her from that tight corner. "Dear God," she kept saying over and over, "don't let them come!" Every few minutes, she directed glances of terror toward the door. Señora Isabel noticed that she would sometimes turn pale, and then redden like a poppy.

"Listen, Elisa, if you're not feeling well . . ."

"Yes, Mother, I feel ill," she replied gladly envisioning the possibility of leaving the room.

"All right, go to bed then; you must be getting a cold."

The girl could ask for nothing more. Dropping the work she had in her hands, she disappeared swiftly through the little door into the back of the store. She bounded up the stairs as if pursued by demons; but when she had reached the parlor she stood as if turned to stone, hearing Don Cipriano's voice in the store.

He and Don Telesforo had in fact come in at that very moment.

"Good evening, ladies and gentlemen."

"Good evening," they all replied.

The schoolmaster's wife was very much surprised, for she and Don Telesforo had had a quarrel a long time ago and he never frequented the store. After a silent and somewhat embarrassing moment, Don Cipriano inquired affably:

"Where is little Elisa?"

"She's just gone to bed; she doesn't feel very well," replied Señora Isabel.

"Well, I'd like to have a few little words with her," replied the judge, continuing to use diminutives.

The woman turned very pale, for she had divined the truth.

"Very well, I'll call her," she said in a thick voice, getting up from her chair.

"You needn't disturb yourself; I'll go upstairs, if she hasn't already gone to bed."

"We'll both go up whenever you wish . . ."

The judge held out a hand to detain her, saying:

"Permit me, Señora Isabel . . . The business we have to discuss is private . . . Don Telesforo is the only one who may go up with me."

The schoolmaster's wife fixed him with a vicious stare. Don Cipriano turned pink.

"I'm very sorry, señora, but it has to be done . . ."

And in order to escape the old woman's eyes, he

hastily went upstairs to the living quarters, followed by the Town Clerk.

The venerable Don Claudio, deeply affected by that scene, let the unlucky *Maclovia* fall to the floor, and forgot to pick it up. Staring at his wife, his eyes opened so wide it was a miracle from Heaven that they didn't fall out of their sockets. She was standing motionless, stopped in her tracks where Don Cipriano had left her, his eyes glued to the door through which he had gone.

"Well," she said at last with concentrated fury, as she rubbed her face, "the girl's in heat. She'll have to get married in a hurry."

"What do you mean get married?" queried Don Claudio.

His wife withered him with a look, and turning to the people around her, who were struck dumb, not knowing what was going on, she added:

"What, haven't you all caught on to it yet? . . . Well, it's as clear as daylight; that scoundrel of the widow's needs money and he wants to get Elisa away from me."

José heard her words perfectly and he started as if he had been stung. Don Fernando tried to quiet him by laying a hand on his shoulder, but he was far from calm himself. However much he stroked his long white beard until he almost pulled it out by the roots, the unfolding of the drama within was having its effect upon him.

"I thought," said one of the regulars, "that it was all over a long time ago."

"To all appearances it was," said Señora Isabel, "but you can see for yourselves how that drunkard has fixed things so as to coax her back into the trap."

"But that is an act of rebellion on Elisa's part, and it deserves an exemplary punishment," Don Claudio exclaimed. "I'd lock her up in the cellar and keep her there for fifteen days on bread and water."

"And I'll lock you up in the stable for being a donkey," said Señora Isabel, turning the full weight of her wrath on her consort.

"Woman! Such harsh words . . . What do you gain by them? . . . Your anger . . . it seems to me it has blinded you."

The schoolmaster's face reflected at the same time both indignation and fear at hearing these words. More than ever he looked like a lapdog, though it is unkind to say so.

Paying him no heed whatsoever, his wife went on talking with outward calm.

"Well, now the widow will be satisfied! . . . We ought to be glad, for otherwise she'd have a stroke some fine day."

"But who would ever have thought that a good girl like Elisa! . . ." cried one of the old women.

"The poor thing's been greatly deceived," said Señora Isabel. "She imagines there are towers and mountains of gold in this house and that they're all hers . . . She and her lover are in for a disappointment!"

"Señora Isabel," said the judge who had come downstairs at that moment, "Elisa has filed a petition for a change of domicile in order to marry, and she has just ratified it . . . I have no choice but to authorize it . . . I'm very sorry to have to cause you such vexation . . . but the law . . . I can do nothing else."

The mother glared at him and made a scornful gesture with her lips.

"Don't be so sorry, Don Cipriano; you'll make yourself ill."

A great rush of blood suffused the sensitive official's face.

"Señora, remember whom you're speaking to."

"To Pepe, the bakerwoman's son," she said, lowering her voice and turning her back on him.

Captain Don Cipriano was in fact the son of a humble bakerwoman, and he had come up in the world after becoming a soldier. He was not one of those who tried to conceal his origin, nor did he think himself dishonored by it; but the tone of disdain with which Señora Isabel pronounced those words wounded him so deeply that he could not utter a word. His lips moved several times without a sound until finally he burst forth, saying in a tremulous voice:

"Be quiet, evil tongue . . . or by the living God I'll carry you off to jail."

The woman made no reply, doubtless fearing that the goaded judge might carry out his threat; she contented herself with laughing to her friends.

Don Cipriano, recovering, or at least convalescing, from his painful emotions, said authoritatively:

"Let me see . . . you are to designate the person

who is to take charge of your daughter while she remains a ward of the court."

Señora Isabel turned her head, looked at him with another stare of contempt, and began to sing to her friends:

"Tra la la, the figs are green."

When Don Cipriano heard this, he said still more authoritatively:

"Come here, Don Telesforo . . . I want you to be a witness here that the señora has not wished to designate anyone to undertake to keep her daughter as a ward in his home during the period of court custody."

After issuing this order, he left the store and went into the hall. Elisa was there in the dark, shaking with fear. When he had exchanged a few words with her, he went back in.

"By virtue of the power invested in me by law, I designate Doña Rafaela Morán, godmother of the party of the first part, to have her in her custody until the expiration of the term of the petition."

While Don Telesforo was filling out the proper documents, the sailors and the women commiserated with Señora Isabel, and began to comment with infinite variations on the scene that had taken place. Once recovered from the surprise they had experienced, their tongues were so loosened that the store sounded like a henhouse.

"But how did that girl dare take such a step!" said one.

"After all, what can you do about it? . . . You might as well take it calmly, Señora Isabel," said an old woman who was not at all perturbed by the other woman's mortification.

"As for me, if I were in your place," said another, even less concerned, "I wouldn't be the least bit put out . . . Let the girl leave home . . . God's blessing on her! Give her what's hers, and that'll be the end of it!"

The mother threw her a quick, angry glance. The speaker's lips wore a trace of a smile. She knew very well she had wounded the señora to the quick.

"The worst thing of all is the example, Don Claudio," said the man from Astorgas.

"You're right, the example, the example!" replied the schoolmaster, raising eyes and hands to heaven.

"I had already begun to sniff that Elisa had a secret," remarked an old sailor. "Twice I saw her talking with Don Fernando on the road to Mount San Esteban, and I noticed that as soon as they caught sight of me, they rushed off, one in one direction, one in another."

"Something similar happened to me," said the harbor master. "I was going toward Peñascosa one afternoon, and about a half a mile from here, I met Don Fernando and Elisa with their heads together; I noticed, too, that the widow of Ramón de la Puente had just left them."

"It had already occurred to me that the fine Italian hand of the lord of the great House of Manure must be at work here," exclaimed the schoolmaster's wife.

Hearing that gross and unforgivable insult, Don

Fernando could not contain himself, and he stormed into the store like a hurricane, his cheeks pallid and his eyes flashing.

"See here, you trollop, wash your mouth out before you speak of the House of Meira."

"What did I tell you!" cried Señora Isabel with a strident laugh. "So now we have with us the Marquess of the Holey Hose!" And turning to face him, she added sardonically, "How many crusts of bread did they give you to take care of this business, Señor Marquess?"

The hangers-on laughed. The poor gentleman was crushed. His anger and outrage rose in his throat and threatened to choke him. Realizing the impossibility of pitting himself against the shamelessness and insolence of such a woman, he left the store, pale and trembling. But the woman, seeing her prey about to escape her, shouted after him:

"Go on, they filled up your belly so you'd act as their go-between, didn't they? Go on, get out, and don't come back, parasite, sponger, pickpocket!"

Struck in the back by that grapeshot of insults, the noble Señor de Meira wheeled around, shook his fists, and summoned the strength to cry:

"Is there no one who will drive a hot spike through the tongue of that infamous woman?"

Doubtless he was harking back to the awesome punishments inflicted on insolent vassals by his forbears. But these terrifying words were received in the store with general laughter.

Meanwhile, Don Telesforo had completed his writing. The Judge, finding the schoolmaster's wife increasingly offensive, said to the Town Clerk:

"Be kind enough to notify the mother of the girl that she must give her her bed and clothing for her use."

"I'll give her nothing; everything in this house is mine," said the old woman, abruptly turning sober.

"Tell the lady," the Judge went on, speaking to Don Telesforo, "that we shall see about that. For the moment, let her hand over the bed and the clothing granted to the ward by law."

"Indeed, I will hand over nothing."

"Then we shall seize them!" exclaimed Don Cipriano, outraged. "Let's see, two of you come with me to act as witnesses . . ."

And pointing to a pair of seamen, he obliged them to go upstairs with him to Elisa's room. She, meanwhile, was sobbing in the doorway as she listened with fear to the terrible insults her mother was pouring out on her, her sweetheart and his family, as she padded around the store like a wild beast.

In a moment or two, Don Cipriano came downstairs.

"Elisa, come up with me and show me your clothing."

"For the love of God, Judge! Let me alone, for God's sake! I don't want to take anything."

Out of respect for the girl's distress and his own delicacy, Don Cipriano was loth to insist. But he went into the street looking for José, led him upstairs, and

ordered him to take charge of Elisa's clothing and bed. Then he made her leave the hallway between Don Fernando de Meira and himself, and turned toward the godmother's house, escorted by the Town Clerk and various women and seamen who had collected at the door of the store. José went ahead, trotting under his precious load.

XV

The three months prescribed by law for awaiting a response from the parents had elapsed. The time had not passed as happily as might have been expected. Elisa was not content in her god-mother's house. The woman was old and self-centered, so peevish that she railed unceasingly all day long at the hens, the pig, and the cats. She was so in the habit of this constant grumbling and nagging that she soon looked upon her god-daughter as one of the domestic animals, and spoke to her in the same manner. From time to time she would directly or indirectly throw in the girl's face the favor she was doing her, a favor the girl had promised to repay as soon as she came into possession of her property. Moreover, her rebellion against her mother weighed upon her: she was remorseful, and she wept frequently. More than once she felt tempted to go home, throw herself at Señora Isabel's feet, and beg her forgiveness. José sustained her with his strong yet tender love during those moments of weakness, so seemly in a good, innocent daughter.

She seldom went out into the street. Only at dusk when her sweetheart was coming home from the sea

would she talk with him for a few short moments at the door of the house in the presence of her god-mother, who never left them alone, more for the pleasure of meddling than to watch over her god-daughter. Once in a great while, the three of them would go for a walk along some lonely road where no one could see them. The innocent girl fancied that her conduct was severely judged in Rodillero and that everyone disapproved of her. It was not true. The villagers, without exception, found her decision justified and they were not a little pleased at it. Señora Isabel was generally loathed.

Another thing happened that affected both her and José very deeply, and caused a considerable stir in the village. Don Fernando of the House of Meira had disappeared from Rodillero a few days after he had arranged for Elisa's custody. He said good-bye to no one, and no one knew where he had gone. All inquiries made to determine his whereabouts were fruitless. José felt deeply concerned. He had just succeeded in setting aside three thousand *reales* from the bonito catch, and had intended to pay it immediately to the old man against the ten thousand *reales* he had received, thinking, not without reason, that the money left over from the fourteen thousand *reales* Don Anacleto had paid for the house must be very nearly spent. He was worried to death by the thought that perhaps the good old gentleman to whom he owed so many favors might be wandering about in the world, driven by necessity and unwilling to shame himself by asking for anything. Leaving his boat and his work, José went immediately in search of Don Fernando. After four days of scouring the countryside and ranging to various distant parts of the province, asking questions at every stop, he was obliged to turn back without a clue. This upset him.

The bonito catch had been as good as during the previous year. The boat José had bought from a Biscayan shipowner worked admirably all summer. The crew, among whom were numbered the facetious Bernardo and the awesome Pirate, were more than happy, not only because of the profits they were making, but also because they could see that poor José, whom they all genuinely liked, was overcoming his misfortunes and was on the eve of happiness. Without noteworthy variations, the episodes at the beginning of this tale were repeating themselves. Bernardo was playing tricks on the crew and especially on the Pirate, tricks as amusing as the old one with the stone. José was not exempt from them either. Bernardo would often ask: "When are we going to see this play, boy? If you don't watch out, the players will be leaving." Everyone knew what that meant, and they would laugh and remind José of the promise made to them a year earlier that on his wedding day he would give them the money to go to Sarrió to see a play. The only difference this year was that there were plenty of sardines, and that worried them not at all. While the younger men went far out after bonito, the old men fished off the shore in small boats and every morning and afternoon they came back loaded with fish. Within a few months the village had grown prosperous. The fish-processing plants were running day and night. The streets were crowded with dealers and with wagons piled high with barrels. The horn of plenty had suddenly spilled out over Rodillero. And as always at such times, everyone poured his money into the taverns and the shops instead of putting a little aside for a rainy day. Among fishermen saving is almost unknown. There is some excuse for this. The constant danger in which their lives are spent dulls the faculty for looking ahead which is so highly developed among country people. The rough, monotonous work to which they have given themselves makes them crave the moments of expansiveness and noisy gayety that wine affords.

What happened was to be expected. After good times came bad. At the end of the bonito run, and with the sardine fishing almost finished, the boats were beached for a time, awaiting the arrival of the hake and the congers. During this period of idleness, the seamen lived in the taverns or strolled about in groups along the beaches, watching the sails bobbing along the horizon and exchanging opinions as usual. In a few days they had consumed what was left them of their rich summer earnings.

But the winter promised to be a hard one. When they started to go out after congers and hake, they came home most days with nothing or a very small catch. Moreover, they began to feel the whiplash of the northeast wind on several occasions, sounding a warning to them. Then they left off deep sea fishing and waited for the right moment to go out after bass. December proved even rougher and stormier than November. Yet since they had no choice but to put out to sea or starve, or go begging through the villages, something they would do only as a last resort, they started to work on the bass run, watchful and ready for anything. The weather went from bad to worse. A few calm days aroused the hope that it might improve; but the sky abruptly turned ugly and threatening again. A rumor that spread through the region filled them with even greater foreboding. It was said that for several nights a young boy had seen three of the boats put out from the beach manned by men dressed in white, and that after two or three hours, he saw the boats come back empty. The terror this news aroused in the village, especially among the women, cannot easily be imagined. The men, too, were downcast and apprehensive, but they concealed it.

To a great degree, Elisa and José shared the general depression which reigned in the village, and an event that touched their hearts added to their sorrow. They learned that Don Fernando de Meira had been found dead on a mountain road in the hill country of León. Among the villagers, it was taken for granted that the old gentleman was on his way by night to raise some money, as he used to do, and that he had died as the consequence of a fall. But some, without any respect for the memory of the governor of Villaplana, the solicitor of the parliament of Toro, the President of the Council for Italy, and the justice of the Royal Tribunal of Mexico, declared that Don Fernando had gone begging and had died of hunger and cold. Be that as it may, his death saddened the entire village, for he was generally loved. Elisa wept for him as for a father; José went about silent and withdrawn for days. Finally, preparations for their wedding dried their tears and occupied all their attention. They had planned to be married early in December. But that proved impossible, owing to certain obstacles the priest placed in their way and which had to be removed; also because they could not find a house. José was resolved not to live with his mother. Knowing Teresa's temperament, he realized that Elisa would have trouble with her, even though Teresa now loved the girl with all her heart. The wedding was finally set for the new year. The pre-nuptial festivities, always so delightful to lovers, were curtailed, owing to the special circumstances of their case and to the atmosphere of melancholy which lay heavy over the village.

The weather continued so rough and the fears of the seamen remained so great that when the masters of the boats met they agreed to sail every night in groups of three to reconnoiter the sea and sky, and to decide on the basis of their observations whether or not to call out the crews. Furthermore, since they usually set sail before dawn, the boat that put out first and took the lead was to place a light in the bow as a precaution in the event that it was found dangerous to proceed. This would signal the others to put back. Two nights before the happenings we are about to relate, it was José's turn to sail with two others to reconnoiter. The sky looked threatening and they were reluctant to advise the boats to sail. But several days had already gone by without any fishing, and hunger was starting to nibble. Some of the men in the tavern were muttering against their decision. The day had improved a little, but not much. That night three other masters were to reconnoiter; they hesitated a long time before giving the boy the order to call out the boats, for the sky was ugly and it had seldom looked dirtier. In the end the order was given, because of the village's need, or perhaps in fear of protest.

José was one of the first to arrive on the beach.

"Mother of God, what weather!" he exclaimed, staring at the sky. "And what a night to decide to go to sea!"

But he was too prudent to alarm his crew and too brave to refuse to sail. He held his tongue, and with the aid of his crew, launched his boat. As it was the nearest to the water, it was soon afloat and the first to be rigged. When the crew were all aboard, they began to row out. As usual, there were more men now than during the summer, partly because the men do not disperse to other work during the winter, and partly because of the frequent calms when more men are needed at the oars. There were fourteen men in José's boat.

When they had left the port a mile behind, José ordered them to set the sails. The Asturian boats always carry five sails, which are in order of their size: the mainsail, the staysail, the foresail, the forestaysail, and the storm sail. The storm sail, which is the smallest, carries the dreadful name of Extreme Unction, because it is hoisted only when they are face to face with death.

"What sail do you want set, José?" one of them asked.

"The foresails," he replied dryly.

The sailors raised the forestaysail on the forestay and the foresail on the foremast, for that was what the order had signified.

The night was dark but not overcast. At moments the sky was clear. The round, black clouds were scudding with unusual velocity, clearly indicating that the wind was near hurricane force aloft, although it had not yet made its strength felt below. José was worried and brooding, never taking his gaze from the sky for any length of time. All the men were silent and glum. The cold benumbed their hands, and the fear they were unable to hide stilled their tongues. They cast frequent looks at the firmament, across which the clouds were running with increasing fury. The sea looked heavy and forbidding.

They proceeded for a quarter of an hour in this way, until José suddenly broke the silence with an exclamation:

"This is a dirty trick on us! Not even a dog would put to sea on a night like this!"

Three or four of the seamen hastened to add:

"You're right. This is foul weather, good for pigs, not men."

"Don't go ahead on our account, José," another one said. "If you think best, put back . . ."

José made no answer. After a moment or two of silence, he suddenly got to his feet and said in a tone of resolution:

"Light that lantern, boy . . . We'll come about."

The boy lighted the lantern and placed it in the bow with evident satisfaction. The seamen executed the maneuver with equal satisfaction, though they concealed it.

The boat began to luff toward Rodillero. Within a few moments they saw in the distance the lights being lit, one after another, on all the boats. This meant that they had all read the signs and were returning to port.

"We can't do anything else," said one.

"Who wants to put out to sea on a day like this!" cried another.

"But why did Nicolás and Toribio, those donkeys, order us out?"

Everyone's tongue was loosed. But a while after they had begun to talk as they moved along, José noticed the loom of a boat, without a light at the bow, coming in close to his leeward.

"Avast, boys!" he said. "What the devil is this?" he asked. "Where is that boat headed for?"

José stood, and making a megaphone of his hands, he hailed her:

"Ship ahoy!"

"What do you want, José?" came from the other, who had recognized his voice.

"Where are you bound for, Hermenegildo?" asked José, who had also recognized the speaker.

"For the shore," replied the other, coming as near as he could.

"But you didn't light your lantern after I lit mine?"

"Yes, I did, but I know this town too well. They probably displayed the signal to you, and then completely disregarded it themselves. How much will you bet that all the boats will show up on the beach this morning?"

"Damn those envious fellows!" exclaimed José under his breath; and then, addressing the crew: "Come about again . . . Some fine day there's going to be a disaster through such tricks."

The seamen executed the maneuver unwillingly.

"Haven't I often told you, José," remarked Bernardo, "that in this town a fellow would as soon go blind in one eye, provided the next fellow goes blind in both?"

The master made no reply.

"The funny thing is," remarked another, "that those idiots imagine they're going to fool one another, when all the time they don't know themselves which way is up."

"The fun will begin when we all see each other at daybreak," added a third.

"You'll see, when something happens some day, they'll pick somebody to be the scapegoat," said José.

"That always happens," answered Bernardo with comic gravity.

After these words, silence reigned on the boat. The seamen glumly contemplated the horizon. The master studied the state of the weather with increasing anxiety, despite the fact that there came a moment when almost the entire sky was clear. The clouds promptly closed in again. Nevertheless, the wind was not blowing hard aloft where it was growing calmer, too. The sunrise was unusually gray and dirty. Daylight filtered through a triple cap of clouds with great difficulty.

When they neared the shore, they saw that in fact almost all the boats from Rodillero had already cast their lines and were fishing close together. A few others were joining them after striking sail, and in the course of two hours they hauled aboard a few hake. At about ten o'clock, the sky darkened and a shower fell with a gust of wind. Within half an hour another squall came, and the wind rose. Then some of the boats hauled in their gear and set sail to make for land. One after another, the others followed their example.

"We didn't need saddle-bags for this trip," said one of José's crew, securing the lower points of the fore staysail at the bowsprit.

They were some ten or twelve leagues off the coast. Before they had come to within a couple of miles of shore, they saw that the sky toward the west was turning black. It was so dark that the seamen stared at one another in alarm.

"Mother of God, look what's coming!" cried one.

From the beginning, José had ordered the foremast fitted, that is, the foresail half-lowered and the staysail made fast to the forestay as a precaution. He scanned the sky to westward. The blackness was rapidly approaching them. When he felt on his face the chill that was a prelude to a heavy squall, he stood up shouting:

"Let go amain sheets and halliards!"

The crewmen, not yet fully aware of their danger, nevertheless hastened to obey. The sails thudded to the thwarts. Barely in time, for a violent gust went whistling through the rigging and drove the hull violently ahead. The sailors sent José a glance that constituted a vote of thanks and confidence.

"You smelled the whiplash descending, you rascal!" cried one.

But as they turned their eyes to the sea, they saw that one of the boats had capsized. Again they turned blanched faces to José.

"Did you see that, José?" asked one in a hoarse, unsteady voice.

The master blinked in affirmation. But the boat boy in the bow, becoming aware of what had happened, commenced to wail:

"Ah, Most Blessed Virgin! What is going to become of us? Mother of God, what is going to become of us?"

"Pipe down, you fool, or I'll throw you overboard right now!"

The frightened boy shut up.

"Hoist the foresail halfway and the fore staysail close to the bowsprit," he ordered then.

This was done with all speed. José bore off to leeward as much as he dared, taking care not to deviate from a straight line to Rodillero. The boat began to fly over the water with extraordinary speed, for the wind was coming hard and was rising. Before many minutes had passed, a huge freak sea or "tidal wave" rose, cutting off their view of the other boats; rain was coming in heavy squalls. The chop troubled them, and several of the men had to keep bailing the boat constantly. But José was concentrated less on all this than on the wind. It was blowing so unevenly and treacherously that the slightest carelessness would certainly cause them to capsize. Twice he was obliged to strike sail again to avoid a catastrophe. Finally, seeing the impossibility of making headway with two sails, he ordered them both lowered, and just the storm sail set. The sailors watched it being hoisted with consternation. Several of the hands were trembling as they executed the maneuver.

"We'll have to go under bare poles," said José, his voice hoarse from shouting. "We can't put back to Rodillero. We'll have to make for Sarrió."

"Not Sarrió either, I think," said an old hand in a low tone.

"No flinching, boy! Courage! This isn't anything!" replied the master forcefully.

From the moment they resigned themselves to being unable to put back to Rodillero, and accordingly turned stern to the wind, the gale ceased to worry them, particularly since they carried so little sail.

But the ocean was acting up ominously. The freak sea, aided by the high tide during the night, had become a veritable tidal wave, terrible and imposing. They were taking such a hard and continual pounding at the stern that they were finally obliged to luff a little, presenting the side of the ship to the waves. All the while the crew never stopped bailing. The seas kept rising, each higher than the last. The boat disappeared beneath them and emerged only by a miracle. One heavy sea carried away the rudder. José hastily seized the emergency rudder; but as he was making it fast, a second sea tore it from his hands and washed aboard several barrels of water.

The boat boy again exclaimed, sobbing: "Oh, Blessed Mother, we're done for."

"Pipe down, you lubber, or I'll kill you!"

José threw at his head the stick of the rudder, which had fallen on a seat.

Seeing the terror on the faces of some of the crew, he glared at them ferociously and said:

"Anyone who sounds off is going to get his neck wrung!"

That ferocity was needed. If panic seized the crew and they stopped bailing for a second, they would certainly founder.

He made an oar fast in the stern to serve as a jury rudder. It is impossible to steer with an oar if the sails are set; but as they were carrying nothing but the storm sail, José could keep the boat under control with great effort. Each blow they took sent a vast amount of water into the boat. And though a man working hard could bail a hogshead of water with the ship's bucket in eight or ten minutes, it was impossible to get it all out; they were in water almost to their knees all the time. José never stopped shouting encouragement with what voice he had left.

"Bail, boys, bail! Courage, boys . . . ! Bail, boys!"

One of the seas carried away Bernardo's beret.

"Go on!" he shouted furiously. "Take my head with it!"

The situation was desperate. Although they all tried to conceal their terror, it had taken possession of them. Then, José, seeing that their strength was flagging, said:

"See here, boys, we're running through a violent storm. Do you want to ask the help of the Christ of Rodillero to get us out of this?"

"Yes, José," they all replied with a promptness that revealed their anxiety of mind.

"All right, let's all take a vow to go to hear a mass in our bare feet, if you'd like to . . . But we'll do it to keep up our courage . . . Don't be afraid. Courage, and bail, boys, bail!"

The vow gave them confidence, and they went on working with faith in their hearts. They had thrown out most of the water in a minute or two, and the boat rode easier. José noticed that the mainmast was hampering them.

"Let's unstep the main mast," he said, and he balanced himself to seize hold of the base of it.

At that very instant they saw an immense sea coming toward them, high as a mountain and black as a cavern.

"José, there won't be any wedding feast now!" cried Bernardo, resigned to his death.

The blow was so hard it knocked José to his hands and knees, and threw him against the thwarts. The boat was all but swamped. But though he was stunned, José sprang gallantly to his feet, shouting:

"Bail, bail! This is nothing!"

XVI

What was going on in Rodillero?

The few boats that had obeyed José's signals returned to port before dawn. Their crews were chagrined and glum, thinking they had been meanly tricked but more so at the thought of facing the ridicule they feared from their wives at home.

"You always have to be the fool! When are you going to realize whom you're dealing with, my dear man? I'll give you something to make you seasick today . . . you'll see!"

As usual, the men would not talk, knowing the truth when they heard it. Inwardly they swore to themselves they would not fall into the trap a second time.

But as the day wore along, they changed their minds a little. The aspect of the sea was so threatening, and the sky so dirty, that their idleness began to weigh lightly on them. As the first blast from the northwest was felt when a squall hit the village, some of them turned to their wives with a smile:

"What do you think now? Would you like me to be out on the sea now?"

It was the women's turn not to answer. The second blast, much stronger than the first, brought the whole village to life. Men and women went down to the beach, and from there they climbed San Esteban through a rain that was falling in torrents. Fear and dismay were soon written on all their faces, giving overt testimony to the superstitious uneasiness which had reigned in the town all winter. The women glanced at the old salts out of the corners of their eyes. These old-timers were sniffing the wind. Some of the women ran to them to ask:

"Is it bad, Uncle Pepe?"

Uncle Pepe answered without taking his eyes off the horizon:

"It's not good . . . But the sea hasn't said 'I'm here' yet."

He spoke too quickly. The storm struck suddenly with fury. The sea changed strikingly and began to break on the Huesos de San Pedro, the nearest bay along the coast. Soon it was breaking on El Cobanín, too, the nearest cove on the other side. The crowd standing on top of Mount San Esteban watched the progress of the storm with great fear. Some of the women started to weep.

According to the old-timers, however, there was no cause to mourn as yet. The port was still clear. Accordingly, unless they capsized (and this was up to them, for it lay in their hands to avoid it), they could enter Rodillero with no danger. Someone remarked:

"What about the heavy seas? Will they have time to bail?"

"Of course they'll have time! . . . Why anyone

would think we'd never seen big seas before! There never was such a village for getting upset over nothing," said a sour old sailor.

The emphasis with which he spoke made the pessimists hold their tongues and calmed the women. Unfortunately his triumph was short-lived. Within a few moments the sea was breaking on El Torno, another of the sandbanks at the mouth of the harbor.

Near San Esteban's chapel there was a hut where a laborer lived who was in the employ of the harbor guild to light signal fires on days and nights of danger in return for a small annual stipend. Although this workman had had little first-hand experience on the sea, he knew it as well as anyone actively sailing. After watching the panorama closely for a good while and hesitating several times, he brought a load of dried broom and furze from the backyard of his hovel, and piling it on the highest point of the mountain, set it afire. It was the first signal to the fishermen.

Elisa, who was among the crowd, near her godmother, felt her heart contract when she saw the bonfire. She recalled the terrible curse of the sacristan's wife, and all the forebodings and superstitious terrors dormant in her mind suddenly awoke. She tried to repress them through shame; but she began to wander among the groups, listening with ill-concealed anxiety to the speculations of the seamen. Every word left her more tense.

There was little talking and a great deal of watching among the people. The wind whipped the last drops of the squall into their faces. The sea was rising rapidly. Following the breakers on the Huesos de San Pedro the Cobanín, and the Torno, came new breakers on another bay farther along the coast.

"She's breaking on La Furada! . . . Manuel, you'd better light another fire!" cried one of the seamen.

Manuel ran back to his house, brought another load of furze, and lighted it near the first. This was a signal of imminent danger. If the men on the sea failed to make land soon, they were exposing themselves to finding the harbor closed.

"Can you see any of the boats, Rafael?" asked a girl whose cheeks were wet with big round tears.

"Not just now; the choppy sea has cut off most of our view."

Not a sail was visible along the line of the horizon. The watchers were so overwhelmed by solicitude and anxiety that minutes went by without a voice being heard. Everyone had his eyes on El Carrero, a short open stretch in the sandbank at the mouth of the Rodillero harbor where the boats could come in safely even when the sea was turbulent. Elisa felt a cold sweat on her forehead, and she clutched her godmother to keep from falling.

A quarter of an hour went by in this fashion. Suddenly a cry rose from the crowd, a wail weaker but sadder than the roaring of the sea. A breaker had just foamed over El Carrero. The sandbank had become a line of whitecaps. The port was closed.

Manuel, pale and silent, went for a new load; he

lighted it alongside the other two. The rain had stopped and the bonfires, fanned by the wind, blazed brightly.

Hearing the cry from the crowd, Elisa shuddered. With an involuntary impulse, like an inspiration, she went running away from the scene, down the path among the pines, through the empty village, up the road to the church. She came to its doors, panting and disconsolate. She paused a moment to catch her breath; then she made the sign of the cross, knelt, and traversed the nave to the main altar on her knees; once there she turned to the right and began painfully to climb the spiral staircase leading to the shrine of the Christ. It was the stairway of penance whose stone slabs had been worn by the knees of the devout. When she reached the top, Elisa's knees were bleeding.

The shrine was a dark chapel hung with images and offerings. A grilled window opened into the church through which the faithful could see the sacred image on the days when mass was said on its altar. As usual, the Christ was hidden by a velvet curtain. Elisa ran to the curtain and prostrated herself, trembling. In a moment or two, other women came one by one to the shrine and prostrated themselves, like her, in silence. A sob that could not be suppressed occasionally disturbed the mystery and the majesty of the little chapel.

By afternoon, the sea was beginning to subside. Thanks to this, a small flotilla of boats was able to put in, not without risk. Later several more came, but by nightfall five were still missing. One of them was José's. The seamen, guarded in their opinion of his fate (for they had seen one boat lost), refused to say a word about this; they responded with evasions to the swarm of questions put to them. No one knew anything; no one had seen anything. The beach was still filled with people late at night; but, as the hours passed, discouragement grew. Little by little, the beach was emptying. Only the families of those still on the sea were left. Finally they, too, their hope almost gone, abandoned the spot and went into the village with death in their hearts.

That was a terrible night! The broken wails of the wretched wives, of the children crying for their fathers, still ring in my ears. The village was grim and forbidding. People wandered through the streets in groups, clotted at the doorways of the houses. Everyone was shouting. The taverns were open, and there the men argued heatedly, blaming one another for the disaster. From time to time a disheveled woman would run through the streets screaming to make your hair stand on end. Moans and sobs could be heard from inside the houses.

Those first moments of confusion and clamor were succeeded by a sadder, and—if possible—a more melancholy composure. People shut themselves up in their dwellings and their mourning took on some degree of resignation. How many tears were shed in those poor cottages! In one of them, an old woman whose two sons were still missing, was screaming so shrilly that the few people passing in the street stood still, horror-stricken. In another, a wretched woman who had lost her husband was sobbing in a corner while two little tots of three and four were playing near her and eating hazelnuts.

When daylight came, the village looked like a cemetery. The priest ordered the bells rung to summon the congregation to church, and promised the faithful gathered there that he would say a requiem mass the next morning for the repose of the souls of the men who had perished.

But toward midday word came by an unknown messenger that some of the boats from Rodillero had made the port of Banzones, about seven leagues distant. The news roused tremendous excitement among the people. Hope, already dead, was quickly reborn in their hearts. Once more confusion and noise reigned in the street. Runners were sent to ascertain the truth. An endless variety of commentaries and theories sped through the chattering groups. The remaining hours of the day and the night were spent in painful worry and anxiety. The poor women ran from group to group, pale, weeping, hoping to snatch some encouragement from the conversation of the men.

Finally at noon came the news that only two boats had reached Banzones. Which ones were they? The messenger did not know, or did not want to say. But it was soon whispered that one was José's and the other Toribio's.

Later in the afternoon, a boy, bathed in sweat, out of breath, and hatless, came running:

"They're here! They're here!"

"Who are they?"

"Lots of them, lots of them are coming!" he managed to pant through his breathlessness. "They ought to be at Antromero about now."

An indescribable stir swept through the village. All the people, without exception, rushed out of their houses, boiled in the street a moment or two, and then forming a compact mass, rushed out of the town. The whole crowd took the road to Antromero, along the shore, in a state of excitement and dread it is difficult to describe. The men were chattering, speculating on what their fellow seamen might have done to save themselves. The women trudged along in silence, dragging their children who cried in vain for a rest. When they had covered half a league, they could see, through an open stretch, a group of seamen in the distance, their oars on their shoulders. A great clamor arose from the crowd. The fishermen answered it with a cheer, waving their berets. Another shout from the crowd; another answer from afar. Thus the two groups approached each other and soon they came together.

What a joyful and at the same time heartbreaking scene! As the small group mingled with the larger one, cries of grief and joy burst forth. The women strained their eyes searching for their men, and those who failed to find them began to moan pitifully, dropping to the ground and wringing their hands in despair. The fortunate, finding a beloved husband or adored son, threw themselves on their men like wild women and clung as though no force on earth could separate them. The poor shipwrecked men, finding themselves the objects of such an ardent welcome, smiled, trying to hide their emotion; but tears rolled down their faces in spite of themselves.

Among the crowd was Elisa, who felt such a tight lump in her throat on seeing José that it threatened to strangle her. She put her hands to her face and sobbed quietly. He was caught and nearly suffocated in his mother's arms, but over her shoulder his eyes eagerly sought his promised wife. Elisa raised her face to him and their eyes met as they kissed.

After the first moment of excitement, the mass of people slowly turned back toward the village. Instantly each of the shipwrecked men was surrounded by a group of his fellows who questioned him eagerly and often on the incidents of his trip. Their women walked behind them. Occasionally they would call them by name, to make sure they had come back alive; and when the men turned around, the women had nothing to say.

Everyone agreed that afternoon to give thanks to God on the following morning at a solemn high mass. It turned out that almost all the seamen who had survived had offered to hear mass at the altar of the Christ in their bare feet. It was the accepted offering in Rodillero during moments of peril, one that had come down from father to son. Accordingly the next morning they gathered on the beach, and each crew with the master at its head, moved slowly, barefoot and bareheaded, toward the church. They marched silently, soberly, their calm eyes shining with a simple faith, though none of them had ever had anything but hardship from life. The women walked behind them with the children and the few men of the upper classes. They, too, were silent, moved by seeing those men, so strong and rough, humbling themselves like helpless babes. The widows and orphans of those who would never come home from the sea were there also, come to pray for the repose of the souls of their men. All of them had put on a black kerchief, apron, or beret, any black thing they could lay hands on at a moment's notice.

In the little church of Rodillero, the miraculous Christ awaited them, hanging from the cross with arms open. He, too, had been a poor shipwrecked man, rescued from the waters through the piety of a few fishermen; like them He had known sorrow and the solitude of the sea, the bitter salt of its waters. They knelt and bowed their heads, uttering prayers learned in childhood but never pronounced with greater fervor. The candles surrounding the sacred image sputtered sadly. A gentle murmur arose from the crowd. The cracked and quavering voice of the priest saying the mass broke the majestic silence of the shrine from time to time.

At the conclusion of the ceremony, Elisa and José met in the vestibule of the church and exchanged tender smiles. And with that innocent and pardonable selfishness of those in love, they instantly forgot all the sadness prevailing around them and went together down the path to the village in gay and lively conversation. Before they had reached their homes, they had fixed the day for their wedding.